TREASURE FOR THE HEART

NATIONAL DISTRIBUTORS

UK (and countries not listed below)

CWR, PO Box 230, Farnham, Surrey GU9 8XG.

Tel: 01252 784710 Outside UK (44) 1252 784710

AUSTRALIA: CMC Australasia, PO Box 519, Belmont, Victoria 3216.

Tel: (03) 5241 3288

CANADA: CMC Distribution Ltd., PO Box 7000, Niagara on the Lake, Ontario L0S 1J0.

Tel: 1 800 325 1297

GHANA: Challenge Enterprises of Ghana, PO Box 5723, Accra.

Tel: (21) 222437/223249 Fax: 226227

INDIA: Crystal Communications, Crystal Crest, Plot No. 83, Sesachella Society, Entrenchment Road, East Marredpally, Secunderabad - 500 026, Andhra Pradesh.

Tel: (40) 7732511/7730577

KENYA: Keswick Bookshop, PO Box 10242, Nairobi.

Tel: (02) 331692/226047

MALAYSIA: Salvation Book Centre (M) Sdn. Bhd., 23 Jalan SS 2/4, 47300 Petaling Jaya, Selangor.

Tel: (603) 78766411/78766797 Fax: (603) 78757066

NEW ZEALAND: CMC New Zealand Ltd., Private Bag, 17910 Green Lane, Auckland.

Tel: 09 5249393 Fax: 09 5222137

NIGERIA: FBFM, (Every Day with Jesus), Prince's Court, 37 Ahmed Onibudo Street,
PO Box 70952, Victoria Island. Tel: 01 2617721, 616832, 4700218, 2619156

PHILIPPINES: Praise Incorporated, 145 Panay Avenue, Cor Sgt Esguerra St, Quezon City.

Tel: 632 920 5291 Fax: 920 5747

REPUBLIC OF IRELAND: Scripture Union, 40 Talbot Street, Dublin 1.

Tel: (01) 8363764

SINGAPORE: Campus Crusade Asia Ltd., 315 Outram Road, 06-08 Tan Boon Liat Building, Singapore 169074.

Tel: (65) 222 3640

SOUTH AFRICA: Struik Christian Books (Pty Ltd), PO Box 193, Maitland 7405, Cape Town.

Tel: (021) 551 5900

SRI LANKA: Christombu Books, 27 Hospital Street, Colombo 1.

Tel: (1) 433142/328909

TANZANIA: City Christian Bookshop, PO Box 33463, Dar es Salaam.

Tel: (51) 28915

UGANDA: New Day Bookshop, PO Box 2021, Kampala.

Tel: (41) 255377

USA: CMC Distribution, PO Box 644, Lewiston, New York 14092-0644.

Tel: 1 800 325 1297

ZIMBABWE: Word of Life Books, Shop 4, Memorial Bldg., 35 S Machel Ave., Harare.

Tel: 781305 Fax: 774739

For e-mail addresses, visit the CWR web site: www.cwr.org.uk

TREASURE FOR THE HEART

DAILY INSPIRATIONS FROM

Selwyn Hughes

FEATURING THE PAINTINGS OF LARRY DYKE

NASHVILLE, TN

0–8054–2428–8

Published by Broadman & Holman Publishers, Nashville, Tennessee

Dewey Decimal Classification: 242.2
Subject Heading: DEVOTIONAL EXERCISES

Printed in Belgium
1 2 3 4 5 04 03 02 01 00

CONTENTS

Publisher's Foreword	vi
Introduction	vii
Topical Index	viii
Songs of Ascents	2
The Divine Eagle	64
The Lord's Prayer	128
The Armor of God	193
Hinds' Feet on High Places	258
Your Father and My Father	320
How to Use the Bible	384
Background	386

PUBLISHER'S FOREWARD

A painting captures a moment in time: a golden shaft of sunlight, the mischievous smile of a child, clouds soaring overhead in fanciful shapes. But even before the brush strokes are dry, the moment passes and is gone, leaving only an image on canvas and the feelings it stirs.

It's human nature to want the world to be like a painting —perfect and never-changing. Experience tells us there's nothing we can do to make time stand still for us. Yet the wonderful message Selwyn Hughes shares in *Treasure for the Heart* is that there's one point of reference in our lives that never changes: the timeless, immortal perfection of God.

Like a storm-swept lighthouse standing strong and unmoving against the driving rain and crashing breakers, God's presence in the world is our rock of assurance no matter what goes on around us. It is the inerrant guidance we long for in a culture where absolutes of right and wrong are challenged at every turn, and where Christians who earnestly and sincerely want to follow God's path so often find themselves not knowing which way to go.

Through whatever spiritual storm life brings our way, the beacon of God's law, love, and assurance shines with undimmed brilliance year after year, age after age. The source of this great light—now and always—is the Bible. If God is the energy that creates the Light, His Word is the filament that sends it out into even the darkest corners of the world, bringing hope, guidance, and assurance to everyone who will follow its beam. In this book, Selwyn Hughes brings us into the light of God by helping us understand God's Word.

As in previous volumes of the Every Day Light series, these daily devotions are divided into six two-month sections, each introduced with a painting and a short observation. Every day's study includes a Bible reading with verses for special emphasis, a brief message, prayer, additional Scripture references, and a couple of questions to consider as you go about your day.

They are treasures for the heart that will draw you closer to the unchanging love of God.

L.G.G.

INTRODUCTION

Treasure. What an evocative word. It conjures up images of fortune-filled caskets, spilling over with a lifetime's wealth of gold coins and sparkling precious jewels.

I think this is the picture that Jesus presented to His disciples when He warned them: "Do not store up for yourselves treasures on earth, where the moth and rust destroy, and where thieves break in and steal. But store up for yourselves treasures in heaven, where moth and rust do not destroy, and where thieves do not break in and steal. For where your treasure is, there your heart will be also." (Matt. 6:19–21)

Jesus wants us to have a special treasure—the heavenly kind—and He tells us that increasing our heavenly investment is a matter of the heart, not the pocket.

Nearly eight hundred references to the heart in the Bible make it clear that the heart is the place from which our whole life flows. It governs our motives, our actions and our speech. As Solomon says, "Above all else, guard your heart, for it is the wellspring of life," (Prov. 4:23).

We have to choose what is valuable to us and that choice determines where our treasure chest is—on earth or in heaven.

I hope that the six themes I have chosen for this edition of Every Day Light will help you to maintain your heavenly focus and encourage you to increase your investment that's waiting for you in heaven.

Selwyn Hughes

adoption 316–323

TOPICAL INDEX
(BY DAY)

adventure 87–93
armor of God, the 184–245

complacency, spiritual 80–86
contentment 32–34, 60
Creator 313–315

deliverance 17–20, 60
disappointment 291–297
disciple 2
doubt 277–283, 337

Eagle, the Divine 61–121
'El-Shaddai' 132
evil 23, 177
faith 7, 24, 25, 35, 44–45, 50, 52, 101–107, 212–218
fatherhood of God 125–128, 304–365
fear 298–303
forgiveness 40, 164–170, 290, 346–349

growing up 108–114
guilt 165–170

hinds' feet on high places 246–304
honesty 256–269
hope 17, 40–42, 46–47, 52–53, 60

Jerusalem 1, 11, 13, 21–22,

24, 34, 47, 56–58
joy 25–27, 60

kingdom of God 87, 93, 110, 124, 143–149, 178–182

Lord's Prayer, the 122–183

mercy 16
motherly qualities of God 324–330
Name of God 136–142
nest, disturbed 61–5

obedience 47–53, 60
peace 165
perseverance 35–38, 60
pilgrim 2, 25–27, 49–50, 57–58, 60
praise 57–61
prayer 4, 24, 39, 45, 122–183, 233–244, 250–251
pride 43
prosperity 73–79

relationships 31
renunciation 3–6, 60
repentance 342–345
righteousness 198–204

salvation 219–225
Satan 148, 185–197, 199,

TOPICAL INDEX
(BY DAY)

201–206, 211, 214–216
security 7–9, 21–24, 60
self–acceptance 94–100
service 14, 60
sin 197, 284–290, 360
Songs of Ascents 1–60
Spirit, Holy 38, 55, 80–86, 144, 171, 212, 227–234, 321–323
steadfastness 205–211
suffering 36, 39, 350–351

temptation 171–177
thirst for God 270–276
trials 66–72
trust 22, 44–46, 60
truth 193–197

unity 54–56, 60, 115–121

war 6
will of God 8, 13, 31, 41, 82, 139, 150–156
Word of God 226–232
work 28–31, 60
worship 1, 10–14, 28, 34, 52, 57, 60

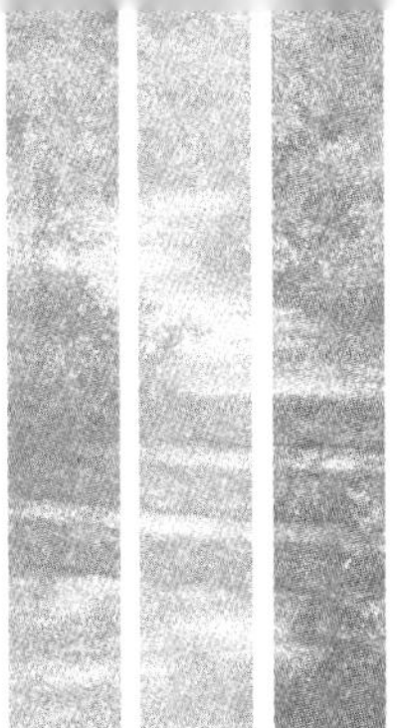

SECTION ONE

Songs Of Ascents

Songs of Ascents

One of the joyous things about travel is that it almost guarantees you'll face surprises along the way. Larry Dyke has visited and painted places ranging from placid golf courses to dramatic jungle waterfalls, and encountered plenty of unexpected situations—some good, others not so good. However, as much as he has enjoyed them, these journeys are insignificant compared with the spiritual journey along the path that leads to Christ.

In this section of *Treasure for the Heart,* Selwyn Hughes highlights a collection of psalms written to accompany us on our spiritual journey. These "songs for the road" were composed to uplift the spirits of God's people as they moved along seeking his way. They celebrate the joy of the journey, and encourage and inspire us the same way they did the readers and listeners (and seekers) of the Old Testament. They put us on notice that there will be challenges and hardships ahead. But at the same time they reassure us that everything that will happen takes place under the providence of God's will. And it's only by following God's path that you'll end up where you're truly supposed to be, safe and content.

Songs give travelers a way to share the experience of the journey with each other. Sometimes singing is a way to share each other's burdens, as when soldiers sing while they march to take their minds off of the battle ahead; other times it is a joint celebration of triumph, as when mountain climbers mark a successful ascent with whoops of victory.

In the case of a spiritual journey, the reward at the end of the trail is the treasure of a lifetime: the eternal blessings of God that are there waiting for each of us. These wonderful psalms make our way clearer, the jagged places less ominous, the climb less steep, and all of us travelers more confident and hopeful.

They're songs that will speed you on your way by transforming even the rockiest, most treacherous spiritual pathway into a fragrant garden walk.

L.G.G.

SECTION ONE

Songs For the Road

For reading & meditation—Mark 10:32–45

"They were on their way up to Jerusalem, with Jesus leading the way …" (v.32)

Together we stand on the threshold of a year of Bible readings. What do the next 365 days hold for us? How can we prepare ourselves? I know of no better way than by focusing on that section of the book of Psalms known as "The Songs of Ascents."

These songs, fifteen in number (Psalms 120 to 134), are thought by scholars to have been sung by Hebrew pilgrims as they made their way to Jerusalem to attend the three great festivals of worship—the Feasts of Passover, Pentecost, and Tabernacles. We know from the Gospel of Luke that our Lord at the age of twelve "went up" to Jerusalem for the Feast of the Passover (Luke 2:41–42), and a similar phrase is used in our reading today: "They were on their way up to Jerusalem."

I wonder how many of you reading these lines will identify with the disciples and the people in this passage who were "astonished" and "afraid." Are you feeling apprehensive as you set your feet on the road that lies ahead of you? Does the prospect of the unexpected and the unknown fill your heart with trepidation? Then I think I have an answer for you. Learn to sing with me the fifteen psalms of the Songs of Ascents and you will find your fears are quieted and your feet become firm and steady. These "songs for the road," as Eugene Peterson calls them, are a song book and a guidebook combined. They not only cheer the flagging spirit but provide direction when the path is dark and unclear. Let's learn to sing them well.

FURTHER STUDY

Matt. 4:1–5; Isa. 1:26; 48:2; Jer. 3:17

1. How is Jerusalem described?

2. What will it be called?

O God, on this the first day of a new journey I put my hand firmly in Yours. Help me travel the new road not with a sigh but with a song. Teach me to sing well, with an ear for the lyrics as well as the tune. In Jesus' Name I pray. Amen.

DAY 2

SECTION ONE

"Long Obedience"

For reading & meditation—Hebrews 12:1–13

"... let us run with perseverance the race marked out for us." (v.1)

Before looking in detail at the Songs of Ascents we pause to make the point that everyone who travels the road of faith requires help and encouragement from time to time. We need cheering up when our spirits flag and direction when the way ahead is confusing and unclear. The Songs of Ascents provide us with some of the best spiritual encouragement I know.

Eugene Peterson (on whose thoughts I am drawing heavily in this edition) points out that there are two biblical designations for the people of faith: disciple and pilgrim. We are disciples because we are apprenticed to a Master, Jesus Christ, and pilgrims because we are people who spend our lives going somewhere—going to God. He points out also that religion in our day has been captured by a tourist mindset. We spend our time visiting attractive religious sites when we have adequate leisure, for instance when we make our weekly visit to church, and we occasionally dip into the Bible, go to see the newest Christian personality on the scene or investigate the latest blessing. Tourists want only the high points, but a Christian cannot come to maturity that way.

Friedrich Nietzsche is quoted as saying: "The essential thing in heaven and earth is ... that there should be long obedience in the same direction." Long obedience in the same direction. Nietzsche said many strange things, but he seemed to be thinking clearly when he made this statement. Where can we go in Scripture to learn the art of "long obedience?" Many parts of it, of course, but most effectively to the Songs of Ascents.

FURTHER STUDY

Gal. 6:1–9; 1 Cor. 15:58; Heb. 12:7; James 1:12

1. What does Paul exhort the Galatians?

2. Who does James call blessed?

Prayer

O Father, forgive me if I approach the Christian life more as a tourist than a pilgrim. Prepare my heart now for the days that follow as I seek to understand and put into practice the art of "long obedience." In Christ's Name I pray. Amen.

SECTION ONE

Disappointments

For reading & meditation—Psalm 120:1–7

"I call on the Lord in my distress, and he answers me." (v.1)

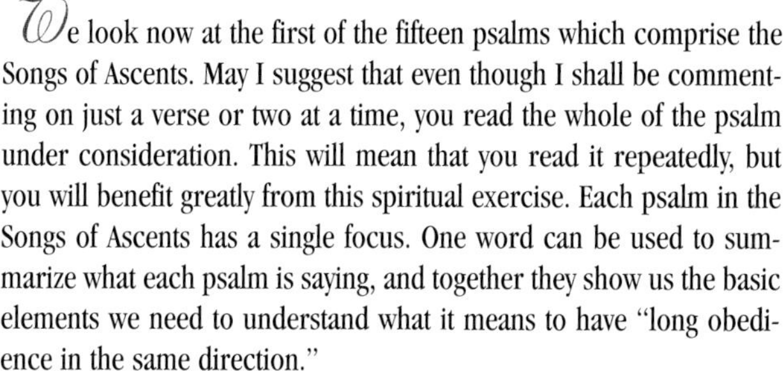

We look now at the first of the fifteen psalms which comprise the Songs of Ascents. May I suggest that even though I shall be commenting on just a verse or two at a time, you read the whole of the psalm under consideration. This will mean that you read it repeatedly, but you will benefit greatly from this spiritual exercise. Each psalm in the Songs of Ascents has a single focus. One word can be used to summarize what each psalm is saying, and together they show us the basic elements we need to understand what it means to have "long obedience in the same direction."

The psalmist begins by telling us he is in distress. Clearly, he has been the victim of lying and deceit (v.2). His soul was in pain over what was going on in the world, yet he did not repress his feelings and pretend that he was not feeling the way he did. Many Christians think that admitting to pain and disappointment concerning the way things are is pure negativism. If indulged in it can become that, but to admit to something is not necessarily to indulge in it. We must not stay there but we must start there. Sometimes we have to be thoroughly disappointed with the way things are before we find the motivation to cast ourselves fully on the Lord.

This might seem a discordant note to strike as we embark on our journey, but the more keenly we allow ourselves to feel the disappointment that the world brings the more motivated we will be to pursue the Christian way.

FURTHER STUDY

Eccl. 2:17–26; Job 8:8–19; 11:20

1. Why do the pursuits of life disappoint?

2. What can we learn from former generations?

Prayer

Father, help me see that dissatisfaction with the world is the first step in preparing to set out on a new journey with You. The more disillusioned I am with the world the more my appetite is whetted for grace. I am grateful. Amen.

SECTION ONE

Before You Can Say "Yes"

For reading & meditation—Psalm 120:2

"Save me, O Lord, from lying lips and from deceitful tongues." (v.2)

The more disillusioned we are with the world, the more motivated we will be to pursue the Christian way. If we are not willing to face the reality that we live in a fallen world, that the latest invention is not going to bring us Utopia, that possessions fail to give any lasting happiness, then we are not going to move along the rugged road of faith with a steady tread.

My favorite word to summarize the message of this, the first of the Songs of Ascents, is renunciation. The psalmist seems to have made a decision to move away from the lies he has heard, and we too must make a similar decision. We must renounce lies such as: human beings are basically good; we are not responsible for the way we are; we can find happiness independently of God. The truth of God does not begin to dawn upon us until we realize that what we have assumed was the truth—that we are the masters of our fate—is in fact a lie. It is painful to admit that we have been taken in by the world's lies but until we accept that we have, and confess it, we are not ready to move on into all that God has for us.

If the psalmist was writing today he might have worded his prayer like this: "Save me, O Lord, from the lies of those who think they know the answer to life, but don't." We must discover that before we can say "Yes" to God we must first learn to say "No" to the world.

FURTHER STUDY

Luke 21:29–36;
Rom. 12:1–2;
Col. 3:2

1. What does Paul admonish the Romans?
2. What did he encourage the Colossians to do?

Prayer

Father, I would make the prayer of the psalmist my prayer also. Rescue me from those who would represent the world to me in terms that are not entirely true. I turn from the untrue to the True. Help me dear Lord. In Jesus' Name. Amen.

SECTION ONE

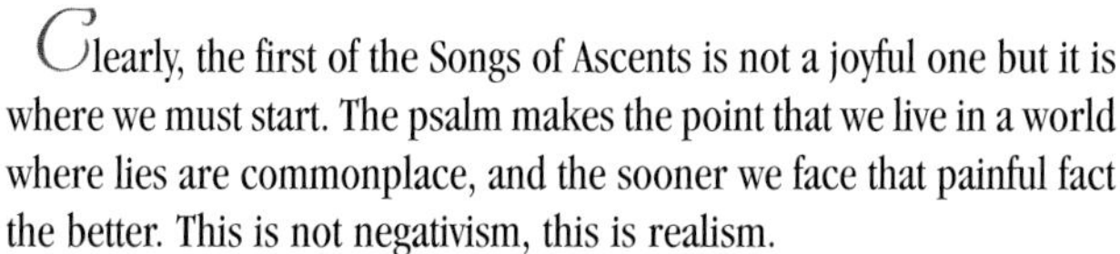

Vindictive-free

DAY 5

For reading & meditation—Psalm 120:3–4

"He will punish you with a warrior's sharp arrows ..." (v.4)

Clearly, the first of the Songs of Ascents is not a joyful one but it is where we must start. The psalm makes the point that we live in a world where lies are commonplace, and the sooner we face that painful fact the better. This is not negativism, this is realism.

In verses 3 and 4 the psalmist tells us that God has sharp arrows which He aims at those who persist in deceitfulness. The Moffatt translation of the Psalms gives this rendering: "What will you get from Him, O crafty tongue, what punishment in full? Sharp arrows poured on you, and burning coals!" What is the psalmist saying here? And why such strong language? Doubtless the psalmist's persecutors had used forceful language to make their point and to impress others with the "truth" of what they said about him, but he reminds them that the strength of their vindictiveness will be met by the strength of the Almighty. As they have shot their arrows of vindictiveness at him so the Lord will send His arrows of fiery judgment on them.

We should remember, however, that God's arrows are judgments designed to lead a person to repentance. How unlike God we are in this respect. If we are honest, we enjoy seeing those who have hurt us going through some painful experiences themselves. The psalmist, I believe, prays for his persecutors not out of a spirit of vindictiveness but with the desire that through the pain of judgment they might be brought to the path of peace. How wonderful it would be if that same spirit was among us.

FURTHER STUDY

Rom. 12:17–21; Matt. 5:39; Lev. 19:18; 1 Pet. 3:9

1. What is written?

2. How are we to overcome evil?

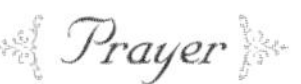

Prayer

My Father and my God, help me keep my spirit free of all vindictiveness. May I, like Your own beloved Son, manifest the attitude that says to all who hurt or disappoint me: "Forgive them ... for they know not what they do." In Jesus' Name. Amen.

DAY

6

SECTION ONE

A Prod to Get Us Moving

For reading & meditation—Psalm 120:5–7

"Woe to me that I dwell in Meshech, that I live among the tents of Kedar!" (v.5)

It is interesting, as Eugene Peterson points out, that one of the first words in this psalm is "distress" and the last word is "war". From start to finish the psalmist pours out his heart to God concerning the pain he feels at living in a world full of deceitfulness and lying.

The reference he makes to Meshech and Kedar is designed to show how uncongenial it was for him to be living with people who acted more like foreigners than friends. The tribe of Meshech lived between the Black Sea and the Caspian Sea, and Kedar were Arabian nomads. They typified barbarian society and represented the strange and the hostile. The psalmist is implying that the people in his community treated him more like an outsider than one of themselves. "I am 'a man of peace,'" he says, "but those around me seem to be bent on hostility and combat." Paraphrased, his words might read: "I live in the midst of people who behave like barbarians." This complaint is made not simply to give vent to his feelings but to let his pain motivate him to move from confidence in people to confidence in God. His anguish penetrates his despair and stimulates him to make a new beginning.

Renunciation is the prod we need to get us moving. There is nothing joyful about this psalm but it gets our footsteps started. Having rejected the world and the lies it tells us about life, we turn more readily to the truth. The rejection is also an acceptance, the leaving an arriving, the "No" to the world a "Yes" to God.

FURTHER STUDY

Phil. 3:1–21; Ps. 118:9; Isa. 2:22; 31:1

1. What does Paul renounce?

2. How does Paul evaluate maturity?

Prayer

O Father, help me realize that I am called to be a pilgrim, not a tourist. I am on a path that leads away from the world, one that leads upwards to You. I renounce all the world's false assumptions to follow the path of truth. Thank You, my Father. Amen.

SECTION ONE

Able to Keep

For reading & meditation—Psalm 121:1–8

"... where does my help come from? My help comes from the Lord ..." (vv.1–2)

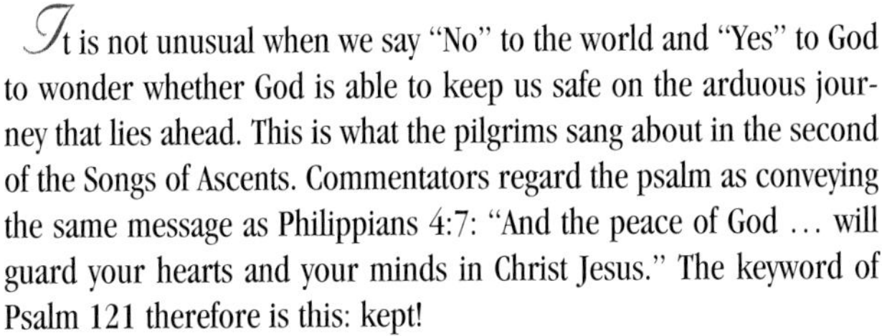

It is not unusual when we say "No" to the world and "Yes" to God to wonder whether God is able to keep us safe on the arduous journey that lies ahead. This is what the pilgrims sang about in the second of the Songs of Ascents. Commentators regard the psalm as conveying the same message as Philippians 4:7: "And the peace of God ... will guard your hearts and your minds in Christ Jesus." The keyword of Psalm 121 therefore is this: kept!

Let's face it, travelling along the road of faith is not easy. Many Christians are surprised at the number of difficulties they encounter on the way. A fairly new Christian said to me on one occasion: "I thought becoming a Christian meant floating to heaven on a bed of ease. But I have been rudely awakened." So what do we do when, on the walk of faith, we meet with some major difficulty? Often when in trouble we scan the horizon hoping that someone will appear and come to our aid. However, the psalmist is making the point that we should not look to the hills for help but to the God of the hills. This is not to say, of course, that the beauty of nature possesses no calming influence—it does. But it is powerless to heal by itself alone. The hills cannot answer back. The mountains cannot love or laugh or weep.

The panacea we need when troubles come is not to be found in nature. When troubles come we must look much higher than the hills. Our help comes from the Lord.

FURTHER STUDY

Ps. 34:1–10; Isa. 40:25–26; Dan. 4:34–35

1. What was David's testimony?

2. When was Nebuchadnezzar's sanity restored?

Prayer

O God, forgive me that so often I look around when I need help rather than looking up. Give me the attitude of the psalmist and all the pilgrims who have gone before me who looked not to creation but to the Creator. In Jesus' Name. Amen.

SECTION ONE

Why Accidents?

For reading & meditation—Psalm 121:3–6

"He will not let your foot slip—he who watches over you will not slumber ..." (v.3)

What are we to make of these verses in which we are told of three hazards that faced travelers in the ancient world? One, stepping on a loose stone and hurting or breaking one's ankle. Two, the peril of severe sunstroke. Three, the effect of the moon on the emotional system, which has been feared for centuries.

I know many Christians who have become deeply disillusioned because of these verses. They have taken them as God's promise that they will not be physically or emotionally hurt. Thus, when they have been involved in an accident, or a serious illness has struck them down, their faith has fallen apart. We must be careful that we do not hold God to promises He has never made. Once, when in Kota Kinabulu, East Malaysia, just minutes before I was due to commence a seminar, a member of my team slipped and seriously chipped her ankle. It was a painful time for her until she received medical attention. Later one person said to me: "How could God let that happen when she was so clearly doing the work of the Lord?"

Are we to conclude from these verses that Christians should never get sick, never break a leg or sprain an ankle, never get a headache, never get sunstroke? Some of the finest Christians I know have suffered from serious setbacks. Some people say that if you are involved in an accident then you must have stepped out of the will of God. I certainly don't believe that, and I hope you don't either. We will explore this in a deeper way tomorrow.

FURTHER STUDY

Gen. 28:10–22; Ps. 57:1; 2 Tim. 1:12

1. What did God promise to be to Jacob?

2. What was Paul's testimony to Timothy?

Father, I see that today's reading and thoughts are a parable of life. There are some days when I don't get answers and have to wait until the next day. In the meantime, help me to hold on to You in perfect trust. In Jesus' Name I ask it. Amen.

SECTION ONE

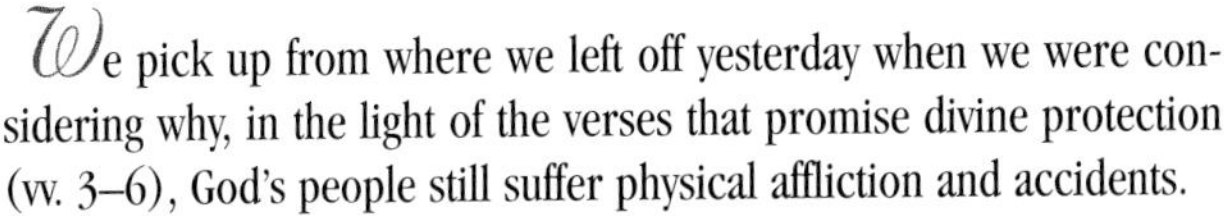

Our Traveling Companion

For reading & meditation—Psalm 121:7–8

"The Lord ... will watch over your life ..." (v.7)

We pick up from where we left off yesterday when we were considering why, in the light of the verses that promise divine protection (vv. 3–6), God's people still suffer physical affliction and accidents.

These words have to be set in the context of the whole of Scripture, and nowhere in the Bible is there the faintest suggestion that the life of faith exempts us from problems. In terms of the physical there is the promise of healing (and that must not be minimized), and there are many instances of divine protection and deliverance from danger in the Scriptures, but we are not to assume that because we are believers we shall never suffer physically. The promise of this psalm is not that a believer will be kept from accidents or sickness but that these and similar difficulties do not have the power to affect us spiritually.

Notice again what the psalmist says in verse 7: "The Lord will keep you from all harm." The New King James Version says: "The Lord shall preserve you from all evil." The promise then is not that we will be kept from hurt but from harm. The two are quite different. Six times in this psalm the Lord is described as the Keeper—the One who watches over us. "He may not," as someone has put it, "stop the waves from buffeting us on the outside, but He will stop them from buffeting us on the inside." Each step we take on life's journey we must sing of the fact that though evil may come to us, it will not cause our downfall.

FURTHER STUDY

2 Cor. 11:16–33;

Phil. 4:11–12

1. What are some of the experiences Paul suffered?

2. What was he able to say?

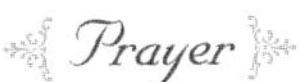

My Father and my God, help me sing this song too—the song that tells of my constant traveling Companion who assures me that though sometimes the envelope gets tattered and torn, the letter inside stays safe. Hallelujah! Amen.

SECTION ONE

Inner Health

For reading & meditation—Psalm 122:1–9

"I rejoiced with those who said to me, 'Let us go to the house of the Lord.'" (v.1)

We come now to the third of the Songs of Ascents. In the first song we saw that the keyword was renunciation. In the second, kept. Here the keyword is worship. This is a psalm that focuses on the delights and joys that come from worshiping God.

Some reading the psalm for the first time might think that the opening words are the attempt of an enthusiast to stir people up to give praise. But they are not. They are the reflections of a person who has experienced the benefits that come to the soul through the worship of God. The author C. S. Lewis told how, after becoming a Christian, he found a stumbling block in the demand so glamorously made by the psalmist that we should worship God, still more in the suggestion that God commanded it. Then he realized that it is through worship that God communicates His presence to us. The essence of the Jewish sacrifices, he pointed out, was that when men and women gave bulls and goats to God, He gave Himself to them.

The idea that God craves our worship in the same way that a vain person may hunger for compliments is an unworthy one. God is thinking more of us than Himself when He bids us worship Him. For it is in the worship of Him that we complete ourselves. Our souls find their highest potential as we pour out our hearts in worship and adoration. Perhaps this is what C. S. Lewis had in mind when he said: "Worship is inner health made audible."

FURTHER STUDY

Ps. 95:1–7; 96:1–13

1. How does the psalmist express his worship?

2. What are some of his exhortations to us?

Prayer

Father, I see that when my soul draws near to You in worship I am all the better for doing so. Yet I worship not because of the benefits but because it is right. You are worthy to be worshiped. And I do so, like the psalmist, with delight. Amen.

SECTION ONE

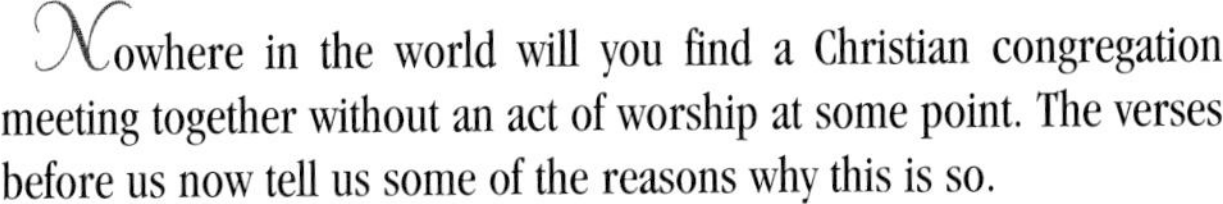

Knowing Where We Stand

DAY 11

For reading & meditation—Psalm 122:2–3

"Jerusalem is built like a city that is closely compacted together." (v.3)

Nowhere in the world will you find a Christian congregation meeting together without an act of worship at some point. The verses before us now tell us some of the reasons why this is so.

First, worship provides us with the structure we need in order to live life effectively. The psalmist tells us that Jerusalem was a city "closely compacted together." Miles Coverdale translated these words "that is at unity with itself." Jerusalem was a beautifully designed city where everything fitted together harmoniously. No loose stones, no awkward gaps, no unsightly buildings; it was well built, compact and "at unity with itself." It was the place also where all the tribes went up to give thanks to the Lord. What was true architecturally was also true socially. The tribes coming from different parts of Israel, with their different accents and local customs, were drawn together in a single entity as they opened their hearts in worship to God.

How do we get the framework, the sense of structure we need to be able to move effectively from one day to another, in a world where everything that seemed to be nailed down is coming apart? What is the coordinating point that pulls together our confused thoughts and feelings as we look out at the comedy we call a civilization? It is to be found in our worship of God. We enter into the presence of the Lord and lo, His unity becomes our unity. Things that were once loose and sloppy become strong and firm. Worship helps us get our heads together. It helps us know where we stand.

FURTHER STUDY

Ps. 26:1–8; 23:6; 27:4; 84:10; 122:1

1. What was David's commitment?

2. What was the psalmist's preference?

Prayer

O God, now I see why it is that I feel so "put together" after I have spent time in worshiping You. All the loose parts of me are restored to their rightful order as Your unity contributes to mine. I am so deeply, deeply thankful. Amen.

DAY 12

SECTION ONE

Feelings Can Be Liars!

For reading & meditation—Psalm 122:4–5

"... the tribes go up ... to praise the name of the Lord according to the statute given to Israel." (v.4)

Today we look at the fact that worship is commanded by God: "That is where the tribes go up ... to praise the name of the Lord according to the statute given to Israel."

I am so glad God has given us a command to worship Him for if not we would be left to the vagaries of our feelings. We would say: "I'll praise God when I feel like it," and the consequences would be harmful to our souls. The biblical position is this: whether or not we feel like it, we should instruct our souls to worship the Lord. Feelings very often are liars. Feelings are important, of course, but we must never let them be our masters; we must make them our servants. Paul Scherer in his book *The Word God Sent* points out that: "The Bible wastes very little time on the way we feel." The age in which we live has been called "the age of sensation" because we think that if we don't feel something then there is little point in it. But it is possible to act ourselves into a new way of feeling just as it is possible to feel ourselves into a new way of acting.

I like the way Eugene Peterson puts it: "Worship is an act which develops feelings for God, not a feeling for God which is expressed in an act of worship." When we obey the command to worship God and offer Him our worship even though we do not feel like it then something happens in our souls that is quite amazing. Try it and see.

FURTHER STUDY

Deut. 5:1–21; 10:1–12; 1 Chron. 16:1–36; Ps. 29:1–2

1. What was the focus of the tablets of stone?

2. Why was the ark so important?

Prayer

O Father, help me when there is a clash between my feelings and Your decrees to vote against my inclinations and for Your commands. I would make my feelings my servants, not my masters. Help me maintain this position. In Jesus' Name. Amen.

SECTION ONE

Shalom!

For reading & meditation—Psalm 122:6–9

"Pray for the peace of Jerusalem . . ." (v.6)

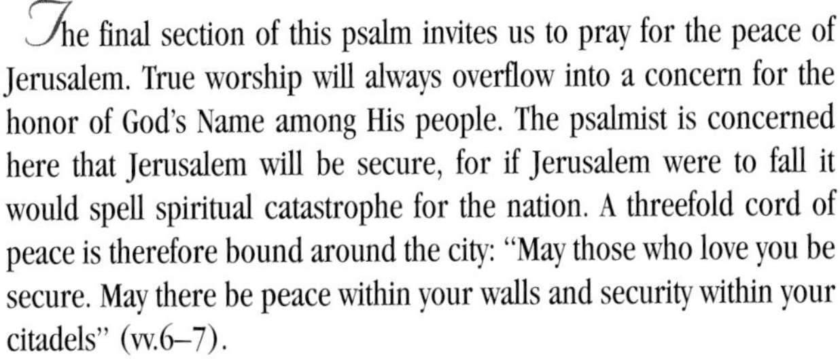

The final section of this psalm invites us to pray for the peace of Jerusalem. True worship will always overflow into a concern for the honor of God's Name among His people. The psalmist is concerned here that Jerusalem will be secure, for if Jerusalem were to fall it would spell spiritual catastrophe for the nation. A threefold cord of peace is therefore bound around the city: "May those who love you be secure. May there be peace within your walls and security within your citadels" (vv.6–7).

The words "peace" and "security" in Hebrew—*shalom* and *shalvah*—play on the sounds in the name Jerusalem—Jerushalom, the place of worship. *Shalom* is one of the most beautiful words in the Bible. The closest we can come to it in English is "peace," but that poorly represents the richness of what is contained in the Hebrew. One commentator says: "You can no more define shalom by calling it peace than you can define a person by his or her social security number. It gathers all aspects of wholeness that result from God's will being completed in us." Shalvah, meaning security, is an almost untranslatable word also. Its root meaning is leisure—the relaxed stance of someone who knows that all is well because God is on His throne.

The theme of this psalm is worship. In worship we find the coordinating point our souls need to bring all the loose ends together. Ancient pilgrims sang this song over and over again on the way to the summit—Jerusalem. It is a song we too must never stop singing.

FURTHER STUDY

Heb. 4:1–16; Matt. 11:29; Phil. 4:6–7

1. How can we enter God's rest?

2. What is God's promise to us?

Prayer

O God, help me sing this song and sing it well, and remember also that the more I give myself to You in worship the more You can give Yourself to me. I would worship You in spirit and in truth. Teach me how, dear Father. In Jesus' Name. Amen.

SECTION ONE

Is God Weightless?

For reading & meditation—Psalm 123:1–4

"I lift up my eyes to you, to you whose throne is in heaven." (v.1)

So far in reflecting on the Songs of Ascents we have been given three great themes to add to our spiritual treasury—renunciation, security and worship. In the psalm now before us we have a picture of what it means to be a true servant of the Almighty. Psalm 123 is a song of service.

Where does our service for God begin? It begins with an upward look: "I lift up my eyes to you, to you whose throne is in heaven." Why is it that so often in the Old Testament the patriarchs and prophets looked up to God? Not around, not down, but up. It is because they saw God first and foremost as transcendent—high and lifted up. In today's culture we are so preoccupied with God's immanence—the closeness of His presence—that we are in danger of losing sight of how great and mighty He really is. Dr. Larry Crabb, speaking on this issue, put it like this: "In today's culture God has been brought so near that He is no longer there." I see this tendency to regard God as immanent rather than transcendent when moving among Christian counselors. They present God as Someone from Whom to obtain things rather than as a Person to humbly worship and sacrificially serve. As a result, God is becoming, as David Wells provocatively put it, weightless.

The Old Testament saints saw God as a transcendent God—a God Who is there, a God Who is weighty. He is also immanent, of course, but that great truth, glorious though it is, must never be put before His transcendence.

FURTHER STUDY

Gen. 14:17–24; Ps. 21:7; 82:6; Dan. 4:17; Isa. 6:1–4

1. How is God described?

2. What was Isaiah's experience?

Prayer

O God, high and lifted up, grant that I may never lose the vision of Your Almightiness. Give me, I pray, a clearer understanding of Your weightiness, Your omnipotence, Your unending strength. In Jesus' Name I ask it. Amen.

The Posture of a Servant

For reading & meditation—Psalm 123:2

"As the eyes of slaves look to the hand of their master … so our eyes look to the Lord …" (v.2)

If our primary vision of God is of Someone we look up to then we will more easily see ourselves as servants. For that really is what we are—men and women who do His bidding.

In parts of today's Church there is a strong emphasis on understanding our authority in Christ, of claiming (sometimes even demanding) what God has promised. We must be careful that this emphasis does not become a primary focus. Eugene Peterson makes the point that because God presented Himself to us in Jesus Christ in the form of a servant, we can come perilously close to regarding God as Someone we can order around, Someone we can exploit. God did not become a servant so that He could be exploited but in order that we could bring our lifestyle into line with His. This is not to say there is no place for exercising our authority in Christ, of rejoicing in the fact that we are seated together with Him in the heavenlies (plus all the implications of that fact). But we can only exercise that ministry correctly when we keep the thought ever before us that He is the Master and we are His servants.

God, as we have said, is a God we must look up to. And when we look up to Him (as opposed to looking down on Him) then, at that moment, we are in the posture of a servant. It is important that we understand clearly the relationship that exists between us and the Almighty. He is not here to do our bidding; we are here to do His.

FURTHER STUDY

Phil. 2:1–11; Ps. 2:11; Eph. 6:7

1. What does the Lord require?

2. How are we to serve?

O God my Father, help me ever to remain in the posture of a servant. I would not have it any other way. I am at the feet of the One who has washed my feet. Thank You, Lord Jesus. Amen.

SECTION ONE

Under His Mercy

For reading & meditation—Psalm 123:3

"Have mercy on us, O Lord, have mercy on us . . ." (v.3)

If we are to function effectively as servants then we need to have a clear understanding of the God we serve. Nothing can be worse for a servant than to have a master who is unpredictable, who doesn't know his own mind.

We, however, who claim to be God's servants know quite well what to expect from our Master. It is mercy. Three times this word appears in this short but powerful psalm: ". . . our eyes look to the Lord our God, till he shows us his mercy. Have mercy on us, O Lord, have mercy on us" (vv.2–3). How important it is for all who serve the Lord to see Him as One who desires their highest good. He does not treat us in the way we deserve to be treated but according to His wise purposes and His eternal plans. God is not, as J. B. Phillips so rightly says in his little classic *Your God is Too Small*: "a Cosmic Policeman who strides through His universe watching for one of His children to step out of line and then comes down on them with a heavy hand, threatening to put them in jail if they become argumentative or obstreperous." No, He is a Potter who works with the clay of our lives, digging out the grit, forming, shaping, reforming our lives until they are in accord with His good and wise purposes.

The servants of the Lord do not cower in terror before Him, afraid of His lash. They serve with true freedom and joy, knowing they live not under their Master's menacing frown but under His mercy.

FURTHER STUDY

Ps. 103:1–22; 108:4; Lam. 3:22–26; Titus 3:5

1. How does the psalmist depict God's mercy?

2. What perspective does Paul put on mercy?

Prayer

O merciful and gracious Master, how can I ever sufficiently thank You for delivering me from the slavery of sin so that I could become a servant of righteousness? Now I serve with joy—Your willing slave forever. Thank You, my Father. Amen.

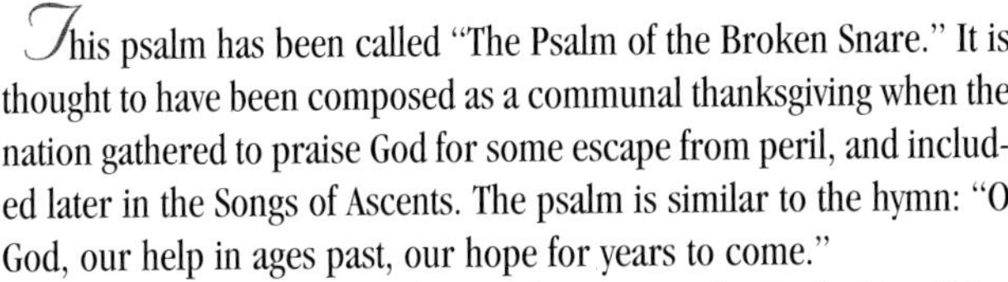

For reading & meditation—Psalm 124:1–8

"If the Lord had not been on our side ..." (v.1)

This psalm has been called "The Psalm of the Broken Snare." It is thought to have been composed as a communal thanksgiving when the nation gathered to praise God for some escape from peril, and included later in the Songs of Ascents. The psalm is similar to the hymn: "O God, our help in ages past, our hope for years to come."

The key thought in this psalm is deliverance. It begins by identifying the most critical period in Israel's history—the Exodus—and ends by giving praise to God for His great deliverance. The repetitive nature of the first lines reflects the fact that the precentor would have sung the first line then the rest of the singers would have taken up the strains.

Some consider it pointless to reflect on the past, choosing rather to turn their eyes to the future. I have noticed that new Christians often ask: Why are we always singing about the things God has done in the past; shouldn't our eyes be focused on the challenges that lie ahead? We do so in order that we might not forget the kind of God we are related to and Whom we serve. "We are so dull and stupid as the result of sin," said Dr. Martyn Lloyd-Jones, "that we might even forget the death of the Son of God and His agony and His shame on the Cross ... if the Lord Himself had not ordained that we should meet together, break bread and drink wine." Sometimes it is only when we focus on the past that hope can be found for the present.

FURTHER STUDY

Ps. 99:1–9; 1 Cor. 10:1–13; Heb. 1:1–2; 3:1–11; Rom. 15:4

1. What did Paul not want the Corinthians to be ignorant of?

2. What does the Holy Spirit say?

Father, I am so grateful that I can bring yesterday into today simply by reflecting on Your goodness in the past. May the deliverances You have wrought in my life in the past quicken my hope for the present and future. In Jesus' Name. Amen.

DAY

18

SECTION ONE

"If the Lord ..."

For reading & meditation—Psalm 124:3

"... when their anger flared against us, they would have swallowed us alive ..." (v.3)

God's ability to deliver the Israelites is identified in this psalm in two ways. First, when they were in danger of being overcome by the might of their enemies, and second, when in danger of being drowned by floods. "If the Lord had not been on our side," the Israelites reminded themselves, "they would have swallowed us alive" (vv.1, 3).

When I was young I heard a stirring sermon given by a Welsh preacher on the three words with which this psalm begins: "If the Lord ..." He recounted the great spiritual events of history—the deliverance from Egypt, the entrance into the Promised Land, the return of the exiles to Jerusalem, the coming of Christ to the world, the great outpouring of the Spirit at Pentecost—his point being that if the Lord had not intervened then history would have been completely different and humanity would have been lost and without hope. Then he brought his message right up to date and invited the congregation to think of where they might have been at that moment if the Lord had not been at work in their lives. The sermon was a powerful one and I saw the point as never before of how grateful we should be for God's intervention in our lives.

Where would you and I be at this moment if the Lord had not been merciful to us? I shudder to think. Our very survival to this present time and our safety can be traced back to God's hand —must be traced back to God's hand. "If the Lord ..." Three little words but they open up worlds.

FURTHER STUDY

Luke 17:11–19; Col. 3:12–16; Luke 19:37; Heb. 13:15

1. What are we often guilty of?

2. What are we to continually express?

Prayer

O my Father, when I think of where I might have been now had it not been for You, my heart is filled with gratitude and praise for Your intervention in my life. I shall never cease to praise You. Blessed be Your wondrous Name forever. Amen.

"The Broken Snare"

For reading & meditation—Psalm 124:6–7

"We have escaped like a bird out of the fowler's snare ..." (v.7)

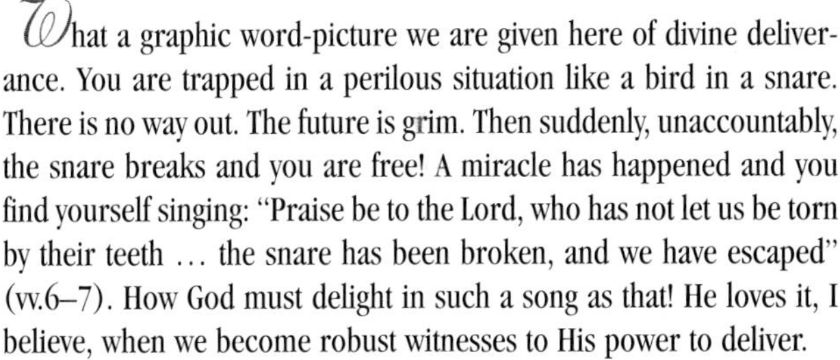

What a graphic word-picture we are given here of divine deliverance. You are trapped in a perilous situation like a bird in a snare. There is no way out. The future is grim. Then suddenly, unaccountably, the snare breaks and you are free! A miracle has happened and you find yourself singing: "Praise be to the Lord, who has not let us be torn by their teeth ... the snare has been broken, and we have escaped" (vv.6–7). How God must delight in such a song as that! He loves it, I believe, when we become robust witnesses to His power to deliver.

Life on this planet is hazardous. We have no idea what will happen to us. Before this day is over we may have to deal with such matters as serious illness, physical or emotional pain, death, a financial reverse, a broken relationship, rejection, perhaps even a national or world emergency. We live on the edge of danger, and sometimes we become caught up in situations from which there seems just no way out. Then God comes in glorious deliverance. The trap is broken and our soul is set free.

That doesn't always happen as quickly as we would like, and it doesn't always happen the way we would like; it happens in the way that God sees best. He steps in, releases the snare and our soul soars, like a bird set free, to sing at the door of heaven.

Take a moment now to count up some of the deliverances God has wrought in your life. Aren't they worth a song?

FURTHER STUDY

2 Tim. 4:9–18; Ps. 91:1–7; Isa. 46:4; 2 Cor. 1:10

1. Of what was Paul confident when he wrote to Timothy?
2. What was the psalmist's conviction?

Prayer

O yes, dear Lord, I reflect on all the deliverances You have wrought in my life, and my heart sings in praise and gratitude to You. Blessed be Your Name forever. Amen.

SECTION ONE

Something to Sing About

For reading & meditation—Psalm 124:8

"Our help is in the name of the Lord, the Maker of heaven and earth." (v.8)

Psalm 124 began with the statement that the Lord is on our side; it ends with that same truth: "Our help is in the name of the Lord ...." Israel had proved God to be their great Deliverer, and with this incontrovertible fact in mind they faced the future not with a sigh but with a song. Psalm 124, then, is a song about hazards and help. God allows us to get into difficulties, but He is always at hand to deliver.

How different our days would be if, instead of lamenting the state of the world, we would give more consideration to the fact that God is on our side. Eugene Peterson says: "Christians are not fatigued outcasts who carry righteousness as a burden in a world where the wicked flourish." Christians are people who sing: "Our help is in the name of the Lord, the Maker of heaven and earth."

I heard of a missionary to Korea who went into the marketplace one morning and sang as he made some purchases. Soon a small crowd gathered and begged him to sing another song. He did, and again they asked him to sing to them. "I'll sing you another song on one condition," he said, "and that is you must sing a song for me." There was silence for a while and then a little girl spoke up: "But sir, we have nothing to sing about." Her statement was revealing. You can only sing, really sing, when you have something to sing about. Christians have Someone to sing about: "The Lord, the Maker of heaven and earth."

FURTHER STUDY

Isa. 41:1–16; Ps. 28:7; 40:17; Heb. 13:6

1. What was God's promise to Israel?

2. What can we say with confidence?

Prayer

My Father and my God, I am so thankful that my song is not a ditty sung in order to divert me from reality. Instead, I sing because I can't help it. It is not so much a case of me singing a song but the song singing me. I am so thankful. Amen.

SECTION ONE

Stirred, But Not Shaken!

For reading & meditation—Psalm 125:1–5

"Those who trust in the Lord are like Mount Zion, which cannot be shaken but endures forever." (v.1)

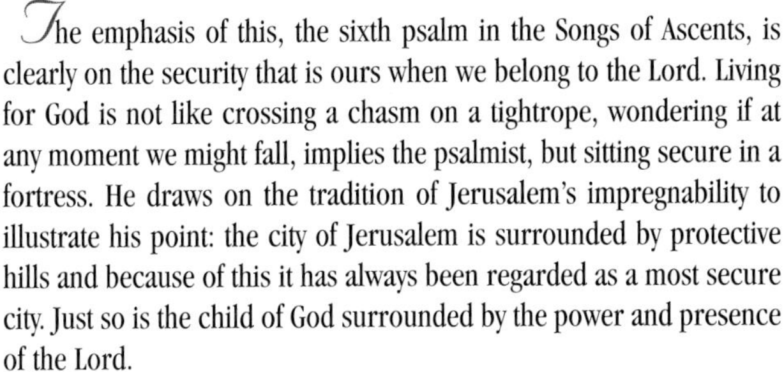

The emphasis of this, the sixth psalm in the Songs of Ascents, is clearly on the security that is ours when we belong to the Lord. Living for God is not like crossing a chasm on a tightrope, wondering if at any moment we might fall, implies the psalmist, but sitting secure in a fortress. He draws on the tradition of Jerusalem's impregnability to illustrate his point: the city of Jerusalem is surrounded by protective hills and because of this it has always been regarded as a most secure city. Just so is the child of God surrounded by the power and presence of the Lord.

Though this all sounds wonderful, is it possible to be so sure of God that we cannot be shaken? I believe it is, and I think that as I get older and more experienced in the Christian life I am learning how. When we experience major problems the first thing that is affected is our feelings. Now feelings are important; they keep us aware of what is happening. However, they tell us next to nothing about God, who He is and how He operates. In the moments when my feelings are being stirred I try to remember that my security comes from knowing who God is, not how I feel.

Spiritual poise comes from living by what I know about God, not by what I feel about Him or about myself and my circumstances. Living this way doesn't stop me from feeling stirred but it does stop me from being shaken.

Prayer

My Father and my God, I am so thankful that in You I can find real peace and joy and never be shaken. I may tremble on the Rock but the Rock never trembles under me. I am eternally grateful. Amen.

FURTHER STUDY

Rom. 8:28–39; Job 11:18; Ps. 112:7

1. What is our response to our calling to be?

2. What was Paul convinced of?

SECTION ONE

A Simple Test

For reading & meditation—Psalm 125:2

"As the mountains surround Jerusalem, so the Lord surrounds his people ..." (v.2)

Someone has referred to the text before us today as "a thrilling spiritual equation." "As the mountains surround Jerusalem, so the Lord surrounds his people." As—so. But how deeply do we believe what the psalmist is telling us? We have no difficulty with one side of the equation, the side that says: "As the mountains surround Jerusalem," because we can easily verify the geography. But what about the other side, the side that says: "so the Lord surrounds his people?" That we have to take on trust.

How good are you at trusting? The degree of your trust in God will be the degree to which you are secure as a person. One of the best tests I know to evaluate how secure I am in God is to examine my heart when I encounter an anxiety-provoking situation. Psychologists who study human reactions tell us that we have elaborate defense mechanisms built into us on which we can draw to guard ourselves against anxiety. They have names for these mechanisms, such as repression, denial, projection and displacement. The challenge for me as a Christian is to decide in times of anxiety whether to rely on my psychological defenses to meet the situation or on God.

The psalmist says in Psalm 46:1: "God is our refuge and strength, an ever-present help in trouble." Lovely sounding words, but are they true? Of course they are. It is on theology, not psychology, that I must base my trust. If you can't bank on anything else you can bank on what God says. Not to bank on it gives rise to insecurity.

FURTHER STUDY

Ps. 37:1–11; 118:8; Prov. 3:5–6; Isa. 26:4

1. What does the psalmist David exhort us not to do?

2. What is his alternative strategy?

Prayer

O God, I would be a secure person. Forgive me that sometimes I have more confidence in my psychological defenses than I have in You. Help me develop a deeper trust. In Jesus' Name. Amen.

SECTION ONE

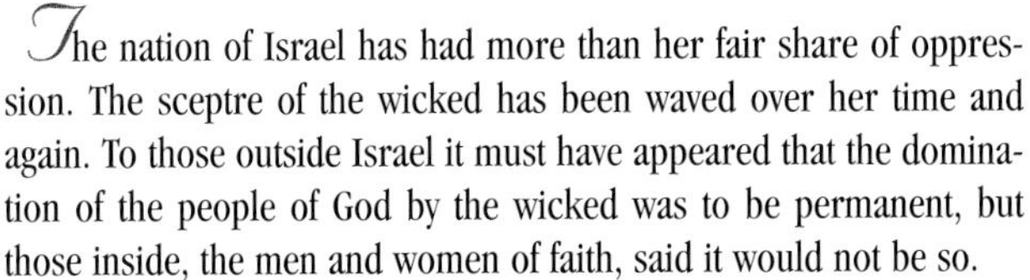

Evil Has a Short Leash

DAY 23

For reading & meditation—Psalm 125:3

"The scepter of the wicked will not remain ... for then the righteous might ... do evil." (v.3)

The nation of Israel has had more than her fair share of oppression. The sceptre of the wicked has been waved over her time and again. To those outside Israel it must have appeared that the domination of the people of God by the wicked was to be permanent, but those inside, the men and women of faith, said it would not be so.

If evil is everlasting, if there is no prospect of it being overcome, then even the strongest believer can break: "... for then the righteous might use their hands to do evil." But God will not permit such a situation. The history of the ages bears witness to this fact. Evil advances and is then overthrown. It makes its forays into the ranks of the people of God and is then hurled back. "Evil is always temporary," says one preacher, "the worst does not last."

This is the confidence we have as God's people living in this world—evil is on a short leash. Nothing that runs counter to God's justice can survive into eternity. The word "evil" is the word "live" spelled backwards. Evil cannot prevail. It has the stamp of death on it. Dangers, difficulties and oppression will never be too much for us. In New Testament language: "God is faithful; he will not let you be tempted beyond what you can bear. But when you are tempted, he will also provide a way out so that you can stand up under it" (1 Cor. 10:13). Be encouraged—the eternal God who watches over every one of us knows when to say: "That's enough."

FURTHER STUDY

Rom. 7:1–8:39; 2 Cor. 10:4; 1 Tim. 6:12

1. How does Paul describe the struggle with evil?

2. How does he describe the outcome?

Prayer

O Father, thank You for this. It is my anchor in times of storm. Help me develop confidence in the fact that You know just how far to let things go, and that You allow nothing to extend further than Your grace. Amen.

SECTION ONE

Relax!

For reading & meditation—Psalm 125:4–5

"Do good, O Lord, to those who are good, to those who are upright in heart." (v.4)

These final verses of Psalm 125 comprise both a prayer and a warning. The psalmist prays for those who are faithful in heart and are endeavoring to maintain the standards God has laid down. Though it looked as if their enemies were on the winning side, the psalmist reminds God's people, Israel, that to abandon the traditional faith would bring them spiritual and national disaster.

His last sentence: "Peace be upon Israel," is colloquial and could, bearing in mind the context, be expanded thus: "Compose yourself. Remember your true security is found in God. Nothing will happen to you that He can't turn to good. Because of this you are as safe in God as you would be sitting in the middle of the fortress Jerusalem."

Walking the upward road of faith is difficult, but it should never be regarded as impossible. The word "impossible" does not feature prominently in a true believer's vocabulary. When God breathes into situations then the aspirate transforms the word into Himpossible. The storms may come but they can never turn back the person whose heart is in touch with the Lord. Some think being a Christian in today's world is an uncertain business. On a plane recently a man said when he discovered I am a preacher and a writer: "It must be very difficult trying to help people maintain their faith in a world such as this." I replied: "I'm not the one responsible for that. God is." I don't think he understood what I meant, but I am sure you do. We are secure because God is secure. So relax!

FURTHER STUDY

Ps. 46:1–11; 37:7; 4:6–8; 127:2

1. What is a sure sign of being able to relax?
2. What do we find difficult?

Prayer

O Father, what reassurance this gives me. I may let go of You but You will never let go of me. You have held the world up for millenniums and never let it slip. Neither, I know, will You let me. I am so thankful. Amen.

SECTION ONE

Of Its Own Accord

For reading & meditation—Psalm 126:1–6

"When the Lord brought back the captives to Zion, we were like men who dreamed." (v.1)

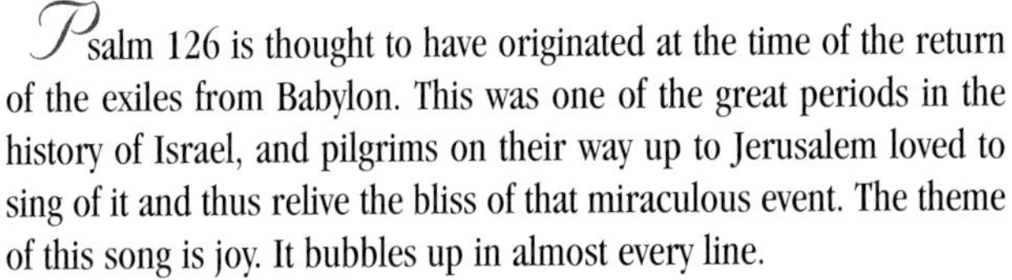

Psalm 126 is thought to have originated at the time of the return of the exiles from Babylon. This was one of the great periods in the history of Israel, and pilgrims on their way up to Jerusalem loved to sing of it and thus relive the bliss of that miraculous event. The theme of this song is joy. It bubbles up in almost every line.

Joy is a characteristic of all who walk the road of faith. Dourness is not a fruit of the Spirit. Joy is. Sometimes people mistake happiness for the joy that is to be found only in God. Worldlings have their pleasures. And indeed, there are many pleasures in life—sweet, God-given things. Samuel Butler said: "All the animals, excepting man, know the principal business of life is to enjoy it." Yet pleasure and Christian joy cannot be equated. Pleasure depends on circumstances. Christian joy is completely independent of circumstances. Pleasures come and go. The joy of God is constant. It rises to rise again. Pleasures are superficial. Joy is deep. It wells up from inner contentment. The smile is not merely on the lips and in the eyes but in the heart. It may flame into rapture or sink into peace.

Godly joy is not something a pilgrim is required to have, but is rather a consequence of having been set free from the bondage of sin and knowing, like the prodigal, that one's feet are on the road that leads to the Father's house. We don't have to acquire joy. It comes to us when we experience salvation, of its own accord.

FURTHER STUDY

Prov. 19:23; 1 Tim. 6:6–8

1. What is great gain?

2. What is a hallmark of this generation?

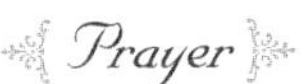

Prayer

O Father, words just cannot express the wonder in my heart that I have found true joy, an unshakable joy, an immeasurable joy. Or rather, it has found me. I am eternally grateful. Thank You, my Father. Amen.

SECTION ONE

Too Good To Be True?

For reading & meditation—Psalm 126:2–3

"... it was said among the nations, 'The Lord has done great things for them.'" (v.2)

Joy, as we have been saying, characterizes a Christian pilgrim. It arises from having been set free from sin's bondage and the realization that one is in communion with the Creator of the universe. D.L. Jacks, in his little book *The Lost Radiance of the Christian Religion*, wrote: "There is no religion which throws off the burden of life so completely, which escapes so swiftly from our moods, which gives so large a scope for the high spirits of the soul as the Christian religion."

We can only imagine what joyful memories the following words would have triggered in the minds of the pilgrims who sang this song: "It was said among the nations, 'The Lord has done great things for them.'" Even those outside of Israel were impressed with the miracles that God had accomplished, and, not to be outdone by pagans, Israel expressed glad and simple appreciation for God's great acts of deliverance.

What were those "great things"? The Old Testament fairly bulges with accounts of them. God has done great things for us, too, has He not? We who live in the Christian era can sing a song that compares with the thoughts uttered in this psalm: "To God be the glory, great things He has done." We too can share the psalmist's sentiment: "We were like men who dreamed" (v.1). What God has done for us in Christ seems too good to be true. But also, too good not to be true.

FURTHER STUDY

Isa. 61:1–10; Jer. 15:16; 1 Pet. 1:8; Rom. 14:17

1. What was Isaiah able to say?
2. What is the kingdom of God a matter of?

O Father, help me take my birthright of joy and live the life for which I'm made. You have set laughter in my heart. May it show itself more often on my face. In Jesus' Name I pray. Amen.

SECTION ONE

Joy! Joy! Joy!

For reading & meditation—Psalm 126:4–6

"Restore our fortunes, O Lord, like streams in the Negev." (v.4)

Joy is nurtured by anticipation of what God will do in the future. In the remaining three verses of this psalm that thought is wonderfully brought into focus by two colorful images.

First: "Restore our fortunes, O Lord, like streams in the Negev." The Negev, the southern part of Israel, is a vast desert, but when it rains it is transformed and becomes ablaze with color. Suddenly plants appear. This is how it is with the people of God, the psalmist is saying—long years of waiting are interrupted by the rain of God's blessing upon our lives.

The second image is: "He who goes out weeping, carrying seed to sow, will return with songs of joy, carrying sheaves with him" (v.6). Every farmer knows sowing seed in the bare earth is hard work and may seem unrewarding, but it is done in anticipation of a good harvest. Eugene Peterson comments: "All suffering, all pain, all emptiness, all disappointment is seed: sow it in God, and He will, finally, bring a crop of joy from it." Notice, too, that the presence of joy in a pilgrim's heart does not mean there will be no tears. Joy does not exclude weeping. Tears are part of our lot too. But they can never displace joy. It has been there in our past and it will be there in our future too. God will not change His way of working with us. What we have known of Him we will know of Him. This is a song for the road every pilgrim can and must sing: Joy! Joy! Joy!

FURTHER STUDY

Ps. 30:1–5; 16:11; Isa. 12:3; 35:10

1. What remains for a night?

2. What lasts a lifetime?

O Father, I am thankful that Your redemption, which includes joy, extends to the roots of my being and goes deeper than all the effects of my sorrows and disappointments. Joy is rooted in me. How wonderful. Thank You, Father. Amen.

DAY

28

SECTION ONE

Don't Work in Vain

For reading & meditation—Psalm 127:1–5

"Unless the Lord builds the house, its builders labor in vain." (v.1)

A subject on which most people have strong views is that of work. Those who are out of work or cannot work because of some injury or disability find the subject a distressing one. Those who have work and enjoy what they do find it deeply rewarding and fulfilling. There is a minority who, while they like the thought of financial reward, are not so keen to make the effort necessary to earn that reward.

The theme of Psalm 127 is, as you have guessed, work. It puts the whole subject into clear spiritual focus. Work is a major component of our lives. It is the one area of life perhaps above all others where, as Eugene Peterson has put it: "Our sin can be magnified or our faith mature." The ancient Israelites saw work in the same light that they saw worship. To them there was no difference between the sacred and the secular. Everything they did they did under the eye of God, and each activity had to square with the divine will.

"Unless the Lord builds the house … Unless the Lord watches over the city, [all is] in vain" (v.1). Note the word "unless". It presupposes that God works also. He builds and He watches. Because of that, unless we link everything we do to Him then it will be in vain. I really mean that. A house can be built by human hands but it can only become a home when God is in it. God must be at work in our work otherwise our work is in vain.

FURTHER STUDY

Gen. 2:1–15; Prov. 10:5; Eccl. 9:10; Eph. 4:28; 2 Thess. 3:12

1. What was part of God's plan for Eden?

2. What should be our attitude to work?

Prayer

Father, I remember what Your Son said when He was on earth: "My Father is always at his work … and I, too, am working" (John 5:17). Show me how to link my work with Your work so that what I do becomes a natural, inevitable and faithful development of Your work. Amen.

Pointless!

For reading & meditation—Psalm 127:2

"In vain you rise early and stay up late . . ." (v.2)

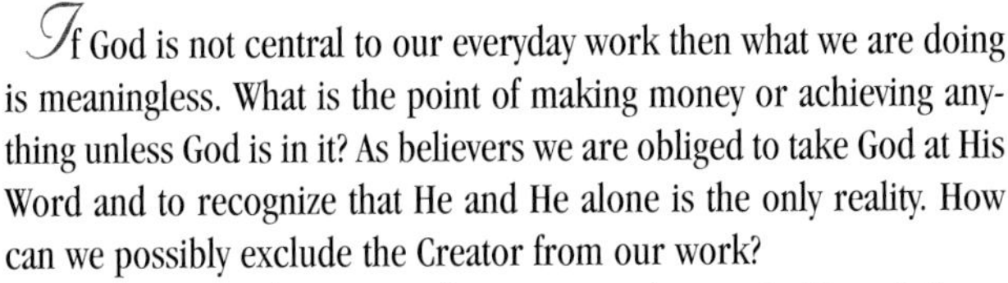

If God is not central to our everyday work then what we are doing is meaningless. What is the point of making money or achieving anything unless God is in it? As believers we are obliged to take God at His Word and to recognize that He and He alone is the only reality. How can we possibly exclude the Creator from our work?

Three times in the space of two verses the words "in vain" are repeated. The psalmist does this to emphasize that God and His children are involved together in everything, and none of us dare dispense with our senior Partner. Many of God's children (some of whom may be reading these lines today) spend long working hours and sleepless nights struggling to be successful in business, and fail because they have never seen the necessity of consulting their senior Partner about every matter. I have known many believers who have embarked on a business project without reference to the Lord, and only when things have gone wrong have they tried to bring God into it. Then they have become frantic and started taking measures such as tithing their profits in the hope that He will rescue them from distress.

No Christian ought to embark on any venture or business project without first consulting the Lord. And if you are sure God is not in your work or business then you should not be involved in it. It's pointless to expend your energy on matters in which God is not involved. Hear the words again: "Unless the Lord builds the house, its builders labor in vain."

FURTHER STUDY

2 Tim. 4:1–7; Mark 16:20; 1 Cor. 3:9; Hag. 2:4

1. What did Paul know he had achieved?

2. What is said of the disciples?

Prayer

O God, help me to evaluate my work carefully in the light of what I have read today. I don't want my work to be pointless. I want it to be meaningful, fulfilling Your purposes. Help me, my Father. In Jesus' Name. Amen.

DAY

30

SECTION ONE

Easy Work

For reading & meditation—Psalm 127:3–4

"Sons are a heritage from the Lord, children a reward from him." (v.3)

The first half of the psalm teaches by warning, the second half by example. "Sons are a heritage from the Lord, children a reward from him." Note the words "a heritage from the Lord … a reward from him."

The example the psalmist chooses is a subtle one. Building a home or guarding a city involve strenuous work, suggests Eugene Peterson, but children are the result of the miraculous process of reproduction which involves very little human effort. We cannot deny the painful exertion a mother has to go through in order to give birth, but we must not overlook the fact that a child is largely, though not entirely, the result of reproductive processes which God has built into the human system. We may be responsible for these marvelous beings who appear in our families as tiny infants, then walk and talk and grow tall among us, but we did not make them. We participated in an act of love—and in that sense alone can it be said that we "made a child." But then divine hands went to work in the womb, knitting the child together (as the psalmist put it in Psalm 139:13), and bringing to pass what can only be described as a miracle.

In contrast to the effort one has to put into building a home or guarding a city, the psalmist is saying when it comes to making a child it is largely effortless work. When God and His children team up then He takes over the major share of the project. We put in a little; He puts in a lot.

FURTHER STUDY

Ps. 139:13–18; 8:3–9; 100:3; Acts 17:21–28

1. What does the psalmist affirm about human conception?

2. What did Paul declare in his Athens sermon?

Prayer

Father, I stand in awe of Your goodness and Your grace. I see from this example that You are calling me to a new understanding of Your involvement in my life. You are willing to take the heaviest end of all my work. I am so grateful. Amen.

SECTION ONE

Intimate Relationships

For reading & meditation—Psalm 127:5

"Blessed is the man whose quiver is full of them. They will not be put to shame ..." (v.5)

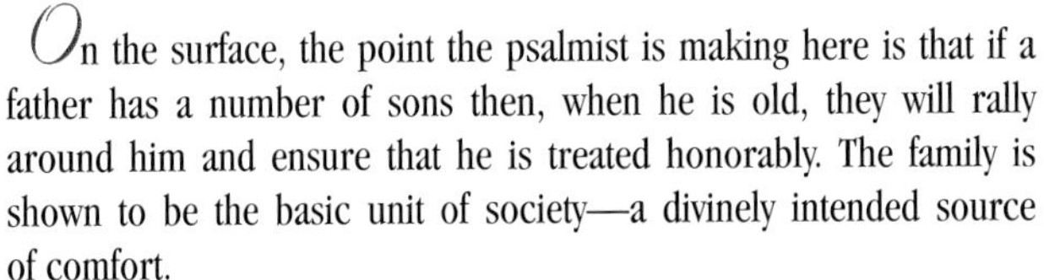

On the surface, the point the psalmist is making here is that if a father has a number of sons then, when he is old, they will rally around him and ensure that he is treated honorably. The family is shown to be the basic unit of society—a divinely intended source of comfort.

But I think there is a deeper truth here which we need to see—the truth concerning intimate relationships. Jesus, you will remember, said on one occasion: "Whoever does the will of my Father ... is my brother and sister and mother" (Matt. 12:50). In the light of that statement we cannot go far wrong if we see the psalmist's "sons" as representative of our personal relationships. By joining those words with the words of Psalm 127 we begin to get a picture of life and a way of working which is not focused on the acquisition of things but on the development of meaningful and rich relationships.

Life really is all about relationships—our relationship with God and relationships with others. Respect for people must be at the center of all our work if we are Christians. I am again indebted to Eugene Peterson for putting this truth much more powerfully than I could: "The character of our work is shaped not by accomplishments or possessions but in the birth of relationships. ... Among those around us we develop sons and daughters, brothers and sisters even as our Lord did with us." Making money is part of work, but developing relationships is part of it too. Happy are those who have their "quivers" full of them.

FURTHER STUDY

Eph. 2:11–22; Matt. 12:50; Rom. 8:17; Eph. 3:15; Heb. 2:11

1. How does the New Testament depict our new-found relationships?

2. What are the implications?

Prayer

O Father, I think again of the words of Your Son: "My Father is always at his work ... and I, too, am working." What sort of work are You both involved in? Can it be the building of relationships? That must be the greatest part of my work too. Help me. In Jesus' Name. Amen.

SECTION ONE

Kick-Back!

For reading & meditation—Psalm 128:1–6

"Blessed are all who fear the Lord, who walk in his ways." (v.1)

The view generally held by people of the world is that living as a Christian involves so many austerities that life becomes drained of all its color. But is this so? Not according to the psalmist. He claims that the true followers of the Lord are recipients of the divine blessing. "Blessed are all who fear the Lord, who walk in his ways." The word "contentment," I think, best summarizes the thoughts of the psalmist here.

Those who are blessed by God fulfil two conditions: they fear Him and walk in His ways. It is not that we should be scared of God but that we should approach Him with a sense of awe. It has been well said that God made us in His image and we return the compliment by trying to make Him in ours. Too often we think of God as an earthly friend. He is that of course. Abraham was called God's friend (James 2:23). We must be careful that we don't think of Him only in these terms. We are dealing with the God of creation who is majestic, holy, vast and wondrous. Let us never forget that.

We must not only let God be God—the real meaning of reverence—but we must "walk in his ways." We must do the things that please Him. When we walk in His ways we get results; when we walk contrary to His ways we get consequences. More bluntly: we can't do as we please and get away with it. Those whose lives are lived for "kicks" will find there is a twin called "kick-back."

FURTHER STUDY

Gen. 24:34–36;
Matt. 5:1–12; 6:33

1. What was the servant's testimony of Abraham?

2. What are some of the characteristics of the blessed?

Prayer

Father, I see that there are laws in the spiritual realm just as there are in the natural realm. The universe responds with results or consequences. I follow You, and You follow me—with blessings that cannot be numbered. I am so deeply, deeply thankful. Amen.

The Characteristic of Blessing

For reading & meditation—Psalm 128:3–4

"Your wife will be like a fruitful vine … your sons will be like olive shoots …" (v.3)

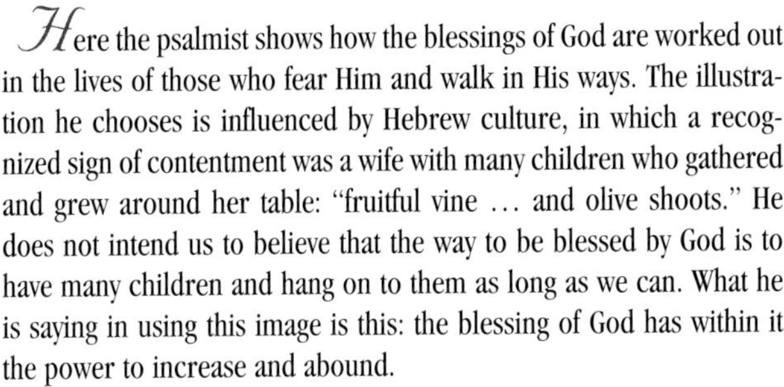

Here the psalmist shows how the blessings of God are worked out in the lives of those who fear Him and walk in His ways. The illustration he chooses is influenced by Hebrew culture, in which a recognized sign of contentment was a wife with many children who gathered and grew around her table: "fruitful vine … and olive shoots." He does not intend us to believe that the way to be blessed by God is to have many children and hang on to them as long as we can. What he is saying in using this image is this: the blessing of God has within it the power to increase and abound.

The *Theological Dictionary of the New Testament* says on this point: "Life consists in the constant meeting of souls, which must share their contents with each other. The blessed give to the others, because strength instinctively pours from him and up around him … The characteristic of blessing is to multiply." The world thinks that blessing and contentment comes from getting, but Scripture says that is more blessed to give than to receive. The problems of those countries in the Third World where there is famine and great hunger could be resolved overnight if governments and authorities were to pursue the well-being of others in the same way that they pursue their own.

The blessing of God flows to those who have learned that it is more blessed to give than to receive. Givers will find that when they give their vitality increases and the people around them become "fruitful vines" and "olive shoots" around their tables.

FURTHER STUDY

Luke 6:27–38; Matt. 10:8; Acts 20:35; Rom. 12:8; 2 Cor. 9:7

1. Why are we to freely give?

2. How are we to give?

Prayer

O God my Father, help me lay hold on the truth that I have been confronted with today that "the characteristic of blessing is to multiply." May I model this in every way and every day. For Jesus' sake. Amen.

DAY

34

SECTION ONE

Godly Contentment

For reading & meditation—Psalm 128:5–6

"May the Lord bless you from Zion all the days of your life ..." (v.5)

In these final verses we move from the homely scene of a woman with many children gathered around her table to the wider image of the city of Jerusalem. "The holy city," as it is called, was not only a political center but a religious one also. Here stood the Temple, and from it God's blessing radiated out to the people who lived in the city and those who visited it to worship. As Jerusalem remained and prospered so would the blessing of God be upon the people.

The psalmist closes with the wish that God's blessing would extend to people living long enough to see their grandchildren. Only those who have grandchildren can fully understand what that means!

His final words, "Peace be upon Israel," are ones which we have commented on before, so let us draw together now in summary form the message of this psalm. It speaks to the restlessness of modern-day life in a powerful way by reminding us, as Paul told Timothy, that "godliness with contentment is great gain" (1 Tim. 6:6). This does not mean that the godly life is protected from problems, but that all difficulties take on a quite different perspective when compared with the blessings that God pours into the souls of those who fear Him and serve Him. As the great hymn writer Isaac Watts put it:

Blessings abound where'er He reigns;
The prisoner leaps to loose his chains;
The weary find eternal rest;
And all the sons of want are blest.

FURTHER STUDY

Luke 3:1–14; Prov. 15:16; 1 Tim. 6:8–10; Heb. 13:5

1. What did John the Baptist tell the soldiers?

2. What has God promised that ought to keep us content?

Prayer

Gracious and loving heavenly Father, help me be a contented person. I see the secret of contentment is to fear You and walk in Your ways. May I do so not only today but all the days of my life. In Jesus' Name. Amen.

SECTION ONE

Down, But Not Out

For reading & meditation—Psalm 129:1–8

"… they have greatly oppressed me from my youth, but they have not gained the victory over me." (v.2)

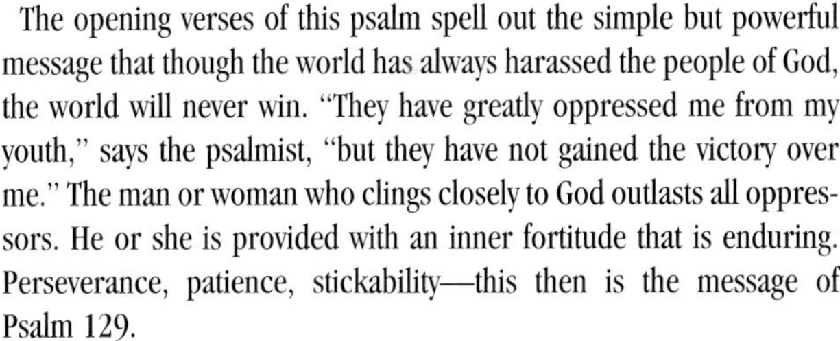

The opening verses of this psalm spell out the simple but powerful message that though the world has always harassed the people of God, the world will never win. "They have greatly oppressed me from my youth," says the psalmist, "but they have not gained the victory over me." The man or woman who clings closely to God outlasts all oppressors. He or she is provided with an inner fortitude that is enduring. Perseverance, patience, stickability—this then is the message of Psalm 129.

There is no better way of seeing the persistency of faith than by setting it in the context of history. God's people have been ostracized, ridiculed, humiliated, scorned, persecuted and beaten, but in the midst of the most horrific trials they have continued to serve God. If the persistence that flows from faith was merely a fad, then we would not be talking about it now.

Faith, persistent faith that is, is not a fad; it is a fact. It runs like a thread throughout all history and is shared by the men and women of every generation. Those who think of the Christian faith as a plant that flourishes only in good weather ought to take a look at history.

Faith is a hardy perennial that survives all weather conditions—drought, storm, even floods. J. B. Phillips, in his brilliant paraphrase of the New Testament, sums it up admirably: "We may be knocked down but we are never knocked out!" (2 Cor. 4:9). A preacher friend of mine puts it equally well when he says: "We may be floored but we are not flattened."

FURTHER STUDY

James 1:1–27; 5:1–11; Gal. 6:9; Heb. 12:1

1. What is Paul's exhortation?

2. What will enable us to persevere?

Prayer

Gracious Father, help me see that my perseverance is not so much a matter of me persevering but You persevering in me. I supply the willingness, You supply the power. Together we will make it, You and I. All glory be to Your wonderful Name. Amen.

SECTION ONE

The Lord Is Righteous

For reading & meditation—Psalm 129:3–4

"Plowmen have plowed my back and made their furrows long." (v.3)

Let us look now at the graphic way in which the psalmist describes the suffering which he had gone through because of his commitment to the Lord—suffering which was shared by many in his day: "Plowmen have plowed my back and made their furrows long." People had crossed God's purposes for his life and seemingly cut God's designs to ribbons.

Read the next phrase, however: "But the Lord is righteous; he has cut me free from the cords of the wicked" (v.4). The imagery here is striking. The psalmist is saying that though Israel's enemies thought they were plowing deep furrows into the backs of God's people, their plows of persecution had been unhitched. The Lord is an expert at unhitching plows. If the wicked would just take a look behind them they would see that their plows have been disconnected. Those who think they can outmaneuver God are stupid.

The words "But the Lord is righteous" (v.4) are the key to all we are considering here. When the Bible says that God is righteous it means that He is just and equitable in all He does. We can depend on the fact that in His relationship with us He operates from a perfect standard which is rooted in His moral nature. The psalmist knew that because God's dealings with him were fair and just, he could make a song out of what he had experienced. When we have a God who relates to us in this way then our survival is not merely the result of our stamina but of His sustaining power within us.

FURTHER STUDY

Jer. 23:1–6; Ps. 48:10; 97:2; 119:37

1. What is one of God's names?

2. What fills God's right hand?

Prayer

Father, I see more clearly than ever that my perseverance is not the result of my determination but of Your faithfulness to me. I survive because You are in me. I am eternally grateful. Amen.

SECTION ONE

DAY 37

Still Here!

For reading & meditation—Psalm 129:5–7

"May they be like grass on the roof, which withers before it can grow ..." (v.6)

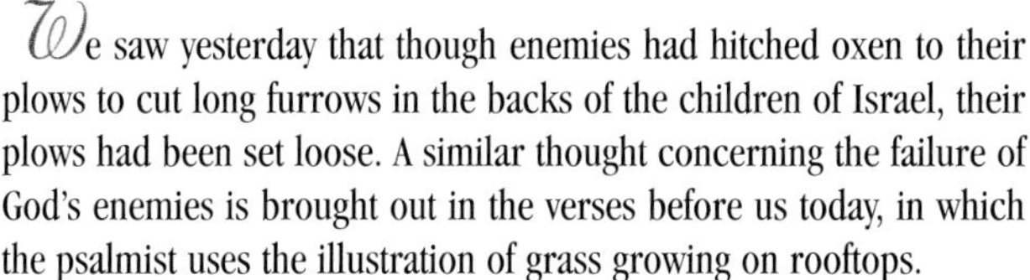

We saw yesterday that though enemies had hitched oxen to their plows to cut long furrows in the backs of the children of Israel, their plows had been set loose. A similar thought concerning the failure of God's enemies is brought out in the verses before us today, in which the psalmist uses the illustration of grass growing on rooftops.

Houses in the psalmist's day were, as you know, flat-topped, with dirt spread on them for insulation. Any seeds that sprouted in this dirt would last for only a short time as the soil was too shallow to support life for long. Eugene Peterson says that there were "no reapers upon the roofs. No one going along the road would ever look up and shout out, 'Great harvest you have there. God's blessing upon you!'" The psalmist is using this rather humorous illustration to show that opposition to God's chosen people is futile. There is nothing to be gained by it.

The world's antagonism towards God's people may cause discomfort, even distress, but because God is at work in us it can never achieve what it sets out to achieve—our downfall and destruction. The Lord's enemies think they are getting somewhere by riding roughshod over His people and interfering with His purposes, but such an idea is as naive as believing it is possible to obtain a harvest from grass sprouting in shallow soil on a rooftop.

FURTHER STUDY

Isa. 54:11–17; Deut. 7:24; Josh. 1:5; 21:44; 23:9; Rom. 8:31

1. What assurance did God give to His people?

2. What was His promise to Joshua?

Prayer

O Father, how comforting it is to know You are committed to ensuring that the efforts of the enemies of Your people come to nought. People can oppose me because of You, but because of You they cannot overcome. Amen.

SECTION ONE

Purposes Last

For reading & meditation—Psalm 129:8

"May those who pass by not say, 'The blessing of the Lord be upon you ...'" (v.8)

Many are troubled by the words the psalmist uses to begin and end this second section of the psalm: "May all who hate Zion be turned back in shame ... May those who pass by not say, 'The blessing of the Lord be upon you'" (vv.5, 8). They see in these words vindictiveness and pique.

But did not the Lord say of Israel: "Whoever touches you touches the apple of his eye" (Zech. 2:8)? I therefore rather think that the psalmist is expressing the biblical idea that those with a hostile attitude towards God would find in the end that that would be His attitude towards them. This did not mean that the Israelites should indulge in tit-for-tat. It simply meant they could not bless in God's Name those who were antagonistic towards Him.

Modern-day pilgrims who are on the road to the new Jerusalem will do well to learn how to sing this song along with the others—its refrain is the thrilling truth that because we have a righteous God who is committed to us, and whose purposes last, it is possible to persevere no matter how flinty the road.

In his book *The Journey* Eugene Peterson refers to Charles Williams's short drama *Grab and Grace*. In it there is a dialogue between Grace and a man who is experimenting with different religions, trying out one approach after another. When Grace mentions the Holy Spirit the man says: "The Holy Spirit? Good. We will ask him to come while I am in the mood, which passes so quickly and then all is so dull." Grace answers: "Sir, purposes last."

FURTHER STUDY

Isa. 14:24–27; Eph. 1:9; 3:11

1. What has God declared?

2. How is God's purpose primarily understood?

Prayer

Gracious Father, I am grateful that despite the constant attempts of the world to defeat Your purposes, its strategies come to nought. They are worthless and unfruitful. Thank You, Father, that I belong to One whose purposes last. Amen.

SECTION ONE

No Denial of Reality

For reading & meditation—Psalm 130:1–8

"Out of the depths I cry to you, O Lord ..." (v.1)

As the psalmist begins this psalm it is clear that he is greatly vexed: "Out of the depths I cry to you, O Lord ... hear my voice" (vv.1–2). This is an anguished prayer. Whatever the cause of his pain, it brought forth a cry from the very depths of his heart.

It is when we suffer that we enter the depths of our spirit. Then we are at the heart of things; we are near to where Christ was on the cross. Eugene Peterson quotes P.T. Forsyth, a famous theologian, and the quote is worth considering in full: "The depth is simply the height inverted, as sin is the index of moral grandeur. The cry is not only truly human, but divine as well. God is deeper than the deepest depth in man. He is holier than our deepest sin is deep. There is no depth so deep to us as when God reveals His holiness in dealing with our sin ... [And so] think more of the depth of God than the depth of your cry. The worst thing that can happen to a man is to have no God to cry to out of the depth."

Whenever pain or suffering enters our souls we must be ready to face it and feel it. Denial of our pain is an attempt to move away from reality. In effect we are saying: "God is not able to hold me in the midst of this so I will pretend it is not happening." The ancient Israelites took a supremely realistic view of life. So must we.

FURTHER STUDY

Rom.8:18–27; Job 30:1–20

1. What 3 groans does Paul refer to?

2. What was Job's experience?

Prayer

O Father, help me to set all my pain and suffering squarely, openly, honestly before You. Fortify me so that I shall not shrink from or deny any encounter with reality. In Christ's Name I pray. Amen.

DAY 40

SECTION ONE

The Wonder of Forgiveness

For reading & meditation—Psalm 130:3–4

"If you, O Lord, kept a record of sins, O Lord, who could stand?" (v.3)

Did the psalmist consider that his own sin might be responsible for the plight he was in? It would seem so from these verses. He is conscious of a great gulf that divides people from God, particularly himself, and he makes the assertion that if God kept a strict tally of mankind's sins there would be no hope for anyone. But then come some of the most beautiful and wondrous words in the Old Testament: "But with you there is forgiveness; therefore you are feared" (v.4). The Living Bible paraphrases the verse like this: "But you forgive! What an awesome thing this is!"

Eight times the divine name "Lord" is used in this psalm, and as we observe how God is addressed we see what a difference knowing Him makes whatever plight we find ourselves in. He is addressed in the first couple of verses as the God who hears, and then, in verses 3 to 4, as the God who forgives. What a wonderful thing it is that God forgives. It is, as the Living Bible puts it, awesome.

As Christians we are so used to hearing about God's forgiveness that we are in danger of taking it for granted. Heinrich Hein, when lying on his deathbed, was asked by a friend: "Do you think God has forgiven you?" Hein replied: "Of course God will forgive me. That's His job." I hope none of my readers will approach the subject of divine forgiveness with such cynicism. The fact that God forgives and forgets is something we will never fully understand, but it must never be taken for granted.

FURTHER STUDY

Ps. 104:1–35; Eph. 1:7; 1 John 1:9

1. Why was the psalmist filled with praise?
2. How did he describe the removal of sins?

Prayer

O Father, forgive me if I have thought that divine forgiveness is just the result of You doing Your job. Grant that my reaction to being forgiven will not be one of complacency but of constant reverence and holy awe. In Jesus' Name I ask it. Amen.

SECTION ONE

Waiting for the Dawn

For reading & meditation—Psalm 130:5–6

"My soul waits for the Lord more than watchmen wait for the morning ..." (v.6)

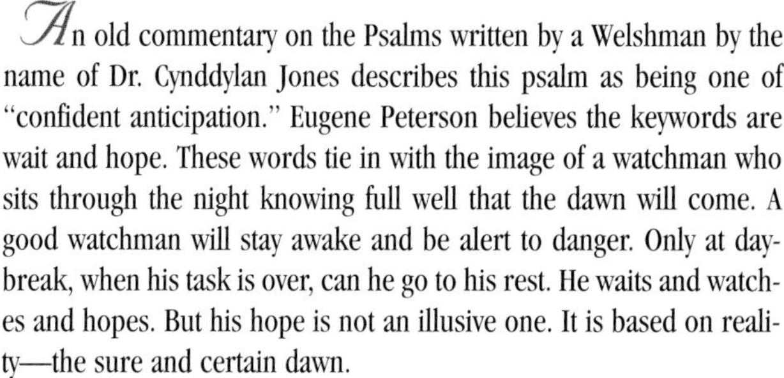

An old commentary on the Psalms written by a Welshman by the name of Dr. Cynddylan Jones describes this psalm as being one of "confident anticipation." Eugene Peterson believes the keywords are wait and hope. These words tie in with the image of a watchman who sits through the night knowing full well that the dawn will come. A good watchman will stay awake and be alert to danger. Only at daybreak, when his task is over, can he go to his rest. He waits and watches and hopes. But his hope is not an illusive one. It is based on reality—the sure and certain dawn.

In describing himself as a watchman the psalmist is saying, I believe, that he is as sure of God as he is of the dawn. His hope (and ours also) is founded on that same conviction—the assurance that God is at work in His world and will bring His purposes to pass no matter how dark things may appear. Waiting and hoping demonstrate a willingness to let God have His way. It is the very antithesis of making plans and then telling God to put them into effect. That is not hoping in God but bullying God.

Some see waiting as nothing more than resignation. They say: "I'm resigned to the will and purposes of God." Resigned? The will of God is not something we should be resigned to; it is something we should rejoice in. And why? Because His will is always our highest good.

FURTHER STUDY

Rom. 4:1–25; Prov. 14:32; Col. 1:5; 1 Pet. 1:3

1. What was Abraham's hope based on?

2. What springs from hope?

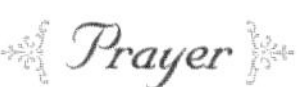

Prayer

Father, give me the condition of soul that waits for Your purposes to come to pass with the same certainty and confident hope with which a watchman waits for the dawn. In Your Word I put my hope. Amen.

DAY 42

SECTION ONE

Knowing God

For reading & meditation—Psalm 130:6–8

"O Israel, put your hope in the Lord, for with the Lord is unfailing love ..." (v.7)

In these concluding verses the psalmist moves from the personal to the general by calling on the whole nation of Israel to put their hope in the Lord. In the previous verses of this psalm God is seen as the One who forgives sin, who comes to those who wait and hope for Him, and now here He is shown to be the One who is characterized by unending love and plenteous redemption.

Knowing God in this way makes a difference. Eugene Peterson puts it like this: "When we suffer we attract counselors as money attracts thieves. Everybody has an idea of what we did wrong to get ourselves into such trouble and a prescription for what we can do to get out of it ... But none of that is what we need ... We need to know that we are in relation to God." I don't agree with the cynicism that underlies these words, but I certainly agree with the last sentence: "We need to know that we are in relation to God." An experienced and professional counselor wrote to a friend of mine: "I'm more and more convinced the greater need is to know God rather than understand and sort through psychological issues. Understanding what the issues are and how they come about does not always help. Getting a focus on God will."

Knowing God is what gives the depths a bottom and makes the heights limitless. When we concentrate on knowing Him and wait for Him with a confident hope then this gives Him the room to work out our salvation and move us on to maturity.

FURTHER STUDY

Phil. 3:1–10; John 17:3; Col. 1:10

1. What was Paul's desire?

2. How did Jesus define eternal life?

Prayer

O God, more than ever I long to know You. Not just to know about You but to know You in a deep and intimate relationship. Help me take to heart what I have read today so that I might put my hope fully in You. In Jesus' Name. Amen.

SECTION ONE

The Deadliest Sin

For reading & meditation—Psalm 131:1–3

"My heart is not proud, O Lord, my eyes are not haughty ..." (v.1)

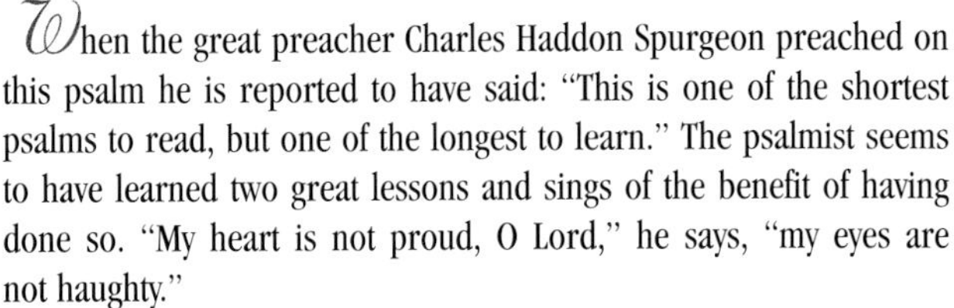

When the great preacher Charles Haddon Spurgeon preached on this psalm he is reported to have said: "This is one of the shortest psalms to read, but one of the longest to learn." The psalmist seems to have learned two great lessons and sings of the benefit of having done so. "My heart is not proud, O Lord," he says, "my eyes are not haughty."

It is a matter of surprise to some people that theologians insist on the pernicious nature of pride and describe it as the most destructive of the seven deadly sins. Today pride is often extolled as a virtue and urged as a necessity. "Pride is so harmless," say the men and women of the world. "It is not like murder or fraud or rape." But the heart of this grave sin lies just here: in the fact that individuals put themselves in the center of the picture and make themselves the standard and measure of all things.

Our place in the universe is that of a creature. The discerning and truthful mind echoes the words of another psalm: "It is [God] who made us, and we are his; we are his people, the sheep of his pasture" (Ps. 100:3). The undiscerning cry with the poet William Henley: "I am the master of my fate, I am the captain of my soul." That is the germ that creates this disease of the soul. It puts self in the center where God ought to be. It dethrones the Creator and enthrones the creature. Pride is indeed a deadly sin. Only Christ can cure it. Only Christ.

FURTHER STUDY

Luke 18:9–14; Prov. 11:2; Rev. 3:14–22

1. What did Jesus teach on pride?

2. How is the Laodicean pride described?

Prayer

O God, I want to be a person without sham or pretense or pride. I want to be the person You intend me to be. Then I shall stand with simplicity and dignity in Your will and purpose. Cure me of my pride, my Father. In Jesus' Name. Amen.

DAY

44

SECTION ONE

On Leaving Things to Him

For reading & meditation—Psalm 131:1

"... I do not concern myself with great matters or things too wonderful for me." (v.1)

Can there be anything more beautiful to behold than a person who clings to God not with a desperate fear or out of the panic of insecurity but with a firm and confident trust? The words before us now suggest this is the place that the psalmist had come to—the place of mature trust. He does not busy himself with things that are beyond him but leaves them in God's good hands. In the words of the hymnist Anna L. Waring: "[He does] not have the restless will that hurries to and fro, seeking for some great thing to do, or secret thing to know."

This attitude must not be seen as passivity or lack of ambition but rather the calm and confident trust that says: "I will give my attention only to those things that God wants me to be concerned about and leave everything else to Him." I heard someone define trust as "accepting only those responsibilities God intends you to have."

"I am so afraid that something will go wrong and prevent me doing what I believe God wants me to do," I told my pastor once. "How can I be sure God will keep my life on the right track?" "Tell me," said my pastor, "Did God rule the world before you were born?" "Of course He did," I replied. "And will He rule it after you have gone from this world?" "Most assuredly," I retorted. "Then why not let Him take care of things in the present too?" My faith was stirred and in a few minutes my heart was at peace.

FURTHER STUDY

Ps. 3:1–8; 20:6–8;

Isa. 12:1–6

1. What contrast of trust did the psalmist make?

2. How are salvation and trust linked?

Prayer

Gracious and loving Father, help me focus on those things that You want me to be concerned about and leave the rest of the universe to You. Bring me to that place of calm, confident trust that the psalmist enjoyed. In Jesus' Name. Amen.

SECTION ONE

Weaned!

For reading & meditation—Psalm 131:2

"But I have stilled and quietened my soul; like a weaned child with its mother …" (v.2)

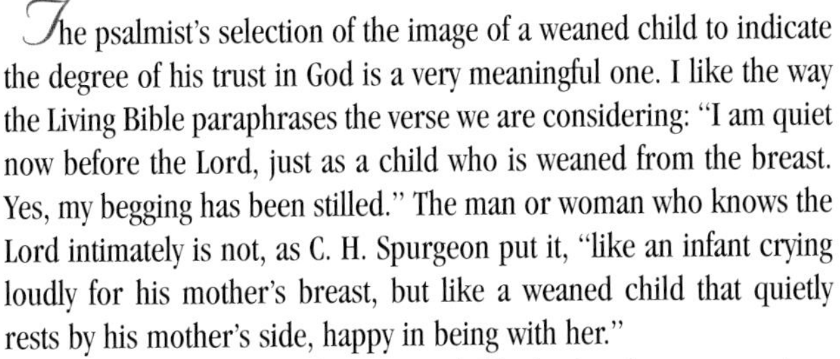

The psalmist's selection of the image of a weaned child to indicate the degree of his trust in God is a very meaningful one. I like the way the Living Bible paraphrases the verse we are considering: "I am quiet now before the Lord, just as a child who is weaned from the breast. Yes, my begging has been stilled." The man or woman who knows the Lord intimately is not, as C. H. Spurgeon put it, "like an infant crying loudly for his mother's breast, but like a weaned child that quietly rests by his mother's side, happy in being with her."

In the normal course of events a child who has been weaned no longer views mother as an object for his own satisfaction but learns to love her for her own sake. So it is with us also. When we are spiritually "weaned" we learn to love God for Himself and not as a means to fulfilling our own wishes.

The image of the weaned child suggests too that the psalmist had not reached the place of trust without a struggle with his self-centered soul. The transition from sucking infant to weaned child is not easy. I often meet Christians (especially those who have not been converted long) who say: "I no longer feel like I did when I first became a Christian. Has God abandoned me? He doesn't seem to answer my prayers in the way He once did. Why?" The answer is this: you are being weaned. You are being set free to enjoy God for who He is, not for what He does.

FURTHER STUDY

1 Cor. 13:1–11; 14:20; 3:1–2; Heb. 6:1; 2 Pet. 3:18; Heb. 5:12

1. What did Paul exhort the Corinthians?

2. What was the complaint of the writer to the Hebrews?

Prayer

Father, I accept that the time of weaning is marked with noise and misunderstanding. Forgive me for my slowness in realizing this. Help me to come through to maturity of trust with as little commotion as possible. In Jesus' Name. Amen.

DAY

46

SECTION ONE

As Content As a Child

For reading & meditation—Psalm 131:3

"O Israel, put your hope in the Lord both now and forevermore." (v.3)

The last verse of this psalm addresses the quality of newfound freedom that we talked about yesterday—the freedom of being able to enjoy the Lord for who He is and not what He does.

"Put your hope in the Lord," says the psalmist to the nation of Israel, "both now and forevermore." The implication behind his words is this: come to the Lord as a weaned child comes to his mother, knowing that in Him is comfort even though some particular form of comfort may have been denied. To quote C. H. Spurgeon again: "It is a blessed mark of growth out of spiritual infancy when we can forego the joys which once appeared to be essential and can find our solace in Him who denies them to us."

Now we begin to see the key thought of this psalm: childlike trust. Our Lord, you remember, rebuked His disciples on one occasion because they were turning away the children parents were bringing to Him for Him to bless. Our Lord declared: "Anyone who will not receive the kingdom of God like a little child will never enter it" (Mark 10:15). The Master used a child as a model of how to accept the Christian faith not because of a child's helplessness but because of a child's willingness to trust. How wonderful when we come to the place where we can sing like the psalmist: "I don't pretend to 'know it all.' I am quiet now before the Lord, just as a child who is weaned from the breast. Yes, my begging has been stilled" (vv.1–2, TLB).

FURTHER STUDY

Isa. 58:1–11; Psalm 17:15; 63:5

1. What satisfied the psalmist?

2. What do you find satisfaction in?

Prayer

Father, I think I understand; the meaning of life becomes plain. I am to turn away from pride. I am not to pretend I "know it all." I am to trust you as a child trusts his mother. Help me now to turn the theory into fact. In Christ's Name. Amen.

SECTION ONE

DAY 47

The Cause of Lost Battles

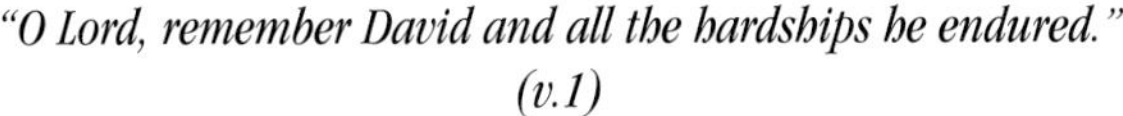

For reading & meditation—Psalm 132:1–9

"O Lord, remember David and all the hardships he endured." *(v.1)*

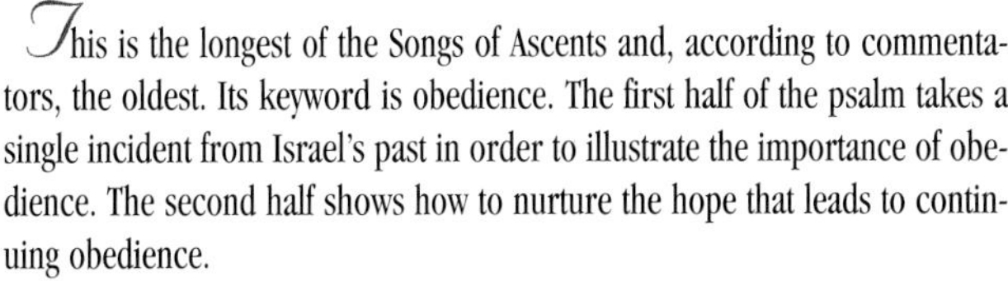

This is the longest of the Songs of Ascents and, according to commentators, the oldest. Its keyword is obedience. The first half of the psalm takes a single incident from Israel's past in order to illustrate the importance of obedience. The second half shows how to nurture the hope that leads to continuing obedience.

Originally this psalm was sung to commemorate King David's moving of the ark of the covenant to Jerusalem. David labored strenuously to bring the ark from Kiriath Jearim and planned for it to have a permanent home in Jerusalem (see 2 Samuel 6 and 1 Chronicles 28). He made a solemn promise not to give up until that plan was realized (vv.2–5). King David had many black marks against him, but in this matter he is the exemplar of godly obedience. "The true knowledge of God," said John Calvin, "is born out of obedience." To put that another way—no one can hope to know God unless he or she is prepared to obey Him.

Many of our difficulties in the Christian life stem from this fact—we are not obedient. During World War II the Allied Forces lost many battles in North Africa, and General Montgomery, a professing Christian, was sent to remedy the situation. He soon found the reason for failure. "Orders," he said, "were being seen as a basis for discussion rather than action. I was determined to stop this state of affairs at once." Our Lord's orders are not a basis for discussion among Christians. They are to be obeyed. No obedience—no discipleship. It is as simple and as stark as that.

FURTHER STUDY

Josh. 1:8; Acts 5:29

1. What did God promise Joshua would be the result of obedience?

2. What strong stand did Peter and the apostles take?

Prayer

O God, help me see that by obeying Your commands I am not entering into bondage but into freedom. For Your laws are my life. They are what I was made for. Deepen my understanding of this. In Jesus' Name. Amen.

SECTION ONE

The Story of the Ark

For reading & meditation—Psalm 132:6–9

"... arise, O Lord, and come to your resting place, you and the ark of your might." (v.8)

This psalm has been referred to as "The Psalm of David's Obedience." King David promised God that he would find a permanent place for the ark of the covenant, and he did not give up his attempts to fulfil that promise. Before we pursue that thought further, let's take a moment to remind ourselves what the ark signified and its place in Jewish history.

The ark of the covenant was a box made of acacia wood measuring about 4 feet by 2.5 feet by 2.5 feet. It was overlaid with gold, and at each end of the solid gold lid was a cherub. The lid was called the "mercy seat," and it was from between the two cherubs that God communed with His people (see Exodus 25:10–22). The ark was a symbol of God's presence among His people. Constructed in the wilderness, it had accompanied the children of Israel on their journey into the Promised Land, finally coming to rest in Shiloh. During a battle with the Philistines it was captured, and was held by them until it caused them problems (see 1 Samuel 4–7). It was then returned to Kiriath Jearim in Israel, where it remained until David decided to bring it to Jerusalem.

The story of the ark is a reminder that we must have God with us in everything we do and not use Him to advance our own purposes. We get into all kinds of difficulties when we attempt to persuade God to follow us rather than following Him ourselves. We are here to carry out His purposes. He is not here to carry out ours.

FURTHER STUDY

Ex. 25:10–22; 1 Sam. 4:1–7:17; 2 Sam. 6:1–23

1. Why did the Philistines want to get rid of the ark?

2. What did the children of Israel do wrong when they moved the ark?

Prayer

O God, forgive me that so often I am more interested in getting You to endorse my plans than in seeking to know Yours. Drive this truth deep within me that You are not here to advance my glory. I am here to advance Yours. Amen.

SECTION ONE

The Purpose of History

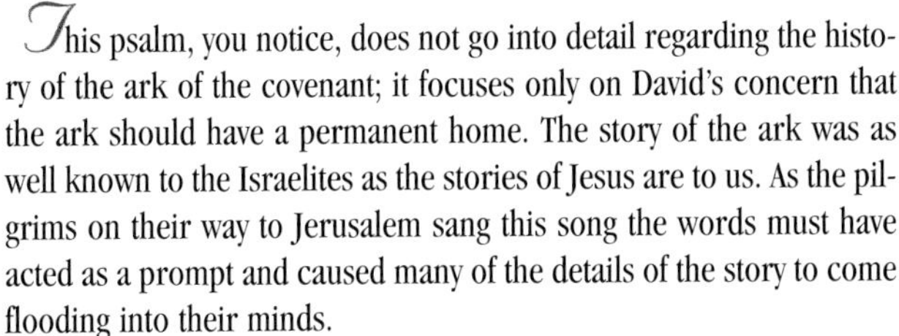

For reading & meditation—Psalm 132:6–7

"We heard it in Ephrathah, we came upon it in the fields of Jaar ..." (v.6)

This psalm, you notice, does not go into detail regarding the history of the ark of the covenant; it focuses only on David's concern that the ark should have a permanent home. The story of the ark was as well known to the Israelites as the stories of Jesus are to us. As the pilgrims on their way to Jerusalem sang this song the words must have acted as a prompt and caused many of the details of the story to come flooding into their minds.

"We heard it in Ephrathah, we came upon it in the fields of Jaar." When David learned where the ark was located he vowed to God that he would go and get it, and he kept that vow (see 2 Samuel 6). He gathered the people together and said: "Let us go to his dwelling place; let us worship at his footstool" (v.7).

In this psalm history is not so much retold as remembered. I remind you again of the purpose of history. Without history we are at the mercy of our whims. Biblical history provides us with information we can use to evaluate situations and make decisions. This is one purpose of getting into the Bible daily—we need more data to move effectively into life than our own experience can give us. Biblical history shows us what works and what does not work. If it wasn't for Scripture we would have to begin every day from scratch, spending much of our time backtracking, correcting, or starting all over. Christian pilgrims walk along well worn paths. Obedience has a history.

FURTHER STUDY

Heb. 9:1–4; Rev. 11:19; Heb. 8:8; 9:15; 12:24

1. What does Hebrews tell us about the ark?

2. Why do we no longer need an ark of the covenant?

Prayer

O God, thank You for all the truth and information You have given me in the Scriptures. Where would I be without Your Word? Each day as I read it let it trigger within me greater faith and inspiration. In Jesus' Name I pray. Amen.

DAY

50

SECTION ONE

"Modest Proofs"

For reading & meditation—Psalm 132:8–9

"... arise, O Lord, and come to your resting place, you and the ark of your might." (v.8)

As we have said, when the pilgrims on their way to Jerusalem sang this song some great memories of their history were revived and relived. They would remember with joy the time when David and the people of his day cried: "Arise, O Lord, and come to your resting place, you and the ark of your might." They would see in their mind's eye both the garmented priests and the people singing and dancing with joy. And they would be reminded also, as they sang, that despite their failures and backsliding there was a rich heritage of compliance with the divine will. Many years previously the ark of the covenant had been carried on the shoulders of the priests along the very road that their feet were treading.

The ark of the covenant, however, was not always carried in the right way or with the right motives. On one occasion, as we briefly mentioned two days ago, the Israelites went up to fight against the Philistines without a clear direction from God and thought because the ark was with them they would be blessed with victory. Such was not the case, though, and the ark was taken captive (see 2 Samuel 4).

The singing of Psalm 132 activated faith's memory and brought home to every pilgrim that obedience (as in the case of King David) had its roots in historical fact. The theologian Karl Barth put it admirably when he said: "Each act of obedience by the Christian is a modest proof, unequivocal for all its imperfection, of the reality of what he attests."

FURTHER STUDY

1 Sam. 15:1–22;

Gen. 6:22;

Josh. 11:15

1. What was Samuel's reply?

2. What is said of Noah?

Prayer

Father, as this psalm activated the faith of the ancient pilgrims may it have the same effect on me also. May the reminders of what You have done in the past instill in me new hope and confidence for the future. In Jesus' Name. Amen.

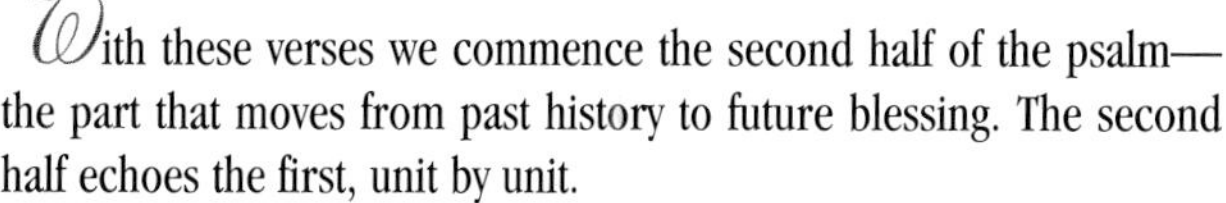

The Promise-Keeper

For reading & meditation—Psalm 132:11–12

"The Lord swore an oath to David, a sure oath that he will not revoke ..." (v.11)

With these verses we commence the second half of the psalm—the part that moves from past history to future blessing. The second half echoes the first, unit by unit.

We read in verse 2 that David "swore an oath to the Lord and made a vow to the Mighty One of Jacob" that he would not rest until he had found a permanent dwelling place for the ark of the covenant. In the verses before us today we read how God responds to David's oath with one of His own: "The Lord swore an oath to David, a sure oath that he will not revoke." David's concern for God's glory and honor is matched by God's concern for David's throne. David himself, rather than the contemporary Davidic king, is addressed, but the point being made is that God will not go back on the commitment He made to David and to David's line. God keeps His promises.

An ancient proverb says: "When a man repeats his promises again and again take care because he means to fail you." This is not so with God, however. He repeats His promises over and over again in Scripture not because He is insecure but because we are insecure. We live in a world of broken promises but God has never broken one of His promises. Listen to what Solomon said to the people when the Temple was dedicated: "Not one word has failed of all the good promises he gave through his servant Moses" (1 Kings 8:56). What a thrilling assertion. Not one has failed. Not one!

FURTHER STUDY

2 Cor. 1:1–20;

1 Kings 8:56;

2 Pet. 1:4

1. What did Paul declare?

2. What is imparted through the promises?

Loving heavenly Father, in a world filled with broken pacts and promises how reassuring it is to know that I am linked to a God whose Word is His bond. What inner security this gives me. I am eternally grateful. Amen.

SECTION ONE

The Trigger for Hope

For reading & meditation—Psalm 132:13–16

"I will bless her with abundant provisions; her poor will I satisfy with food." (v.15)

Yesterday we said that the second half of this psalm echoes the first unit by unit. We saw how David's oath to the Lord was matched by the Lord's oath to David. The verses before us now are intended to parallel verses 6 to 9, which talk about the ark being brought to Zion. The divine promises in this section are God's answers to the prayers and wishes of the petitions made earlier.

Note how each of these promises is rooted in Israel's history. "I will bless her with abundant provisions; her poor will I satisfy with food" (v.15). This would have triggered in the minds of those singing this psalm memories of how God had provided for His people in their wilderness wanderings. He supplied them with everything they needed—water, bread and meat. Again: "I will clothe her priests with salvation, and her saints shall ever sing for joy" (v.16). Has any other group of people had such a good time with their faith as the people of Israel? The occasions of public worship were times of great joy, renewing the life of redemption. Sadness resulted from Israel's frequent disobedience, but joy accompanied the restoration of their relationship. Take Moses' song of deliverance at the Red Sea, for example (see Exodus 15). We sing similar songs in our churches to this very day. The joy has overflowed to us.

But we should bear in mind that none of the hopes for the future is unrelated to history. Each develops from what a person with a good memory knows happened. Obedience is fulfilled by hope.

FURTHER STUDY

Isa. 1:17–20;
1 Kings 11:38;
Deut. 11:26–28;
Luke 11:28

1. What did God promise as a result of obedience?
2. When did Jesus say we would be blessed?

Prayer

My Father and my God, help me not to take an antiquarian interest in the past—reveling in it for its own sake—but to use it as a traveler uses every bit of information to help him get where he is going. In Jesus' Name. Amen.

SECTION ONE

Simple but Sublime

For reading & meditation—Psalm 132:17–18

"Here I will make a horn grow for David and set up a lamp for my anointed one." (v.17)

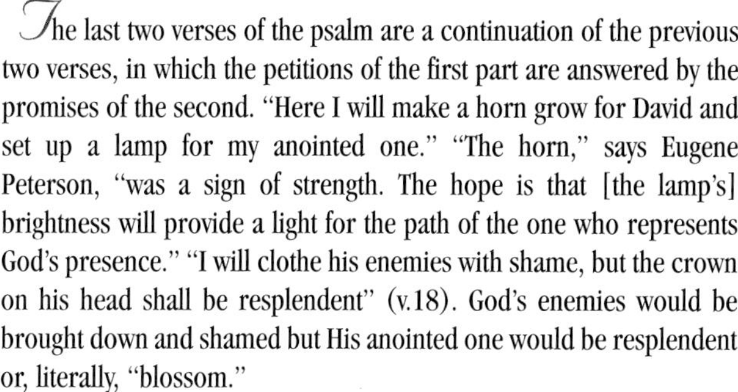

The last two verses of the psalm are a continuation of the previous two verses, in which the petitions of the first part are answered by the promises of the second. "Here I will make a horn grow for David and set up a lamp for my anointed one." "The horn," says Eugene Peterson, "was a sign of strength. The hope is that [the lamp's] brightness will provide a light for the path of the one who represents God's presence." "I will clothe his enemies with shame, but the crown on his head shall be resplendent" (v.18). God's enemies would be brought down and shamed but His anointed one would be resplendent or, literally, "blossom."

The purpose of these promises is to stimulate obedience by showing that God has kept His Word in the past. Our expectations for the future, too, have their roots in what God has already accomplished. In this section of the psalm God is not simply promising to bless His people in the future in the same way that He blessed them in the past, but that the blessings that lie ahead will be greater than those of the past. The assurance is similar to that which our Lord gave to His disciples: "Anyone who has faith in me will do what I have been doing. He will do even greater things than these ..." (John 14:12).

We must not forget that the key to God's blessing is first and foremost obedience. A little boy in Sunday school when asked "What is Christian obedience?" gave this reply: "Obedience is doing what God tells us." Simple but sublime.

FURTHER STUDY

Gen. 22:1–24;
2 Kings 18:6;
Acts 26:1–19;
James 1:25

1. What was Paul able to say to Agrippa?
2. What does James say is the road to blessing?

Prayer

O Father, may the things that You have accomplished for us in the past do more than cultivate our memories. May the reminder of them nurture a hope that leads to even greater obedience. In Christ's Name we ask it. Amen.

SECTION ONE

One Big Happy Family?

For reading & meditation—Psalm 133:1–3

"How good and pleasant it is when brothers live together in unity!" (v.1)

The first few words of this psalm disclose its keyword and main theme: unity. Before we can understand what unity is we must first be clear about what it is not. Unity is not unanimity—everyone agreeing with everyone. Neither is it uniformity—everyone looking and behaving alike. Unity has been defined as "the bond that exists between one person and another in which they know that the things that unite them are deeper and more important than the things that might separate them."

An example of what unity is not is provided by a true story about the minister of a small congregation in the United States. On one occasion he declared: "When I say Christian I mean Baptist. And when I say Baptist I mean Bible-believing Baptist. And when I say Bible-believing Baptist I mean born again by the Spirit. And by that I mean to have the Spirit indwelling. And the only place I know where you can find people like that is right here in this church."

The true people of God are a family. That metaphor is often used to describe them in the Scriptures. But are they one big happy family? Regrettably, no. It is probably one of the greatest embarrassments of the modern-day Church that the mirror which is meant to reflect to the world the unity which exists between Christ and His Father—the people of God—is broken and fragmented (see John 17:11). I said embarrassing—scandalous might be a more appropriate word. To live in unity is good and pleasant. To live in disunity is scandalous.

FURTHER STUDY

John 17:1–26; Eph. 3:14–4:16

1. How does Paul describe God's people?

2. What are we to make every effort to do?

Prayer

God my Father, I see that Your way is not merely a way of theology but of life. For You have set us in relationships. Where our relationships are wrong help us to put them right. In Jesus' Name. Amen.

SECTION ONE

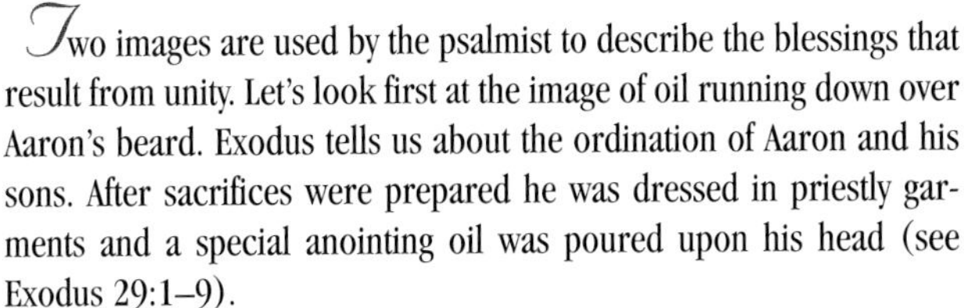

The Basis of Community

DAY 55

For reading & meditation—Psalm 133:2

"It is like precious oil poured on the head … running down on Aaron's beard …" (v.2)

Two images are used by the psalmist to describe the blessings that result from unity. Let's look first at the image of oil running down over Aaron's beard. Exodus tells us about the ordination of Aaron and his sons. After sacrifices were prepared he was dressed in priestly garments and a special anointing oil was poured upon his head (see Exodus 29:1–9).

Oil, as I am sure you are aware, is used in Scripture as a symbol of the Holy Spirit. "The anointing oil," says one commentator, "because it contained sweet-smelling spices, bestowed upon the person on whom it was lavished a delightful fragrance." No sweeter smell rises to God's nostrils than that which comes from His people when they dwell together in unity. And it needs to be said—no smell is as foul as that which ascends to Him from those who are disunited. The main point of this image, however, is the fact that pouring the anointing oil over a person marked him out as a priest. Dwelling together in unity means seeing our brothers and sisters as priests.

Eugene Peterson quotes Dietrich Bonhoeffer as saying: "Not what a man is in himself as a Christian, his spirituality and piety, constitutes the basis of our community. What determines our brotherhood is what that man is by reason of Christ. Our community with one another consists solely in what Christ has done to both of us." How different our relationships would be if we could see that we are set apart to serve one another. We mediate to one another the mysteries of God.

FURTHER STUDY

1 Cor. 10:1–17;
Rom. 12:1–12;
Gal. 3:28

1. What picture does Paul give us of oneness?
2. What barriers does he describe that have been removed?

Prayer

O Father, thank You for reminding me that our brotherhood is determined by what we are by reason of Your Son. You have anointed us with Your Spirit and thus set us apart for service to one another. Help me grasp this thrilling truth. Amen.

SECTION ONE

The Dew of Hermon

For reading & meditation—Psalm 133:3

"It is as if the dew of Hermon were falling on Mount Zion." (v.3)

We look now at the second image that is used to describe the benefits and joys of unity—the morning dew that descends on Mount Hermon. Hermon, just to the north of Israel, is the highest mountain in the area and rises to 9,000 feet. I have never been to the summit but people who have camped high on its slopes tell me that at certain times of the year the dew is so heavy that they have to protect themselves from being soaked.

Dew is always a picture in the Bible of morning freshness, of being cleansed to start a new day. But note how the writer leaps in his imagination to the drier, barren country of Judea when he talks about the dew of Hermon falling on Mount Zion, which, as you know, is the hill on which Jerusalem was built. What can be in his mind as he makes this strange but intriguing mental vault? He is thinking, I believe, of the way unity, when it is practiced, reaches out to refresh those who are feeling spiritually bereft and barren. The more unity is enjoyed in the Church of Jesus Christ the more it will be enjoyed. By that I mean unity spreads and carries its influence like refreshing dew into all parts of Christ's Body.

The dew descending from Hermon's slopes and extending into the regions beyond gives a picture of unity's far-reaching influence. Oil and dew. Two things that make the pilgrim way both "good" and "pleasant." How powerful the Church would be if the unity spoken of here was our chief characteristic.

FURTHER STUDY

1 Cor. 1:1–10;
2 Cor. 13:11;
Phil. 1:27; 1 Pet. 3:8

1. What was Paul's plea to the Corinthians?

2. How are we to contend for the Gospel?

Prayer

O Father, may Your Church worldwide this day rise to the challenge to be as united in our purposes as You and Your Son are in Yours. Fuse us together in the bonds of this great endeavor. In Jesus' Name we ask it. Amen.

SECTION ONE

The Last Word

For reading & meditation—Psalm 134:1–3

"Praise the Lord, all you servants of the Lord who minister by night ..." (v.1)

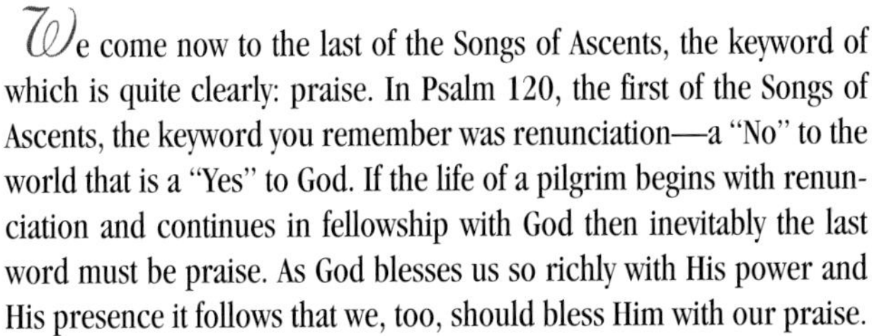

We come now to the last of the Songs of Ascents, the keyword of which is quite clearly: praise. In Psalm 120, the first of the Songs of Ascents, the keyword you remember was renunciation—a "No" to the world that is a "Yes" to God. If the life of a pilgrim begins with renunciation and continues in fellowship with God then inevitably the last word must be praise. As God blesses us so richly with His power and His presence it follows that we, too, should bless Him with our praise.

The first verse of this psalm invites the priests to lead the people in worship and addresses those "who minister by night in the house of the Lord." The priests, I am informed, often worked in shifts, especially during the celebratory feasts, and it was not unusual for services to go on through the night (see Isaiah 30:29). Imagine yourself as a pilgrim to Jerusalem for the first time, and unable to sleep because of all the excitement. What could you do, say, at 3 o'clock in the morning? Well, you could go to the Temple and watch the priests worshipping and praising God.

I don't know if you have already discovered this, but listening to people praise is contagious. Many times in my life when I have not felt like praising God the sight and sound of others doing so has kick-started my own spirit and caused it to open up to Him in joyful praise. Praise that begins in duty is guaranteed to end in delight.

FURTHER STUDY

1 Pet. 2:1–9; Ps. 9:11; 33:2

1. What is a fourfold reason to declare praise?

2. What are we to continually do?

Prayer

O God, forgive me that so often my soul is sullen and sour when it ought to be soaring in joyous praise. Even in the darkest of life's experiences help me respond to You not with a sigh but with a song of praise. In Jesus' Name. Amen.

SECTION ONE

Lift Up Your Hands

For reading & meditation—Psalm 134:2

"Lift up your hands in the sanctuary and praise the Lord." (v.2)

The first verse of this psalm is an invitation to praise. The second verse is a command. "Lift up your hands in the sanctuary," the psalmist says, "and praise the Lord."

The view held by some commentators is that this, the last of the Songs of Ascents, was sung as pilgrims actually entered the city of Jerusalem. They had been on the road for many days, but now they had arrived. What would they do? There were many possibilities. They could visit the bazaars and see the craftsmen at work, or meet up with friends, or visit the upper city to admire the fine buildings. This psalm, however, would help them focus on the real reason for their visit—to honor and glorify the Lord. The words of this psalm seem to be telling us: "Think about how the Lord has blessed you. Now it's your turn to bless Him."

Some Christians rebel at the fact that God commands us to praise Him. "I won't be a hypocrite," they say, "I'll praise Him when I feel like it." The biblical response to that attitude is this: "Lift up your hands … and praise the Lord." If you are not physically disabled you can lift up your hands, regardless of how you feel. You may not command your heart in that way but you can command your arms. And sometimes when you don't feel like lifting your heart in blessing just lifting your hands can help your heart get the message. Go through the motions of blessing God, and your heart will pick up the cue. Try it and see.

FURTHER STUDY

1 Tim. 2:1–8; Ps. 63:4; Lam. 2:19

1. What did Paul want men everywhere to do?

2. Why not lift your hands in prayer and praise today?

O Father, I need to take to heart the message that feelings must not run the show because there is a reality that is deeper than feelings. Help me live by that reality—the reality that You are worthy of praise no matter how I feel. In Jesus' Name. Amen.

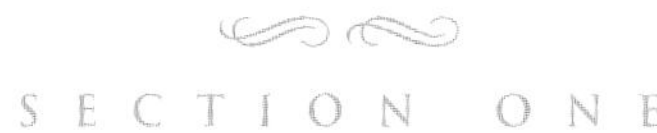

SECTION ONE

"The Circle of Blessing"

For reading & meditation—Psalm 134:3

"May the Lord, the Maker of heaven and earth, bless you from Zion." (v.3)

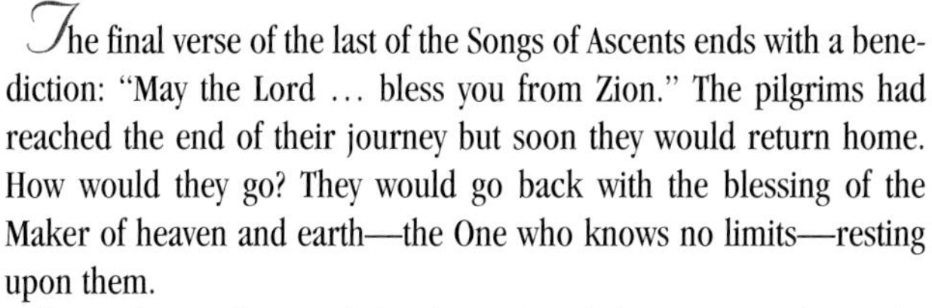

The final verse of the last of the Songs of Ascents ends with a benediction: "May the Lord ... bless you from Zion." The pilgrims had reached the end of their journey but soon they would return home. How would they go? They would go back with the blessing of the Maker of heaven and earth—the One who knows no limits—resting upon them.

This psalm is often entitled "The Circle of Blessing" as it begins by inviting people to bless God and ends with God's promise of blessing upon them. For the Israelites to go home knowing that God's blessing rested upon them was worth more to them than all the riches in Israel. "Which would you rather have," Saint Augustine once asked, "all the riches of the land but without God's blessing, or to have none of these treasures yet to live under His blessing?" I know which I would choose. Do you?

Some of the last words in the Bible are: "Blessed are those who wash their robes, that they might have the right to the tree of life" (Rev. 22:14). The verse speaks of the blessing that awaits us at the end of the road—the eternal world. But how glad we should be that we don't have to wait until we reach our destination to get what is at the end of the road. The blessing of heaven, of course, is much greater than any blessing we can know here on earth. Yet because God's blessing rests upon us in the present, we have a little bit of heaven to go to heaven in.

FURTHER STUDY

Prov. 10:1–22; Ps. 24:1–5; Eph. 1:18; James 2:5

1. Who will receive the blessing of the Lord?

2. What was Paul's prayer for the Ephesians?

Prayer

O God, to live under Your blessing is the greatest desire of my heart. I shudder to think what life would be like if Your hand of blessing was to be removed from me. Let Your hand be upon me for good, my Father. Now and ever more. Amen.

DAY

60

SECTION ONE

Epilogue

For reading & meditation—Jeremiah 12:1–17

"If you stumble in safe country, how will you manage in the thickets by the Jordan?" (v.5)

We have seen in our meditations on the Songs of Ascents that each psalm describes an aspect of the life of the spiritual traveller that needs to be carefully considered, indeed sung about, as we move along the pilgrim way. These aspects once again are: renunciation, being kept, worship, service, deliverance, security, joy, work, contentment, perseverance, hope, childlike trust, obedience, unity and praise.

I cannot guarantee you in the days that lie ahead a new set of circumstances. There will be many difficulties to face. No year has ever passed which did not bring them. And if there were such a time it would be debilitating to our soul. But what I can guarantee is this: as you learn to sing these songs and keep ever before you the truths they underline, you will find faith and hope growing steadily in your heart. William Faulkner says of these psalms: "They are not monuments, but footprints. A monument only says, 'At least I got this far,' while a footprint says, 'This is where I was when I moved again.'" The poet Susan Lenzkes puts it beautifully when she reminds us how grateful we ought to be that the pilgrims who have gone before have left us "faithful footprints and the lilting strains of summit songs rehearsed along the way."

The world in which these fifteen psalms were sung remains in some senses unchanged. The pilgrims' struggles are our struggles, their problems our problems. But we have the same songs to sing—songs of deliverance, songs of joy, songs of hope. My brother, my sister, sing them well!

FURTHER STUDY

Ps. 95:7–11; 81:1;
1 Cor. 14:15;
Eph. 5:19

1. What is to happen in our hearts?

2. What did Paul say he would do?

Prayer

Father, I realize as the old hymn puts it: "We are marching upward to Zion." It is an uphill climb and an arduous task. But I have songs to sing that can cheer my way. Songs that others have sung before me. Help me sing them well. In Jesus' Name. Amen.

SECTION TWO

The Divine Eagle

The Divine Eagle

We admire eagles not only because they look so majestic and beautiful, but also because they're such a clear symbol of power, speed, strength, and intelligence. It's no wonder the eagle was chosen as a symbol of the United States (even though Benjamin Franklin lobbied for the turkey instead!).

As a native of Wales, Selwyn Hughes didn't grow up surrounded by eagles on coins, currency, and mail boxes like most of us did. Even so, he has incisively captured one of this bird's most remarkable characteristics and compared it to our relationship with God: its intuitive knowledge of when to nurture its young and when to force them to strike out on their own.

The eagle is a fitting symbol for God—solitary, powerful, soaring above all it surveys. It loves its young and nurtures them lovingly, diligently protecting them from harm. But one day the time comes when the eagle instinctively knows that, for the sake of assuring their survival, its young have to fend for themselves.

Have you ever felt that God pulled the rug out from under you? Have you ever said, "God, everything was going along fine, and now this had to happen!"? In God's perfect timing, the moment comes when He has to drag us kicking and screaming out of our comfort zones in order to make us grow, strengthen us, and shape us for his holy purpose.

There are certainly times when we disagree with God's new arrangement because we were perfectly happy with the old one. The Scripture tells us we see dimly, as through a mirror. We will never have the capacity to understand His plan for our lives as part of His infinite creation. But He is the Divine Eagle, watching over us, protecting and nurturing us until the day He deems it time for us to leave safe, familiar surroundings and be about His work.

The day He knows it's time for us to soar.

L.G.G.

SECTION TWO

Out of the Nest

For reading & meditation—Deuteronomy 32:1–14

"Like an eagle that stirs up its nest and hovers over its young, that spreads its wings to catch them and carries them . . ." (v.11)

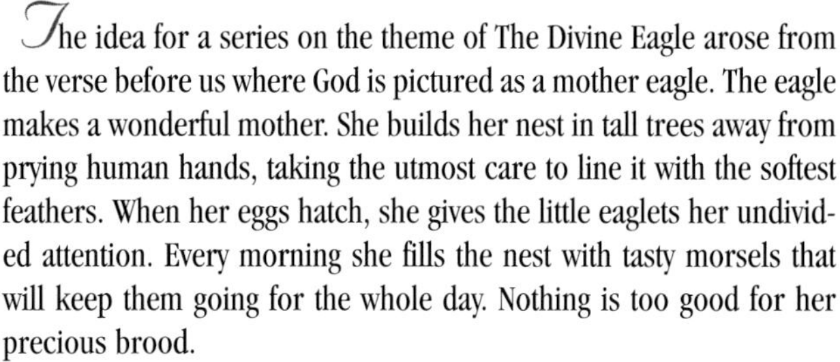

The idea for a series on the theme of The Divine Eagle arose from the verse before us where God is pictured as a mother eagle. The eagle makes a wonderful mother. She builds her nest in tall trees away from prying human hands, taking the utmost care to line it with the softest feathers. When her eggs hatch, she gives the little eaglets her undivided attention. Every morning she fills the nest with tasty morsels that will keep them going for the whole day. Nothing is too good for her precious brood.

After several weeks of this tender, loving care, the mother eagle's behavior suddenly changes. It is now time for her eaglets to leave the nest and learn to fly. So, reaching down into the nest, she rips out the feathers, breaks up the twigs and overturns their nice, comfortable home. The little eaglets are frightened out of their wits. Gently she nudges one of them toward the edge of the overturned nest and pushes it out into the air. The little bird, of course, falls like a bullet to the ground, squawking with fright, but just as it is about to hit the ground, the mother eagle swoops beneath it, catches it on her broad wings and carries it safely up into the sky. Then she tilts her wings and the bird falls once again, but this time, as it flaps its wings in fright, it discovers it can fly!

This is what God does. He pushes us out of our comfortable nests in order that we might expand our wings and soar toward His highest purposes.

FURTHER STUDY

Ps. 91; Ex. 19:4; Deut. 33:27

1. List some of the Psalmist's descriptions of the Lord.

2. How does God show His care and support?

Prayer

Father, I am on the tiptoe of expectation. I've been in the nest far too long. Teach me to expand my wings—and fly. In Jesus' name. Amen.

SECTION TWO

"The Growing Edge"

For reading & meditation—Exodus 3:7–18

"But Moses said to God, 'Who am I, that I should go to Pharaoh ...?'" (v.11)

We saw yesterday that God deals with us as a mother eagle. He pushes us out of the nest in order to make us fly. When once the mother eagle has taught the first of her eaglets to fly, she repeats the process with all the others until every one of her offspring is out of the nest and safely in the air. This gripping truth of God pushing us forward into greater usefulness—the Divine Eagle throwing us out of the nest to make us fly—is a divine principle that is deeply embedded in Scripture. If we miss it, or fail to comprehend it, we deprive ourselves of an important spiritual insight.

It is illustrated in the book of Exodus where the captivity of the Children of Israel in Egypt is described. There can be no doubt that the Israelites were not greatly motivated to set out on the long march to the "Promised Land" until God permitted Pharaoh to put such pressure upon them that they regarded any measures as better than their present distress. The oppression opened a door!

Our discomforts, sorrows, disappointments and overturned nests become what Howard Thurman calls "the growing edge." They become the starting points of progress. The deprivations we experience motivate us toward greater usefulness. How many of us would be where we are today had not God overturned our lives, changed our circumstances, allowed us to be disappointed and deprived, permitted us to walk through the deepest darkness in order that we might find ourselves on "the growing edge"? God had to upset us in order to set us up.

FURTHER STUDY

Ps. 18; Isa. 41:10; 46:4

1. How did David view his distresses?

2. Why was his response so positive?

Prayer

O Father, help me when I find myself on "the growing edge" not to look down at the hard twigs beneath me but to the broad wings above me. Give me, I pray, a new vision of Your almightiness. In Jesus' Name. Amen.

SECTION TWO

Prevenient Grace

For reading & meditation—Genesis 45:1–15

"So then, it was not you that sent me here, but God …" (v.8)

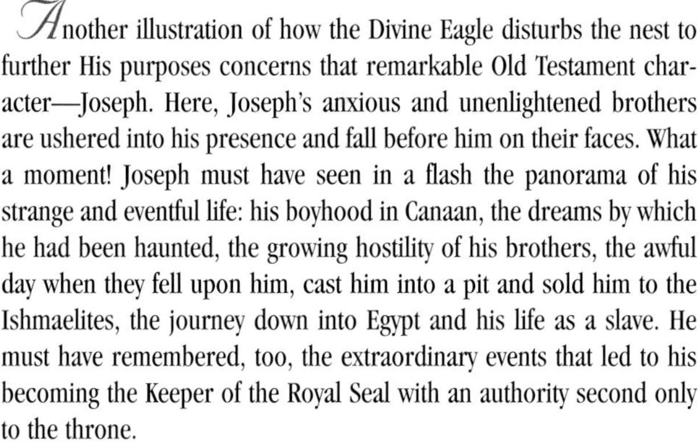

Another illustration of how the Divine Eagle disturbs the nest to further His purposes concerns that remarkable Old Testament character—Joseph. Here, Joseph's anxious and unenlightened brothers are ushered into his presence and fall before him on their faces. What a moment! Joseph must have seen in a flash the panorama of his strange and eventful life: his boyhood in Canaan, the dreams by which he had been haunted, the growing hostility of his brothers, the awful day when they fell upon him, cast him into a pit and sold him to the Ishmaelites, the journey down into Egypt and his life as a slave. He must have remembered, too, the extraordinary events that led to his becoming the Keeper of the Royal Seal with an authority second only to the throne.

But it is not the events, significant as they are, that interest me most, but the conclusions to which he comes as he ponders the past: "Be not grieved, nor angry with yourselves," he says: "that ye sold me hither: for God did send me …" Three times he says it: "God sent me before you …" and "It was not you that sent me hither, but God …" The astonishing thing is that there was no anger or bitterness in his heart. And why? Because he recognized the work of the Divine Eagle who had pushed him out of the nest in Canaan in order that he might be the provider for his family in time of famine. God moved him into a position of greater usefulness. "You sold me," he said: "but God sent me."

FURTHER STUDY

Gen. 37; 47:11–12, 27; 50:15–21

1. How was Joseph used as an instrument in God's hand?

2. What was his final response to his brothers?

Prayer

O Father, as I look back, the whole meaning of my life is made plain. Many times I have rebelled against the stirring of my own nest, but now I see it was for Your glory and my eternal good. I am so thankful. Amen.

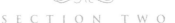

SECTION TWO

Broken—in Order to Be Better

For reading & meditation—Acts 8:1–4

"… there was a great persecution against the church which was at Jerusalem; and they were all scattered …" (v.1, KJV)

We said yesterday that the principle of God throwing us out of the nest in order to make us fly, is a truth that is found everywhere in the Scriptures. We saw it illustrated in an Old Testament setting—the Exodus from Egypt—and now today we look at it in a New Testament setting: the scattering of the believers who formed the first Christian church in Jerusalem. On the face of it, it seems strange that God should permit the church at Jerusalem to be broken up by persecution. It was a great spiritual center—a veritable hive of spiritual industry.

Why then did God overturn their nest? There are two main reasons. First, God knew that Christianity could not come into its own in Jerusalem. The church, great as it was, was too rigid, too racial, too authoritarian. The grave clothes of Judaistic outlook and customs still clung to them, hindering the church from becoming a clear model for future generations to follow. The matrix of Jerusalem was too narrow to be universalized, so God overturned their nest and, through it, brought about the establishing of a new church and a better model at Antioch (Acts 11:19).

Second, the church at Jerusalem tended to be introspective. Some evangelism flowed out to the surrounding areas, but largely they were too inward-looking. When persecution came, they scattered everywhere and, as they did, they carried with them the seeds of the Gospel, causing New Testament churches to spring up all over the place. The persecution, instead of stopping them, furthered them. They didn't simply bear it—they used it.

FURTHER STUDY

Matt. 28:16–20; 26:31; Acts 11:19–21; 1:8

1. What was the prophecy and also the commission of Christ?

2. In what 2 ways was this brought about?

Prayer

Gracious Father, help me to see that when You permit the good to be taken away, it is only because You want to introduce me to the better. Make me more aware of this than I have ever been before. For Jesus' sake. Amen.

SECTION TWO

Gone—But Nearer than Ever

For reading & meditation—John 16:1–16

"... my going is for your good. If I do not depart, the Helper will not come to you ..." (v.7, Moffatt)

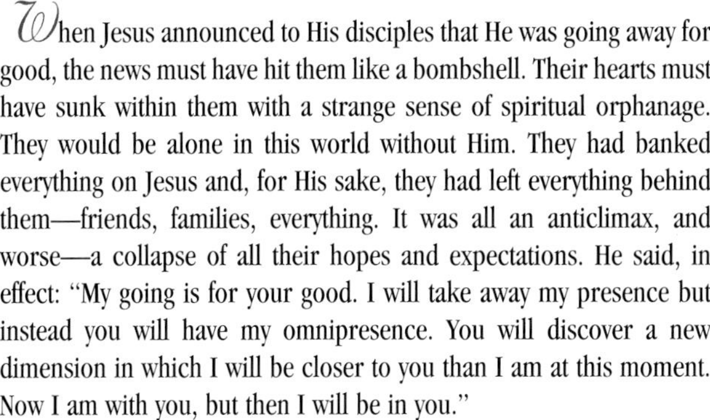

When Jesus announced to His disciples that He was going away for good, the news must have hit them like a bombshell. Their hearts must have sunk within them with a strange sense of spiritual orphanage. They would be alone in this world without Him. They had banked everything on Jesus and, for His sake, they had left everything behind them—friends, families, everything. It was all an anticlimax, and worse—a collapse of all their hopes and expectations. He said, in effect: "My going is for your good. I will take away my presence but instead you will have my omnipresence. You will discover a new dimension in which I will be closer to you than I am at this moment. Now I am with you, but then I will be in you."

And isn't this precisely what happened? At Pentecost He came back—He did change His presence for His omnipresence. He came into the inner recesses of their hearts—burningly, blessedly near. They didn't simply remember Christ—they realized Him. They must have said to one another: "He's gone—yet He is nearer than ever." And not only was His presence available, but His power was available—unlimited resources at their disposal at any and all times. When this happened, they knew He was right in taking away the comfort of His bodily presence to give them His spiritual presence—intimate, available and within. The Divine Eagle never disturbs our nest but for a good purpose and He never takes away the good without giving something much better.

FURTHER STUDY

Luke 24:13–53;
Mark 16:12–14;
John 20:24–28

1. Why were the disciples so disillusioned?

2. What was the response when Jesus explained the purpose of His death?

Prayer

Gracious Father, when my nest is stirred and I feel threatened and afraid, help me to see that You want to turn all my good into better, all my better into best. Amen.

SECTION TWO

When Trouble Comes . . .

For reading & meditation—James 1:1–16

"When all kinds of trials and temptations crowd into your lives ... don't resent them as intruders, but welcome them as friends!" (v.2, J. B. Phillips)

Now that we have established from Scripture the principle that God overturns our nest in order to push us forward into greater usefulness, we must focus our attention on some specific occasions when God is likely to be implementing this principle in our lives. He does it, for example, when He overturns the nest of our calm experiences and tips us out into the midst of fiery trials. Have you gone through periods in your life when it seems that everything is running smoothly and you haven't a care in the world—then suddenly calamity strikes, and you find yourself saying: "Just when everything seemed to be going fine—this had to happen."

Many Christians, when faced with such a situation, think that sudden calamity is an indication that God is punishing them for some sin. This attitude makes victory impossible. We must recognize, of course, that this is a world of moral consequences and that sin does bring trouble, but we are indebted to Jesus for showing us that sin and calamity are not always directly connected. In His comment on the fall of the tower at Siloam and on those who lost their lives, Jesus said the sufferers were not worse sinners than the rest (Luke 13:4, 5). When trouble comes our attitude should be that of our text for today: "Greet it as pure joy, my brothers, when you encounter any sort of trial" (Moffatt). And why? Because what happens to us can help us to expand our wings and soar to new heights and new discoveries of God. Our inner attitudes determine the results.

FURTHER STUDY

Heb. 12; Job 23:10; 2 Cor. 4:17

1. How does God use trials and testings to further His purposes?

2. What trial are you facing at the moment?

Prayer

O Father, help me to lay hold on this sacred secret, for when I do then I am invulnerable and invincible. If life hits me on the chin, it will but lift my face to see higher. Amen.

SECTION TWO

"There is No Bad Weather"

For reading & meditation—Proverbs 30:7–19

"The way of an eagle in the sky ..." (v.19)

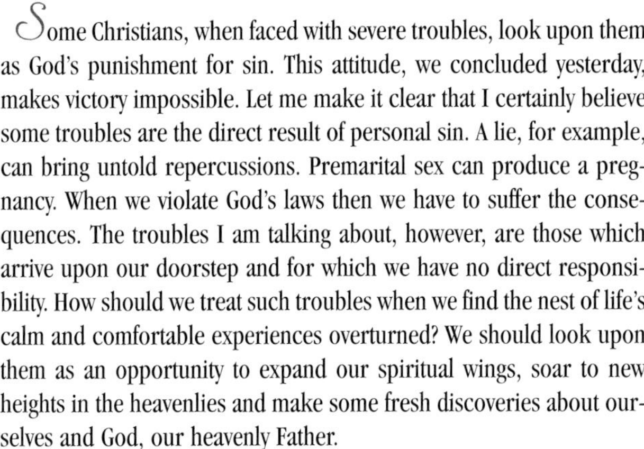

Some Christians, when faced with severe troubles, look upon them as God's punishment for sin. This attitude, we concluded yesterday, makes victory impossible. Let me make it clear that I certainly believe some troubles are the direct result of personal sin. A lie, for example, can bring untold repercussions. Premarital sex can produce a pregnancy. When we violate God's laws then we have to suffer the consequences. The troubles I am talking about, however, are those which arrive upon our doorstep and for which we have no direct responsibility. How should we treat such troubles when we find the nest of life's calm and comfortable experiences overturned? We should look upon them as an opportunity to expand our spiritual wings, soar to new heights in the heavenlies and make some fresh discoveries about ourselves and God, our heavenly Father.

Ruskin said: "There is no bad weather; there are only different kinds of good weather." There is no bad weather except as you take it badly. Adverse weather is only perverse weather as we fail to harness it to our purposes. The writer of Proverbs says that among the mysteries of the universe is "the way of an eagle in the sky." And why? Because although an eagle can soar higher than any other bird, it does so without flapping its wings. The eagle understands the air currents (or thermals) and waits for the right moment, then ascends without any great effort. Adverse winds cans lift you higher into the presence of your loving, heavenly Father—if you know how to tilt your wings!

FURTHER STUDY

2 Cor. 12:1–10; James 1:2; 1 Pet. 1:5–9

1. What was Paul's, Peter's and James' "thermal"?

2. What "thermal" are you currently rising on?

Prayer

Father, I am so glad that the word trouble is not to be found in Your dictionary. When I look for it there, I find that it is spelled T-r-i-u-m-p-h. I am so thankful. Amen.

SECTION TWO

Don't Get Into a Flap

For reading & meditation—Isaiah 40:25–31

"But they that wait upon the Lord ... shall mount up with wings as eagles ..." (v.31, KJV)

Did you notice that Isaiah says of the eagle that she "mounts up" and not "flaps up"? Of course, an eagle is well able to is use its wings to fly, but typically it "soars." An eagle will sometimes perch on a high rock and wait for a while—testing the winds. When it feels that the right wind is blowing, it expands its broad wings and is at once lifted by the breeze into the great heights. In every difficulty that God allows to come our way, there is a breeze that, if we wait for it and take advantage of it, will lift us clean beyond the clouds where we will see the face of God.

Life is determined more by our reactions than by our actions. When God allows difficulties to crowd into your life, it is then that reaction counts. You can react in self-pity and in frustration, or with confidence and courage and turn the trouble into a triumph. When trouble strikes and your nest is overturned—don't panic. Wait for the breeze that is springing up; it will lift you into the presence of God. Those that wait, says the Scripture, are those that mount up. This is the eagle's secret of being able to soar so high—waiting. A man wrote to me: "My life was in ruins. But I just knew that God would not let me down. I waited for God to get me out—and He did. His timing was perfect." It always is. When troubles come, don't flap—soar!

FURTHER STUDY

Ps. 27; Eph. 3:16;
Col. 1:11–12;
John 3:8

1. Why are we able to "mount up with wings as eagles?"
2. What is the breeze upon which we mount?

Prayer

Gracious God, teach me the secret of getting on top of Your breezes so that I can ascend to higher heights with You. This I ask in Jesus' name. Amen.

"Let It Hurt—Good"

For reading & meditation—Revelation 2:18–29

"I will grant him to see the Morning-star." (v.28, Moffatt)

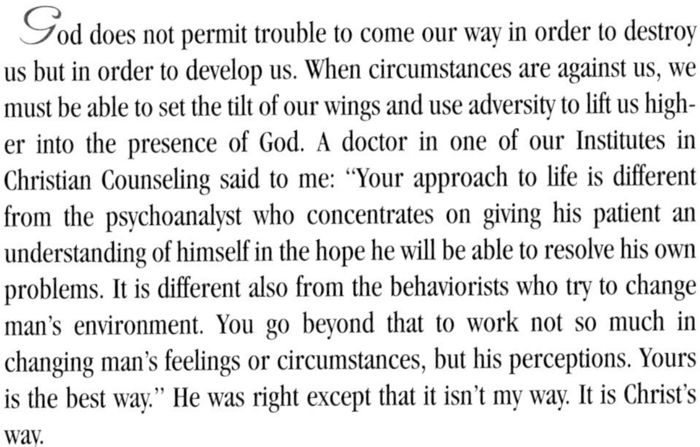

God does not permit trouble to come our way in order to destroy us but in order to develop us. When circumstances are against us, we must be able to set the tilt of our wings and use adversity to lift us higher into the presence of God. A doctor in one of our Institutes in Christian Counseling said to me: "Your approach to life is different from the psychoanalyst who concentrates on giving his patient an understanding of himself in the hope he will be able to resolve his own problems. It is different also from the behaviorists who try to change man's environment. You go beyond that to work not so much in changing man's feelings or circumstances, but his perceptions. Yours is the best way." He was right except that it isn't my way. It is Christ's way.

Christians can meet adversity and trouble head-on because they know that through it they will develop more Christlikeness. In India some farmers winnow wheat by holding up a basket of wheat and chaff, shaking and tipping it up, letting the contents slowly fall so that the wind can blow through them, driving the chaff away and leaving only the wheat to fall to the ground. The winds of adversity and affliction may blow through your spirit but they do nothing except separate the chaff from the wheat. You become a sifted soul—sifted of everything that is not worthwhile. The Moffatt translation of Psalm 119:67 puts the issue of why God allows trouble in clear perspective. "Before my trouble I went wrong: now I do thy bidding."

FURTHER STUDY

Ps. 66; Zech. 13:9; 1 Pet. 1:7

1. How does fire refine?

2. What is the end result?

Father, You are teaching me to understand, to understand by undergoing. I could never learn otherwise. So let it hurt—good. In Jesus' name. Amen.

The Tilt of Our Wings

For reading & meditation—Romans 8:28–39

"And we know that all things work together for good to them that love God . . ." (v.28, KJV)

We are seeing that nothing need beat us if we have the right attitude of mind. When the storm strikes the eagle, if its wings are set in a downward tilt, it will be dashed to pieces on the ground; but if its wings are tilted upward, it will rise, making the storm bear it up beyond its fury. The Christian faith, providing we interpret it correctly and apply it to our circumstances, will set the wings of our spirit in the right direction, so that when calamity strikes, we go up and not down. The calamity that strikes one Christian finds him with his spiritual wings tilted in the direction of the earth so he writhes in anguish in the dust. The same calamity strikes another, one with his wings set upwards, and he soars above it—calm and serene.

Some students, discussing Romans 8:28, asked a professor in a theological college: "You don't believe that all things work together for good—all the pain, suffering and misery—do you?" The professor replied: "The things, in themselves, may not be good, but God can make them work together for good." That afternoon his wife was killed in an automobile accident. Before leaving the college, he left this message: "Romans 8:28 still holds good." When the professor died a year later, his friends and relatives inscribed Romans 8:28 on his tomb. Many a student has stood at that tomb and prayed that he might have that same spiritual insight. But it is not enough to have Romans 8:28 inscribed on our tomb, it must be inscribed in our life convictions.

FURTHER STUDY

Isa. 43:1–21; Ps. 30:5, 34:19

1. How can we be sure that "ALL THINGS work together for good"?

2. How does your own testimony bear this out?

Prayer

O Father, I don't need to look any further for the secret of successful Christian living. I have the secret in these words of Romans 8:28. You can make all things work together for good. Inscribe this on my heart I pray. Amen.

SECTION TWO

"God's Passion Flower"

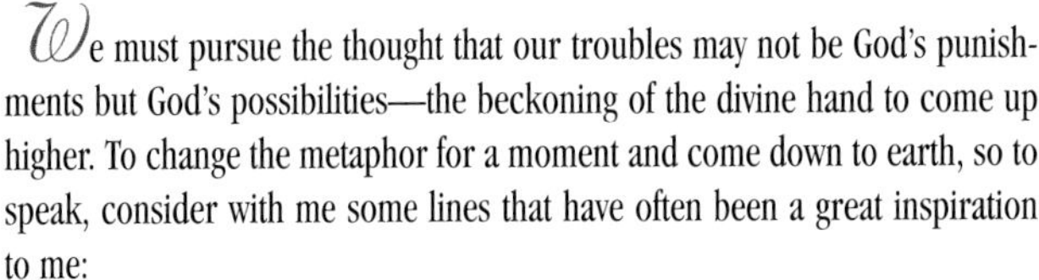

For reading & meditation—Matthew 26:36–46

"Then he said to them, 'My soul is overwhelmed with sorrow to the point of death ...'" (v.38)

We must pursue the thought that our troubles may not be God's punishments but God's possibilities—the beckoning of the divine hand to come up higher. To change the metaphor for a moment and come down to earth, so to speak, consider with me some lines that have often been a great inspiration to me:

Why do I creep along the heavenly way
By inches in the garish day.
Last night when darkening clouds
Did round me lower,
I strode whole leagues in one short hour!

The darkening clouds may only serve to quicken your pace toward Home. An Indian proverb says: "The bursting of the petals say the flowers are coming." So when your heart bursts with grief at the overturning of your comfortable nest remember that the bursting is only the bursting of the imprisoning sheath petals to let the flower out. One writer says: "The heartbreak of Gethsemane was the bursting of the sheath that let the Passion Flower out. And now the whole world is filled with that Perfume." As someone said: "It is wonderful what God can do with a broken heart—if He can get all the pieces." Is your heart bowed low at this moment because of the troubles you face? Has God overturned your nest and sent you plunging into depths of despair and uncertainty? Don't weep over the spoiled nest. God wishes to make you new. Your spiritual resolve has been weakened by too much dependence on things other than Himself.

FURTHER STUDY

Job 1–2, 42:10–17; Ps. 41:3; Rom. 8:18; 1 Pet. 4:12–13

1. What lessons can be learned from Job?

2. Why can we rejoice in our sufferings ?

Prayer

O God, I pray, help me not to whine and whimper when my nest is overturned, but to see that it is not so much what happens to me but what I do with it that determines the result. Amen.

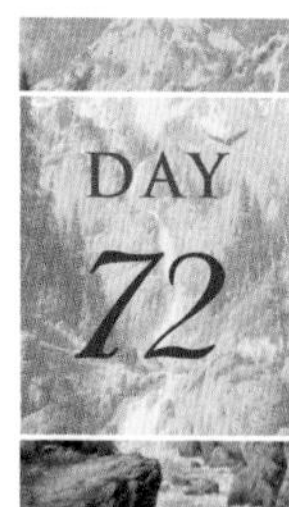

SECTION TWO

Jolting the Glory Out

For reading & meditation—Romans 8:14–27

"... our present sufferings are not worth comparing with the glory that will be revealed in us." (v.18)

God overturns the nest of our comfortable experiences and tips us out into the midst of problems, not in order to destroy us but to develop us. Hudson Taylor was seated in a room with a new missionary to China. He filled a glass with water, placed it on a table, and then struck the table with his fist. As the water splashed out, he said to the young missionary: "You will be struck by the blows of many sorrows and troubles in China, but, remember, they will only splash out of you what is in you." Out of some splash the emotions of bitterness, resentment and despair. Out of others splash joy, forgiveness and victory. Says Edwin Markham:

Defeat may serve as well as victory
To shake the soul and let the glory out.
When the great oak is straining in the wind
The boughs drink in new beauty, and the trunk
Sends down a deeper root on the windward side.

An elderly Christian stood in the corridor of a train as it was coming into a station. The train lurched several times before it stopped, throwing him from one side of the corridor to the other. When he hit one side, those near him heard him quietly say: "Glory!" When he hit the other side, they heard him say: "Hallelujah!" The jolting brought out what was in him. What does trouble do to you? Does it shake the glory out? If so, then you have victory!

FURTHER STUDY

Acts 16; John 7:38; Phil. 2:13

1. What was Paul's reaction to his adversity?

2. How do you react to your adversities?

Prayer

O Father, help me to respond to trouble in the same way as this dear old Christian. If situations jolt me, they shall but jolt the glory out. Amen.

SECTION TWO

"Summer Sang in Me"

DAY 73

For reading & meditation—Matthew 6:25–34

"But seek first his kingdom ... and all these things will be given to you as well." (v.33)

We turn now to consider another nest that God often overturns in our lives—the nest of material prosperity. This question of material possessions is a sharp one. Some Christians prefer not to face it as it raises all kinds of emotions in their hearts. But if we don't face it, we leave God with no alternative but to deal firmly with us. God will not have our heart fixed on things. He wants our gaze fully focused on Himself. There is nothing wrong with being the possessor of great riches, providing these are held in trust for God and that we see our role not as proprietors but as stewards of the Lord's treasury.

I have seen many Christians become preoccupied with riches and I have watched with interest as God overturned their nest. A Christian with a brilliant business mind launched an enterprise that made him a fortune. When I talked to him about his spiritual life, I was reminded of the words of Edna Vincent Millay:

I cannot say what loves have come and gone.
I only know that summer sang in me
A little while, and in me sings no more.

The winter of materialism had set in, chilling his spiritual life. But then God overturned his nest. He was stripped of everything he owned. At first he was stunned and crushed. Out of the bewilderment and pain, however, came a new vision of God. He rose up to build a new and better business—one in which God was the principal shareholder.

FURTHER STUDY

Matt. 19:16–26;
Deut. 8:13–14, 18;
Ps. 62:10

1. Which commandments were not mentioned?

2. What is the danger of riches?

Gracious Father, help me to learn the ways of the kingdom and to put You first in everything. Help me to see myself as a steward and not a proprietor. In Jesus' Name. Amen.

DAY 74

SECTION TWO

Sitting by the Treasury

For reading & meditation—Mark 12:41–44

"And Jesus sat down opposite the place where the offerings were put and watched ..." (v.41)

It is a solemn moment when we review our relationship to our material possessions with Jesus sitting beside us, watching the effect of money on us. The real question for us to ask is: Who owns my possessions, God or me? Whether we acknowledge it or not, we do not in reality own anything. We are only in possession of our possessions for a brief period. A prominent minister was invited by a rich farmer to his house for dinner. The farmer took him to the top of a hill and waved his hand toward the beautiful, broad acres stretched out before them and said: "You mentioned in one of your sermons that no one really owns anything. It all belongs to God. If I don't own these acres, who does?" The minister thought for a moment and replied: "Ask me that question a hundred years from now." If we don't own our possessions then the obvious thing to do is to say to God: "I'm not the owner. I'm only the ower. Teach me how to work out that relationship." We do not need to look very far for instruction on this issue because in the Bible God teaches us how to acknowledge His ownership—by giving Him one-tenth. But, remember, when we give one-tenth we are not really giving, we are only paying an obligation. When we give out of the remaining nine-tenths, only then are we giving. A Christian businessman put it wisely when he said: "God has prospered me. Now I want to know how much of God's money I can keep for my own needs."

FURTHER STUDY

Luke 12:15–34; Job 20:28; Prov. 23:5

1. Which word is used more than any other in this parable?

2. List the things we are to consider.

Prayer

Father, when You touch the issue of my relationship to my money then You have Your finger on a nerve center. I wince but I do not withdraw. Help me to be faithful and open to all You have to show me. In Jesus' Name. Amen.

SECTION TWO

"Under Orders"

For reading & meditation—1 Timothy 6:7–16

"For the love of money is the root of all evil . . ." (v.10, KJV)

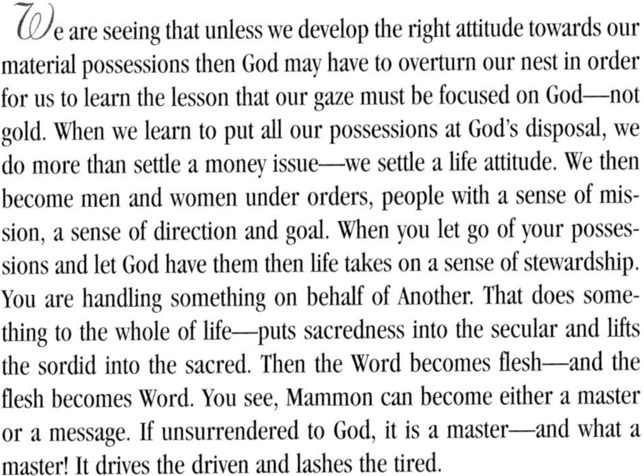

We are seeing that unless we develop the right attitude towards our material possessions then God may have to overturn our nest in order for us to learn the lesson that our gaze must be focused on God—not gold. When we learn to put all our possessions at God's disposal, we do more than settle a money issue—we settle a life attitude. We then become men and women under orders, people with a sense of mission, a sense of direction and goal. When you let go of your possessions and let God have them then life takes on a sense of stewardship. You are handling something on behalf of Another. That does something to the whole of life—puts sacredness into the secular and lifts the sordid into the sacred. Then the Word becomes flesh—and the flesh becomes Word. You see, Mammon can become either a master or a message. If unsurrendered to God, it is a master—and what a master! It drives the driven and lashes the tired.

A doctor I know, who treats a lot of businessmen in Surrey's stockbroker belt, refers to his patients as not having high blood pressure but "high blood-money pressure." The craving for money drives people mad—or to the mortuary. If surrendered to God, however, it can be a beautiful thing. Brother Lawrence put it this way: "Sanctification is not changing your work, but is doing everything which you have done for yourself for the glory of God." Surrender of your possessions to God makes them sanctified and sanctifying. Your Christianity functions in and through the material.

FURTHER STUDY

Prov. 3; 13:7;
Matt.6:19–21

1. What is more precious than rubies?

2. What happens when we give what we have back to God?

Prayer

Heavenly Father, I hold all I have at Your disposal. You know my needs and the needs of the world. Relate them, through my surrender. In Jesus' Name. Amen.

DAY 76

Called—To Make Money?

For reading & meditation—Luke 12:13–21

"... a man's life does not consist in the abundance of his possessions." (v.15)

I once heard an old Welsh preacher begin a sermon: "I want to speak on the subject: 'What Jesus talked about most.'" Immediately I tried to work out what it was. I thought to myself, could it be "prayer" or "faith" or "heaven?" No, I concluded, it was none of these. It must be: "Salvation." Imagine my surprise when the preacher said: "The subject Jesus talked about most was a man's relationship to his possessions." Consider the facts for yourself. Half of Jesus' parables focus on the issue of money. In Matthew's Gospel alone Jesus talks about money close on 100 times. In fact, extending the argument further than the Gospels, although in the New Testament there are about 500 references to prayer, there are over 1,000 references to a person's relationship to his possessions.

I believe that God calls some people to go into business as definitely as He calls some to go into the ministry of the Church. There they can use their powers of organization and administration to make money for God. Sir Christopher Wren, the great architect, asked three men who were building St Paul's Cathedral, what they were doing. One said "I'm laboring here until 5 o'clock which is knocking-off time." Another said "I'm working for money." The third replied: "I'm helping Sir Christopher Wren build this cathedral." In this life, money is important and every dollar we make counts. Find God's plan for yourself and work that plan. Then you feel that you are part of a vast design and you will grow big in that vastness. You are a creator under the Creator.

FURTHER STUDY

Matt. 25:14–30;
Prov. 10:22;
1 Cor. 4:2

1. What is Jesus teaching in Matt. 25?
2. Find out what the talents are to which Jesus refers.

Prayer

O Father, I live in an acquisitive society where worth is judged by wealth. As I am a Christian, my judgments must be different. Help me to decide the Christian way in everything. For Jesus' sake. Amen.

SECTION TWO

Making Money for God

For reading & meditation—Romans 12:1–18

"... if it is contributing to the needs of others, let him give generously ..." (v.8)

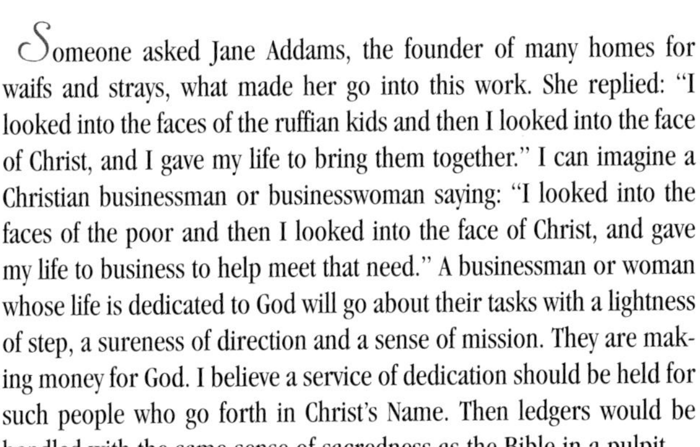

Someone asked Jane Addams, the founder of many homes for waifs and strays, what made her go into this work. She replied: "I looked into the faces of the ruffian kids and then I looked into the face of Christ, and I gave my life to bring them together." I can imagine a Christian businessman or businesswoman saying: "I looked into the faces of the poor and then I looked into the face of Christ, and gave my life to business to help meet that need." A businessman or woman whose life is dedicated to God will go about their tasks with a lightness of step, a sureness of direction and a sense of mission. They are making money for God. I believe a service of dedication should be held for such people who go forth in Christ's Name. Then ledgers would be handled with the same sense of sacredness as the Bible in a pulpit.

This fits in with Howard Lowry's definition of religion: "It conceives of all man does as a calling and all of life as a piece, a unity of richly component parts." "Of all man does as a calling": that fits in with the New Testament idea of people working out God's plan. Livingstone's motto should become the motto of every Christian in the world. Repeat it to yourself slowly through the day: "I will place no value on anything that I have or possess except in relation to the kingdom of Christ." If it furthers the kingdom—it has value, it can stay. If it is useless to the kingdom—it must go.

FURTHER STUDY

James 2; Prov. 25:21; Eccl. 11:1

1. How can we combine faith and works practically?

2. When was the last time you gave to someone in need?

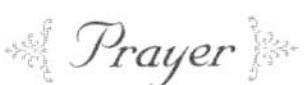

Prayer

O Father, help me to evaluate all I do in the fight of Your kingdom's demands, and to streamline my life to fit Your eternal purposes. In Jesus' Name. Amen.

SECTION TWO

The Generous Eye

For reading & meditation—Matthew 6:19–24

"... if your Eye is generous, the whole of your body will be illumined." (v.22, Moffatt)

Unless we have the issue of material possessions straight then we may soon find our nest overturned. God will not have our gaze focused on things but only on Himself. Once the central issue of who owns our possessions is fixed—God and not ourselves—we are then free to cultivate generosity. We must decide that our outlook on everything should be to find the good, further the good and do good in every situation. Someone has said: "If we do not give according to our resources then God will make our resources according to our giving." Does this make God a tyrant? Not if we understand things correctly, for the more we give to others, the more beautiful we become in ourselves. The giving are the living—in themselves!

Our text for today says that if our eye, our outlook on life, our whole way of looking at things and people, is generous then our whole personality is illuminated. We become better by our giving. A rich Christian businessman who decided to donate some important medical equipment to a hospital in China, went to see the ship on which it was being carried. At the dockside he met another Christian and the businessman shared with him what the moment meant to him. "I, too, have a gift on board that ship," said the other Christian. "My daughter is on board, going to China as a missionary." The businessman said "My brother, my sacrifice is nothing compared to what you have given." Both, however, were stewards of the entrustments of God. Both could say: "Such as I have, I give."

FURTHER STUDY

Luke 10:25–37; Acts 20:35; Luke 6:38; 2 Cor. 9:6

1. What is the philosophy of the world?

2. Why is it more blessed to give than to receive?

Father, help me to keep my money in my hands and not in my heart. This I ask in Jesus' Name. Amen.

SECTION TWO

Undedicated Possessions

For reading & meditation—Matthew 13:1–23

"... the worries of this life and the deceitfulness of wealth choke [the word] ..." (v.22)

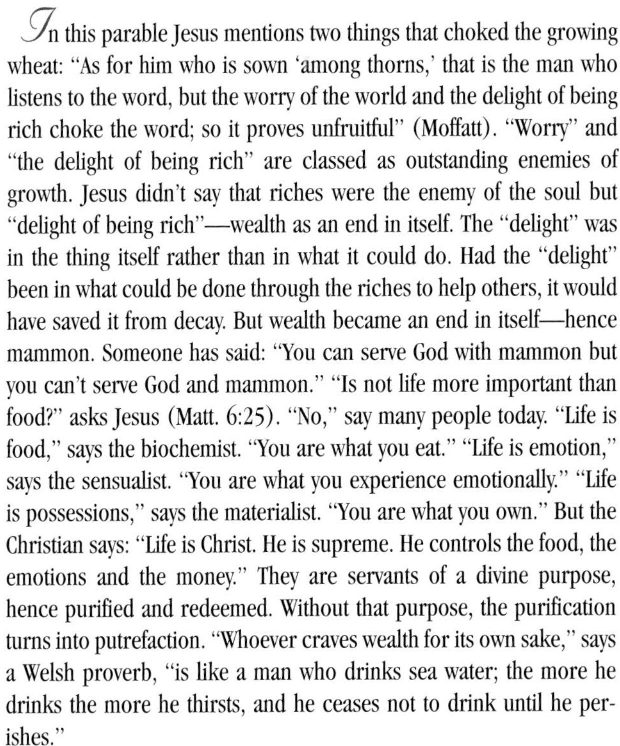

In this parable Jesus mentions two things that choked the growing wheat: "As for him who is sown 'among thorns,' that is the man who listens to the word, but the worry of the world and the delight of being rich choke the word; so it proves unfruitful" (Moffatt). "Worry" and "the delight of being rich" are classed as outstanding enemies of growth. Jesus didn't say that riches were the enemy of the soul but "delight of being rich"—wealth as an end in itself. The "delight" was in the thing itself rather than in what it could do. Had the "delight" been in what could be done through the riches to help others, it would have saved it from decay. But wealth became an end in itself—hence mammon. Someone has said: "You can serve God with mammon but you can't serve God and mammon." "Is not life more important than food?" asks Jesus (Matt. 6:25). "No," say many people today. "Life is food," says the biochemist. "You are what you eat." "Life is emotion," says the sensualist. "You are what you experience emotionally." "Life is possessions," says the materialist. "You are what you own." But the Christian says: "Life is Christ. He is supreme. He controls the food, the emotions and the money." They are servants of a divine purpose, hence purified and redeemed. Without that purpose, the purification turns into putrefaction. "Whoever craves wealth for its own sake," says a Welsh proverb, "is like a man who drinks sea water; the more he drinks the more he thirsts, and he ceases not to drink until he perishes."

FURTHER STUDY

Phil. 3;
Eph. 1:18; 3:8

1. Why did Paul "count all things but loss"?

2. What was his pursuit?

Prayer

Lord Jesus, You who enriched the world with riches, help me to take my riches, small and great, and make them the instrument of Your purposes. For Your own dear Name's sake. Amen.

Life Unlimited

For reading & meditation—John 10:1–1

"... I am come that they might have life, and that they might have it more abundantly." (v.10, KJV)

We look now at yet another nest which God seeks to overturn in our lives—spiritual complacency. Many Christians are content to live at a level far below the best. It might be comfortable in the nest, but it is far better to expand one's wings, launch out into the clear, blue sky and live life to its fullest potential. God's desire is to get you out of the nest and up into the air.

I am thinking particularly of those Christians who, although soundly saved and fully committed to Jesus Christ, have never experienced all the fullness of the Holy Spirit. Although every Christian has the Holy Spirit (1 Cor.12:3), the Holy Spirit does not have every Christian. When you surrendered your life to Jesus Christ, the Holy Spirit came in to regenerate you, give you a new birth, but now you need to experience another encounter with the Spirit that lifts you clean out of the nest and up into the air.

The text before us today claims that Jesus came not merely to give us life but to give it—abundantly. One writer says of this verse: "At conversion, Christ gives us life, but when we experience the fullness of the Spirit, we encounter not merely life but life that is abundant. In conversion, God's life is imparted to us. In the fullness of the Spirit, God's life inundates us." A sign over a shop read: "Life Ltd." A sign could be put over our individual and collective lives: "Life Ltd." And yet Jesus said that the purpose of His coming was to give life more abundantly.

FURTHER STUDY

Acts 1–2; John 7:38–39; 1 Cor. 3:16; Rom. 8:11 (KJV)

1. What caused the disciples to soar to new heights?

2. What does the word "quicken" mean?

Prayer

O Father, take me from life limited to Life Unlimited. I have lived far too long in the nest. Now I want to get up into the air. Amen.

SECTION TWO

Belief—Not an Experience

For reading & meditation—Ephesians 5:17–33
"... be filled with the Spirit." (v.18)

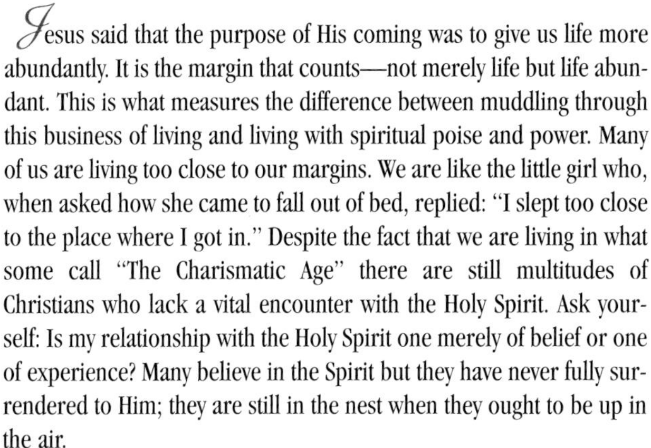

Jesus said that the purpose of His coming was to give us life more abundantly. It is the margin that counts—not merely life but life abundant. This is what measures the difference between muddling through this business of living and living with spiritual poise and power. Many of us are living too close to our margins. We are like the little girl who, when asked how she came to fall out of bed, replied: "I slept too close to the place where I got in." Despite the fact that we are living in what some call "The Charismatic Age" there are still multitudes of Christians who lack a vital encounter with the Holy Spirit. Ask yourself: Is my relationship with the Holy Spirit one merely of belief or one of experience? Many believe in the Spirit but they have never fully surrendered to Him; they are still in the nest when they ought to be up in the air.

Rufus Jones remarks that by the time when the creeds were written, all the Church could say was: "I believe in the Holy Spirit." At great length the Church outlined the facts of the life of Jesus—the Incarnation, Crucifixion, Resurrection, Ascension—but the Holy Spirit was mentioned as a belief instead of an experience. Many present-day Christians need to know and experience the energizing power of the Spirit pulsing through the warp and woof of their lives, moving them from the ordinary to the extraordinary, from the mediocre to the magnificent, from the nest where all is calm and complacent, to the sky where all is bright and brilliant.

FURTHER STUDY

Acts 10:34–48; Matt. 3:11; Luke 11:13; 24:49

1. What happened when Peter preached?

2. What was Luke's testimony of Jesus?

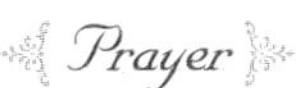

O Father, I have believed in the Holy Spirit as a doctrine. Now I want to experience Him as life. Make everything clear to me. In Jesus' Name. Amen.

SECTION TWO

Another Crisis?

For reading & meditation—Romans 8:1–14

"... because through Christ Jesus the law of the Spirit of life set me free from the law of sin and death. " (v.2)

Must we, in seeking the fullness of the Spirit, face another crisis similar to conversion? Yes, I think that usually we must. Some people have such a dramatic conversion that they seem to appropriate all God has for them from the word "Go." Most of us, however, would share the experience of a great "Holiness" preacher of a past generation, who said: "The soul gets on by a series of crises." The spiritual movements that are making the greatest headway in today's Church all converge on one fact—the necessity of bringing the whole life into line with the will of God. There must be an absoluteness about the whole thing. And they would agree that while conversion begins this process, some further crisis is necessary to bring everything into line. Are they all wrong about this? I think not. They may be wrong in certain emphases, but in the one central thing, I believe they are profoundly right.

In my own life and in the lives of thousands of others with whom I have dealt intimately, I have seen the principle at work, that when we come to the end of our own strength, we can either sink back and become a mediocre Christian or give ourselves in total abandonment to the person of the Holy Spirit, for Him to empower us, enlighten us and energize us.

Permit me to ask you a very personal question: Are you living a Spirit-filled life? Are you conscious of His residency and presidency in your heart? If not, you are still in the nest. It's time you got up into the air.

FURTHER STUDY

Ps. 42; Isa. 55:1; Matt. 5:6; Ps. 63:1

1. What is the promise for the thirsty?

2. How does this apply to the Holy Spirit?

Prayer

Father, You are stripping my nest of all the comforts on which I have relied for a long time. You know how I hate to be challenged, but I realize You are disturbing me to develop me. Help me not to miss what You are saying to me at this important moment. Amen.

SECTION TWO

The Baptism in the Spirit

For reading & meditation—Matthew 3:1–12

"... He will baptize you with the Holy Spirit ..." (v.11)

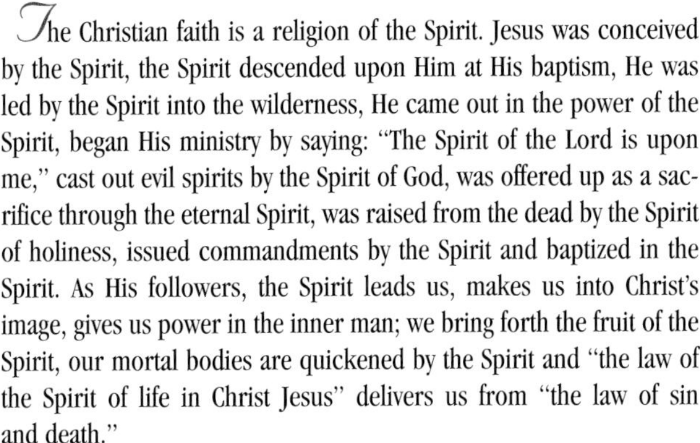

The Christian faith is a religion of the Spirit. Jesus was conceived by the Spirit, the Spirit descended upon Him at His baptism, He was led by the Spirit into the wilderness, He came out in the power of the Spirit, began His ministry by saying: "The Spirit of the Lord is upon me," cast out evil spirits by the Spirit of God, was offered up as a sacrifice through the eternal Spirit, was raised from the dead by the Spirit of holiness, issued commandments by the Spirit and baptized in the Spirit. As His followers, the Spirit leads us, makes us into Christ's image, gives us power in the inner man; we bring forth the fruit of the Spirit, our mortal bodies are quickened by the Spirit and "the law of the Spirit of life in Christ Jesus" delivers us from "the law of sin and death."

Jesus reveals the nature of the Spirit. The Spirit is a Christlike Spirit. This is very important because people have made the Holy Spirit appear strange and even bizarre. A man told me once that the Spirit had told him to take two wives—one to meet his physical needs and the other to meet his spiritual needs. When I suggested to him that the Spirit would never tell him to do anything that contradicted the character of Jesus, he told me he was led by the Spirit not by Jesus. If we are truly led by the Spirit then we will become more like Jesus or it won't be the Holy Spirit that is leading us but some other spirit.

FURTHER STUDY

John 16:1–16; 14:17, 15:26; 1 John 4:6; John 1:14

1. How is Truth revealed to us?

2. What were the characteristics of Christ's glory?

Lord Jesus, I am not afraid of being made like You—I am only afraid I will not be made like You. Help me to surrender to Your Holy Spirit so that I can become more and more like You in every way. Amen.

SECTION TWO

Rabbits Become Ferrets

For reading & meditation—Acts 1:1–12

"But you will receive power when the Holy Spirit comes on you . . ." (v.8)

The nature and operation of the Holy Spirit prior to the coming of Jesus is somewhat difficult to understand. In the Old Testament, for example, the Spirit appears to have no permanent abiding place on the earth. He comes and goes, alights upon men for a specific task, then returns to heaven. On some occasions the Spirit used men whose lives quite clearly lacked dedication and holiness. All this could lead to wrong conclusions about the Spirit. This is why God gave the Spirit sparingly until Jesus came and fixed the content of the Spirit. It is only in Jesus that we see the full and final revelation of the Spirit's work and purpose in the world.

What does the life and teaching of Jesus reveal about the character and content of the Spirit? Two things—He is the Spirit of power and the Spirit of purity. When Jesus was about to return to heaven, He promised His disciples that if they would tarry in Jerusalem for the "promise of the Father," they would receive supernatural power that would transform them from being weak, timid, vacillating disciples into men ablaze and invincible. Did this happen? It most certainly did. In the Upper Room the disciples received such an invasion of power, it completely revolutionized their personalities. Such was the impact it made upon them that someone described it like this: "Before Pentecost, they were like rabbits. After Pentecost, they were like ferrets." This is precisely what the Spirit can do for you—He can turn you from a rabbit into a ferret.

FURTHER STUDY

Acts 19; Mic. 3:8; Zech. 4:6; Luke 4:14

1. List some of the aspects of Paul's ministry in the power of the Holy Spirit.

2. Can we expect the same powerful ministry today?

Prayer

O Father, fill me so full of the Holy Spirit and His power that my life will be completely transformed. I'm tired of being a rabbit, bolting down every hole I see because of fear. I want to be a ferret, fearless and unafraid. Grant this today. In Jesus' Name. Amen.

SECTION TWO

Inner Cleansing

For reading & meditation—Galatians 5:16–26

"… Walk in the Spirit, and ye shall not fulfil the lust of the flesh." (v.16, KJV)

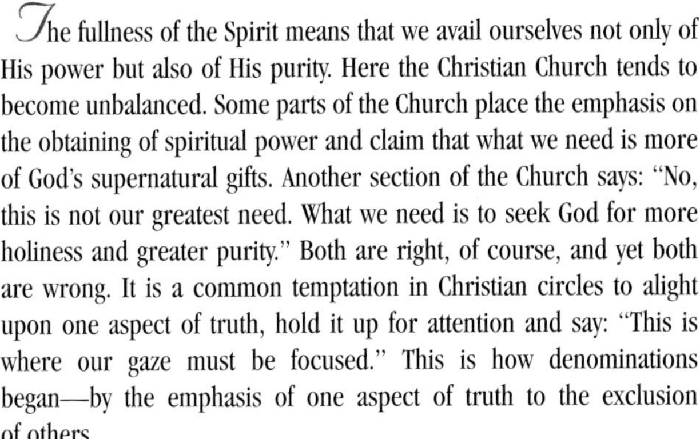

The fullness of the Spirit means that we avail ourselves not only of His power but also of His purity. Here the Christian Church tends to become unbalanced. Some parts of the Church place the emphasis on the obtaining of spiritual power and claim that what we need is more of God's supernatural gifts. Another section of the Church says: "No, this is not our greatest need. What we need is to seek God for more holiness and greater purity." Both are right, of course, and yet both are wrong. It is a common temptation in Christian circles to alight upon one aspect of truth, hold it up for attention and say: "This is where our gaze must be focused." This is how denominations began—by the emphasis of one aspect of truth to the exclusion of others.

If we are to become like Jesus then we need both qualities—purity and power. When we examine the Acts of the Apostles, we find that the coming of the Holy Spirit brought both purity and power into the hearts of those early Christians. The fact that they were empowered is seen quite clearly from the evidence in the Upper Room. The frightened disciples became as bold as lions when once the Spirit came upon them. The fact that they were purified is also quite clearly seen, for when Peter interprets the coming of the Spirit upon the Gentiles, he says: "He made no distinction between us and them, but cleansed their hearts by faith" (Acts 15:9, RSV). Cleansing of the heart came as a result of the coming of the Spirit.

FURTHER STUDY

Eph. 5:1–20; Ezek. 36:27; Rom. 8:9,14; John 6:63

1. List some of the works of the flesh.

2. List the fruit of the Spirit and your definition of each one.

O Father, I am so grateful that You have provided for my deepest needs—the empowerment of my personality and the cleansing of my heart. Help me to know the true fullness of the Spirit in every part of my life today. Amen.

SECTION TWO

Power and Purity

For reading & meditation—Luke 11:1–13

"... how much more will your Father in heaven give the Holy Spirit to those who ask him!" (v.13)

Have we by our denominational emphases greatly narrowed the work of the Spirit? Have we conditioned our converts to expect God to work in them and through them according to our own preconceived ideas? Following a dramatic conversion, I made rapid progress in my Christian life, but after a while my victories turned into defeats. I became greatly dissatisfied with my condition, and because I had no one to guide me, I searched the Scriptures for myself in an attempt to discover the answer to my needs. The Spirit showed me that He was the cause of my disturbed condition and it was He who had precipitated this crisis. The Divine Eagle was pushing me out of the nest so that I might experience "the law of the Spirit of life in Christ Jesus" and lay hold upon God in a new environment. I saw my need in two terms—power and purity. I cried out for both. God graciously met me at the point of my need, filled me with such power that it transformed me from a shy, diffident teenager into a preacher of the Gospel, simultaneously dealing a death blow to the carnal lusts and desires that up to that time had filled my heart.

My Pentecostal friends would say that in that crisis I received the baptism in the Spirit. My Holiness friends would say that my heart was sanctified by faith. All I know is that in that never-to-be-forgotten experience, God met my need for both power and purity. And, my dear friend, what He did for me, He can do for you.

FURTHER STUDY

John 11:33–46;
2 Cor. 3:17;
Rom. 8:2

1. What is the difference between life and liberty?
2. How is this illustrated in Lazarus' resurrection?

Prayer

Father, here I am on the edge of the nest. I tremble as I am about to take this leap of faith. Hold me on Your wings and teach me all I need to learn about life in the Spirit. In Jesus' Name. Amen.

SECTION TWO

Adventurous Living

For reading & meditation—Proverbs 2:6–22

"... for only good men enjoy life to the full" (v.21, TLB)

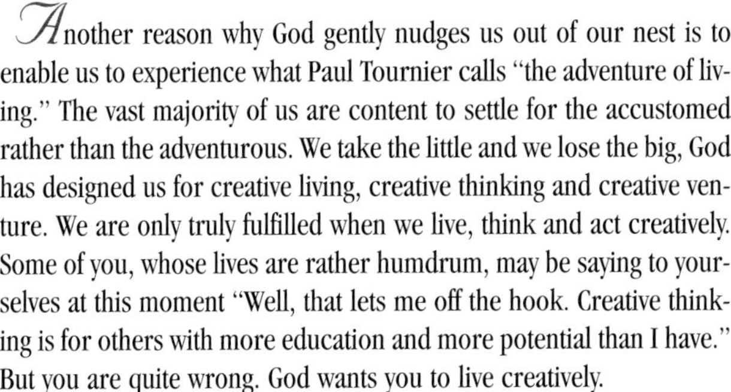

Another reason why God gently nudges us out of our nest is to enable us to experience what Paul Tournier calls "the adventure of living." The vast majority of us are content to settle for the accustomed rather than the adventurous. We take the little and we lose the big, God has designed us for creative living, creative thinking and creative venture. We are only truly fulfilled when we live, think and act creatively. Some of you, whose lives are rather humdrum, may be saying to yourselves at this moment "Well, that lets me off the hook. Creative thinking is for others with more education and more potential than I have." But you are quite wrong. God wants you to live creatively.

Some years ago a famous hotel in California, the El Cortez Hotel, had a serious problem. Its one elevator could not cope with the needs of the guests. The management decided to call in some architects who suggested that another elevator should be installed. To do this, they said, a hole would have to be made from the basement to the roof, and would involve putting the hotel out of service for a whole season. A cleaner, overhearing the discussions, said: "Why don't you build it on the outside?" Astonished, the architects looked at each other. Then someone said: "Why not?" El Cortez Hotel became the first building in history to have an elevator built on the outside. Although all human beings have a capacity to be creative, only a Christian who is wholly dedicated to God has the potential for a fully dynamic and adventurous life.

FURTHER STUDY

Heb. 11; Matt. 17:20; 9:22

1. What is your definition of faith?

2. How is faith creative?

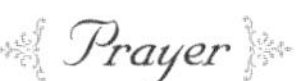

Prayer

O Father, You who created me to be creative, help me to make every day an adventure with You. In Jesus' Name I pray. Amen.

SECTION TWO

"Clinging to His Creeks"

For reading & meditation—Judges 5:13–18

"... Asher remained on the coast and stayed in his coves." (v.17)

One of the greatest mistakes we can make in life is to block the efforts of the Divine Eagle when He attempts to push us out of the nest of the accustomed into the world of the adventurous. Asher did this—the account in the Moffatt translation reads: "Asher sat still by the seaboard clinging to his creeks." Although the metaphor is changed, the principle is still the same. There was Asher sitting by the seaboard, clinging to his creeks, when he could have launched out into the ocean and experienced the joy of a great adventure. In face of the big, he settled for the little. They were "his" creeks and he wasn't going to let the accustomed go to venture into the unaccustomed no matter how great the possibilities.

Asher is a type of the Christian who wants to stay by the safe and secure, and finishes up by doing nothing and getting nowhere. I am not advocating spiritual recklessness nor am I arguing for an unmindful approach to the Christian life, I am simply saying that we ought to be ocean-minded and not creek-minded Christians. The people who try to find inner security by clinging to the creeks are invariably unfulfilled for we are inwardly made for growth and creativity.

A turtle doesn't get anywhere until he sticks his neck out! To cling to our creeks for safety and security is to be upset at every call of the big. We are made for the big and are restless in our littleness. We cannot be content this side of God's purpose.

FURTHER STUDY

1 Sam. 17; Matt. 21:22; Mark 11:24; 1 John 5:14–15

1. In what ways was David adventurous?
2. On what was his adventurous spirit based?

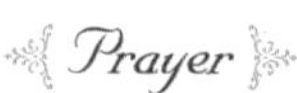

O Father, You are calling and I must come. I drop my littleness and watch it sink into the bigness of Your purpose for me. The great calls and I must come—at any price. Amen.

SECTION TWO

"Let It Soar!"

For reading & meditation—Philippians 4:4–13

"... I can do everything God asks me to with the help of Christ who gives me the strength and power." (v.13, TLB)

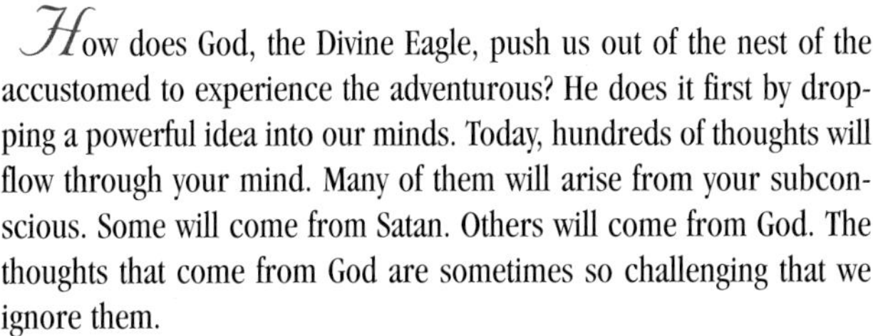

How does God, the Divine Eagle, push us out of the nest of the accustomed to experience the adventurous? He does it first by dropping a powerful idea into our minds. Today, hundreds of thoughts will flow through your mind. Many of them will arise from your subconscious. Some will come from Satan. Others will come from God. The thoughts that come from God are sometimes so challenging that we ignore them.

Many years ago I heard a man say: "The secret of success in doing something for God is to find a need and then set out to meet it." I pondered this for a while and then one day there came into mind the idea that I ought to write some daily thoughts for those Christians who wanted to meet God at the point of the devotional and not simply at the point of the analytical. But I remembered what a tutor had told me in college. "Stick to preaching and teaching," he said. "You will never make a writer." But despite this negative thought in my mind, I allowed the thought that had come from God to soar, and as it did the idea for *Every Day with Jesus* was born. Now millions of words later, I look back and wonder what would have happened if I had not allowed that thought to soar in my mind and then move forward into action.

Today God may drop into your mind a beautiful new thought or idea on how you can minister to someone's need. Don't crush it, resist it or ignore it. Let it soar!

FURTHER STUDY

1 Cor. 1:25–31; Isa. 55:8–9; Phil. 4:8; Rom. 12:2

1. How does God express His thoughts?
2. How can we begin to discover God's thoughts?

O Father, bring me to such maturity that I will he able to recognize immediately the gentle nudges You are giving me to greater service and ministry through the thoughts and ideas You drop into my mind. Begin today, dear Lord. Amen.

SECTION TWO

The Verge of Discovery

For reading & meditation—Proverbs 25:1–13

"It is the glory of God to conceal a thing; To search out a matter is the glory of kings." (v.2)

Our text for today is: *"It is the glory of God to conceal a thing; And it is the glory of kings to reveal it."* God carefully, quietly hides His most precious gifts so that we may become joyous "kings" by discovering them. It is a universal truth that the most valuable treasures are hidden from view. The pearl is hidden within the oyster. The diamond is buried deep within the earth. The gold nugget is concealed in the heart of a mountain. God plans life in such a way that the greatest treasures are concealed, waiting for you to discover them. And there is no thrill like the thrill of making a great discovery. You will feel like a king.

Today you must begin to discover the treasures that God has hidden within your thoughts. Be on the lookout for God's "deposits" in your mind. An idea will come to you and at first you will say: "Go away, go away," but learn to ask yourself: "Is this what God is saying to me?" Don't push a thought away because it is too challenging. Welcome it. This doesn't mean that every big and great idea must be acted upon. It has to be considered, weighed, evaluated and analyzed to see whether it has really come from God. Take more time in looking at your thoughts. Perhaps today while reading these lines, God will drop an idea into your mind that will transform your relationships, your service or your vocation. "It is the glory of God to conceal a thing, and it is the glory of kings to reveal it."

FURTHER STUDY

Ps. 139; 1 Cor. 2:16; Phil. 2:5; 1 Pet. 4:1

1. How can we have the mind of Christ?

2. Where are God's thoughts directed?

Prayer

O Father, I see that one of the places in which you hide Your greatest treasures is in my thoughts. Help me to become a discoverer of these treasures—day by day. Amen.

SECTION TWO

The Ceaseless Creator

For reading & meditation—Psalm 104:1–34

"May he be pleased by all these thoughts ... for he is the source of all my joy." (v.34, TLB)

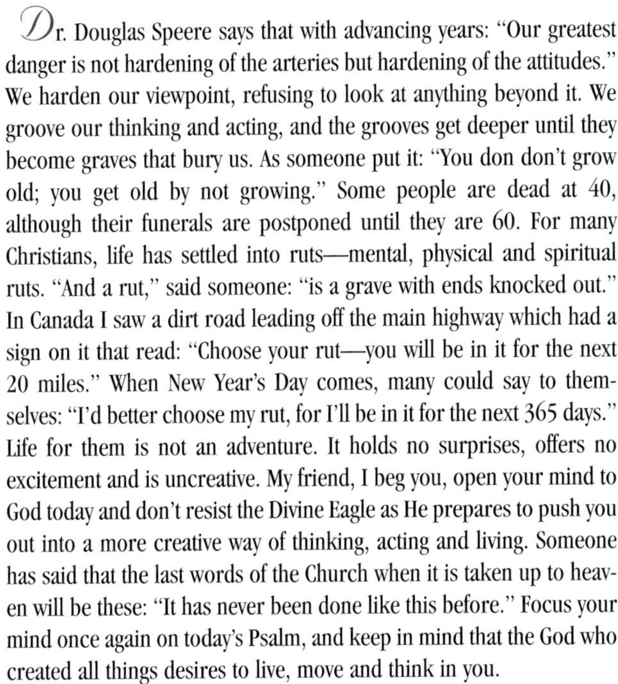

Dr. Douglas Speere says that with advancing years: "Our greatest danger is not hardening of the arteries but hardening of the attitudes." We harden our viewpoint, refusing to look at anything beyond it. We groove our thinking and acting, and the grooves get deeper until they become graves that bury us. As someone put it: "You don don't grow old; you get old by not growing." Some people are dead at 40, although their funerals are postponed until they are 60. For many Christians, life has settled into ruts—mental, physical and spiritual ruts. "And a rut," said someone: "is a grave with ends knocked out." In Canada I saw a dirt road leading off the main highway which had a sign on it that read: "Choose your rut—you will be in it for the next 20 miles." When New Year's Day comes, many could say to themselves: "I'd better choose my rut, for I'll be in it for the next 365 days." Life for them is not an adventure. It holds no surprises, offers no excitement and is uncreative. My friend, I beg you, open your mind to God today and don't resist the Divine Eagle as He prepares to push you out into a more creative way of thinking, acting and living. Someone has said that the last words of the Church when it is taken up to heaven will be these: "It has never been done like this before." Focus your mind once again on today's Psalm, and keep in mind that the God who created all things desires to live, move and think in you.

FURTHER STUDY

Col. 2; Isa. 11:2; Matt. 13:15; 1 Cor. 1:25; Rom. 11:33

1. What are the characteristics of Christ's thoughts?
2. How are they opposed to human philosophy and tradition?

Prayer

O Father, You who are a ceaseless Creator, make me a ceaseless creator. Break the molds of my thinking patterns and give me new ones. In Jesus' Name. Amen.

DAY 92

SECTION TWO

"Bedridden Truths"

For reading & meditation—Ephesians 3:7–21

"God has given me the wonderful privilege of telling everyone about this plan of his; and he has given me his power..." (v.7, TLB)

We continue examining our need to allow God to prod us into greater usefulness and more creative thinking. Dr. Halford Luccock in his book *Marching Off the Map* quotes Gibbons' indictment of the monks of Constantinople, the sterile pedants of the tenth century: "They held in their lifeless hands the riches of their fathers, without inheriting the spirit which had created that sacred patrimony. They read, they praised, they compiled; but their languid souls seemed alike incapable of action and thought." If Jesus were here today He would probably say: "Beware of the monks of Constantinople." If Jesus were to look into our eyes today, would He read there the same sterility?

Here we are in one of the most exciting periods of history. It is true there are great problems, but there are also great possibilities. Science continues to make great strides, crossing frontiers hitherto undreamed of, and showing a quality of thinking that is breathtaking. And the Christian Church in such an era is, generally speaking, like those of whom Coleridge speaks: "People with bedridden truths which lie asleep in the dormitory of their minds." Many of us hold truths, but they are bedridden truths—they don't walk and dance and go in procession, with banners waving. I am not referring, of course, to the timeless, changeless truths of the Incarnation, Redemption, etc., but the truths of translating the Gospel message in terms that really communicate to the men and women of this age. How tragic that so many of us are asleep when the world is awake—bedfast when the world is on the march.

FURTHER STUDY

Luke 14:15–24; Amos 6:1; Matt. 7:26; James 4:17

1. What were the excuses of Luke 14?

2. Why did they excuse themselves?

Prayer

O Father, stir me until every truth that lies within me becomes alive and in operation. I want no bedridden truths. In Jesus' Name. Amen.

SECTION TWO

The Stimulus of Christ

For reading & meditation—Philippians 2:1–11

"So by all the stimulus of Christ ..." (v.1, Moffatt)

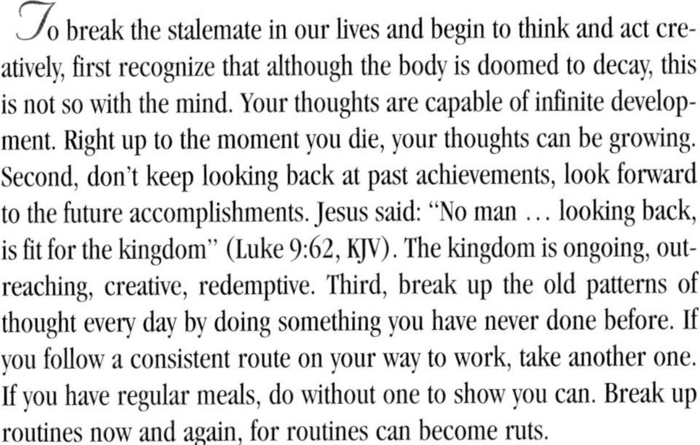

To break the stalemate in our lives and begin to think and act creatively, first recognize that although the body is doomed to decay, this is not so with the mind. Your thoughts are capable of infinite development. Right up to the moment you die, your thoughts can be growing. Second, don't keep looking back at past achievements, look forward to the future accomplishments. Jesus said: "No man ... looking back, is fit for the kingdom" (Luke 9:62, KJV). The kingdom is ongoing, outreaching, creative, redemptive. Third, break up the old patterns of thought every day by doing something you have never done before. If you follow a consistent route on your way to work, take another one. If you have regular meals, do without one to show you can. Break up routines now and again, for routines can become ruts.

Fourth, keep a mental and spiritual wastebasket so that you can discard old ideas. Throw away the bad to get the good, throw away the good to get the better, throw away the better to get the best. A head of a school said, pointing to an incinerator: "Without this the school couldn't keep going." Get rid of old ideas to make way for better ones. Fifth, let Christ stimulate your mind into greater creativity. In Christ you have the most absolutely stimulating force in the universe. He coaxes a summer out of a winter, a bird out of a shell and life out of a dead spirit. Expose your whole being to His stimulus and be the person He designed you to be.

FURTHER STUDY

1 Cor. 2; Dan. 2:22; Amos 3:7; John 15:15; Eph. 1.9

1. How can we know the deep things of God?
2. What things has God been revealing to you recently?

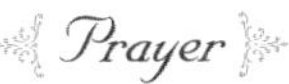

Prayer

Lord Jesus, Your hand once touched the dead, Your voice penetrated to them and they arose. Do it again—to me. Come and think in me, live in me, love in me and make me a more creative person. In Jesus' Name. Amen.

SECTION TWO

Taking Off Our Masks

For reading & meditation—Psalm 51:1–17

"... thou desirest truth in the inward parts..." (v.6, KJV)

Another reason why the Divine Eagle gently nudges us out of the nest is in order that we might learn to become totally honest. Because we don't know how to face the fear, guilt, inferiority feelings and hurts within us, many of us go about pretending they are not there. We instinctively wear a mask and pretend to be someone we are not. We do not accept ourselves enough to be ourselves and so we slip into a role and act out our part in life rather like an actor does on a stage. While it might seem to be a safer life behind this mask, it is also a lonely life. We cease to be authentic, and as persons we cease to grow. We are simply not being ourselves, and when the curtain drops after our performance, we remain the same, immature persons that we were when the curtain went up at the beginning of our act. The trouble about wearing a mask is that it prevents us from being ourselves. It is the authentic self that God wants to use, not someone who is playing a role.

I know that for many the reality of facing themselves as they are, and accepting themselves as they are, is a challenge from which they would shrink. If you feel this way now don't, I beg you, resist the nudge of the Divine Eagle as He gently pushes you toward the edge of the nest. If you let God have His way in your heart and life in this coming week, a new dimension of living can open up for you.

FURTHER STUDY

Ps. 139 (TLB); Jer. 17:9; Ps. 36:2; Gal. 6:3

1. What was the prayer of David?

2. Why was he able to pray such a prayer?

Prayer

Father, I sense I am on the verge of a great challenge and some great discoveries. As I am about to go over the edge of the nest, show me again how broad and expansive are Your wings. In Jesus' Name. Amen.

How God Deals With Us

For reading & meditation—Hebrews 12:1–13

"For when he punishes you, it proves that he loves you ..." (v.6, TLB)

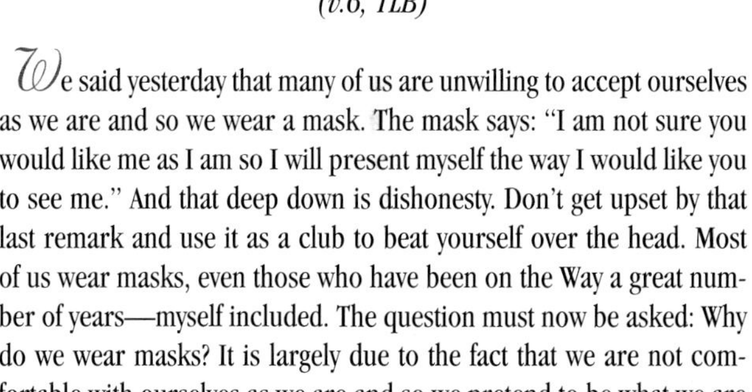

We said yesterday that many of us are unwilling to accept ourselves as we are and so we wear a mask. The mask says: "I am not sure you would like me as I am so I will present myself the way I would like you to see me." And that deep down is dishonesty. Don't get upset by that last remark and use it as a club to beat yourself over the head. Most of us wear masks, even those who have been on the Way a great number of years—myself included. The question must now be asked: Why do we wear masks? It is largely due to the fact that we are not comfortable with ourselves as we are and so we pretend to be what we are not.

At this point someone might raise an objection and say: "But how can we be comfortable with ourselves, our faults, our failures, our mistakes, our blunders and our inadequacies, until we have reached spiritual maturity?" Accepting ourselves as we are does not mean that we will not dislike our failures, our mistakes and our inadequacies. It means that we will not be bowled over by them or intimidated by them to the extent that we lose our spiritual balance. Whenever we make a mistake, commit a sin or make a foolish blunder, God begins to work in our lives to correct the situation. But His corrections and His disciplines are always motivated by love and compassion. He is never punitive, judgmental or authoritarian. And the way God deals with us is the way we must deal with ourselves.

FURTHER STUDY

2 Tim. 3:16; Deut. 8:5; Ps. 94:12

1. In what 4 ways does Scripture help us?

2. In what ways does God reprove us?

O Father, I have so many misconceptions about You. Most of these have developed in my growing years. Help me, whenever I err or stray, to be as gentle on myself as You are. In Jesus' Name. Amen.

SECTION TWO

Loving Yourself

For reading & meditation—Mark 12:28–34

"... You must love others as much as yourself ..." (v.31, TLB)

I have always been an idealist, wanting to resolve all my personal problems and hang-ups so that I could get on with the business of living and teaching others how to live. At times I have been intensely angry at my own immaturity. I wanted to grow up quickly, find the answers to all of my questions, resolve all my inner conflicts and present myself to the Church as "Mr. Perfect." The gap between what I was and what I felt I ought to be was something I struggled to close. So much so, that in one period of my life I became greatly disillusioned and dejected. I was being harder on myself than God was, and my own punitive and harsh self-judgments worked to compound the problem rather than resolve it. It was in the midst of this predicament that God revealed Himself to me and showed me that He accepted me as I was—faults, failures, mistakes, misunderstandings notwithstanding—and that the gap between what I was and what I knew I ought to be could only be closed by resting in His love rather than by frantic struggle and inward striving.

God enabled me to accept myself and to live in the knowledge that day by day the gap would close, and that I would grow toward the goal that He has set for my life. I have learned to accept myself as God accepts me, and to discipline myself as God disciplines me—in love. The pressure to grow is no longer a harsh one. I am learning to love myself as God loves me.

FURTHER STUDY

Rom. 12:1–6; 1 John 3:20; 1 Sam. 16:7; 2 Cor. 3:18

1. How does God look at us?

2. Does God condemn us? (John 3:17)

Gracious Father, I want so much to be myself. Help me to accept myself as You accept me, and to follow Your design in everything. Amen.

SECTION TWO

Seeing Ourselves as God Sees Us

For reading & meditation—Colossians 1:9–14

"... We are asking God that you may be filled with such wisdom and that you may understand his purpose." (v.9, J. B. Phillips)

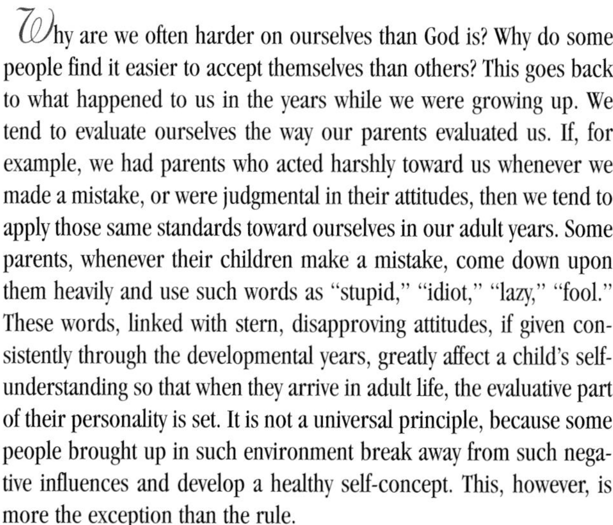

Why are we often harder on ourselves than God is? Why do some people find it easier to accept themselves than others? This goes back to what happened to us in the years while we were growing up. We tend to evaluate ourselves the way our parents evaluated us. If, for example, we had parents who acted harshly toward us whenever we made a mistake, or were judgmental in their attitudes, then we tend to apply those same standards toward ourselves in our adult years. Some parents, whenever their children make a mistake, come down upon them heavily and use such words as "stupid," "idiot," "lazy," "fool." These words, linked with stern, disapproving attitudes, if given consistently through the developmental years, greatly affect a child's self-understanding so that when they arrive in adult life, the evaluative part of their personality is set. It is not a universal principle, because some people brought up in such environment break away from such negative influences and develop a healthy self-concept. This, however, is more the exception than the rule.

If we are to accept ourselves as we are, we must look at the way God views us. Whenever we make a mistake, commit a sin or err in some way, God begins to discipline us. But His discipline is never given in anger but always in love. He corrects us not because He delights to punish us, but because He loves us too much to let us get away with things that will hinder our spiritual growth. And that, I say again, is the same attitude we must show toward ourselves.

FURTHER STUDY

Col. 2; Eph. 1:4–6; 2 Cor. 5:9

1. What does it mean to be accepted?

2. Does this mean there is no need for change?

Prayer

Father, slowly the truth is dawning on my spirit. What a wonderful Parent You are. Help me to break free from the negative attitudes of my formative years, and to see myself from Your point of view. In Jesus' Name. Amen.

SECTION TWO

Conversion—Not a Cure-All

For reading & meditation—Colossians 1:28–2:10

"... so that we may bring every man up to his full maturity in Christ Jesus." (1:28, J. B. Phillips)

Many of the attitudes we have toward ourselves are hangovers from our past relationships. Doesn't conversion eliminate these difficulties and give us new understanding and enlightenment? Not always. Conversion must not be viewed as a cure-all for our problems. This is not to devalue conversion but to understand it.

Some years ago I was present in a meeting where a very sincere and well-meaning girl said: "Since my conversion a few years ago I have never had one single problem." I thought to myself: "How fortunate." That is not my experience, and I am sure it is not yours either. In fact, conversion sometimes intensifies our problems because it forces issues to the surface in our lives which we are obliged to deal with if we are to move on to spiritual maturity.

What, then, does conversion mean? It means we have started but not finished. If, for example, someone grows up experiencing little love, affection or kindness, there are problems created in that person's life which conversion does not always cure. God comes in at conversion to help that person work through those problems, and such is the miracle of His presence, that the very deprivation becomes an opportunity to experience more of God's power and love than would otherwise be possible. The groaning point, hurt and deprivation, now becomes the growing point to a greater awareness of God and the reality of His love. Maturity doesn't mean having all my problems solved, but learning to accept myself and live with myself, recognizing all the time that God is quietly nurturing me, developing me and changing me.

FURTHER STUDY

Matt. 4:18–20; Acts 2.14–41; Matt. 18:3; Acts 3:19; Ps. 19:7

1. List some of the challenges in Peter's life from Matt. 4 to Acts 2.

2. Why did Jesus allow Peter to work through these things?

O God, I am thankful for the discovery that the hurts and deprivations of my life can now become the doors through which I can gain an understanding of You that otherwise would not have been possible. Thank You, Father. Amen.

SECTION TWO

Self-Acceptance

For reading & meditation—Matthew 6:27–34

"... Consider the lilies of the field, how they grow ..." (v.28, KJV)

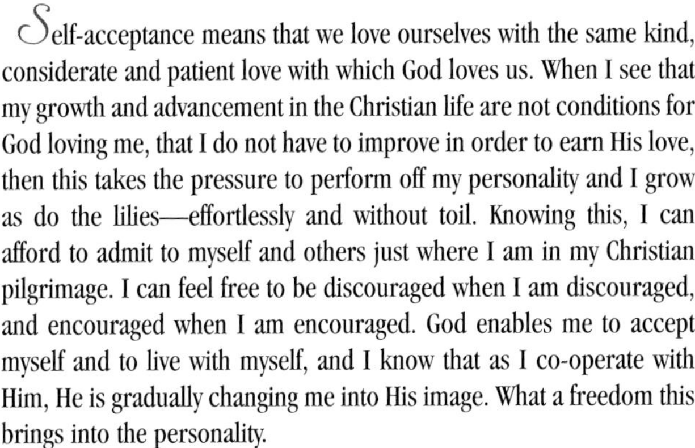

Self-acceptance means that we love ourselves with the same kind, considerate and patient love with which God loves us. When I see that my growth and advancement in the Christian life are not conditions for God loving me, that I do not have to improve in order to earn His love, then this takes the pressure to perform off my personality and I grow as do the lilies—effortlessly and without toil. Knowing this, I can afford to admit to myself and others just where I am in my Christian pilgrimage. I can feel free to be discouraged when I am discouraged, and encouraged when I am encouraged. God enables me to accept myself and to live with myself, and I know that as I co-operate with Him, He is gradually changing me into His image. What a freedom this brings into the personality.

A man in a group with whom I once shared this truth said: "The thing that scares me about removing my mask is finding that you won't love me as I am." I asked him if he loved himself in the true biblical sense of that phrase and he admitted he didn't. When he came to accept himself, he was able to remove his mask and say: "This is what I'm really like. You may not like me as I am but this is all I've got. God loves me and I love myself, so even if you don't love me, it is better for me and you that I am honest, for in honesty lies a power that makes for my positive development and growth."

FURTHER STUDY

Eph.2; John 15:9;
Rom. 8:35;
1 John 3:1

1. What does God's love provide in my life?

2. How does this affect how we see ourselves?

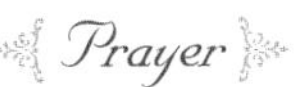

Prayer

Father, I am still struggling with this challenge to remove my mask. But hold me to the issue, I pray, so that I won't miss one lesson You are trying to show me. In Jesus' Name. Amen.

DAY 100

Ministry Out of Weakness

For reading & meditation—2 Corinthians 12:1–10

"... My power shows up best in weak people ..." (v.9, TLB)

Removing our mask is risky, but it is equally risky not to remove it. The truth is, the harder we try to please everyone, the more certain it is that we will please no one. You must be yourself—in Christ.

Does this mean that I must now go about shocking people into reality by saying: "Look, this is what I am really like. How do you like the real me?" Dr. Paul Tournier was once asked at a conference just how much openness one should practice with others. He replied: "Be prepared to say it all, but say only what you feel God is leading you to say." Wise advice. Being prepared to say it all relieves us of our fear of exposing ourselves or being exposed, so that we can respond to another in loving honesty without the fear of saying too much. In being free to say it all, we are also free to be silent when we should be. So often we want to share our strengths but not our weaknesses.

Once, in a counseling session, a woman shared with me about a matter that brought her great discouragement. It so happened that something similar had happened to me around the same time, and I shared with her my discouragement. She was overcome and said: "I never thought you could be discouraged. This puts a whole new perspective on my problem." Later she said that my frankness brought her great hope, and out of it God ministered to her need. Christ ministered to this woman out of my weakness, not out of my strength!

FURTHER STUDY

2 Sam. 12:1–25; Gal. 6:2; James 5:16

1. How did the Lord reveal David to himself?

2. What is the Lord revealing to you about yourself?

Prayer

Gracious Father, slowly the truth of being myself is opening up to me. Now bring the whole thing into sharp and clear focus so that I might truly be myself. In Jesus' Name I pray. Amen.

SECTION TWO

Through Trouble to Triumph

For reading & meditation—1 Peter 2:18–25

"When they hurled their insults at him, he did not retaliate …" (v.23)

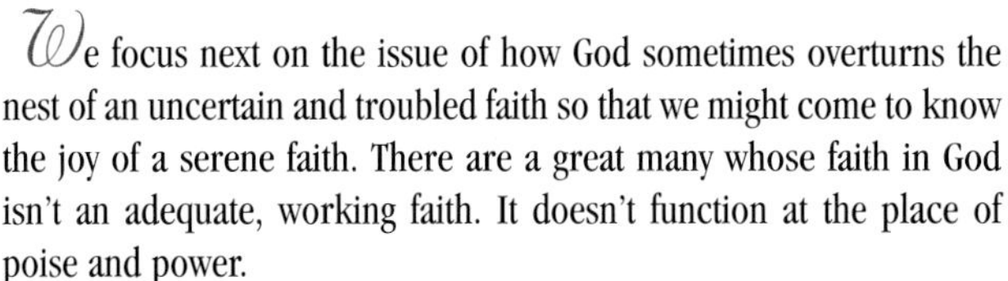

We focus next on the issue of how God sometimes overturns the nest of an uncertain and troubled faith so that we might come to know the joy of a serene faith. There are a great many whose faith in God isn't an adequate, working faith. It doesn't function at the place of poise and power.

A headmaster in India was invited to attend a Christian gathering where a famous missionary would answer questions on matters relating to the Christian faith. The headmaster declined to attend, saying: "At the moment I have a satisfactory faith but if I come to that meeting, a non-Christian might ask a question which will upset my faith." His faith was a troubled one—not a triumphant one.

How does God go about the task of getting us to experience a serene, assured faith rather than one that is uncertain and inadequate? Does He keep dark and desolating doubts from us? Does He protect us from the incisive questions of non-believers? No. He gently nudges us out of the nest, forces us to face the reality of a world where our faith is put to the test, makes sure that we come face to face with issues that have to be grappled with, for He knows that it is by grappling that we grow. Someone has said: "The Church is no candle—blow on." He was referring to the fact that the Church is indestructible. But the same can be said of the Christian faith. We can face all the doubts and questions people throw at us. The Christian faith "is no candle—blow on."

FURTHER STUDY

Heb. 11; Luke 17:5; Prov. 3:1–5; Isa. 26:4

1. What is faith?

2. List some of the exploits achieved through faith.

Prayer

Father, help me to come to a place in my life where my faith can stand anything a non-Christian world throws against it. In Jesus' Name I ask it. Amen.

SECTION TWO

"Science Frightens Me"

For reading & meditation—Colossians 1:15–23

"... all things were created by him and for him." (v.16)

A woman wrote in great distress to the editor of a Christian magazine: "I see in the newspapers that a space probe is being sent to certain planets in order to discover if there is any life in other parts of the universe. What will happen to the Christian faith if they make such a discovery? Science frightens me." She had a faith, but it could hardly be called a faith; it lacked central assurance. Discoveries on other planets would upset it.

There are two major approaches to life, the Christian approach and the scientific approach. The Christian approach works from divine revelation down to life; the scientific approach works from facts up to conclusions. Both come out at the same place—they say the same thing. Not one single fact has been discovered in the heavens above, or in the earth beneath, to invalidate a single thing as it is contained in the Christian faith that centers in Jesus. Invalidate Him? Such a thing would be impossible. The discoveries of science have done nothing but corroborate Him, for His laws are written into the very nature of reality. All that science does is uncover those laws. The God of nature and the God of the Bible are not two different gods—they are one God, and that one God is the Father of our Lord Jesus Christ. The laws of the universe, the laws of our relationships, the laws of our physical bodies, the laws of our minds are turning out to be the laws of Christ. They fit.

FURTHER STUDY

Rom. 1:18–32; 10:17; 5:1; Heb. 11:6

1. What is the result for those who look to science?
2. To what does the Christian look to increase his faith?

O Father, I see so clearly that You are not just the Author of my being but also the Finisher of it. In You, I feel the sum total of reality behind me. Amen.

God Never Invalidated

For reading & meditation—Genesis 1:1–10

"In the beginning God created the heaven and the earth." (v.1, KJV)

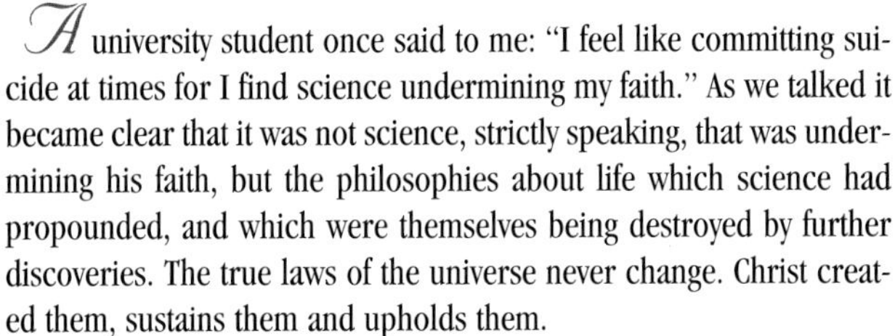

A university student once said to me: "I feel like committing suicide at times for I find science undermining my faith." As we talked it became clear that it was not science, strictly speaking, that was undermining his faith, but the philosophies about life which science had propounded, and which were themselves being destroyed by further discoveries. The true laws of the universe never change. Christ created them, sustains them and upholds them.

Another university student said to me: "I wish I had been born a hundred years ago for the intellectual climate then was traditional not scientific. Now everything has to be verified for science believes in verified knowledge." Can the knowledge in the classroom be verified and the knowledge in the Church be unverified? This is an impossible dualism and many of our young people are caught up in it. Together we must work our way through this scientific climate, and hopefully come out not simply with a faith that we sustain but with a faith that sustains us. We must not be afraid of our own time with its great scientific advances, its space shuttles, its nuclear energy and its amazing discoveries. Neither must we shrink from facing fearlessly the challenge this age brings us in terms of our faith. The young man I referred to who wishes he had been born a hundred years earlier because of the pressure this scientific age put upon his faith, needed to know (as perhaps you do) that science can never invalidate God. It only confirms Him.

FURTHER STUDY

Ps. 104; Neh. 9:6; Job 26:7; Acts 14:15

1. List from Ps. 104 some of God's creative acts.

2. Write a short psalm yourself.

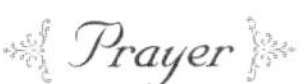

Father, I want my faith to be deepened to the point where nothing can assail it. Grant that this shall take place as I face these issues this coming week. Amen.

SECTION TWO

The Scientific Method

For reading & meditation—Luke 4:1–15

"And Jesus returned in the power of the Spirit ..." (v.14, KJV)

Can we take the same steps in verifying the Christian faith as science takes in verifying knowledge of things that can be weighed and measured? I believe we can. There are five steps in the scientific method: (1) The statement of the problem. (2) The selection of a hypothesis to meet the problem. (3) Experimentation with the hypothesis. (4) Verifying the hypothesis on a wide scale. (5) A simple and humble sharing of the verified results.

Let us apply this method to the realm of the spiritual. First—the statement of the problem—how to develop a serene and joyous faith in the midst of a world beset by so many difficulties. Next comes the selection of a hypothesis to meet the problem. Let your mind sweep the horizon of possibilities as to who best illustrates a serene and joyous faith, and who do you come up with? Christ. We have but to turn to the account of His life to find so. Every line speaks of poise and every line speaks of power. And yet the poise and power were manifested in the midst of great problems and difficulties. He went into the wilderness for 40 days and was tempted by the devil there. We would expect to see Him emerge from that shattered and exhausted. On the contrary, the account says that He "returned in the power of the Spirit." That which was intended to weaken Him ended only by strengthening Him. Here is the authentic attitude we are looking for—an attitude that uses everything, transforms everything and grows by grappling with difficulties, not withdrawing from them.

FURTHER STUDY

Heb. 1; John 1:3; 1 Cor. 8:6; Col. 1:16

1. What is the Bible's "statement"?

2. What does this do for our faith?

O Father, this is what I have been looking for—an attitude that meets everything and masters everything, and does it with serenity and poise. Help me to experience it. In Jesus' Name. Amen.

His Faith Becomes Our Faith

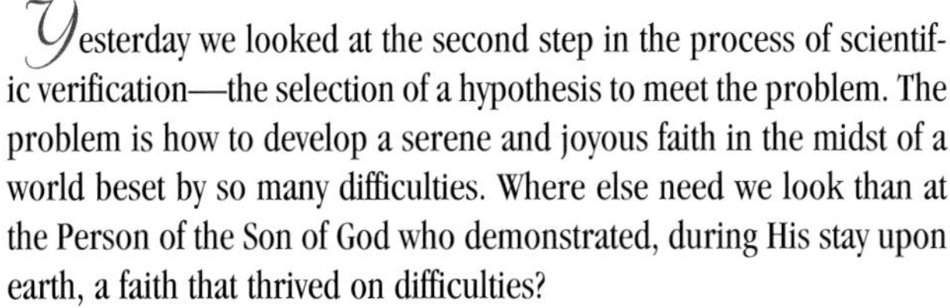

For reading & meditation—Acts 4:1–13

"... they took note that these men had been with Jesus." (v.13)

Yesterday we looked at the second step in the process of scientific verification—the selection of a hypothesis to meet the problem. The problem is how to develop a serene and joyous faith in the midst of a world beset by so many difficulties. Where else need we look than at the Person of the Son of God who demonstrated, during His stay upon earth, a faith that thrived on difficulties?

Next we come to the third step in the scientific verification—experimentation with the hypothesis. Isn't Christ's faith something that is unique, incapable of being duplicated? An examination of the New Testament shows that not only did Jesus possess a serene and joyous faith in the midst of great difficulties, but He seemed to be able to pass on to His followers the same spirit of victory over all things. In living fellowship with Him, His disciples had the very same serenity. If this was not true then Christ's movement would now be a monument, instead of a living organism that has spread across the face of the earth. We have only to link ourselves with Jesus Christ, live in daily fellowship with Him, draw from His unending supplies, and His faith becomes our faith.

I used to be the most negative person in the little Welsh village where I lived until I met Jesus Christ. Instantly my life changed. Where before I withdrew from life, I found I wanted to face everything. All my "No's" turned to "Yes's." I stopped having conferences with fear and instead I had them with faith. It was Jesus who made the difference.

FURTHER STUDY

Matt. 17:14–21; John 6:28–29; Matt. 8:13; 9:27–30; Mark 9:23

1. What was hindering the disciples' ministry?
2. What was the promise of Christ?

Prayer

O Father, I am so thankful that You are able to put nerve within my nerves, quiet amid my agitation and turn up all my inadequacies into adequacies. Blessed be Your Name forever! Amen.

DAY 106

SECTION TWO

The Language of the Redeemed

For reading & meditation—Revelation 7:9–17

"... there before me was a great multitude that no one could count, from every nation ..." (v.9)

We come now to the fourth step of scientific verification—verifying the hypothesis on a wide scale. In the Christian Church we have the world's greatest collective verification. It stretches into all countries, races, colors and cultures. Although separated by different languages, the members of Christ's Body unite to speak a common language—the language of a tried and proven faith. It is the language of an experience of God in Christ. That language is the language of certainty. The accents differ, the language is the same. I have heard this language in every part of the world as I have traveled around. It is a language with a lift in it, with a note of redemption from evil, of triumph over difficulties. It is the purest language spoken on this earth. And it is not confined to any one group or denomination. Anywhere the heart is open to Christ in simple surrender and obedience, it works. And it works with an almost mathematical precision.

If collective verification has been tried and found workable, this is it. This gives universal backing to our conviction. In Christ we have our roots in the historical. Jesus is someone who is rooted in fact, not fancy. In Christian consciousness, we have our roots in the experiential—faith in Christ speaks certainty to the very depths. In the Christian Church, we have our roots in the collective—verification of my personal experience as evidenced in the lives of others. This lets me know that I am not off the track. This is it. All these coming together give me what I need—total backing.

FURTHER STUDY

Eph. 4; 1:22; 5:23; Col. 1:18

1. How does Paul describe the Church?
2. List some of its characteristics?

Prayer

O God, I am so grateful that in You I find certainty that sweeps right down to the depths of my being. And in Your Church I find the verification that what works for me is the only way life is meant to work. I am so thankful. Amen.

Sharing the Results

For reading & meditation—2 Corinthians 4:1–15

"It is God ... who has given us this wonderful work [of telling his Good News to others] ..." (v.1, TLB)

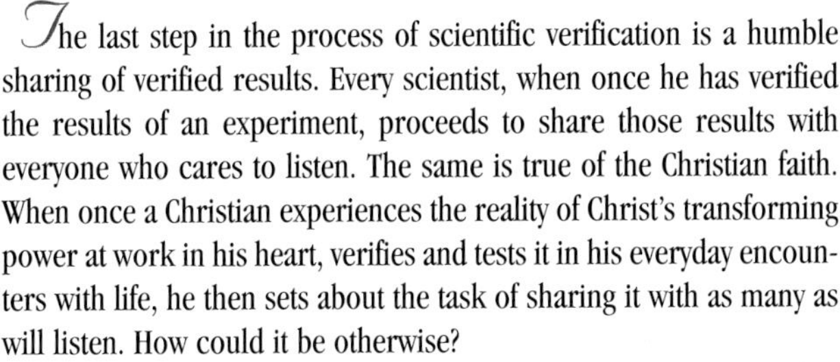

The last step in the process of scientific verification is a humble sharing of verified results. Every scientist, when once he has verified the results of an experiment, proceeds to share those results with everyone who cares to listen. The same is true of the Christian faith. When once a Christian experiences the reality of Christ's transforming power at work in his heart, verifies and tests it in his everyday encounters with life, he then sets about the task of sharing it with as many as will listen. How could it be otherwise?

A boy of 23, dying in a hospital, said to his pastor: "Everybody has been so good to me. I haven't a thing in the world to leave anybody. Couldn't I leave my eyes to somebody?" He offered his all—and he was happy in the offering.

Actually, each one of us propagates something—whether we realize it or not. When we meet people, they give us a dominant impression—of inner conflict or of serenity. The dominant impression we must leave with people is one of faith—not faith in our own faith but faith in His faith. We said before that in today's scientific climate, many are concerned that their faith will not develop. But this is simply not true. When we allow the Divine Eagle to nudge us out of the nest, we may feel, when faced with the biting challenge of today's society, that our faith will fail us. But such will not be the case. Confronted with challenge, a troubled faith has the very opportunity it needs to become a triumphant faith.

FURTHER STUDY

Rom. 5; James 2:17;
1 John 5:4;
Eph. 6:16

1. How can we implement our faith?

2. What are you going to do today to demonstrate and exercise your faith?

O Father, I long for more than a weak, inadequate faith. I want a faith that can stand up to every test, weather every storm, and come out all the better for it. Help me to experience it. In Jesus' Name. Amen.

SECTION TWO

Games People Play

For reading & meditation—1 Corinthians 13:1–13

"... when I became a man, I put away childish things." (v.11, KJV)

Another reason why the Divine Eagle nudges us out of the nest is because He wants us to grow up. Many of us are adults, yet still behave like children. Inwardly we carry the same attitudes to life that we had when we were young. Eric Berne has shown in *Games People Play* that many of us go through life playing childish games. The word game here is not to be understood as similar to "Snakes and Ladders," but as an attitude we adopt when relating to other people, in which we become defensive rather than honest.

In the passage before us, Paul talks about putting away childish things. The Greek word used here is a very forceful one—*Katageo*—which means to cut off, render inoperative, disassociate from. Paul came to a place in his life where he realized he was acting childishly so he took the decision to stop acting that way—and grow up.

A man once said to me: "At work I think about my family, and realize I am not acting toward them the way I should. I decide to be more loving but strangely, when I enter the door all my good intentions stay outside. I become sullen, morose and cantankerous." Actually, he was playing a game. In childhood, whenever he acted like this, he received more attention from his parents. Now as an adult he was acting in the same way. When I shared with him what might be happening, he recognized it immediately. "What a fool I've been," he said. "It's time I grew up." He did—and so must you.

FURTHER STUDY

1 Cor. 3; Prov. 22:15; Jer. 4:22

1. What are some characteristics of childishness?

2. How did Paul speak to the Corinthians about being babes?

O Father, how childish and foolish many of my attitudes must appear to You. Yet despite everything You still love me. Help me to believe that You nudge me out of the nest of my childish attitudes to help me deal with life more realistically and honestly. In Jesus' Name. Amen.

"Yes . . . But"

For reading & meditation—Exodus 4:1–17

"Moses answered, 'What if they do not believe me . . .?'" (v.1)

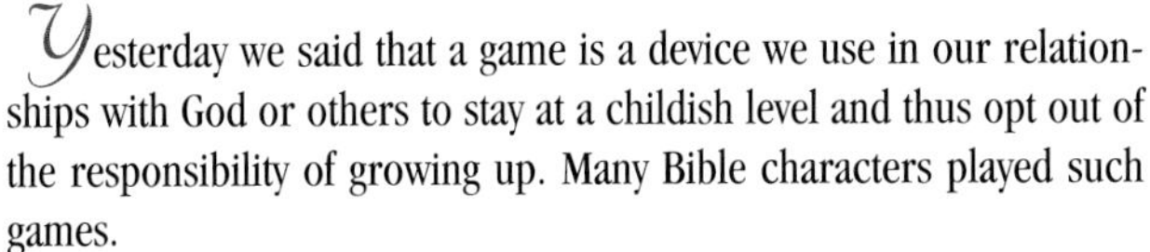

Yesterday we said that a game is a device we use in our relationships with God or others to stay at a childish level and thus opt out of the responsibility of growing up. Many Bible characters played such games.

Take Moses, for example. The children of Israel had been in bondage for hundreds of years. In the midst of their groanings, God heard their request and chose a leader who was to be their deliverer. But when God approached Moses at the burning bush, announced to him that He had confidence in him and would give him His support, Moses began to play one of the most repeated games of history. It is called: "Yes … but." God would never have approached Moses and given him this great commission if He didn't believe him to be capable of it, but Moses reverted to a game that many of us play. We say: "Yes, Lord, I hear what you say … but … I'm afraid … and I have this problem …"

The game is that we attempt to discount ourselves in the hope that God will pass over us. We are so afraid of failure, so entrenched in our own negative beliefs, so committed to self-humiliation, that we fail to see that God always equips when He calls. Do you play such games with God? If so then it's time to grow up. God wants to relate to you on a more adult level. He has tasks for you to perform, responsibilities for you to face. Decide to "katageo" (disconnect) your childish attitudes—now.

FURTHER STUDY

Gal. 4; 5:1;
1 Cor. 14:20; Eph. 4:14; Heb. 5:12

1. What is Paul teaching about sonship?

2. What is his admonition to the Galatians?

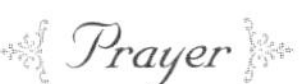

Prayer

O God, I see so clearly that I need to grow up. Today, by an act of my own volition, supported by Your Spirit, I take the decision to sever my childish attitudes and become a more responsible Christian. Help me, dear Lord. In Jesus' Name. Amen.

"Uproar"

For reading & meditation—Genesis 4:1–16

"… 'How should I know?' Cain retorted. 'Am I supposed to keep track of him …?'" (v.9, TLB)

We continue examining the concept of "Games People Play," selecting Bible characters to observe this theory at work in the lives of some of God's people. Today we look at Cain. Although Cain undoubtedly knew that God must be approached by an offering taken from the animal kingdom, he decided to offer instead an offering selected from the vegetable kingdom. It was an incorrect offering and he knew his gift would be unacceptable. Cain discounted God's commands and also the offering of his brother. Here we see Cain initiate a game called "Uproar"—a game where conflict is purposefully started to avoid intimacy. It happens when a non-Christian, feeling drawn toward God and His kingdom, sets up some argument or point of conflict in an attempt to prevent himself reaching the place where he has to surrender to God.

Early in my Christian life, I could never understand why a person, when close to the kingdom of God, would say something like: "Why does God allow suffering?" Or: "Why did God create the devil?" I came to see that such questions (not all) were really an unconscious attempt to keep God out of their hearts. You see, when God comes close to a person, their inner life is greatly disturbed. It must inevitably be so for inbred sin must be repented of, confessed and put away.

But this game is not only played by unbelievers, it is played by some Christians also. When God draws near to your heart, you can choose to open yourself or create an issue which avoids spiritual intimacy. Is this a game you sometimes play?

FURTHER STUDY

1 John 2; 1 Pet. 2:2; Ps. 131:2; Mark 10:15; Luke 18:16; Heb. 5:14

1. What are the characteristics of maturity?

2. What is the difference between childishness and childlikeness?

Prayer

O Father, I want to cooperate with You in bringing myself to maturity. If I have been making foolish and childish moves to keep You away then help me to grow in my understanding, and to stop playing such games. In Jesus' Name. Amen.

SECTION TWO

"If It Weren't for You"

For reading & meditation—Genesis 3:1–12

"'Yes,' Adam admitted, 'but it was the woman you gave me who brought me some, and I ate it.'" (v.12, TLB)

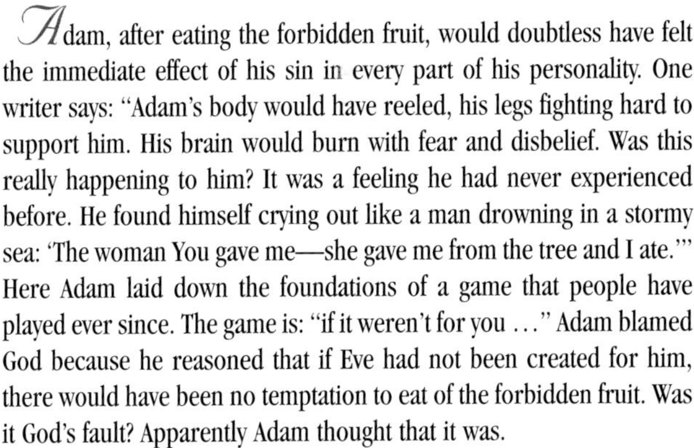

Adam, after eating the forbidden fruit, would doubtless have felt the immediate effect of his sin in every part of his personality. One writer says: "Adam's body would have reeled, his legs fighting hard to support him. His brain would burn with fear and disbelief. Was this really happening to him? It was a feeling he had never experienced before. He found himself crying out like a man drowning in a stormy sea: 'The woman You gave me—she gave me from the tree and I ate.'" Here Adam laid down the foundations of a game that people have played ever since. The game is: "if it weren't for you …" Adam blamed God because he reasoned that if Eve had not been created for him, there would have been no temptation to eat of the forbidden fruit. Was it God's fault? Apparently Adam thought that it was.

How many times have you done the same thing? Something happens to you and you immediately blame someone else, perhaps even God. Many of us excuse ourselves with such statements as: "If God had given me a different wife …" "If only I had been born into a different family …" "If my circumstances had been different …" If … If … If.

A man who accidentally ran into a door said: "What's that door doing there?" No one ever grows in the Christian life until they accept the responsibility for the decisions they make, stop blaming others for their predicament and face the present realistically—and not defensively.

FURTHER STUDY

Ex. 32; 1 Sam. 15; Rom. 1:20

1. What was the response of Aaron and Saul?

2. How did Samuel respond to Saul?

Prayer

O God, the fears within me make me want to fasten on to some compromise, some half measure. Save me from this. Help me to face life responsibly and realistically. In Jesus' Name. Amen.

SECTION TWO

"See If You Can Catch Me"

For reading & meditation—Jonah 1:1–17

"But Jonah ran away from the Lord …" (v.3)

Who hasn't heard of Jonah? The story of his encounter with the big fish is probably the most well-known of all the Old Testament stories—even though critics deny its validity. Personally I find no difficulty in believing the literal account of the story, especially when Jesus validates its significance in His statement in Matthew 12:40: "For as Jonah was in the great fish for three days and three nights, so I, the Messiah, shall be in the heart of the earth three days and three nights" (TLB).

Jonah's game was: "See if you can catch me." A grown man makes himself a fugitive in his own mind, sinks into despair and crawls into a dark corner of a ship to hide from the Lord. We play this game whenever we are unsure of ourselves (or of God), and go out of our way to get others to prove their interest in us by constant attention. It's similar to a game we all played in childhood entitled "Hide and Seek." It is extremely childish to put ourselves in positions where we continually apply pressure upon those who love us (God or people) to prove their love. We say, albeit unconsciously: "If you love me then prove it by dogging my footsteps, putting aside your own interests and engaging in ways that show me you are not willing to give me up." This is immaturity at its worst. Maturity recognizes that the best way to be loved is to be the initiator, not the receiver. The rewards of loving are to be loved.

FURTHER STUDY

1 Kings 19:1–18; Josh. 7:7; Jer. 15:10; Luke 24:14–17

1. How did God deal with Elijah's self-pity?

2. Where does despondency originate?

Prayer

O Father, here again Your knife cuts deep. If I've been manipulating others in order to get them to love me then forgive me I pray. Help me not to run from others but to run to them. For Your own dear Name's sake. Amen.

SECTION TWO

"Stupid"

For reading & meditation—Luke 22:47–62

"Peter replied, 'Man, I don't know what you're talking about!'" (v.60)

Today we look at a game called "Stupid". Simon Peter played this game. Picture the scene. Peter, the big fisherman, strong, resolute, determined, firm in his declaration of love for Christ, denies all knowledge of the Master. Why? He had walked with the Master for three whole years, heard Him speak the most wonderful words, saw Him heal the sick, raise the dead, cleanse the lepers and work other amazing miracles. Yet when he is asked if he knows Jesus, his response is one of withdrawal. In other words, he plays stupid.

Eric Berne claims that whenever we play games, it is always for a reward. What was Peter's reward? It was the reinforcement of his fear. Why should the reinforcement of his fear be a reward? Well, the more deeply he believed that he was afraid, and the more he did to reinforce that fear, the easier it would be to excuse himself for his failure to stand up for Jesus when confronted. The final pay-off was to protect himself from danger.

A Christian schoolteacher told me that at an educational conference, someone happened to remark that the Bible was a fable. The man then turned to the schoolteacher and said: "What do you think?" He told me that his first impulse was to play stupid and say: "I am not sure," or "I don't know." He caught himself just about to play the game, but instead accepted the challenge of the situation and responded with some positive comments. To play the game of "Stupid" may bring temporary benefits, but the dishonesty involved greatly upsets one's spiritual balance.

FURTHER STUDY

Acts 5:1–10; Ps. 63:11; Prov. 19:5; Jer. 9:5

1. When we play "Stupid" what are we really doing?

2. How serious is it?

Prayer

O Father, help me to he an honest person. Help me to absorb Your love in such a measure that it will dissolve every fear. Then strengthen me to face life—fearless and unafraid. Amen.

DAY 114

SECTION TWO

"Let God Do It"

For reading & meditation—John 2:1–11

"His mother said ... 'Do whatever he tells you.'" (v.5)

Although everyone plays games in life—both Christians and non-Christians—the favorite game we Christians play is this: "Let God do it." Let me illustrate. Some time ago a lady asked me if I would pray with her about the difficulty she was having in her relationships with people. She said she felt rejected, no one seemed interested in her, and the people in her church just ignored her. I asked her: "What are you doing about your problems?" She said, "Well, I pray every morning and evening about them." I said: "That's fine—but what else are you doing?" She looked at me in amazement and said: "What else can I do? If I pray enough about it, and get others to pray along with me, then won't God make the people who reject me a little more friendly toward me?"

There was nothing wrong with her praying, but really she was playing a game. It was this: "Let God do it." She wanted God to do what He had already done—give her the ability to relate, share and have fellowship with others. What she needed to work on was her own attitudes. Someone has said: "To have friends—be friendly." Fortunately she took the advice I gave her, worked on it and began to see some success.

If we are to get up out of our nests, soar into the air and enjoy the freedom of being mature then we must be able to differentiate between what we should be doing ourselves and what God alone can do in our lives and circumstances.

FURTHER STUDY

James 2; Phil. 2:12–13; Matt. 7:24–27; James 4:17

1. How do we "work out our own salvation"?

2. How do works and faith fit together?

Prayer

O Father, I know that there is a fine line between my responsibility to do something for myself and letting You work where only You can work. Give me the wisdom to know the difference. Amen.

SECTION TWO

Christian Unity

For reading & meditation—John 17:20–26

"That all of them may be one ..." (v.21)

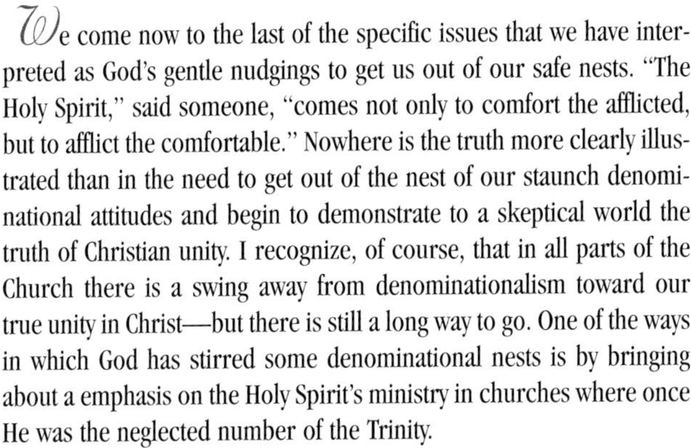

We come now to the last of the specific issues that we have interpreted as God's gentle nudgings to get us out of our safe nests. "The Holy Spirit," said someone, "comes not only to comfort the afflicted, but to afflict the comfortable." Nowhere is the truth more clearly illustrated than in the need to get out of the nest of our staunch denominational attitudes and begin to demonstrate to a skeptical world the truth of Christian unity. I recognize, of course, that in all parts of the Church there is a swing away from denominationalism toward our true unity in Christ—but there is still a long way to go. One of the ways in which God has stirred some denominational nests is by bringing about a emphasis on the Holy Spirit's ministry in churches where once He was the neglected number of the Trinity.

I remember in 1963 when it was reported that Anglicans, Baptists and others were receiving and manifesting the gifts of the Spirit, a well-known Pentecostal leader said to me: "I feel greatly threatened by what is taking place. I had considered, up until now, that 1 Corinthians 12 was the playground of the Pentecostals, but now I see I was wrong. I pray God will forgive me for my bigotry, and may He sweep the whole of His Church toward a new Pentecost." That man, along with many others at that time, came to see that God is bigger than a denomination, and that although the Holy Spirit is thought of as a Dove, He also functions in the capacity of an Eagle.

FURTHER STUDY

Eph. 4; Romans 12:5; 1 Cor. 10:17; Gal. 3:28

1. What is the basis of our unity?

2. What does Paul say about the unity of the Spirit and the unity of our faith?

Prayer

Blessed Holy Spirit, I am thankful although You are a Dove, gentle and brooding, You are also an Eagle, forceful and provocative. Amen.

DAY 116

SECTION TWO

Forced to Reassess

For reading & meditation—Acts 10:1–48

"... But God has shown me in a vision that I should never think of anyone as inferior." (v.28, TLB)

In the Early Church the gulf between Jew and Gentile was very wide. Peter, being a strict Jew, had to undergo a shaking of his nest before he was prepared to minister to the Gentiles gathered in the house of Cornelius. The shaking came in a vision from God concerning all manner of four-footed beasts that a strict Jew would regard as unfit for human consumption. When God said: "Rise, Peter; kill, and eat," the command helped to shatter his bigotry, and from here on he rises to be the means in God's hands of bringing the Holy Spirit to the Gentiles. Later when Peter is questioned by the leaders of the Church in Jerusalem as to why he went to a Gentile congregation, he recounts his God-given vision and tells what happened in Cornelius's home: "As I began to speak, the Holy Spirit came on them as he had come on us at the beginning ... if ... God gave them the same gift as he gave us ... who was I to think that I could oppose God?" (Acts 11:15, 17).

The entire episode in the house of Cornelius forced the Early Church to examine their attitudes, check their preconceived ideas and be open to change. The time has come for us to do something similar. We must examine our hearts and distinguish between principles and prejudices, between man-made traditions and unchanging truths of God. There is a great shaking going on at the moment in many churches and fellowships. May we emerge from it as did Peter—with a new vision and a new task.

FURTHER STUDY

James Ch. 4; 2 Tim. 2:14; 1 Cor. 1:11–12; 3:3

1. Where do strivings come from?
2. What does James suggest is the antidote?

Prayer

O Father, cleanse from my heart this day all prejudice and bigotry, and help me to clamber out of my nest to share with the whole Church the joy of fellowship and unity in You. Amen.

SECTION TWO

The Next Great Step

For reading & meditation—Ephesians 4:1–16

"Make every effort to keep the unity of the Spirit through the bond of peace." (v.3)

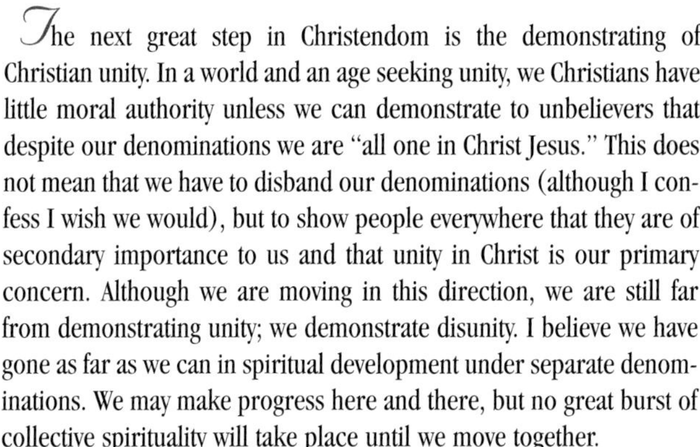

The next great step in Christendom is the demonstrating of Christian unity. In a world and an age seeking unity, we Christians have little moral authority unless we can demonstrate to unbelievers that despite our denominations we are "all one in Christ Jesus." This does not mean that we have to disband our denominations (although I confess I wish we would), but to show people everywhere that they are of secondary importance to us and that unity in Christ is our primary concern. Although we are moving in this direction, we are still far from demonstrating unity; we demonstrate disunity. I believe we have gone as far as we can in spiritual development under separate denominations. We may make progress here and there, but no great burst of collective spirituality will take place until we move together.

But, you ask, how can we come together unless we agree on everything? We do not make that a prerequisite of fellowship in a home. The home can be united in spite of differences in temperament and belief. The one thing that binds us together is the fact that we are children of the same parents. So it is in the family of God. Let that suffice. The differences are needed so that they can become growing points.

The music of the Hindus is based on melody and not on harmony as is Western music. A Hindu hearing some black-spiritual singing said: "What a pity they can can't all sing the same tune!" Had they done so it wouldn't have been harmony. The very difference made for richness!

FURTHER STUDY

Rom. 12; 1 Cor. 1:10; 2 Cor. 13:11; Phil. 1:27; 1 Pet. 3:8

1. How can we overcome our denominationalism?

2. What steps have you taken to do this?

Prayer

O Father, it is obvious that we will never get melody-unity in Your Church for we cannot all sing the same part but we can have harmony-unity—and that will be far richer. Help us toward this, dear Lord. In Jesus' Name. Amen.

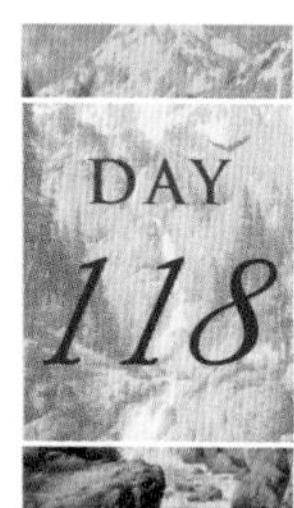

SECTION TWO

The Movement for Unity

For reading & meditation—Luke 9:46–56

"… Master, we saw one casting out devils in thy name; and we forbad him …" (v.49, KJV)

We continue examining the important issue of Christian unity. Someone has said: "The measure of our maturity can be and is measured by the breadth and depth of our capacity for fellowship with other Christians. We are as mature as our fellowships." So if we cannot fellowship with other Christians, even though they belong to other denominations, we reveal our immaturity. What then is the basis of Christian fellowship? One thing and one thing only. Everyone who belongs to Christ belongs to everyone else who belongs to Christ. The basis of our fellowship is not around this doctrine or that doctrine. It is around Christ.

When John said, in the passage before us today, that the disciples had seen a man casting out devils in Christ's Name and they had forbidden him they were simply revealing their immaturity. They would probably have said in justification that they were concerned about protecting their movement from impurities, irregularities and such like, but actually they were trying to protect their own prestige. The Pharisees came all the way from Jerusalem on one occasion to see the awakening under Jesus, but all they could see was that the disciples of Jesus ate with unwashed hands (Matt. 15:2). The movement of Jesus swept past them and left them grand relics.

The same can be seen today. The movement for unity created by the Holy Spirit is sweeping across the world. Many sit clinging to a mode of baptism, a line of succession, an interpretation of doctrine and many other things. They let unity sweep right past them and they finish up—high and dry.

FURTHER STUDY

Acts 2; 4:32–37; Mal. 3:16; Phil. 1:3–5; 1 John 1:7

1. What was the characteristic of the Early Church?

2. What was the outworking of their fellowship?

Prayer

O Father, I am so thankful that the movement of the Spirit has begun bringing Your Church toward greater unity. Help me to be a worthy part of this glorious fellowship. May I be a miniature of the glorious future. In Jesus' Name. Amen.

SECTION TWO

Love—and More Love

For reading & meditation—Galatians 3:26–29

"... for you are all one in Christ Jesus." (v.28)

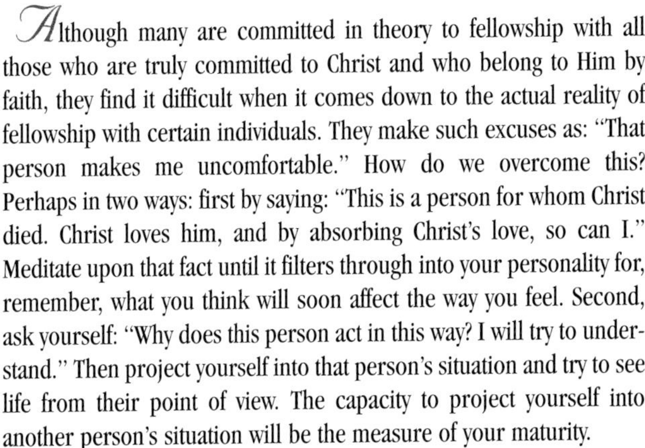

Although many are committed in theory to fellowship with all those who are truly committed to Christ and who belong to Him by faith, they find it difficult when it comes down to the actual reality of fellowship with certain individuals. They make such excuses as: "That person makes me uncomfortable." How do we overcome this? Perhaps in two ways: first by saying: "This is a person for whom Christ died. Christ loves him, and by absorbing Christ's love, so can I." Meditate upon that fact until it filters through into your personality for, remember, what you think will soon affect the way you feel. Second, ask yourself: "Why does this person act in this way? I will try to understand." Then project yourself into that person's situation and try to see life from their point of view. The capacity to project yourself into another person's situation will be the measure of your maturity.

A famous businessman, questioned about the chief characteristic of an executive, said: "The willingness and the ability to project oneself into another person's situation, and to see things from his point of view." If you come across someone with whom you constantly find it difficult to have fellowship, find out the reason, and if the reason is unreasonable, then dissolve it by your love. If the amount of love you give does not dissolve it, give more love. God fellowships with you not on the basis of you being worthy of that fellowship, but because of who He is. You are to fellowship with everyone because of who you are—a lover of Christ.

FURTHER STUDY

Luke 10:25–37;
Matt. 9:36; 20:34;
Mark 1:41;
Luke 7:13

1. What was Jesus' teaching about reaching out to others?
2. How did He demonstrate this?

Prayer

Father, if You fellowship with me in spite of what I am then I will fellowship with everyone else in spite of what they are. Help me. In Jesus' Name. Amen.

SECTION TWO

Agreeing to Disagree

For reading & meditation—Romans 16:17–20

"... watch out for those who cause divisions ..." (v.17)

As Christians, are we entitled to disagree with each other on matters of biblical interpretation? Yes, providing we disagree without being disagreeable. Christian unity does not mean that we have to agree on everything—we simply agree to disagree and go on loving each other as our Master commands us.

Division, however, is another matter. This takes place when a person or a group decides to take their disagreements further and exclude from fellowship those who do not share the same views. If it is true that when we belong to Christ, we belong to everyone else who belongs to Christ then such an action as this disrupts the unity of Christ's Body and wounds the heart of God. Divisions come when people are more motivated by self-centeredness, the urge to be in the limelight, than they are by the proper functioning of Christ's Body. "Watch out for those who cause divisions," says the Scripture. We have a right to hold strong views of Scripture, but we must not let those views prevent us from sharing fellowship with those genuinely committed to Christ, but who may not see eye to eye with us.

A letter to me said: "What a pity that in *Revival* magazine you have a statement that says you believe in the infallibility of the Bible. This excludes millions of Catholics who believe in the infallibility of the Pope." But it doesn't. There I stated what I believe. I do not make that a condition of fellowship. Interestingly enough in the same mail came an invitation to address a meeting in Westminster Cathedral!

FURTHER STUDY

Matt. 20:20–28;
Mark 9:34–37;
1 Cor. 3:3, 11:18;
Rom. 12:10

1. Did the presence of Jesus prevent divisions?

2. What did Jesus say would resolve divisions?

Prayer

Heavenly Father, drive this truth deeply into my spirit that although I am entitled to disagree with my brothers and sisters in Your Body, my disagreement must never be the cause for division. In Jesus' Name. Amen.

God Speaks

For reading & meditation—Luke 9:28–36

"A voice came from the cloud, saying, 'This is my Son, whom I have chosen; listen to him.'" (v.35)

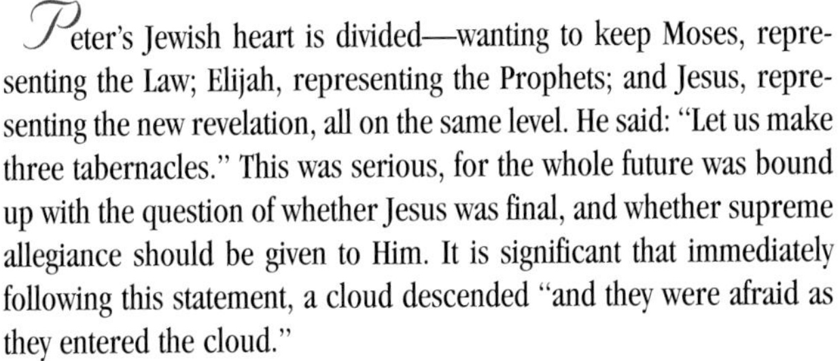

Peter's Jewish heart is divided—wanting to keep Moses, representing the Law; Elijah, representing the Prophets; and Jesus, representing the new revelation, all on the same level. He said: "Let us make three tabernacles." This was serious, for the whole future was bound up with the question of whether Jesus was final, and whether supreme allegiance should be given to Him. It is significant that immediately following this statement, a cloud descended "and they were afraid as they entered the cloud."

Where there is division, there will always be clouds. There are clouds over our churches, and we fear as we enter those clouds. Why are we afraid? The answer is simple—division. Each denomination is thinking in terms of itself, is losing a sense of the collective unity. But out of the cloud comes a Voice. God speaks! The voice is one of evaluation and invitation: "This is my beloved Son: hear him" (v.35, KJV). The clouds will never lift and the fears will never depart until we listen to Christ. And what is He saying? This: "… that all of them may be one, Father, just as you are in me and I am in you … that the world may believe that you have sent me" (John 17:21). Christ must be first, and the unity of His Body must take priority over any denominational allegiance.

As the Divine Eagle nudges His Church toward the edge of the nest in an effort to cause it to soar above denominational divides, I pray that it will not be long before we who share Christ's Name truly become one.

FURTHER STUDY

Matt. 5:21–26; Isa. 11:13; 52:7; John 10:16

1. What steps will you take to build Christian unity?

2. Is there anyone you need to be reconciled to?

Prayer

O Father, I am so thankful that I am part of Your glorious Family. Make me a good member of that Family. May the Family spirit be in all I do and say, for I want others to come into this Family. In Jesus' Name. Amen.

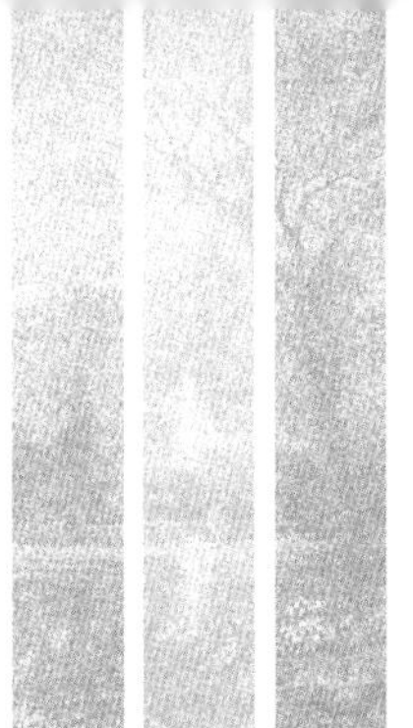

SECTION THREE

The Lord's Prayer

The Lord's Prayer

The Lord's Prayer is one of the first passages of Scripture many of us learn. I expect it's the one most say and read more often than any other. You may have memorized it as a child; many congregations say it aloud in church every week. Even a lot of non-Christians have a passing knowledge of these few dozen heartfelt words spoken by Jesus and recorded in Matthew 6.

As familiar as the verses are, Selwyn Hughes has mined a treasury of insight and illumination from them that help explain why this simple prayer is one of the foundation stones of the Christian faith. He builds a rich, deep, authoritative interpretation of Jesus' words, line by line, even word by word, that carries an understanding of them to new spiritual depths.

Examining each small component of the Lord's Prayer in detail reveals a completely new understanding of the whole. It's like the way a Larry Dyke painting is made up of tiny individual brush strokes. Each stroke in itself has a shape, color, and texture. Together they combine to produce the shadow on a cloud, the sun shining through a branch, or a row of ripples on the water. Shadows and lights form whole cloud banks and forests; then the clouds and forests come together to form the whole image. You can look at a painting across the room a hundred times and get something out of it. But it's not until you examine and comprehend the components that you have a true appreciation for what you're looking at.

The power of the Lord's Prayer, so abundantly clear even with a casual reading, is wonderfully enhanced and intensified by studying its "brush strokes" — its words — more thoroughly. It is tempting to gloss over a passage of Scripture so familiar. But looking deeper, its words, ideas, and inspiration appear in a new light, filled with new meaning, assurance, and hope.

L.G.G.

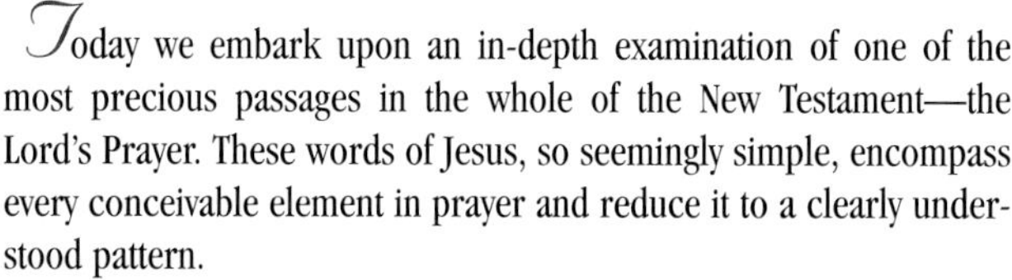

Jesus—Pattern of Prayer

DAY 122

For reading & meditation—Matthew 6:1–13

"This, then, is how you should pray: 'Our Father in heaven, hallowed be your name …'" (v.9)

Today we embark upon an in-depth examination of one of the most precious passages in the whole of the New Testament—the Lord's Prayer. These words of Jesus, so seemingly simple, encompass every conceivable element in prayer and reduce it to a clearly understood pattern.

The Lord's Prayer (or, more correctly, The Disciples' Prayer) is, among other things, a miracle of condensation. In the short compass of 66 words, the Master presents a model of praying that touches on every major aspect of prayer. One writer says of it: "The Lord's Prayer sets the standard for all praying. Everything every man ever needed to understand about prayer is latent in the choice disclosure of these words." That might sound like an astonishing claim, but it is true. No set of theological volumes, no sermon, no series of writings could ever capture the fullness of all that prayer is as does this simple yet profound model.

The more we understand this model, and the more we pray in line with it, the more powerful and productive our prayer life will become. All communication with God begins with prayer, and because this communication is so important, the enemy seeks to disrupt it. This is why we face the necessity to constantly refocus our thinking on the subject, and seek to deepen and enhance our prowess in the art of prayer. If the Lord's Prayer sets the standard for all praying, then we must lay our praying alongside His pattern in order that our prayers might become more and more like His.

FURTHER STUDY

1 Tim. 2:1–8;
1 Chron. 16:11;
Luke 18:1;
1 Thess. 5.17

1. What was Christ's injunction?
2. What is Paul's desire?

Prayer

O God, as I begin this quest for a deeper and more effective prayer life, my heart cries out: "Lord, teach me to pray." For I know that when I learn to pray, I learn to live—vitally and victoriously. Amen.

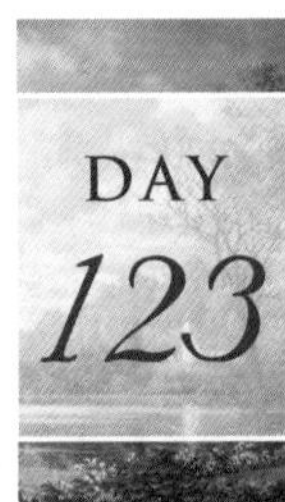

DAY

123

SECTION THREE

More Than a Recitation

For reading & meditation—Matthew 6:7–18

"Don't recite the same prayer over and over as the heathen do ..." (v.7, TLB)

Some Christians think that prayer consists solely of reciting the words of the Lord's Prayer, but, as the great preacher C. H. Spurgeon once said: "To recite the Lord's Prayer and believe that you have then prayed is the height of foolishness." This does not mean, of course, that there is no spiritual value in reciting it, providing we realize that it is not just a prayer to be recited. Personally, I would not want to deprive Christian congregations of the pleasure and joy of reciting together the Lord's Prayer, but I do want to encourage them to view it as a departure point rather than an arrival platform.

If Jesus advised His disciples to avoid "vain repetitions, as the heathen do," would He then immediately follow it by giving us a prayer to simply recite? Obviously, as I have said, one can derive great spiritual pleasure from repeating the words that Jesus gave us, but if we are to obtain the greatest value from the Lord's Prayer, then we must view it as a skeleton on which we have to put flesh. If you view these words, not merely as something to recite, but as an outline from which you must work your way when praying, no matter what you are praying about, then you will experience a growing confidence that you are praying the way Jesus taught. You see, it's one thing to recite a prayer: It's another thing to know how to pray.

FURTHER STUDY

Gal. 4:1–11;

Isa. 29:13;

Matt. 23:14; 6:5

1. What is Paul saying about ritualism?

2. When does prayer become hypocritical?

Prayer

Heavenly Father, I see there can be great value in reciting a prayer, but I want to be able to do more than repeat a prayer—I want to pray. Help me, for without You I can do nothing. For Jesus' sake. Amen.

SECTION THREE

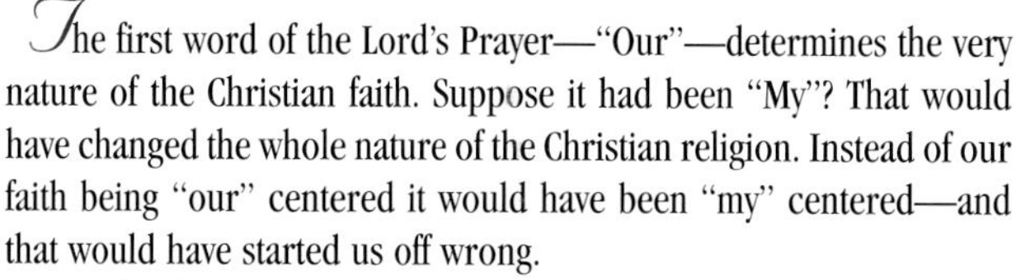

Suppose It Had Been "My"?

DAY 124

For reading & meditation—Luke 11:1–13

"This, then, is how you should pray: 'Our Father in heaven, hallowed be your name …'" (Matt. 6:9)

The first word of the Lord's Prayer—"Our"—determines the very nature of the Christian faith. Suppose it had been "My"? That would have changed the whole nature of the Christian religion. Instead of our faith being "our" centered it would have been "my" centered—and that would have started us off wrong.

In the field of prayer, as in many other fields, to start wrong is to finish wrong. The word "our" involves a shifting of emphasis from me to the Father, and to my brothers and sisters in the kingdom. It implies a renunciation—a renunciation of myself. We see something similar in the first words of the Beatitudes: "Blessed are the poor in spirit" (the renounced in spirit) "for theirs is the kingdom of heaven" (Matt. 5:3). All the resources of the kingdom belong to the renounced in spirit. So, in the first word of the Lord's Prayer, we find an implied demand that we adopt an attitude of self-surrender—surrender to the Father, and to His interests, and the interests of others in His kingdom. If we do this, then everything opens to us. If not, then everything is closed. The rest of the Lord's Prayer has no meaning, and dies if the "Our" is not alive.

And what does this mean? It means that the "Our" must stretch beyond our own fellowship, local church or denomination to include the whole family of God—everywhere. We will never get very far in prayer unless we come to it prepared to sacrifice self-interest, and willing to merge into God's greater plan for the whole.

FURTHER STUDY

Luke 18:9–14;
Mark 10:35–45;
Matt. 23:12

1. How did Jesus answer James and John?

2. What was wrong with the Pharisee's prayer?

Prayer

O Father, cleanse my heart from any limitations I might have in relation to the word "Our". Help me to make it a true "Our" with everybody included—those I like and those I don't like. For Jesus' sake. Amen.

SECTION THREE

A Family Within a Family

For reading & meditation—John 1:1–13

"... to all who received him, to those who believed in his name, he gave the right to become children of God." (v.12)

The second word in our Master's model of prayer is "Father." In Christian circles the term "Father" is probably the most common term used when addressing God, and rightly so, for this is the pattern Jesus set when teaching His disciples the art of effective praying. Prayer should always begin with the recognition that God is our Father.

This raises the much debated question: Is God a Father to all men and women everywhere, or only to those who are committed members of the Christian Church? For many years now liberally minded theologians have taught that God is everyone's Father, so we are all His children, and thus all brothers and sisters. This teaching, known as the universal brotherhood of man, makes conversion unnecessary, and puts to one side the redemptive sufferings of Christ on the Cross.

The Bible teaches that God is a Father in two senses. Firstly, He is the Father of the human family by virtue of creation. Malachi 2:10 says: "Have we not all one Father? Did not one God create us?" In Acts 17:29 Paul said: "We are God's offspring." In the sense of creation, yes, God is our Father. In the sense of a familial relationship, He is not. Jesus said in John 8:44 to the Jewish leaders: "You belong to your father, the devil." Quite clearly, the fatherhood of God is seen in the Bible in two senses. He is the Father of all men and women because He is their Creator, but He has another family—a family within a family—consisting of those who have committed themselves to Jesus Christ, the Son.

FURTHER STUDY

Rom. 8:1–17; Ps. 68:5; Isa. 64:8

1. How have we "received the spirit of adoption"?

2. What is our cry?

Prayer

O God, I am so grateful that I know You as my Father—not only in the creative sense, but in the familial sense. May the wonder of this closer relationship grow within me hour by hour and day by day. For Jesus' sake. Amen.

SECTION THREE

God Is a Father

For reading & meditation—1 John 2:1–15

"... I write to you ... because you have known the Father." (v.13)

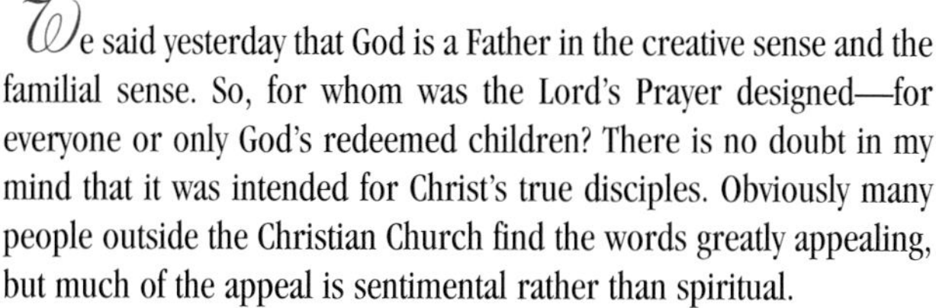

We said yesterday that God is a Father in the creative sense and the familial sense. So, for whom was the Lord's Prayer designed—for everyone or only God's redeemed children? There is no doubt in my mind that it was intended for Christ's true disciples. Obviously many people outside the Christian Church find the words greatly appealing, but much of the appeal is sentimental rather than spiritual.

To understand the Lord's Prayer, and apply its principles in the way our Lord intended, one needs to have experienced a genuine conversion. Then, and only then, does its meaning become apparent. Jesus shows us in the first sentence of His prayer pattern that true prayer must begin with a concept of God as Father. Someone has pointed out that the term "Father" answers all the philosophical questions about the nature of God. A father is a person, therefore God is not an invisible force behind the machinery of the universe. A father is able to hear, therefore God is not an impersonal being, aloof from all our troubles and trials. And, above all, a father is predisposed, by reason of his familial relationship, to give careful attention to what his child says.

When we pray, then, to the Father, we must hold in our minds the picture of our eternal Creator as a being who has a father's heart, a father's love and a father's strength. This, then, must be the second note we strike when praying—God is a Father, and we must come to Him with all the trust and frankness of a child. Otherwise it is not prayer.

FURTHER STUDY

John 5:17–47; 1:12;
2 Cor. 6:17–18;
Gal. 4:5–6

1. How did Jesus speak of His Father?

2. What is God's promise to those who believe?

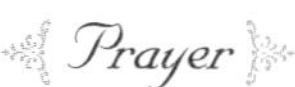

Prayer

O God, I am so grateful that in the word *Father* I discover the greatest truth about You. My heart pillows itself on that glorious and wonderful fact. Thank You—Father. Amen.

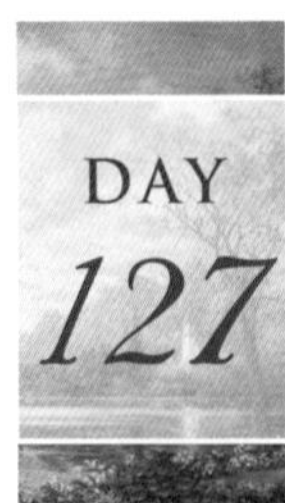

DAY

127

SECTION THREE

What's In a Word?

For reading & meditation—Hebrews 11:1–6

"... anyone who comes to him must believe that he exists and that he rewards those who earnestly seek him." (v.6)

It is not enough that we address God as "Father," simply saying the word with our lips. We must understand the nature of God's fatherhood, for if we don't, then we will never be able to pray the way Jesus laid down for us. No one can rise higher in their prayer life than their concept of God. If you do not hold in your heart a picture of God as He really is, then your prayers will be short-circuited, and, like electricity when it has nowhere else to go, will run into the earth.

What goes on in your thoughts and feelings when the word father is mentioned? Some will have positive thoughts and feelings like warmth, love, affection; while others will experience negative feelings such as remoteness, sternness, or even unconcern. For many people, the word *father* has to be redeemed or amended, because it conjures up memories of unhappy relationships. I believe that this is why Jesus, after laying down the structure of prayer in Luke 11, then went on to teach us, through the parable of the friend who came at midnight, just what God is really like. He is not only a Father, said Jesus, but also a Friend.

Christ, knowing that for some the word *father* would have negative connotations, attempted to fill it with a deeper content, by showing that God was a Father and a Friend. We must make sure that our concept of the word *father* is a positive one, for if it isn't, then we will never be able to approach Him with the confidence of a trusting child.

FURTHER STUDY

John 11:5–36; 15:13–15; 14:18; Prov. 18:24

1. How did Jesus show true friendship?

2. To what length was this demonstrated?

Prayer

O God, I see that my prayer life rises or falls in relation to my understanding of Your Fatherhood. Give me a vision of Your loving care and concern for me that, in turn, will enable me to come to You in childlike trust and confidence. Amen.

SECTION THREE

Jesus Reveals the Father

For reading & meditation—John 14:1–14

"... Anyone who has seen me has seen the Father ..." (v.9)

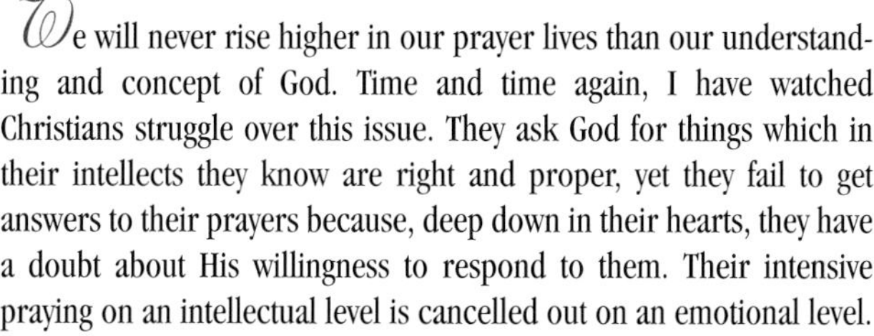

We will never rise higher in our prayer lives than our understanding and concept of God. Time and time again, I have watched Christians struggle over this issue. They ask God for things which in their intellects they know are right and proper, yet they fail to get answers to their prayers because, deep down in their hearts, they have a doubt about His willingness to respond to them. Their intensive praying on an intellectual level is cancelled out on an emotional level.

This is why, if we are to learn to pray the Jesus way, we must seek to develop a clear understanding of the fatherhood of God. But how can we gain a picture of God's fatherhood that is true to reality? We do it by focusing upon Jesus.

"The philosophies of India," said one great writer, "are the high watermark of man's search for God. Here the mind of man strained itself to search for God and speculate about Him. But in all their searching, they never discovered that He was a loving and tender Father. And why? Because they had no Jesus. They had Rama, Krishna, Shankara, Buddha, and many others, but no Jesus." That lack was the vital lack. For Jesus is the expression of the Father in human form. If you want to know what God is like as a Father, then gaze at Jesus. He drives the mists and misconceptions from around the Deity, and shows us that the heart that throbs at the back of the universe is like His heart—a heart overflowing with unconditional love.

FURTHER STUDY

John 17; 10:25–42; 5:17; Luke 2:49

1. How did Jesus show He was of the Father?

2. What did Jesus pray?

Prayer

O Lord Jesus, I am so thankful that no longer need I wonder what the Father is like. He is like You. You have revealed Him as He truly is. This gives a clear focus to my praying. I am deeply grateful. Amen.

DAY

129

SECTION THREE

Getting the Right Focus

For reading & meditation—Isaiah 40:25–31

"Lift your eyes and look ... Who created all these? ..." (v.26)

We turn now to focus on the second clause: "who art in heaven." It might seem astonishing that we can spend a whole week meditating on one clause of this matchless prayer, but one of the wonders of Scripture is its ability to introduce us to vast themes with a minimum of words. In the Lord's Prayer, a library is compressed into a phrase; a volume squeezed into a single syllable. These inspired words and phrases have become the source of numerous writings and expositions, and none of them, this one included, can fully plumb the depths of all that our Lord was saying.

We now ask ourselves: what was in our Master's mind when He taught His disciples to pray: "Our Father who art in heaven ...?" He wanted to teach them (so I believe) the way to achieve a true perspective in prayer. Before we can pray effectively, we must first be convinced who God is (our Father) and where God is (who art in heaven). In other words, the initial focus of our praying should not be on ourselves but on God.

Doesn't this reveal at once a fatal weakness in our praying? We come into God's presence, and instead of focusing our gaze upon Him, we focus it on our problems and our difficulties, which serve, in turn, to increase the awareness of our lack. Perhaps this is the reason why, when praying, we frequently end up more depressed or more frustrated than when we began? This is perhaps one of the greatest lessons we can learn about prayer—the initial focus must be upon God.

FURTHER STUDY

Isa. 40:12–24; Ps. 123:1; John 11:41; 17:1; Acts 7:55

1. How does Isaiah enlarge our vision of God?

2. What did Jesus do when He prayed?

Prayer

O God, I begin to see now where I have so often gone wrong in this vital matter of prayer. I have begun with myself, instead of beginning with You. Help me to get the right initial focus in my praying. For Jesus' sake. Amen.

"Imagineering"

For reading & meditation—Isaiah 26:1–13

"Thou wilt keep him in perfect peace, whose mind (imagination) is stayed on thee . . ." (v.3, KJV)

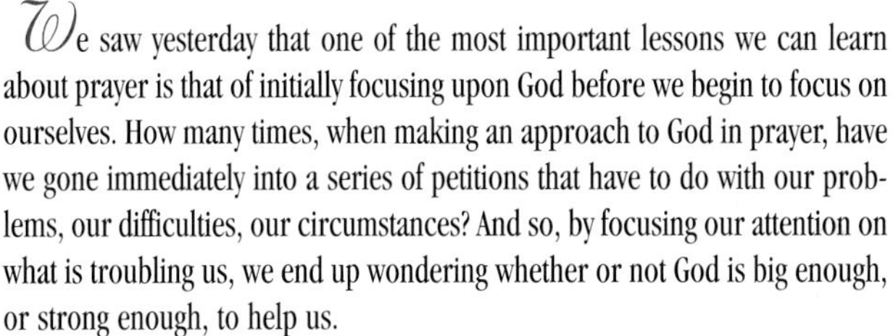

We saw yesterday that one of the most important lessons we can learn about prayer is that of initially focusing upon God before we begin to focus on ourselves. How many times, when making an approach to God in prayer, have we gone immediately into a series of petitions that have to do with our problems, our difficulties, our circumstances? And so, by focusing our attention on what is troubling us, we end up wondering whether or not God is big enough, or strong enough, to help us.

In the first six words of the Lord's Prayer, Jesus shows us a better way. He tells us to take a slow, calm, reassuring gaze at God—at His tenderness, His eagerness to give, His unwearying patience and untiring love. The result of this, of course, is that we develop a calmness and tranquillity in our spirit which means we will find it no longer necessary to plunge into a panicky flood of words.

In some parts of the world one can enroll in courses called "Imagineering"—courses that are designed to stimulate creative imagination. Most of our problems begin in the imagination—hence the instruction in the words of our text for today. "One can never become proficient in prayer," said one great writer, "until the imagination has been redeemed." What did he mean? He meant that when the imagination is redeemed from self-concentration, sex-concentration, sin-concentration, and makes God its prime focus, then it becomes creative-conscious, since its attention is concentrated on the Creator and the Re-Creator. And when the imagination is redeemed, all the doors of the personality fly open.

FURTHER STUDY

1 Cor. 2:1–16; Gen. 6:5; Rom. 1:21; 2 Cor. 10:5 (KJV)

1. How can we "cast down imaginations"?

2. What has God given to us?

Prayer

O God, how can I be calm and tranquil when my imagination is more self-centered than God-centered? Help me to be a God-focused person, not only at prayer times, but at all times. Amen.

SECTION THREE

"God's Postal Address?"

For reading & meditation—Psalm 20:1–9

"... He bears me from highest heaven and sends great victories." (v.6, TLB)

We continue meditating on why Jesus, in the opening words of the Lord's Prayer, taught us to focus first on God before presenting to Him our requests and petitions.

Why did Jesus bid us pray: "Our Father who art in heaven"? What is so important about the fact that God lives in heaven? Someone has suggested that heaven is "God's postal address," and, therefore, the place to which all prayers and petitions ought to be directed. I believe, however, that Jesus, in using the words "who art in heaven," sought to focus our minds, not so much on God's location, but rather His elevation. We are so used to living, as we say: "in a man's world," surrounded by limitations, that we are apt to forget that God exists in a realm where there are no shortages or restraints. Here, on earth, we stagger from one crisis to another, face endless problems—such as economic recessions, strikes, political unrest—but in heaven, where God lives, such situations are non-existent. There are no shortages in the factories of His grace, no disputes on His assembly lines and no faults in His communication system. Ring "Calvary" at any hour of the day or night, and you will be put into direct contact with the King of kings!

Can you now see what Jesus means when He bids us focus on God who is in heaven? He is telling us to elevate our spiritual vision until it breaks free of earth's gravitational pull, and to remind ourselves constantly of the fact that, in our Father's presence, our greatest problems turn into possibilities.

FURTHER STUDY

Rev. 21; Isa. 66:1–2; Matt. 5:34; Rev. 4:2

1. What is the focal point of heaven?
2. How does this elevate our vision?

Prayer

O Father, this phrase "who art in heaven" is like a rocket that launches me beyond earth's limitations into a realm where everything is blessedness and light. Help me never lose sight of this fact—today and every day. Amen.

Settling Down in God

For reading & meditation—Isaiah 6:1–8

"... I saw the Lord sitting upon a throne, high and lifted up ..." (v.1, RSV)

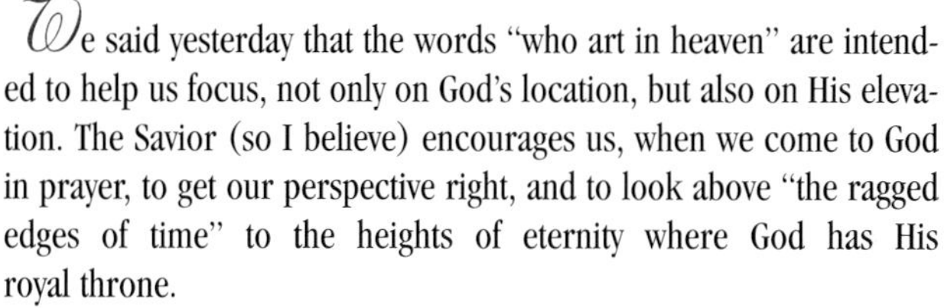

We said yesterday that the words "who art in heaven" are intended to help us focus, not only on God's location, but also on His elevation. The Savior (so I believe) encourages us, when we come to God in prayer, to get our perspective right, and to look above "the ragged edges of time" to the heights of eternity where God has His royal throne.

The old Welsh preachers and theologians such as Christmas Evans, Daniel Rowlands, and others, used to call this aspect of prayer "settling down in God." They taught that when we gain a right perspective of God and heavenly things, then and only then, can we have a right perspective of man and earthly things. It was only when Isaiah saw the Lord "high and lifted up" that he was able to put into focus the events that were happening around him. Our life here on earth can never be abundant unless we realize that we have access to resources which are outside the realm of terrestrial things.

A good working translation of the term El-Shaddai (Gen. 17:1) is "God—the Enough." Actually, of course, He is more than enough, but how comforting it is to know that He is at least that. So, when coming to God in prayer, learn to settle yourself down in God. Remind yourself that His resources so infinitely exceed your requirements; His sufficiency so immeasurably surpasses every demand you may make upon it. Get the divine perspective right and earthly things will fall into their right and proper focus.

FURTHER STUDY

Matt. 19:13–26; Eph. 3:20; 2 Cor. 9:8; Phil. 4:19

1. What was the declaration of Jesus?

2. How did Paul describe "El-Shaddai?"

Prayer

My Father, gently and quietly I breathe the strength of Your Almightiness into every portion of my being. I realize that when I see You "high and lifted up," then all of life is reduced to its proper proportions. I am so thankful. Amen.

DAY

133

SECTION THREE

"Too Close to the Ground"

For reading & meditation—Psalm 92:1–15

"But you, O Lord, are exalted forever." (v.8)

Quietly we are coming to the conclusion that before we can see the events of time in their proper perspective, we must learn to focus our gaze upon God. The reason why our personal problems and difficulties seem so large and ominous is due mainly to the fact that we have not brought God into proper focus. When we see Him as He really is—"high and lifted up"—then all our troubles and anxieties are reduced to their proper proportions.

A minister looked through his study window one day into the garden next door. He saw a little boy there, holding in his hand two pieces of wood, each about eighteen inches long. He heard him ask his mother he could make a weathercock. After getting her permission, he proceeded to nail one piece of wood upright on the low garden wall, then nailed the other piece loosely on top. Soon the loosely nailed piece of wood turned and twisted, first this way and then that, and the little boy danced with delight. He thought he had a weathercock that registered the winds, but all it did was register the draughts. "It turned half a circle," said the minister, "when the back door banged."

From where the minister sat in his study, he could see a real weathercock on the church steeple. It was as steady as a rock in the constant winds that blew in from the sea. There are many Christians, however, who are like the little boy's weathercock—at the mercy of every gust of circumstance, their thoughts of God fluctuating with their personal experiences. They take their direction from a weathercock that is too close to the ground.

FURTHER STUDY

Ps. 8:1–9; 1 Cor. 13:12; 2 Cor. 3:18

1. How did the psalmist focus his gaze on God?

2. How did Paul describe it?

O God, my Father, forgive me that my life is taken up more with the immediate than the ultimate. I have been glancing at You and gazing at my circumstances. From today it will be different—I will glance at my circumstances and gaze at You. Amen.

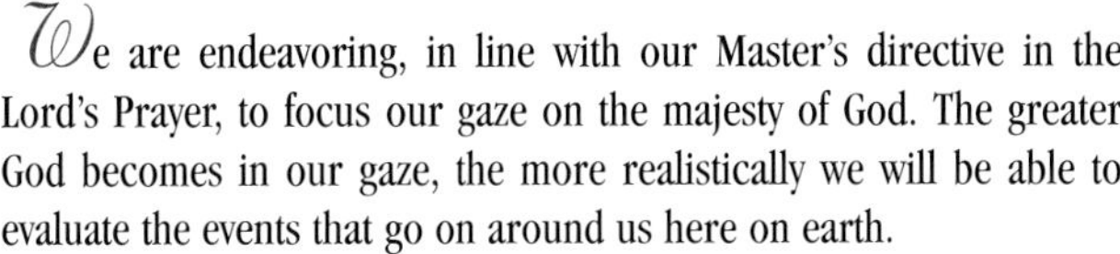

"The Universe Proclaims It"

For reading & meditation—Psalm 19:1–14

"The heavens declare the glory of God ..." (v.1)

We are endeavoring, in line with our Master's directive in the Lord's Prayer, to focus our gaze on the majesty of God. The greater God becomes in our gaze, the more realistically we will be able to evaluate the events that go on around us here on earth.

In the passage we have read today the Psalmist tells us that one way we can focus on the greatness of God is to consider His handiwork in creation. All around us in this wonderful world, we see evidences of His sublime sufficiency. Consider, for example, the vastness of the universe. Scientists tell us that in relation to the myriads of other celestial bodies in outer space, the planet we inhabit is like a tiny speck of dust in a huge railway station in relation to all the other specks of dust around it, or like a single grain of sand among all the sand on all the seashores of the world. They tell us also that if the earth were to fall out of its orbit, and spin away into space, it would create no more disturbance than the dropping of a pea in the Pacific Ocean!

Such word pictures, inadequate as they are, do, nevertheless, help us form some idea of the greatness and power of our God. Who can meditate on the vastness of the universe without experiencing an expansion in their conception of the majesty of God? Why did God construct the universe on such a grand scale? My conclusion is—He did it to show us that He is gloriously sufficient, unchangingly adequate and abidingly faithful.

FURTHER STUDY

Matt. 6:19–34; Luke 12:24; Ps. 45:1– 17

1. How did Jesus focus our attention on God's goodness?

2. Of whom does the psalmist give us a picture?

Prayer

O God, what a fool I am to think that my resources might run dry. Help me to live in the light of the fact that my demand will never exceed Your supply. You are the Enough. I am so thankful. Amen.

DAY

135

"A Time Exposure to God"

For reading & meditation—Psalm 62:1–12

"... twice have I heard this: that power belongs to God." (v.11, RSV)

We have been seeing the futility of presenting our petitions and requests to God before pausing to reflect on His unchanging adequacy and sufficiency. We said that one reason why Jesus directed us to use the words "who art in heaven" was to encourage us to focus our gaze on a God who is unaffected by the restrictions and limitations of earth, and who dwells in a place where the resources never run dry.

Those who plunge into the areas of petition and intercession, before reflecting on the abundant resources that lie in God, will find their praying ineffective. They are praying contrary to God's pattern. The poet says:

What a frail soul he gave me, and a heart
Lame, and unlikely for the large events.

However, I wonder if, more often than not, we haven't given ourselves "a heart lame, and unlikely for the large events" because we rush into God's presence to present our petitions before taking stock of our spiritual resources.

God offers us infinite resources for the asking and the taking—Himself. The first moments of prayer should, therefore, be contemplative, reflective, meditative. As we gaze upon God and His infinite resources, we take, as someone put it, "a time exposure to God." His adequacy and sufficiency are printed indelibly upon us. No matter, then, what difficulties and problems face us—we are more than a match for them. The vision of His greatness puts the whole of life in its proper perspective. "We kneel, how weak—we rise, how full of power."

FURTHER STUDY

Eph. 1; Ps. 5:3; 65:5–7; 1 Chron. 29:12

1. What was Paul's prayer for the Ephesians?

2. Ask God to enlarge your vision in this way.

Prayer

O Father, I am so thankful that my resources are so near at hand. I reflect on Your greatness and wonder in the depths of my heart, and my praying takes on new strength and power. I am so grateful. Amen.

SECTION THREE

Honoring God's Name

For reading & meditation—John 14:12–21

"... I will do whatever you ask in my name, so that the Son may bring glory to the Father." (v.13)

The next clause in Jesus' pattern of prayer is: "hallowed be thy name." What does it mean to hallow the Name of our loving heavenly Father?

To hallow something is to reverence it, or treat it as sacred. It is derived from a very important word in the Bible (Greek: *hagiazo*) which means to venerate, set apart, to make holy. Does this mean that our veneration of God makes Him holy? No, for nothing we do can add to or subtract from His qualities. God is the only Being in the universe who needs nothing, or no one, to complete Him. To venerate God means to give Him the recognition He deserves, to acknowledge His superiority, and to treat Him with admiration and respect. So prayer is much more than a way by which we can talk to God about our problems; it is a vehicle by which God can increasingly reveal to us who He is.

Some Christians think of prayer merely as a means by which they can obtain things from God. Prayer, first and foremost, is a communication system through which God is able to reach deep into our spirits, and impress upon us His superiority, His power and His love. "I will do whatever you ask in my name," said Jesus. And why? "So that the Son may bring glory to the Father." If prayer does not begin by giving God a preminent place in our hearts and minds, then it is not New Testament praying. Isn't it staggering that the first petition in the Lord's Prayer is not on our own behalf but on His!

FURTHER STUDY

John 1:1–14; 13:31; 17:4; 1 Pet. 4:11

1. What was John's testimony of Christ?

2. What was Jesus' testimony of Himself?

O God, help me to build my prayer life according to the pattern which Jesus gave me, and begin by deepening the conviction that my first petition should never be for myself, but for You and Your eternal glory. Amen.

DAY 137

SECTION THREE

What's In a Name?

For reading & meditation—Exodus 34:1–10

"... the Lord ... announced ... 'I am Jehovah, the merciful and gracious God ... slow to anger and rich in ... love ...'" (vv.5–7, TLB)

We ended yesterday by saying that the first petition in the Lord's Prayer is not on our behalf but on God's—"hallowed be thy Name." Arthur W. Pink says in his book *An Exposition of the Sermon on the Mount*: "How clearly, then, is the fundamental duty of prayer set forth. Self, and all its needs, must be given a secondary place, and the Lord freely accorded the pre-eminence in our thoughts and supplications. This petition (hallowed be thy name) must take the precedence, for the glory of God's great Name is the ultimate end of all things."

Today we ask ourselves: what does it mean to hallow God's Name? Are we required to pronounce God's Name in the quietest and most reverential of tones? Does it mean that we develop a mystical attitude toward the term *God*? No. In biblical times names were not just designations, but definitions. They had varied and special meanings. A name stood for a person's character, such as is demonstrated in 1 Samuel 18:30. "David...behaved himself more wisely than all Saul's servants; so that his name was very dear and highly esteemed" (Amplified Bible). The people did not esteem the letters of David's name. The statement means that David himself was esteemed.

In the text for today we are given, not just the Name of God, but some of the characteristics that go under that Name. He is merciful, gracious, long-suffering, and so on. In other words, the Name of God is the composite of all His attributes. When we honor God's Name, we honor Him.

FURTHER STUDY

Ps. 111:1–10; 138:2; Lev. 22:2; Isa. 29:23

1. How does the Psalmist link God's Name and acts?
2. What does "awe-some" mean?

Prayer

O Father, I begin to see that my object in prayer has been to get the things I thought I needed. Now I realize my greatest need is to give You the pre-eminence You deserve. Help me understand and respond to this deep and important truth. For Jesus' sake. Amen.

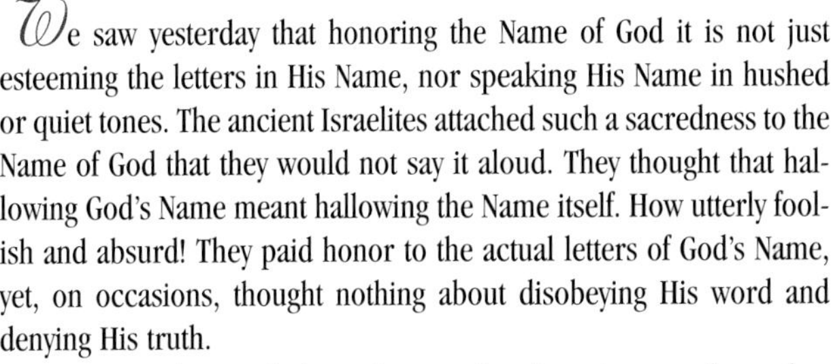

SECTION THREE

"Jehovah"—No Such Word

DAY 138

For reading & meditation—Exodus 3:1–15

"God said to Moses, 'I AM WHO I AM . . .'" (v.14)

We saw yesterday that honoring the Name of God it is not just esteeming the letters in His Name, nor speaking His Name in hushed or quiet tones. The ancient Israelites attached such a sacredness to the Name of God that they would not say it aloud. They thought that hallowing God's Name meant hallowing the Name itself. How utterly foolish and absurd! They paid honor to the actual letters of God's Name, yet, on occasions, thought nothing about disobeying His word and denying His truth.

One great Hebrew scholar points out that there is no such word as Jehovah in the Hebrew language, although it appears in English translations of the Old Testament. The Name of God in Exodus 3:14, where the Almighty gave His Name to Moses, I AM WHO I AM, is Yahweh: the English equivalent of which is Jehovah. The Israelites would not say the word Yahweh, and eventually the vowels were taken out and mixed with the consonants of another Hebrew word to form the word Adonai. This was done as a device to avoid having to say the real word "Yahweh." How ridiculous can you get?

Let us be quite clear, then, about what Jesus meant when He taught us to pray "hallowed be thy name." God's Name stands for who He is—His mercy, His compassion, His love, His power, His eternity, and so on. When, as God's children, we come to Him to honor His Name, we do more than enter into a religious routine—we contemplate all that His Name stands for, and reverence Him for what He is.

FURTHER STUDY

Gen. 15, 22:14;
Ex. 15:26, 17:15;
Judg. 6:24; Ps. 23:1;
Jer. 23:6;
Ezek. 48:35

1. List the names of God.

2. What do they mean?

Prayer

O Father, I see that prayer, true prayer, is not just a technique, it is an art. Help me to learn that art, and to implement all You are teaching me in my prayer life day by day. For Jesus' sake. Amen.

DAY

139

SECTION THREE

In line With God's Character

For reading & meditation—Matthew 26:36–46

"… Yet not as I will, but as you will." (v.39)

Our first consideration, when approaching God, is the reverence of His Name. And why His Name? Because His Name stands for who and what God is. When we reverence His Name, we take into consideration all the ingredients of His character. The phrase "hallowed be thy name" implies that prayer is first and foremost a recognition of God's character and a willingness to submit to it. Jesus put first the determining thing in prayer—God's character. If our petitions are not in line with His character, then, however eloquently or persistently we plead our cause, the answer will be a firm and categorical: "No."

I wonder what would happen if we started our personal petitions with these words: "Father, if what I now want to ask You is not in line with Your character, then show me, for I don't want to ask for anything that does not contribute to Your praise and glory"? That would cause many of our petitions to die on our lips unuttered. Like the Muslim who washes his feet before going into the mosque, this attitude will wash our mouths, our thoughts, our desires, our motives. We would be saying, in effect: "Your character be revered first, before my desires or my petitions."

This kind of praying puts God's character first and our claims second—putting both in the right place. True prayer, then, begins with God, puts self in a secondary place, and seeks to honor and glorify God's Name. It is characterized by a desire for God's will more than our own will. Any other kind of praying is contrary to Jesus' pattern.

FURTHER STUDY

Rom. 12; Ex. 32:29; Prov. 23:26; 1 Thess. 2:4

1. How should we present ourselves to God?

2. How does this "please" God?

Prayer

My Father, thank You for reminding me that the prayers which get answered are those that are in line with Your character. And what squares with Your character is always in my best interests. I am deeply grateful. Amen.

SECTION THREE

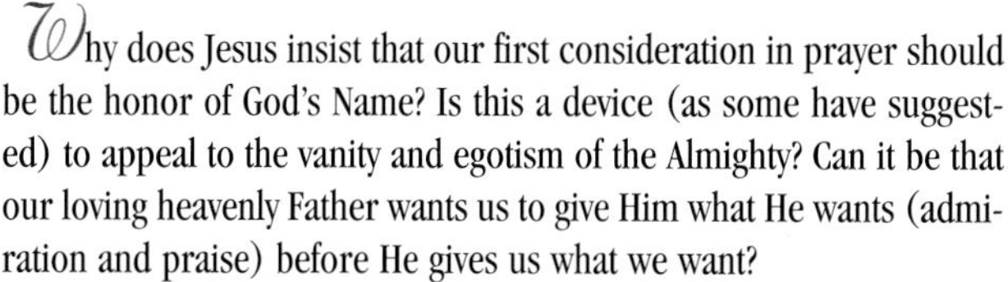

"A Little of Eternity"

For reading & meditation—2 Corinthians 3:7–18

"And we, who … all reflect the Lord's glory, are being transformed into his likeness …" (v.18)

Why does Jesus insist that our first consideration in prayer should be the honor of God's Name? Is this a device (as some have suggested) to appeal to the vanity and egotism of the Almighty? Can it be that our loving heavenly Father wants us to give Him what He wants (admiration and praise) before He gives us what we want?

No, of course not! God encourages us to focus on Himself because He knows that in contemplating Him, we complete ourselves and bring all parts of our personality to health. To admire, appreciate, respect and venerate the character of God is to awaken ourselves to reality. Not to do so is to deprive ourselves and bring about a depletion of our powers. We were designed for the worship and contemplation of God, and when, therefore, we stand before Him and gaze at His majesty and glory, the machinery of our inner being whirrs into activity, and our characters take on the features of His character.

God, therefore, has our interests at heart more than His own when He asks us to venerate Him. We "hallow" His Name and our own name (character) is hallowed. We gaze at His character and our own character is made better for the gazing. A shop assistant put it this way: "I just go quiet and empty into His presence, gaze at His glory and loveliness, and give myself time for His disposition to get through to mine." "Time for His disposition to get through." That's the secret. Give God a little of your time, and He will give you a little of eternity.

FURTHER STUDY

2 Pet. 1; Rom. 8:29;
Phil. 3:21;
1 John 3.2

1. How do we become partakers of the divine nature?
2. List some of these characteristics.

Prayer

O Father, forgive me for the times I rush into Your presence intent only on getting my needs met. Slow me down and make me a more contemplative person. Then Your character can rub off on my character. In Jesus' Name I pray. Amen.

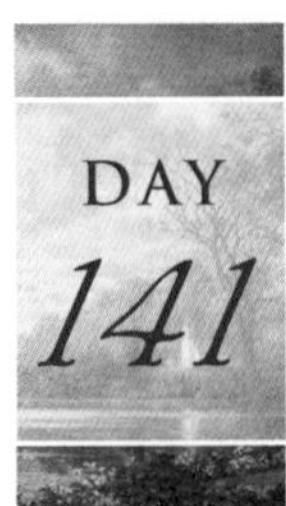

SECTION THREE

Not Just a "Father"

For reading & meditation—John 17:1–11

"... Holy Father, protect them by the power of your name ..." (v.11)

John Calvin said: "That God's name should be hallowed is to say that God should have His own honor of which He is so worthy, so that men should never think or speak of Him without the greatest veneration."

One of the things that saddens me about the contemporary Christian Church is the way that some believers refer to the Almighty in terms that drag Him down to a "good buddy" relationship. They refer to the great God of creation as "The Man Upstairs" or "My Partner in the Sky." When people talk about God in such low-level terms, they do Him an injustice. And it's not so much the terms, but the image of God that lies behind those terms which is the real problem.

We must, of course, strike a balanced note on this issue, as Paul teaches that the Holy Spirit in our hearts prompts us to call God, not merely Father, but "Daddy" (Rom. 8:15). Too much of the "Daddy," however, can lead us, if we are not careful, into sloppy sentimentalism. I believe this is why, after the phrase "Our Father," Jesus introduces us to another aspect of God—hallowed, holy, reverenced be His Name. It is right that we think of God in familiar terms such as "Daddy," but it is right also that we remember that our heavenly Father is a God of majestic holiness and unsullied purity. A.W. Tozer was right when he said: "No religion has been greater than its idea of God." Jesus put it into proper focus when He addressed God, not only as Father, but Holy Father.

FURTHER STUDY

Heb. 12:1–14; Ex. 15:11; 1 Sam. 6:20; Isa. 6:3; Rev. 15:4

1. Where are we to look?

2. How do we become holy?

Prayer

My Father and my God, help me gain a healthy and balanced view of Your person, so that while I enjoy the familiarity of Your Fatherhood, I am exceedingly conscious also of Your holiness. In Jesus' Name. Amen.

A Clear Perspective

For reading & meditation—Psalm 34:1–8

"Glorify the Lord with me; let us exalt his name together." (v.3)

Hallowing God's Name does not mean having some kind of fetish about pronouncing the word *God* in hushed or reverential tones. It is rather hallowing all that God is, His qualities, character and attributes—all the things embodied in His Name. When the Psalmist in Psalm 102:15 said: "The heathen shall fear the name of the Lord," did this mean they feared the letters in the word Yahweh? No, they feared the Lord God Himself.

At the risk of over-simplifying the opening clauses of the Lord's Prayer, what Jesus is teaching us is to come before the Father with this attitude: "Our Father, who cares for us with true tenderness, and who has in heaven the supplies to meet our every need; may Your attributes, Your nature, Your character, Your reputation, Your person, Your whole being itself be hallowed." This, then, is how prayer should begin. Before we start asking for what we want from God, we need to have the right perspective of God.

I have just been reading some words of Gregory of Nyssa who prayed: "May I become through Thy help blameless, just and holy. May I abstain from every evil, speak the truth and do justly. May I walk in the straight paths, sing with temperance adorned with incorruption, beautiful through wisdom and prudence. May I meditate upon the things that are above and despise what is earthly, for a man can hallow God's Name in no other way than by reflecting His character and bear witness to the fact that divine power is the cause of his goodness." Hallowed be the Name of God.

FURTHER STUDY

Ps. 111:1–10; 33:8; 34:9; 86:11

1. What is the beginning of wisdom?

2. What does it mean to fear the Lord?

Gracious Father, I see that if I am to become effective in prayer, then I must get all my values straight. Thank You for giving me a clear pattern to follow, and for reminding me that when I hallow Your Name, You will hallow mine. Thank You, Father. Amen.

DAY 143

SECTION THREE

"Thy Kingdom Come"

For reading & meditation—Matthew 6.25–34

"But seek first his kingdom … and all these things will be given to you as well." (v.33)

We turn now to examine the fourth phrase in the Lord's Prayer: "Thy kingdom come." Jesus, after making clear that the first consideration in prayer is to focus on God's character, puts as the next issue the establishing of God's kingdom. Any pattern of praying that does not make the kingdom a priority is not Christian praying. Our text today tells us: "Seek first his kingdom and his righteousness, and all these things will be given to you as well." If you seek something else first then your life will be off balance.

A newspaper report tells of a small town in Alaska where all the electric clocks were showing the wrong time. The fault, it appears, was in the local power plant. It failed to run with systematic regularity, and thus all the electric clocks were "out." When your primary concern is for something other than the kingdom of God, then everything in your life will be "out," too.

One of the sad things about Church history is that the Church has never really been gripped by the vision of the kingdom of God. There are notable exceptions, of course, but by and large the Church has missed its way in this matter. One theologian points out that when the Church drew up its creeds—the Apostle's, the Athanasian, the Nicene—it mentioned the kingdom once in all three of them, and then only marginally. The Church will never move into the dimension God has planned for it until it puts the kingdom where Jesus put it in this prayer—in a place of primary consideration and primary allegiance.

FURTHER STUDY

Luke 9:51–62; Matt. 5:3; John 3:3; Jas. 2:5

1. What did Jesus teach about the kingdom?

2. What did Jesus say to His would-be followers?

Gracious Father, I begin to see that there is something here that demands my thought and attention, and I don't want to miss it. Prepare me in mind and spirit for what You want to teach me this week. In Jesus' Name. Amen.

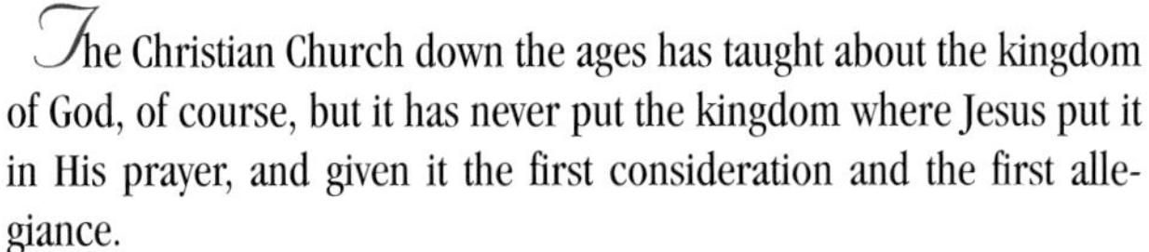

The Missing Note

For reading & meditation—Mark 1:9–28

"... Jesus came into Galilee, preaching the gospel of the kingdom of God." (v.14, KJV)

The Christian Church down the ages has taught about the kingdom of God, of course, but it has never put the kingdom where Jesus put it in His prayer, and given it the first consideration and the first allegiance.

"Thy kingdom come." Three simple words in both English and Greek, yet they open to us something so vast that one approaches them like a child standing on the seashore with a tiny bucket, wondering how to fit the vast ocean into it! There is no way one can adequately and fully expound these words, but I hope I can whet your appetite over these next few days, and then you can spend the rest of your life exploring all that is beyond them.

A couple of decades ago the Church woke up to the fact that there was a missing note in modern Christianity—the Holy Spirit. Gradually at first, and very tentatively, the Church opened itself up to the Person of the Holy Spirit, and now there are comparatively few churches that have not been affected, to some degree at least, by His power and His presence. It seems strange, when we look back, that we could have remained content with a Holy Spirit-less type of Christianity. The same strange omission has taken place in regard to the kingdom of God. There are signs that the message is being emphasized by certain groups and churches, but we are a long way from giving it the priority God demands. No wonder the Church has stumbled from problem to problem when its priorities are lost or only marginally held.

FURTHER STUDY

Dan. 2:36–44; Mark 9:1; 1 Cor. 4:20; John 18:36

1. What was the prophecy of Daniel?

2. What did Jesus say about His kingdom?

Gracious God, You who are always reaching out after me in love, and awakening me to new awareness and understanding, help me comprehend the truth of Your kingdom. For Jesus' sake. Amen.

DAY 145

SECTION THREE

"Our God Reigns"

For reading & meditation—John 18:28–40

"Jesus said, 'My kingdom is not of this world …'" (v.36)

The kingdom of God was the motif running through everything Jesus taught. However, I pick up many Christian books and magazines today and find that, with one or two exceptions, the kingdom of God is not mentioned. Jesus made it the central note of His preaching and also His praying.

It is time now to ask ourselves: what exactly does Jesus mean when He uses the word "kingdom"? The word for kingdom (*basileia* in the Greek) means "rule" or "reign." The kingdom of God, then, is the rule or reign of God, His sovereignty, for which we are to pray. Jesus spoke of the kingdom as being in the present as well as in the future. In Luke 17:21 he said: "the kingdom of God is within you." Wherever there is a heart that is surrendered to the claims and demands of Jesus Christ, there the kingdom exists. But there is a day coming, says Jesus in Matthew 8:11, when both small and great will sit side by side in the kingdom, and realize that in God's order of things there are no favorites.

The Scripture tells us also that God has a kingdom which is established in the heavens (Heb. 12:22–28), and the phrase we are studying "Thy kingdom come"—is a petition for God to let that kingdom extend to every area of the universe where His rule is resisted. We are thus introduced to another great purpose of prayer—transporting to all parts of the universe, across the bridge of prayer, the power that overcomes all sin, all rebellion and all evil.

FURTHER STUDY

Ps. 93; 47:8; Ex. 15:18; Mic. 4:7; Rom. 5:17

1. What does the psalmist conclude?

2. What is Paul's expectation?

Prayer

Father, what can I say? When I see that You have given me the privilege of helping You usher in Your kingdom through my prayer, my heart is overwhelmed. What confidence You place in Your redeemed children. May we be worthy of it. For Jesus' sake. Amen.

A Worldview

For reading & meditation—Revelation 11:15–19

"... The kingdom of the world has become the kingdom of our Lord and of his Christ ..." (v.15)

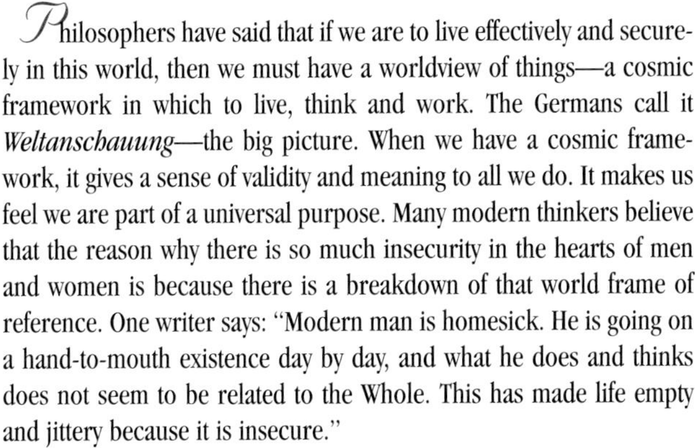

Philosophers have said that if we are to live effectively and securely in this world, then we must have a worldview of things—a cosmic framework in which to live, think and work. The Germans call it *Weltanschauung*—the big picture. When we have a cosmic framework, it gives a sense of validity and meaning to all we do. It makes us feel we are part of a universal purpose. Many modern thinkers believe that the reason why there is so much insecurity in the hearts of men and women is because there is a breakdown of that world frame of reference. One writer says: "Modern man is homesick. He is going on a hand-to-mouth existence day by day, and what he does and thinks does not seem to be related to the Whole. This has made life empty and jittery because it is insecure."

The Chinese have a saying: "In a broken nest there are no whole eggs." The nest, the world in which we live and think and work, has been broken up by sin and, therefore, our central unity has gone. This can be seen on a small scale when the home is broken. Nearly all the boys in reform schools come from broken homes. Why? The framework in which they have lived has broken down and has left them inwardly disrupted and confused. As a consequence morals break down. Can you see now why Jesus taught us to have a world view of things? With our eyes focused on the kingdom, we know that at the heart of things there is utter security.

FURTHER STUDY

Ps. 24:1–10; 2 Chron. 20:6; 1 Tim. 1:17; Rev. 19:6

1. What picture does the psalmist give us?

2. What is his exhortation?

O God, I am so grateful that I am not an orphan in this universe. I have a homeland, the kingdom of God. And because nothing can hinder the establishing of that kingdom, I have a peace that nothing can disturb. I am so grateful. Amen.

A Position of Strength

For reading & meditation—1 Corinthians 15:12–28

"... the end will come, when he hands over the kingdom to God the Father after he has destroyed all dominion ..." (v.24)

If people are to live securely in this world then they must cultivate a worldview. They must see the "big picture." Is this why Jesus, when laying down a pattern for prayer, taught His disciples to focus on the "big picture" of the kingdom of God? Whether it is or not, one thing is certain—when we start off in prayer gripped by the certainty of God's coming kingdom, our prayers are launched from a position of strength.

Just as I was about to begin this page a sales bulletin came in the post, and on it were the words: "Get the idea—and all else follows." I thought to myself, when the idea is God's idea, the kingdom, then, indeed, all else follows. What if we were to begin our prayers, however, by focusing, not on the kingdom of God, but on the kingdoms of this world? We would receive very little motivation from such an action. Man-made empires come and go. Egypt came and went. Syria came and went. Babylon came and went. Greece came and went. Historians tell us that at least 21 former great civilizations are extinct. Earthly kingdoms go the way of all flesh—the debasing power of sin, decay, distress and destruction is inevitable.

The kingdom of God, unlike earthly kingdoms, is destined for success. Call it triumphalism if you like, but the eventual accomplishment of God's kingdom has more reliability about it than tomorrow's dawn. When our minds are permitted to focus on such a tremendous truth, it will not be long before the heart leaps up in confident, believing prayer.

FURTHER STUDY

Ps. 115:1–18; Phil. 2:10; Heb. 1:8; Rev. 11:15

1. How does the psalmist relate heaven and earth?

2. How can we help to bring the kingdom of heaven to earth?

Prayer

Father, I think I get the idea. When I focus my mind on the glory of Your coming kingdom, then, against such a wonderful backdrop, my prayers take on a new boldness and authority. Get the idea—then all else follows. Thank You, Father. Amen.

Another Kingdom

For reading & meditation—John 12:20–36

"Now is the time for judgment on this world; now the prince of this world will be driven out." (v.31)

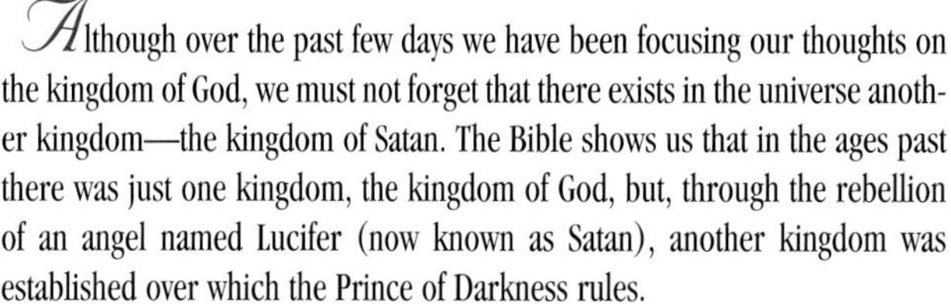

Although over the past few days we have been focusing our thoughts on the kingdom of God, we must not forget that there exists in the universe another kingdom—the kingdom of Satan. The Bible shows us that in the ages past there was just one kingdom, the kingdom of God, but, through the rebellion of an angel named Lucifer (now known as Satan), another kingdom was established over which the Prince of Darkness rules.

Every person since Adam (with the single exception of Jesus Christ), comes under the dominion of Satan, and is, in fact, classified as a citizen of the devil's kingdom (Eph. 2:1–2). When, through conversion, we become followers of the Lord Jesus Christ, we become citizens of the kingdom of God (Col. 1:13). Once we receive this new citizenship whether we realize it or not, we are thrust into the front line of the age-long conflict which has existed between God and Satan, and we become participators in the Almighty's plan to bring about Satan's defeat, and to bring the universe once again under the control of God and His kingdom.

Standing as we do on the cutting edge between the kingdom of God and the kingdom of Satan, the Almighty has given us a weapon with which to fight, that is the most powerful in all the armories of heaven. That weapon is prayer. Our citizenship in God's kingdom entitles and enables us to pray: "Thy kingdom come." And when uttered with sincerity and trust, those words spell out, every time they are spoken, the ultimate triumph of the kingdom of God.

FURTHER STUDY

Eph. 1:17–2:7; 6:1;
2 Cor. 4:4; 11:3

1. What is Christ's position?

2. What is our position?

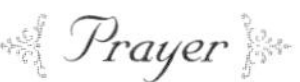

O Father, I confess I am utterly amazed when I realize You have not only taken me out of Satan's kingdom, but You are using my prayer life, when it is in line with Your pattern, to demolish his kingdom and re-establish Yours. Help me to participate with all my might. For Jesus' sake. Amen.

DAY

149

SECTION THREE

Eating Our Own Words

For reading & meditation—Daniel 4:28–37

"... His dominion is an eternal dominion; his kingdom endures from generation to generation." (v.34)

We have been studying over the past six days the phrase used by Jesus in the Lord's Prayer, "Thy kingdom come." We said that one reason why Jesus taught us to focus on the coming kingdom was in order to help us get our spiritual bearings, and thus be better equipped and fortified when praying for other things. Just as the mariner has to get his bearings from the stars to be able to put into the right earthly port, so we have to get our eternal values straight before we begin to concentrate on temporal things.

Nebuchadnezzar, lifted up by pride, was humbled and ate grass like one of the cattle until he realized that not he but God rules from heaven. Then he was restored to reason and to the throne. I am afraid that we will have to eat many of our words unless we learn that the heavens rule and the kingdom of God has the last word. Oh that we could become so preoccupied with the kingdom of God that it would affect every part of our being, our thinking, our working and our praying.

Our own causes are valid only as they accord with the eternal cause of God. When I pray: "Thy kingdom come," I am really praying: "Lord, I pray that You will do whatever advances Your kingdom, whatever brings in Your rule and Your reign." And, we might add—"even though my own 'cause' might have to be pushed aside." What a prayer! What a challenge! No wonder the ancient Jewish Talmud said that "the prayer in which there is no mention of the kingdom of God is no prayer at all." It's only when we get the kingdom values straight that we can pray this prayer with assurance.

FURTHER STUDY

Mark 4:30–41; Isa. 9:7; Dan. 7:13–14; Luke 1:32–33

1. Write out your own definition of "the kingdom."

2. To what did Jesus liken the kingdom?

Prayer

O Father, help me to pray this prayer, not only with my lips, but with my whole heart. May my life be so geared to Your cause that my own "cause" may take second place. In Jesus' Name I pray. Amen.

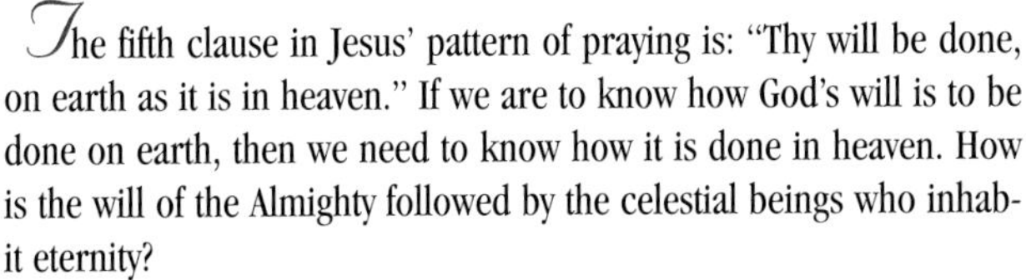

"Thy Will Be Done"

DAY 150

For reading & meditation—Psalm 103:1–22

"Praise the Lord, you his angels, you mighty ones who do his bidding ..." (v.20)

The fifth clause in Jesus' pattern of praying is: "Thy will be done, on earth as it is in heaven." If we are to know how God's will is to be done on earth, then we need to know how it is done in heaven. How is the will of the Almighty followed by the celestial beings who inhabit eternity?

First, it is followed unquestioningly. There is no discussion among the angels over any of the Creator's directives. On earth the Lord has to prod to get His servants moving, but in heaven that is unnecessary. Second, it is done speedily. Once a command is received, the angels move with the utmost speed to do His bidding. They eagerly wait for the next command so they can hurry to accomplish it. How slow are we, His earthly servants, by comparison. Third, it is done completely. The angels carry out His bidding down to the tiniest detail. There are no alternatives, no omissions, no modifications to the divine orders. The will of God is done in full.

A little girl aged seven asked me once: "Does an angel have a will?" I said: "I think so." "Then how many wills are there in heaven?" she asked. "Oh," I said: "there must be millions." "Wrong," she said. "There is only one. There were two once, but one got kicked out. Now God's will has full control." I was amazed at such clarity of thought from a seven-year-old. May the day soon dawn when the will of God is done on earth as it is done in heaven—unquestioningly, speedily and completely.

FURTHER STUDY

Isa. 14:12–15; Neh. 9:6; Luke 10:18

1. Why was Lucifer cast out of heaven?

2. What phrase occurs five times?

Prayer

O God, forgive me for the perfunctory way in which I often respond to Your commands. Help me to be as responsive to Your bidding as the angels of heaven. For Jesus' sake. Amen.

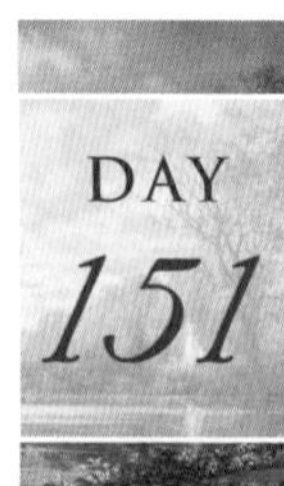

SECTION THREE

God's Totalitarianism

For reading & meditation—1 Corinthians 15:24–28

"... the Son himself will be made subject to him who put everything under him, so that God may be all in all." (v.28)

We continue meditating on the question: How is God's will done in heaven? We saw yesterday that the angels respond to the will of God in unquestioning obedience and perform His bidding with the utmost readiness and willingness. Heaven can, therefore, be described as a totalitarian society.

We are rather afraid of that word here on earth as it brings to mind oppressive regimes where individualism is discouraged or repressed. I recognize that the word has negative connotations because of this, but, make no mistake about it, heaven is a totalitarian community. Those reading these lines who have had some experience of totalitarianism might say: "What? Are we to emerge from one totalitarian system to become involved in another?" The answer is yes. And God's totalitarianism is more thorough going and absolute than any totalitarian regime on earth.

However, there is a profound difference. When you obey the will of God fully and completely, you find perfect freedom. When you obey other totalitarian systems, you find utter bondage, for they are not in line with the way you were designed to live. As the stomach and poison are incompatible, and when brought together produce disruption and death, so your being and other-than-the-will-of-God ways are not made for each other and produce disruption and death. However, as the stomach thrives on good wholesome food, and the two are made for each other, and bring health and life, so the will of God and your being are made for each other, and when brought together produce health, life and fulfillment.

FURTHER STUDY

Heb. 10:1–12; John 14:31; 15:10; Rom. 5:19

1. What was Christ's example?

2. What was His challenge?

Prayer

O God, drive this truth deep into my spirit, that it is only when I submit to Your reign that I truly realize myself. My will is my ruin: Your will is my release. Help me to lose myself in Your will, for it is only then that I can find myself. For Jesus' sake. Amen.

SECTION THREE

"Made For Each Other"

For reading & meditation—Hosea 8:1–14

"I wrote for them the many things of my law, but they regarded them as something alien." (v.12)

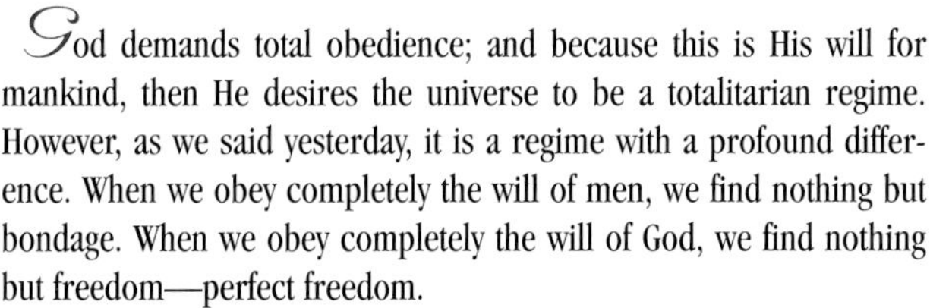

God demands total obedience; and because this is His will for mankind, then He desires the universe to be a totalitarian regime. However, as we said yesterday, it is a regime with a profound difference. When we obey completely the will of men, we find nothing but bondage. When we obey completely the will of God, we find nothing but freedom—perfect freedom.

There are many in this universe who think like Ephraim, of whom God complained: "Were I to write for him my laws, he would but think them foreigners' laws" (Moffatt). Ephraim felt that God's laws were foreign sayings or laws—something disruptive. But the will of God and the human will are not alien. They were made for each other. The expression is inadequate, but it is the best way I know of explaining the fact that my will functions best when it acts and behaves in accordance with His will.

We must take hold of this until it becomes a basic axiom: my will and God's will are not alien. When I find His will, I find my own. I am fulfilled when I make Him my center, I am frustrated when I make myself the center. And if you are afraid that this depletes you as a person, or makes you into a cipher by subduing your individuality, then your fear is quite groundless. You are really at your best only when you are doing the will of God. Then all parts of your personality are drawn to health, vitality and fulfillment.

FURTHER STUDY

Ps. 40:1–8; 143:10; Matt. 12:50; Eph. 6:6

1. What is the psalmist's request?

2. What is the testimony of the psalmist?

Prayer

O God, my Father, thank You for reminding me that Your will and my will were made for each other. When my will and Yours coincide, then I live. When they clash, I do not live. Lord, I want to live. Amen.

DAY 153

SECTION THREE

Forced to Face Reality

For reading & meditation—Romans 12:1–8

"… offer your bodies as living sacrifices … be transformed by the renewing of your mind …" (vv.1–2)

Whenever we pray, we are to pray in accordance with God's will. One Greek scholar says that the words "Thy will be done, on earth as it is in heaven" can be paraphrased in this way: "Your will, whatever You wish to happen, let it happen—as in heaven so in earth." In other words: "God, do what You want." It's not easy to pray this way. If anyone thinks it is, then it is probably because they have never really sounded the depths of self-interest within their own hearts.

It's hard sometimes to pray "Thy will be done" when we know that if God has His way, we will not get our way. Has that ever happened to you? The basic reason for this conflict is due to the major problem of the human heart—self-centeredness. Paul, when describing a self-centered life and its results in Romans 6:21, ends by asking this question: "Well, what did you gain then by it all? Nothing but what you are now ashamed of!" (Moffatt). The end was zero. That is the inevitable end of a self-centered life—nothing. The major thing that stands in the way of God performing His will in our lives utterly and completely is just that—self-centeredness.

Jesus knew, as we now do, that if we are to become effective in prayer, then we must face up to the question: whose will comes first—mine or God's? I must be willing to say: "God, do what You want." That is the bottom line in prayer.

FURTHER STUDY

1 John 5:1–15; Jas. 4:13–17; 1 John 2:17

1. What is the confidence we have?

2. What ought we to say?

Prayer

Gracious Father, I am grateful for the gentle and loving way You are putting Your finger on the obstacles in my life. Give me the attitude that puts Your will first and my will second. For Jesus' sake. Amen.

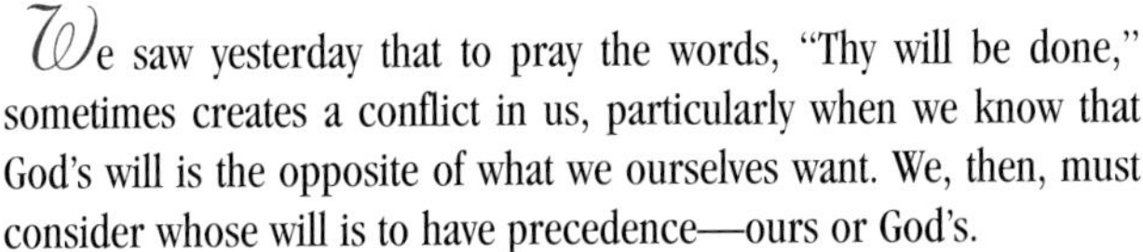

Louder Than "Amen"

DAY 154

For reading & meditation—Psalm 40:1–8

"I desire to do your will, O my God; your law is within my heart." (v.8)

We saw yesterday that to pray the words, "Thy will be done," sometimes creates a conflict in us, particularly when we know that God's will is the opposite of what we ourselves want. We, then, must consider whose will is to have precedence—ours or God's.

There are some Christians who pray, "Thy will be done," but they do it with an attitude of rebellion and resentment. They believe that they cannot escape the inevitable, and they become angry about it. They say the words, "Thy will be done," almost through clenched teeth. Other people say the words with an attitude of passive resignation. They say: "Thy will be done," but what they mean is something like this: "Lord, I'm not very happy about the way things are turning out, but I suppose You know best. So I'll go along with it, and try my best to believe it's for the best."

The proper attitude to the will of God, and the goal for which we should aim, is one of rejoicing. It's not easy to arrive at such an attitude, I know, but nevertheless we must have it before us as the desired end. David, as we saw in the passage before us today, prayed that way, and so, on occasions, did others in the Scriptures. If we can cultivate that attitude as the normal and characteristic reaction to everything that happens around us—sorrow, disappointment, disillusionment, frustration, disaster, loss, bereavement—then such a spirit is more than a match for anything. As someone has said: "The Hallelujah of triumph is louder than the Amen of resignation." It is!

FURTHER STUDY

Ps. 100; John 5:30; Eph. 6:6; Heb. 13:21

1. What is the psalmist's exhortation?

2. What should be our heart attitude?

Prayer

O God, help me drop my anchor into the depths of Your eternal love, and ride out all storms in the assurance that You are willing my highest good. Help me to accept it—joyously. For Jesus' sake. Amen.

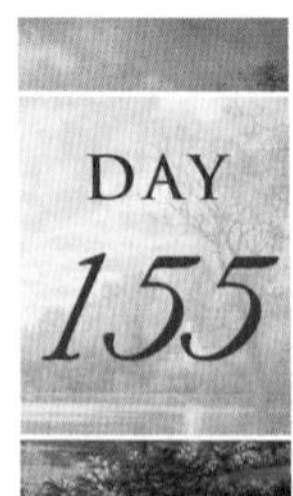

DAY 155

SECTION THREE

"On" or "In"

For reading & meditation—Romans 8:18–25

"... the whole creation has been groaning as in the pains of childbirth right up to the present time." (v.22)

In the phrase "Thy will be done, on earth as it is in heaven," what does Jesus mean by the term "on earth"? Theologians have argued for centuries over the preposition used here. Some say it should be "in" earth, and others say it should be "on" earth. I think that the word "on" is the truer translation, but I take the point that some theologians make when they say: "The phrase 'in earth' more nearly expresses the meaning than 'on earth' because God's ultimate will is destined to triumph not only over the minds of men, but over the disharmony and dissolution that is inherent in planet earth."

Paul put his finger on this issue when, speaking by the Holy Spirit in the passage before us today, he says: "The whole creation has been groaning." Who can doubt it? Despite the beauty of this glorious creation, everything that lives is subject to decay, disease and death. Life seems strangely poisoned near the fount. The lady who wrote the hymn "All Things Bright and Beautiful" was only looking at some aspects of creation. She was being selective. She wasn't seeing nature "whole." But Paul did! If you place your ear to the ground (I speak metaphorically, of course), you will hear the groan of a creation that is crying out to be delivered from the effects of sin. But be assured of this—there is a day coming when the will of God will impose itself, not only "on" the earth, but "in" the earth, and will restore this sin-affected planet to its original beauty and majesty.

FURTHER STUDY

Ps. 8; Gen. 1:26; Matt. 6:26; 12:12

1. What was God's original purpose?

2. How did Jesus illustrate this?

Prayer

O Father, You originally made the earth as You made me—to reflect Your eternal glory. But sin has spoiled both. I take confidence in the fact that one day everything will be restored, and Your redemption be made known in every part of Your universe. Thank You, Father. Amen.

SECTION THREE

Doing His Will—Now

For reading & meditation—Philippians 2:1–16

"... it is God who is at work within you, giving you the will and the power to achieve his purpose." (v.13, J. B. Phillips)

We said yesterday that theologians are divided about whether the statement of Jesus should be translated "in earth" or "on earth." We decided to examine both prepositions, and today we look at the words "on earth."

Most commentators believe the phrase has reference to the world of human beings who have their home on this earth. In other words—us. Fantastic as it may sound, a day will dawn when this earth will be peopled with those who will do the will of God, not with resentment or resignation, but with rejoicing. That day may not be as far distant as we may think, so we ought to double our efforts in prayer, and joyously become involved in bringing our lives in line with His will. One thing is sure—the more you and I conform to His will, the more quickly can His purposes for this earth be realized.

John Wesley famously said: "God does nothing redemptively in this world except by prayer." Can you see what he is saying? The purposes of God for the future will have to cross the bridge of prayer. This raises the question: how committed are you and I to doing the will of God? Are we hindering or are we promoting the interests of His future kingdom? It is vital that we Christians, both individually and corporately, focus our prayers on this issue with fervency and passion, remembering as we do so that the more abandoned we are to the divine will, the more speedily will His purposes come to pass for the world.

FURTHER STUDY

Matt. 3; John 8:29; 1 Thess. 4:1; Heb. 13:16

1. What was the pronouncement from heaven?

2. Could this be said of your life?

O Father, in the light of this challenge today, I feel like praying: "Thy will be done, on earth in me as it is done in heaven." Grant it, I pray, for the honor and glory of Your peerless Name. Amen.

DAY

157

SECTION THREE

A Change of Focus

For reading & meditation—1 Timothy 2:1–7

"I urge, then, first of all, that … thanksgiving be made …" (v.1)

The Lord's Prayer falls naturally into two divisions: the first focusing upon God, and the second focusing on ourselves. The second part of the prayer has to do with our physical, psychological and spiritual needs. This natural division reinforces the truth we have been seeing, that it is only when God is given His rightful place that we can have the proper perspective towards ourselves. Jesus begins this part of the prayer by encouraging us to petition God for our physical needs: "Give us this day our daily bread."

Some Christians believe that it is inappropriate for most of us who live in the Western hemisphere to use to these words, as our problem is not so much where do we get the next meal, but how do we keep from eating it! In an overfed, overweight society, they say, our prayer ought to be: "Lord, teach us self-discipline, and prevent us from eating more than we need."

At first glance, the phrase which Jesus used—"Give us this day our daily bread"—does seem somewhat inappropriate, at least for those of us who live in Europe or North America. This prayer might be better uttered by the inhabitants of India, Cambodia, or some of the countries in Africa. However, to take that view is to misunderstand the deep truth which Jesus wants us to absorb. He invites us to pray: "Give us this day our daily bread," because when we say these words with sincerity, we build a barrier against ingratitude. All that comes from God must be taken, not for granted, but with gratitude.

FURTHER STUDY

Luke 17:11–19;
Deut. 8:10;
Ps. 100:4; Col. 1:12

1. How did the lepers show ingratitude?
2. List some things for which you can give God thanks.

Prayer

Lord Jesus, You whose every statement is filled with light and meaning, unfold to me this coming week the full meaning of these words: "Give us this day our daily bread." You have reminded me already that I need to accept Your gifts with gratitude. Help me be a more grateful person. In Your Name. Amen.

SECTION THREE

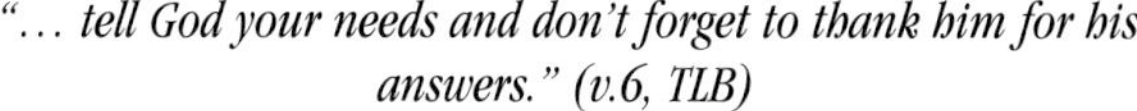

For reading & meditation—Philippians 4:4–9

"... tell God your needs and don't forget to thank him for his answers." (v.6, TLB)

We ended yesterday by saying that one of the reasons why Jesus taught us to pray—"Give us this day our daily bread"—was because He wanted to build in us a barrier against ingratitude.

Do you pray daily for your physical needs? Do you ask God daily for things like food, shelter and the other physical necessities of life? I must confess that when I asked myself that question before writing this page, I had to admit that I did not. Now I have made a decision to apply myself to this part of the Lord's Prayer with greater sincerity.

Of course some people argue that because Jesus said: "Your Father knows what you need before you ask him" (Matt. 6:8), then it is pointless to inform God of our physical needs because He knows them already. But the central value of prayer is that prayer is not something by which we inform God of our needs, and thus influence Him to give things to us. Prayer is designed to influence us—it is we who are in need of this kind of prayer, not God. Of course God knows what we are in need of, but He also knows that unless we come face to face daily with the fact that we are creatures of need, then we can soon develop a spirit of independence, and withdraw ourselves from close contact with Him. Prayer, then, is something we need. God may not need to be told, but we need to tell Him. That's the point. And unless we grasp it, we can miss the primary purpose of prayer.

FURTHER STUDY

Matt. 6:19–34; Ps. 37:5; 118:8; 125:1

1. What should be our attitude to worldly cares?

2. What should be our first priority?

O Father, thank You for showing me that prayer is not begging for boons. It is becoming a boon—to myself. I pray, not to change Your attitude towards me, but to change my attitude towards You. Thank You, Father. Amen.

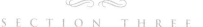

SECTION THREE

Give Thanks to the Lord

For reading & meditation—Psalm 92:1–8

"It is good to praise the Lord ..." (v.1)

We pray because we have a need to tell God Him about our circumstances. To understand the truth of this statement we must ask ourselves: what happens when we neglect to pray for our daily needs and thank God for providing them? If we are honest about it, and examine our lives over a period of time, we will discover a subtle change taking place in our feelings and in our thinking. If we neglect to pray for our needs, we will begin to take the blessings of life for granted, and gradually, without at first realizing it, we will succumb to the senseless notion that we can provide for the necessities of life, and that we are perfectly capable of managing our own affairs, without any help from God.

When we think that way, it is not long before pride steps in, and a kind of spiritual blindness settles upon us—a blindness which blocks our vision in relation to God, ourselves and others. We need, therefore, to constantly remind ourselves that everything we have comes from His hand, and that, at any moment, should He choose to do so, He could turn off the supplies, and we would soon become beggared and bankrupt. The only way, therefore, that we can build a barricade against this awful blight of ingratitude is to pray daily, remembering, as the poet said:

Back of the bread is the snowy flour,
And back of the flour, the mill,
And back of the mill is the field of wheat,
The rain, and the Father's will.

FURTHER STUDY

1 Kings 17; Ps. 23:5; Isa. 41:10; Mal. 3:10

1. How did God test Elijah's faith?
2. How did he respond?

Prayer

O Father, teach me the art of continual thankfulness, and help me never to become bored with acknowledging Your grace and goodness, otherwise life will begin to disintegrate. Help me, Lord Jesus. Amen.

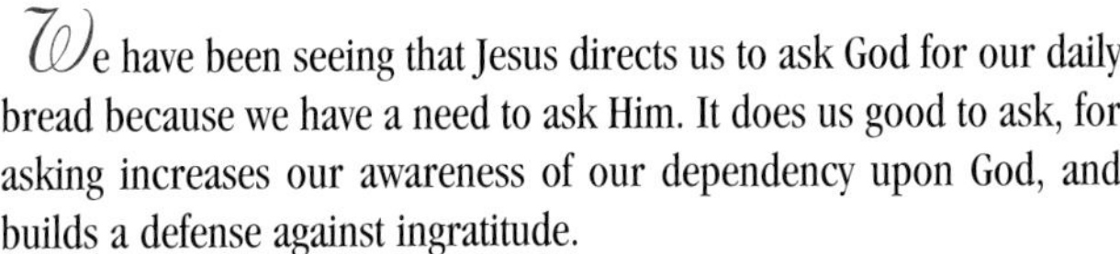

"They Shall Be Satisfied"

DAY 160

For reading & meditation—Psalm 37:1–19

"... in the days of famine they will enjoy plenty." (v.19)

We have been seeing that Jesus directs us to ask God for our daily bread because we have a need to ask Him. It does us good to ask, for asking increases our awareness of our dependency upon God, and builds a defense against ingratitude.

I find it greatly encouraging that the God of creation, who is infinitely holy, and who holds the universe in His hand, cares that my physical needs are met. This implies that God regards our bodies as important. He designed them, and is interested in the way they function. Some Christians regard it as "unspiritual" to pray about the needs of the body, but, as Jesus pointed out, this is really where our personal petitions ought to begin. While Jesus endeavored to get His hearers to keep their values straight, by saying that the spiritual was all important—"Seek first his kingdom" (Matt. 6:33)—He nevertheless put the body in its rightful place, as being a matter of great concern. The Father, we are told, guarantees our physical needs if we seek first the kingdom of God.

Most of the promises in the Bible have to do with spiritual truth, but never to the exclusion of the physical. How much spiritual use would we be to our heavenly Father if He didn't meet our basic physical needs? This is why I do not fear the future. However people might mismanage the resources which God has placed in the earth, I have confidence in the truth of the verse before us today: "in the days of famine they will enjoy plenty."

FURTHER STUDY

John 6:1–15; Ps. 37.25; Joel 2:24; Luke 6:38

1. What was the disciples' attitude?

2. How did Jesus show interest in physical needs?

Prayer

Father, help me not to get bogged down in wrong attitudes about the physical factors of my life, for they are a part of me. Teach me to live, physically and spiritually, as one. For Jesus' sake. Amen.

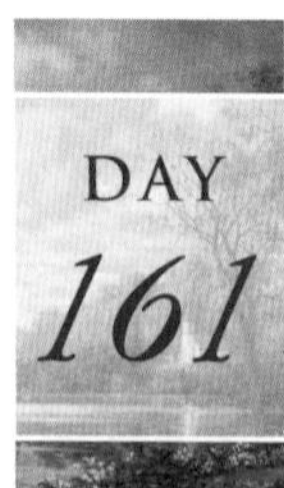

SECTION THREE

God's Pantry

For reading & meditation—Genesis 1:29–31

"Then God said, 'I give you every seed-bearing plant ... They will be yours for food.'" (v.29)

Do we thank God daily for His provision for the physical necessities of life? Some might respond by saying: "But we never eat a meal without saying grace or giving thanks." Ah, but are you really thankful? Do you look up into your Father's face at least once every day, acknowledging that He is the source of everything, and giving Him thanks?

The term *bread* is regarded by most Bible teachers as a broad term for food. Just think for a moment what God has provided in the way of nourishment for His children. He has provided food in the grains of wheat, barley and so on, and, according to Genesis 43:11 and Numbers 11:5, He has provided nuts, vegetables, melons, and a whole host of other things. Keep looking in God's pantry and you will find food plants such as grapes, raisins, olives and apples. In addition to this, there are animals which provide food, such as oxen, sheep and goats, as well as different kinds of fowl. Then there are fish, and according to Leviticus chapter 11, even four types of insects!

How thrilling is His bountiful provision. You and I eat nothing that did not come from the earth, and every element in it is the work of the creative hand of God. Not to recognize that is indeed the height of ingratitude. As the old hymn so aptly puts it:

Its streams the whole creation reach
So plenteous is its store.
Enough for all, enough for each,
Enough forevermore.

Prayer

Father, something is being burned into my consciousness—You are a bountiful and magnanimous God. Keep me awake and alert, day after day, to Your loving concern for my physical and spiritual care. Amen.

FURTHER STUDY

Ex. 16; Gen. 9:3; Ps. 104:14; 136:25; Matt. 6:26

1. What three things did God provide for the Children of Israel?
2. List the things God has provided for you.

SECTION THREE

Pensioners of Providence

For reading & meditation—James 1:12–18

"Every good and perfect gift is from above, coming down from the Father ..." (v.17)

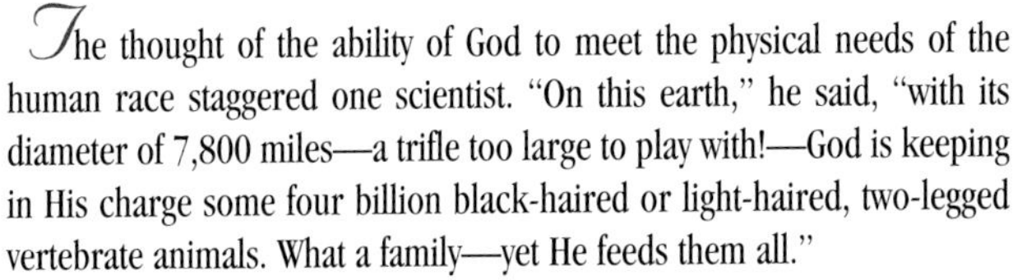

The thought of the ability of God to meet the physical needs of the human race staggered one scientist. "On this earth," he said, "with its diameter of 7,800 miles—a trifle too large to play with!—God is keeping in His charge some four billion black-haired or light-haired, two-legged vertebrate animals. What a family—yet He feeds them all."

There are many difficulties and problems facing us today in relation to economy, but the issue is not really that the earth cannot provide enough food. If there is a failure, it is one of distribution, not in production. The food is there, but it is not properly apportioned. A Prime Minister of India, Mrs. Gandhi, said that there are enough resources in India to feed that nation entirely, and then export two-thirds of what it produces.

How wrong it is to blame God for the fact that thousands of people die of starvation each year. The fault is not in Him, but in us. God has given us His gracious promise: "As long as the earth endures, seedtime and harvest, cold and heat, summer and winter, day and night will never cease" (Gen. 8:22). As Isaac Watts puts it:

Thy providence is kind and large,
Both man and beast Thy bounty share;
The whole creation is Thy charge,
But saints are Thy peculiar care.

Is it not so? Yet how slow we are to pause and reflect that we are, in fact, literally the pensioners of providence!

FURTHER STUDY

Jas. 5; Ex. 23:25; Ps. 81:16; Isa. 30:23

1. What does James say about selfish living?

2. What are we to live in the light of?

Prayer

O Father, when I think of Your bountiful goodness and grace, I find it difficult to express my feelings. I echo the words of the Psalmist: "You open your hand and satisfy the desire of every living thing." For that I am eternally grateful. Amen.

DAY 163

SECTION THREE

Overpopulation—A Myth

For reading & meditation—Psalm 33:1–22

"... the eyes of the Lord are on those who fear him, on those whose hope is in his unfailing love." (v.18)

We must spend one more day in considering the bountiful provision of our great Creator. A modern writer tells how once he asked an old man how he managed to live alone in a single cottage, miles from anywhere. The old man answered cheerfully that he enjoyed it since, as he explained: "Providence is my next-door neighbor."

Despite what many politicians and scientists tell us, the problems of this earth are not physical but spiritual. It is not over-population that requires our attention, but spiritual ignorance. If people came into a knowledge of Jesus Christ as their Lord and Savior, then they would be given the wisdom to use the earth's resources rightly. Murray Norris in his book *The Myth of Overpopulation* says that only fifteen percent of the arable land on the globe is being farmed, and only half of that every year. It goes without saying, of course, that although God supplies the basic necessities, people have to put some effort into harvesting them; but our problem is not lack of resources, nor too many people—it is our lack of dependency upon God.

Paul, in 1 Timothy 4:3, says that God has created all food "to be received with thanksgiving by those who believe and who know the truth." Can you see what this verse is saying? God has provided an incredible abundance of food that we might express our thanks to Him. The rest of the world indulges with little gratitude. Let's make sure that not one day passes without this prayer meaningfully crossing our lips: "Give us this day our daily bread."

FURTHER STUDY

Jas. 2; Rom. 12:11; Prov. 13:11; 2 Thess. 3:10

1. How does James relate faith and works?

2. What is Paul's exhortation?

Prayer

O Father, now that I understand the significance of Your words, "Give us this day our daily bread," help me, every time I utter them, to make them, not just a recitation, but a realization. For Jesus' sake. Amen.

Follow the Pattern

For reading & meditation—Psalm 32:1–11

"Blessed is he whose transgressions are forgiven …" (v.1)

We consider now the second petition of that part of the Lord's Prayer which focuses on us: "And forgive us our trespasses, as we forgive those who trespass against us." I use the word *trespass* in preference to the word *debt* as in our modern society the word *debt* has come to have a monetary significance. The word *trespass* has a wider significance and implies an offense done against another—an intrusion into someone's rights.

This second section of Jesus' pattern of prayer takes in every level of human life: the physical, the psychological and the spiritual. "Give us this day" refers to the physical part of life. "Forgive us our trespasses" has to do with the psychological part of life (the emotions, the thoughts and the will), and "Lead us not into temptation" has to do with the spiritual part of life.

With characteristic accuracy, Jesus puts His finger squarely on the paramount need in human life. If we understand the Lord's Prayer correctly, there is really nothing more to be said when we come to this matter of prayer. This does not mean, of course, that, prayer has to be limited to these statements of Jesus, but it does mean that the issues He deals with, although we can expand upon them, cover the entire gamut of human need, and are the pattern for all adequate and effective praying. When we fail to cover the issues raised in Jesus' pattern of prayer, expanding on them in our own words, we deny ourselves the true power that lies in prayer. Follow the pattern and you find the power.

FURTHER STUDY

Eph. 3; 1:7; Phil. 4:19; Rom. 2:4

1. What is Paul's desire for the Ephesians?

2. What is the "inner being"?

Prayer

O God, in a world torn and fragmented, I need guidance as to how to tap Your resources, and bring Divine Help into my situation. In this matchless model of prayer, You have given it to me. Help me follow it, and discover the power that lies in prayer. For Jesus' sake. Amen.

SECTION THREE

The Biggest Single Problem

For reading & meditation—Psalm 51:1–17

"Create in me a new, clean heart, O God, filled with clean thoughts ... Then I will sing of your forgiveness." (vv.10 & 14, TLB)

Today we begin by asking ourselves a pointed question: What is the biggest single problem which faces us in human life? Some would say ill health; others, lack of money; still others, uncertainty about the future, or fear of dying. My own view is that the biggest single problem with which human beings have to grapple is the problem of guilt. A sense of guilt is the most powerfully destructive force in the personality. We cannot live with guilt, that is, truly live.

When I was a young Christian, I heard some great preaching in my native Wales, most of which focused on how God was able to release us from the guilt of inbred sin. Nowadays, apart from a few exceptions, that message is hardly heard in the pulpits of the Principality, or, for that matter, in many other pulpits. The emphasis ceased to appeal to the modem mind, and so was discarded. However, it is now coming back through the science of psychology. Someone said that the point at which psychology and religion meet is at the point of guilt. Christianity and the social sciences underline what the human heart knows so well—it cannot live comfortably with guilt.

In this simple prayer of Jesus, however, we have an adequate answer: "Forgive us our trespasses, as we forgive those who trespass against us." If we have fully accepted the forgiveness of God, and we know that our sins have been forgiven, then the result is a pervading sense of peace. The human heart cannot be put off by subterfuge: it needs reconciliation, forgiveness, assurance.

FURTHER STUDY

John 8:1–11; Ps. 40:12, 38:4, 73:21

1. What made the Pharisees leave?

2. How did Jesus respond to the woman?

Prayer

O God, my Father, I see that within the ways of men, You have a way—a way that is written into the nature of reality. And that way is a way of forgiveness. May I ever walk in it. For Jesus' sake. Amen.

SECTION THREE

God's Thorn Hedges

For reading & meditation—Romans 3:21–31

"... in his forbearance he had left the sins committed beforehand unpunished." (v.25)

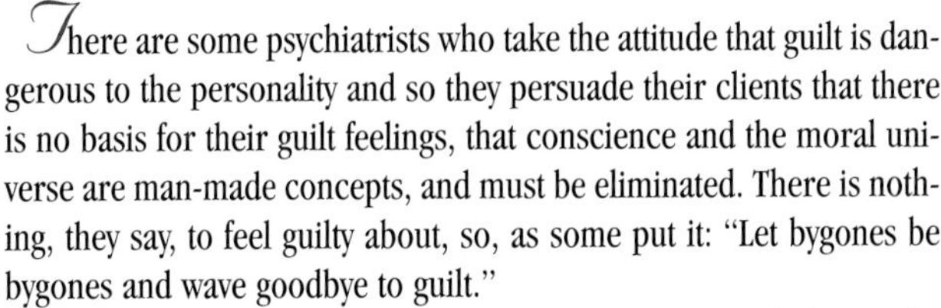

There are some psychiatrists who take the attitude that guilt is dangerous to the personality and so they persuade their clients that there is no basis for their guilt feelings, that conscience and the moral universe are man-made concepts, and must be eliminated. There is nothing, they say, to feel guilty about, so, as some put it: "Let bygones be bygones and wave goodbye to guilt."

It must be acknowledged that some ideas regarding guilt have to be dealt with in that way, for some guilt is false, and needlessly torments many sincere people. However, I am not talking here about false guilt. I am talking about real guilt—the guilt that the human heart carries because it has offended a holy God. You cannot get rid of that by waving your hand and saying: "Let bygones be bygones." Nor can you get away from sin by joking about it. Oscar Wilde said: "The only way to get rid of a temptation is to yield to it." But you do not get rid of temptation by yielding to it. It becomes an act, and then a habit and then part of you.

No, we are hedged in—thorn hedges on either side. The only open door is the mercy of God. And these thorn hedges are His provision, too. They are God's creation enabling us not to live comfortably with evil, for evil is bad for us. God has so arranged the universe that we can only be truly comfortable with that which is good for us. Guilt cannot be banished by subterfuge. Only God can redeem our wickedness.

FURTHER STUDY

Ps. 32; Acts 2:37; Ezra 9:6; John 16:8

1. What was the result of guilt?
2. What did confession produce?

Prayer

O God, I know that although men might be able to help me with my false guilt, only You can help me with real guilt. I bring my guilty heart to You for cleansing, forgiveness and reconciliation. In Jesus' Name. Amen.

DAY 167

SECTION THREE

Nothing Hidden

For reading & meditation—Luke 12:1–7

"There is nothing concealed that will not be disclosed, or hidden that will not be made known." (v.2)

Our text today shows us that no one gets away with anything in this universe. The Moffatt translation puts it thus: "Nothing is hidden that shall not be revealed, or concealed that shall not be made known." It will have to be "revealed" voluntarily, and forgiveness sought, or it will be revealed as an inner complex, conflict or functional disease. In any case, it is "revealed."

The young doctor in A.J. Cronin's book *The Citadel* found his inner problems were revealed. When politics defeated his proposed health measures in a Welsh mining town, he sold his standards for money. After his wife's tragic death, he found in her handbag snapshots of himself taken during his crusading days. It reminded him of the man he might have been. He knew his pain was deserved, and he shouted at himself in a drunken stupor: "You thought you could get away with it. You thought you were getting away with it. But … you weren't."

You cannot get away with guilt, either by waving goodbye to it or by bottling it up within you. It "reveals" itself in your face and in your manner. Lady Macbeth, in Shakespeare's play, said: "What, will these hands ne'er be clean? … All the perfumes of Arabia will not sweeten this little hand." Only the blood of Jesus Christ can erase the stain of guilt upon the human heart. When we pray, "Forgive us our sins," we are asking for the reality that God promises to everyone who asks of Him. And the only way we can fail to experience it, is simply not to ask.

FURTHER STUDY

Dan. 5; Gen. 3:8; 42:21; Heb. 9:14

1. Why did Belshazzar call for Daniel?

2. What was Daniel's pronouncement?

O Father, I am so grateful that when I confess my sins, they are fully and freely forgiven at a stroke. There is no period of moral probation or parole. I ask—and it is done. What clemency! Thank You, dear Father. Thank You. Amen.

SECTION THREE

The Divine Example

For reading & meditation—Luke 23:32–43

"Jesus said, 'Father, forgive them, for they do not know what they are doing.'" (v.34)

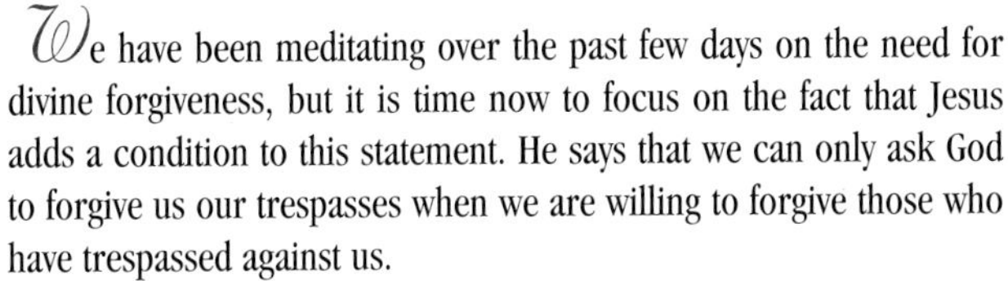

We have been meditating over the past few days on the need for divine forgiveness, but it is time now to focus on the fact that Jesus adds a condition to this statement. He says that we can only ask God to forgive us our trespasses when we are willing to forgive those who have trespassed against us.

Does this mean that before we can be converted to Christ, and have our sins forgiven, we have to search our hearts in order to make sure that we hold no bitterness or resentment against anyone? No. There is nothing in the Scripture that states that a non-Christian receives forgiveness from God on the basis of claiming to forgive everyone else. Jesus is referring here, so I believe, to those who are His followers. They have been forgiven for their sins, but they now need a principle by which they can deal with guilt that arises, subsequent to conversion, through the violation of some biblical standard.

Paul says in Ephesians 1:7: "In him we have redemption through his blood, the forgiveness of sins, in accordance with the riches of God's grace." Grace—that's the basis of our forgiveness when we first come to Christ. But although we have received that forgiveness, we can never enjoy freedom from defilement in our Christian walk unless we are ready to extend the forgiveness God has given us to those who have hurt us. This is an extremely important issue, for if we fail to forgive those who have offended us, we break the bridge over which God's forgiveness flows into us.

FURTHER STUDY

Luke 17:1–10; Mark 11:25; Col. 3:13; Eph. 4:32

1. What did Jesus teach on forgiveness?
2. What was the disciples' response?

Prayer

Blessed Lord Jesus, You who hung upon a Cross, tortured in every nerve, yet prayed, "Father, forgive them," help me this day to forgive all those who have wronged me in a lesser way. For Your own dear Name's sake. Amen.

DAY 169

SECTION THREE

"For Christ's Sake"

For reading & meditation—Ephesians 4:17–32

"Be kind … to one another, forgiving each other, just as in Christ God forgave you." (v.32)

We experience divine forgiveness for our sins only as we extend forgiveness to those who have offended us. That cuts deep.

Perhaps you might be saying at this moment: "But I can't forgive: I have been hurt too deeply." Then, may I say it very tenderly, but very solemnly, you can never, never be forgiven. "But if you do not forgive men their sins," says Jesus, "your Father will not forgive your sins" (Matt. 6:15). In refusing to forgive others (as we emphasized yesterday), you break the bridge over which you yourself must pass.

A man once said to me: "I know I'm a Christian, but someone did such an awful thing to me that I find I can't forgive him." After spending a good deal of time with him, and getting nowhere, I said: "If it is really true that you can't forgive this person, it suggests that you yourself have not been forgiven, and you may be deluding yourself that you are a Christian." He looked at me aghast and went white in the face. My counselling methods are not always as abrupt as that; however, this brought him face to face with reality—and it worked. He got down on his knees, right where he was, and said: "Father, because You have forgiven me, I offer Your forgiveness and my forgiveness to my brother who has offended me, and I absolve him of his offense in Jesus' Name." Then what happened? Instantly the joy of the Lord streamed right into the center of his being, and he laughed and laughed, literally for almost an hour.

FURTHER STUDY

Matt. 18:21–35; 5:7; Luke 6:36; Prov. 3:3

1. How does this parable apply to us?
2. What is the basis of forgiving others?

Prayer

Lord Jesus, You who forgave those who spat in Your face and nailed You to a Cross, help me to open my heart now, and forgive all those who have hurt me. I do it in Your strength and power. Thank You, Lord Jesus. Amen.

Getting to the Root

For reading & meditation—Genesis 41:46–5

"... God has made me forget all my hardship ..." (v.51, RSV)

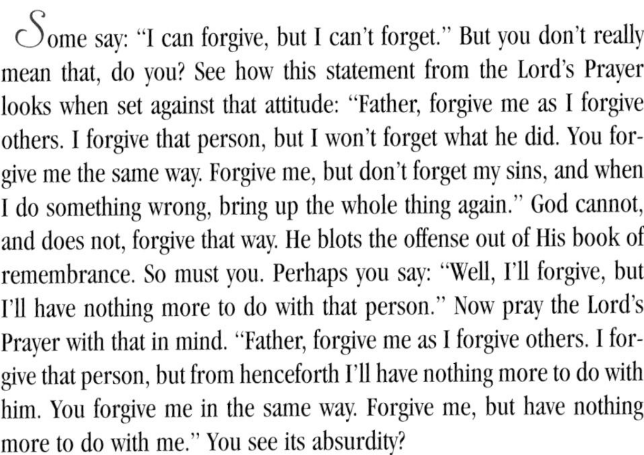

Some say: "I can forgive, but I can't forget." But you don't really mean that, do you? See how this statement from the Lord's Prayer looks when set against that attitude: "Father, forgive me as I forgive others. I forgive that person, but I won't forget what he did. You forgive me the same way. Forgive me, but don't forget my sins, and when I do something wrong, bring up the whole thing again." God cannot, and does not, forgive that way. He blots the offense out of His book of remembrance. So must you. Perhaps you say: "Well, I'll forgive, but I'll have nothing more to do with that person." Now pray the Lord's Prayer with that in mind. "Father, forgive me as I forgive others. I forgive that person, but from henceforth I'll have nothing more to do with him. You forgive me in the same way. Forgive me, but have nothing more to do with me." You see its absurdity?

Don't try to forget things, don't try to smooth them over, and don't drive them into the subconscious. Get them up and out. A woman visited her doctor and asked him to give her a special ointment to smooth over her abscess. When the doctor refused, and said it must be lanced, she left his surgery and went home. In a few days the poison had spread through her system and killed her. Unbelievable? The lady was known to me. I beg you, when facing the issue which is confronting us this week, don't ask for a Band-Aid or a halfway measure. Get it out. Forgive.

FURTHER STUDY

Gen. Ch. 45; Phil. 3:13; Heb. 8:12

1. How did Joseph demonstrate true forgiveness?

2. How did he see God's purposes in what had happened?

Prayer

Heavenly Father, albeit gently and tenderly, You are driving me into a corner. I would escape, but You won't let me. Today, therefore, in Your Name, I forgive all who have hurt or injured me. It's done. In Jesus' Name. Amen.

DAY

171

SECTION THREE

A Knotty Problem

For reading & meditation—James 1:2–18

"... God cannot be tempted by evil, nor does he tempt anyone." (v.13)

We move on now to examine the third petition in that part of the Lord's Prayer which focuses on ourselves: "Lead us not into temptation, but deliver us from evil." The first part of the Lord's Prayer relates, as we saw, to God and His glory. The second part relates to man and his needs. Here, in this third petition relating to our needs, the vital core of human need is touched, as Jesus characteristically puts His finger on the deepest need of the spirit—deliverance and protection.

An immediate problem, however, presents itself in these words, and it is one over which theologians have debated for centuries. The problem is this: if temptation is necessary to our growth (as we grapple—we grow), are we really expected to pray that God will not do what He must do in order to accomplish His work within us? After all, we are told, Jesus was led by the Spirit into the wilderness to be tempted by the devil.

Over the years I have had more letters about this particular issue than probably any other subject. A letter that came recently put the problem like this: "If, as I understand it, the word *temptation* (Greek *peirasmos*) means a test or a trial, why should we pray to be kept from it, particularly as James tells us to 'count it all joy when you fall into temptation?'" You see the difficulty, I am sure. There are a number of interesting answers to this question, which we shall look at over the coming week.

FURTHER STUDY

Matt. 4:1–11; 2 Cor. 2:11; Eph. 6:13; 1 Pet. 1:5–7; 2 Pet. 2:9

1. What is the basis of temptation?
2. How does this become sin?

Prayer

Father, as I come up against this problem, which Your people have debated and discussed for centuries, help me, I pray, to come to clear and certain conclusions. For Jesus' sake. Amen.

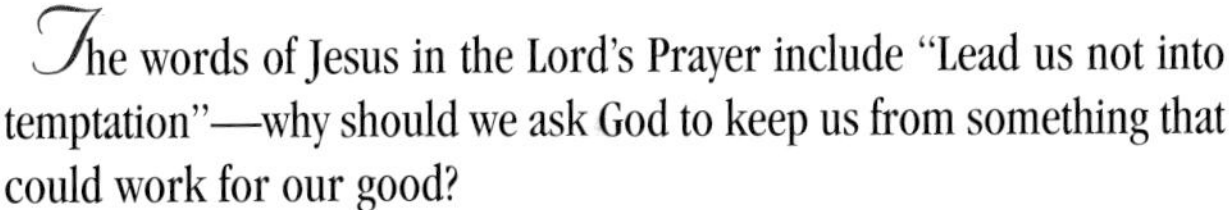

For reading & meditation—Matthew 26:36–54

"Watch and pray so that you will not fall into temptation. . . ." (v.41)

The words of Jesus in the Lord's Prayer include "Lead us not into temptation"—why should we ask God to keep us from something that could work for our good?

One answer to this problem is that Jesus, when using these words, meant not just temptation but unrecognized temptation. The advocates of this interpretation say that when temptation is recognized, it can be resisted, and when it is resisted, it then becomes a source of strength and power in our lives. One writer, who holds to this interpretation, put it this way: "If I am filling out my Income Tax form, and I know that some income has come to me through other than the usual channels, and there is no way of anyone checking it, I am confronted with a temptation to omit it. But I know that is wrong. No one has to tell me. I know it. And when I resist the temptation, I find I am stronger the next time, when an even larger amount may be involved."

There is a good deal of merit in this interpretation, for there is no doubt that evil can be more effectively resisted when it is clearly recognized. Simon Peter is an example of this. Jesus said to him in the garden of Gethsemane: "Watch and pray so that you will not fall into temptation." He did not heed that word, and became involved in a serious act of violence (John 18:10). Peter thought he was doing the right thing, but really his act of violence was due to his inability to recognize what was happening.

FURTHER STUDY

Gen. 3; 1 Thess. 3:5; 2 Cor. 11:3; 2 Pet . 3:17

1. Why did Eve succumb to temptation?

2. What is Paul's warning?

Father, this may not be the precise meaning Your Son had in mind when He gave us these words, but I see that it has some application to life. Help me, therefore, to be alert to every temptation, and give me the spiritual insight to discern it and deal with it in Your strength and power. Amen.

DAY

173

"Lord, Help Me"

For reading & meditation—1 Corinthians 10:1–13

"... God is faithful; he will not let you be tempted beyond what you can bear...." (v.13)

If we pray for the ability to recognize temptation when it comes our way, then we will be able to confront it, and turn it to advantage. Another interpretation of "Lead us not into temptation" is that this is a prayer for us to be kept back from more temptation than we can cope with. It's like saying: "Lord, help us not to get involved in more temptation than we can handle." This interpretation, as I am sure you can see at once, makes good sense, and could well be what Jesus meant.

One of the biographers of an intrepid missionary tells how, in his early days in China, Hudson Taylor met with several great disappointments. One day, after a spate of troubles, he took hold of a guide, who had demanded an outrageous fee from him, and shook him violently. A few hours later, he realized he had denied his Lord by this action, and after searching his heart for the reason why he had succumbed to anger and violence, he realized that he had been so preoccupied with his problems that he had failed to commit his ways to the Lord. His biographer says: "If Hudson Taylor had prayed the prayer, 'Lead us not into temptation,' and committed his ways to the Lord, then perhaps the Spirit would have been able to direct his path so that he would not have faced more temptation than he could bear." It is an intriguing thought. But is it the fullest meaning of Jesus' words? Possibly—but, as we shall see tomorrow, I think it means much more.

FURTHER STUDY

Acts 5:1–11;
Prov. 1:10; 4:14;
Rom. 6:13

1. Why did Ananias and Sapphira yield to temptation?

2. What is Paul's antidote?

Prayer

Father, though the meaning of this phrase is not yet clear, one thing is—I need Your help at every stage of my earthly pilgrimage, for I cannot face temptation alone. So stay with me—every day and every hour. For Jesus' sake. Amen.

SECTION THREE

God's Safety Valve

For reading & meditation—Hebrews 2:5–18

"Because he himself suffered when he was tempted, he is able to help those who are being tempted." (v.18)

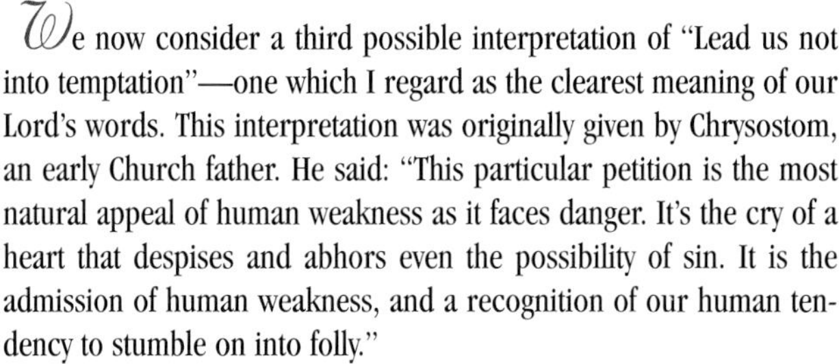

We now consider a third possible interpretation of "Lead us not into temptation"—one which I regard as the clearest meaning of our Lord's words. This interpretation was originally given by Chrysostom, an early Church father. He said: "This particular petition is the most natural appeal of human weakness as it faces danger. It's the cry of a heart that despises and abhors even the possibility of sin. It is the admission of human weakness, and a recognition of our human tendency to stumble on into folly."

Perhaps, in order to see these words of Chrysostom in a clear light, we need to set them against our Lord's experience in the garden of Gethsemane. He prayed "My Father, if it is possible, may this cup be taken from me" (Matt. 26:39). Jesus knew that the only way to accomplish redemption for the human race was by way of the cross. Nevertheless, because He was human as well as divine, He gave expression to His humanity, even though, as the writer to the Hebrews said, He endured the cross for the joy that was set before Him (Heb.12:2).

You see, even though Jesus knew that the cross had to be experienced in all its horror and torment, if men and women were to be redeemed, He still gave expression to His human feelings of dread and apprehension. Jesus did not feel guilty about this demonstration of His humanity, neither was God disappointed by His words: "My Father, if it is possible, may this cup be taken from me." The expression of our human weakness is a necessary part of prayer.

FURTHER STUDY

Phil. 2:1–11; Rom. 8:3; Heb. 4:15; 2 Cor. 12:9

1. What is revealed through Christ's humanity?

2. How is this a strength to us?

Prayer

Father, I think I am beginning to see. These words are the safety valve, built into prayer, which enable me to express my weakness and my true feelings. I am so thankful. Amen.

DAY

175

SECTION THREE

"Emotional—Not Cognitive"

For reading & meditation—Hebrews 4:12–16

"For we do not have a high priest who is unable to sympathize with our weaknesses ..." (v.15)

We continue examining "Lead us not into temptation, but deliver us from evil." Yesterday we touched on the fact that one explanation of these words might be that Jesus was providing a framework through which we could express our feelings of weakness, when faced with the possibility of temptation.

One writer says of the words "Lead us not into temptation"—"They can only be properly understood when they are seen, not as cognitive (mental) but emotional." He meant that this statement of Jesus is something that appeals to the heart. It is as if Jesus were saying: "Even though your mind understands that as you face temptation and overcome it, you become stronger in God, there is still a part of you—your emotions—that feels it would rather not face the pressures. I understand this. I have been in that situation myself. So I will provide a prayer framework for you that will enable you to express, not so much your thoughts, but your feelings. It will be an admission of your feelings of weakness, but it will also be a release, for if your fears are not expressed, they will be repressed, and will go 'underground' to cause trouble. So these words will provide you with what you need—an opportunity to give vent to your inner feelings of reluctance at facing temptation."

The more I ponder this, the more grateful I am to God for recognizing that I am not just an intellectual being but an emotional being, and for building into His pattern of prayer a safety valve that lets me express my inner feelings.

FURTHER STUDY

1 Cor. 10:1–13; Luke 22:31–32; Rom. 16:20; Heb. 7:25

1. What is the way of escape?

2. How can temptation be turned to good?

Prayer

O Father, what can I say? You think of everything. I am overwhelmed with the compassion that You show me, even when attempting to bring me to a higher level of prayer. Amen.

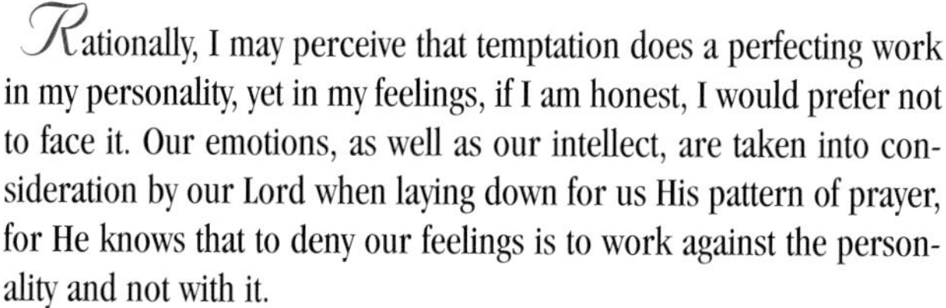

Acknowledge Your Feelings

DAY 176

For reading & meditation—Psalm 42:1–11

"Why are you downcast, O my soul? Why so disturbed within me? . . ." (v.5)

Rationally, I may perceive that temptation does a perfecting work in my personality, yet in my feelings, if I am honest, I would prefer not to face it. Our emotions, as well as our intellect, are taken into consideration by our Lord when laying down for us His pattern of prayer, for He knows that to deny our feelings is to work against the personality and not with it.

Psychologists tell us that the denial of feelings is the first step toward a nervous breakdown. Negative feelings must be handled carefully, for if repressed they are like the Chinese pirates of the past, who used to hide in the hold of a vessel and then rise up when the ship was out on the open sea in order to attempt to capture and possess it. Then there was a fight.

One of the most helpful insights I have found in my study of human personality is the fact that we don't have to act on our negative feelings, but we do have to acknowledge them. If we say with our minds: "Come on, temptation, I'm ready for you," and deny the fact that our emotions feel differently, then this pretense, that the feelings are not there, invites trouble into the personality. When, however, we acknowledge the feelings and admit they are there, we rob them of their power to hurt us. I see this psychological mechanism wonderfully catered for in the words of Jesus which we are considering. They are the framework in which our feelings can have a vote also. Thus, though not acted upon, they are not denied.

FURTHER STUDY

1 Kings 19;
Pss. 28:7; 40:17;
Isa. 41:10

1. How was Elijah able to express his feelings?

2. How did God respond?

Prayer

O Father, how can I thank You enough for taking into consideration every part of my personality in this exciting pattern of prayer? I am so thankful. Amen.

SECTION THREE

Evil Is Bad for Us

For reading & meditation—Romans 12:9–21

"Love must be sincere. Hate what is evil; cling to what is good." (v.9)

Today, in considering the words "Lead us not into temptation, but deliver us from evil," we concentrate on "deliver us from evil." Notice it is not a prayer for deliverance from this or that type of evil, but from evil itself. To Jesus, evil was evil in whatever form it came—whether in the evil of the flesh, the evil of the disposition, whether in the individual will or in the corporate will. Evil was never good, and good was never evil.

Someone has pointed out that the word *evil* is the word *live* spelled backwards. Evil, then, could be said to be anti-life. Non-Christians are finding out how not to live the hard way. They think they know better than God, and follow a way of their own choosing, only to find, like the rats in the scientific experiments who go down the wrong path, that there are wires at the end which carry electric shocks. These shocks are of various kinds: neuroses, inner conflicts, as well as some forms of physical illness.

Society is concerned about a new disease called sexual herpes which apparently comes about through sexual permissiveness. God has made it impossible for us to live against His design or harm ourselves without His protest. And He protests because He loves us. We can decide to have done with evil. The best way to deal with evil is to keep away from it, hence the prayer "Lead us not into temptation, but deliver us from evil." I say again, evil is bad for us, and good is good for us.

FURTHER STUDY

Gen. 39; 1 Cor. 10:6; 1 Thess. 5:22; 1 Pet. 3:11; 2 Tim. 2:22

1. How did Joseph resist temptation?
2. What did Paul advise Timothy?

My Father, You who made me for good, because goodness is good for me, help me to abstain, not only from evil, but from the very appearance of it. For Your own dear Name's sake. Amen.

The Doxology

For reading & meditation—Revelation 11:15–19

"... The kingdom of the world has become the kingdom of our Lord and of his Christ ..." (v.15)

We come now to the final section of the Lord's Prayer: "For thine is the kingdom and the power and the glory, forever. Amen."

This part of Jesus' pattern of prayer—a doxology—is so beautiful that it somehow seems almost irreverent to try to dissect it. Some believe that Jesus did not actually say these words. They claim that they were added by someone else at a later date, which is why they are not included in some versions of the Bible. Some manuscripts have it, and some do not. I have looked long at the evidence for and against their inclusion in the sacred Scriptures, and I am perfectly satisfied myself that they were part of Jesus' original pattern of prayer.

The prayer ends, as it begins, with an assertion of God's majesty and glory "Thine is the kingdom." I believe that the emphasis here should be placed on the word *is*—"Thine *is* the kingdom"—now. Despite all appearances to the contrary, God has never abdicated His position as ruler of the universe. What a heartening thought that is in these days, a thought to fill the soul with song and flood the heart with hope and gladness. It is true that there are many things in the world that militate against His authority—war, poverty, unemployment, drink, gambling, social impurity, and so on. All these seem a flat and final refutation of the phrase "Thine is the kingdom," but their days are numbered. The hour will come when the kingdoms of this world will signal their final surrender and pledge their allegiance to their rightful Lord.

FURTHER STUDY

Matt. 4:1–11; Obad. 21; Heb. 12:28; 2 Pet. 1:11

1. Why was Satan's temptation foolish?

2. How did Jesus respond?

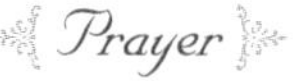

O Father, help me to see, despite all the situations and circumstances which might deny Your eternal Kingship, that You are reigning over the world now. Yours is the final control. I am so thankful. Amen.

DAY

179

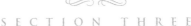

SECTION THREE

"Their Days Are Numbered"

For reading & meditation—2 Thessalonians 2:1–12

"… the lawless one will be revealed, whom the Lord Jesus will … destroy by the splendour of his coming." (v.8)

We continue meditating on the final words of the Lord's Prayer. We said yesterday that, despite all evidences to the contrary, God is in charge of the world's affairs, and that the days of the rebellious kingdoms on earth are numbered. Our God reigns! The "power and the glory" spoken of here are kingdom power and glory. The other type of power and glory, that which is measured by earthly standards alone,and rejected by Jesus in His temptation in the wilderness, is doomed to dissolution and decay.

Ezekiel the prophet, speaking centuries ago of the impermanence of anything not founded on kingdom values, said: "Your doom appears; your sin has blossomed, your pride has budded" (Ezek. 7:10, Moffatt). Note the steps: doom appears, sin blossoms, and pride has budded. And the fruit of all this? Dissolution and decay.

I have spoken before of my fondness for Moffatt's translation, despite his astonishing liberties with some texts, but I know of nothing that excites me more than his translation of 2 Thessalonians 2:3. When speaking of a prominent figure, who will arise in the last days and challenge the authority of God's kingdom, he refers to him as "the Lawless One, the doomed One." Those who are lawless, who break the laws of God's kingdom, which are written into the very nature of things, are doomed. Perhaps not today, nor tomorrow, but inevitably anything that is against God's kingdom is destined to destruction. It carries within itself the seeds of its own dissolution and decay.

FURTHER STUDY

Eph. 6:10–18; John 12:30–31; Heb. 2:14; 1 John 3:8

1. What is Paul's exhortation?

2. How can we take dominion?

Gracious Father, I have looked upon the kingdom of the world until my eyes are tired—tired of looking at death. Now lift up my eyes, and let me look at Life—let me look upon You. And I see You, not as a reclining God, but a reigning God. Hallelujah!

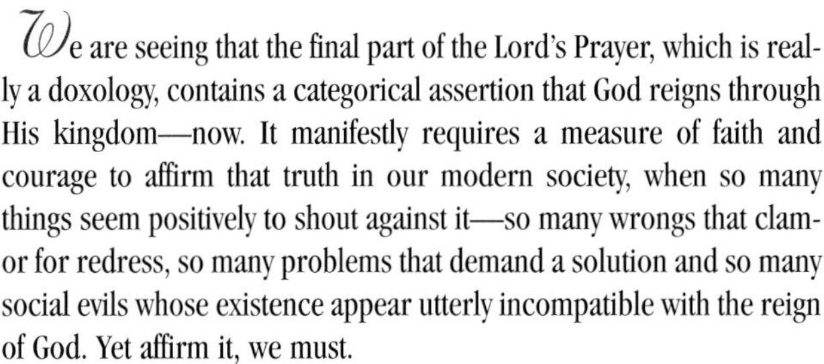

SECTION THREE

He Reigns—NOW

For reading & meditation—Romans 11:33–36

"... To him be the glory forever! Amen." (v.36)

We are seeing that the final part of the Lord's Prayer, which is really a doxology, contains a categorical assertion that God reigns through His kingdom—now. It manifestly requires a measure of faith and courage to affirm that truth in our modern society, when so many things seem positively to shout against it—so many wrongs that clamor for redress, so many problems that demand a solution and so many social evils whose existence appear utterly incompatible with the reign of God. Yet affirm it, we must.

A dear Christian in a letter to me some time ago said, "I look around the world and am appalled. My only comfort is the hymn 'Jesus Shall Reign Where'er the Sun.' I, therefore, sit back and watch and wait the day." I told her that her letter reminded me of some words I heard someone put together in a conference once:

Sit down, O men of God!
His kingdom He will bring,
Whenever it shall please His will.
You need not do a thing!

In my reply I said, "Yes, it's true that one day the kingdom of God shall 'stretch from shore to shore,' but let us not ignore the fact that God is reigning now. Given our cooperation, the Almighty can greatly affect the world through our committed lives. If we fail to see this, then it is possible that we struggle and stumble through life, waiting for Him, while all the time He is waiting for us."

FURTHER STUDY

Rev. 7:9–17; Exod. 24:17; 40:34; Ps. 19:1; John 1:14

1. How can we behold His glory?

2. How is our vision of God enlarged?

Prayer

O God, deliver me from a view of life that says, "Look what the world is coming to." Help me to look at You; then I can say; "Look what has come to the world." Thank You, Father. Amen.

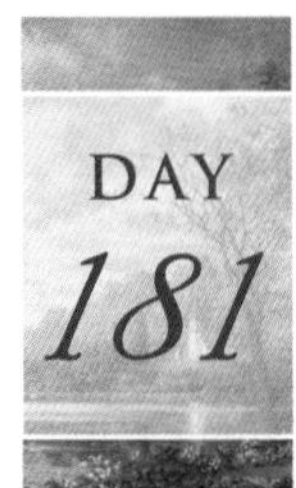

DAY 181

SECTION THREE

"Rise Up, O Men of God"

For reading & meditation—Psalm 93:1–5

"The LORD reigns ..." (v.1)

Although the fullness of God's kingdom is yet to come, there is a sense in which the King is reigning now, and we can say with the utmost certainty, "Our God reigns!"

Yesterday I mentioned a lady who had written to me, indicating her intention to withdraw from life and await the day when God would finally establish His kingdom in power and glory on the earth. I replied with a parody of a hymn that apparently got her thinking. She wrote back in a few weeks and said, "You were right. I was waiting for God, but now I realize He is waiting for me." She ended her letter with the words of the hymn:

Rise up, O men of God!
Have done with lesser things;
Give heart and soul and mind and strength
To serve the King of kings.

This, not the parody I referred to yesterday, must indicate our line of action. Yes, of course, the final ushering in of God's kingdom is yet to take place, but that does not mean that He is taking a back seat in the world's affairs. God wants to reign through us! We need not wait for the day when spectacularly the great God of the universe demonstrates His imperial power. As through these pages, He sounds forth a rallying cry, respond to it, I urge you, with a fresh consecration of purpose, and dedicate yourself to letting Him reign through you.

FURTHER STUDY

Rom. 13:1–14; 2 Cor. 10:4; 1 Tim. 1:18; 6:12; 2 Tim. 2:4

1. How can we overcome the works of darkness?

2. What was Paul's exhortation to Timothy?

Prayer

My God, I see everything clearly. I give myself wholly to You, not only just to live in me, but to reign through me. I gladly submit my whole being to You today. Live and reign in me. For Jesus' sake. Amen.

SECTION THREE

"Follow the King"

DAY 182

For reading & meditation—Psalm 96:1–13

"Say among the nations, 'The Lord reigns,' . . ." (v.10)

We have been saying that when Jesus said, "For thine is the kingdom and the power and the glory, forever. Amen"—it must be seen as an assertion of God's kingly rule—now. The Almighty has never abdicated His throne. He rules—and our task, as His followers, is to affirm this in our attitudes, behavior, and daily living.

On this penultimate day of focusing on the Lord's Prayer, we ask ourselves: what practical steps can we take to substantiate our assertion that God reigns now? Out of many possibilities, let me just focus on two.

We can do it by our lips. Even though so many ugly and obtrusive facts seem to militate against the truth, we must tell men and women that, behind the disordered events of this age, God is at work. We can do it also by our lives. The greatest contribution we can make individually to the world at this present time is to demonstrate, by our lives, that the King of heaven is reigning in us. High-principled, sacrificial and serviceable living is an irrefutable argument for the fact of God's rulership in the world. Tennyson put it in these words:

Follow the Christ—the King!
Live pure! Speak true! Right wrong!
Follow the King! Else wherefore born?

The best guarantee we can give to a sceptical world that "blessings abound where'er He reigns" is that those eminently desirable results have actually been achieved in our own lives.

Prayer

My Father and my God, I want to be at my very best for You. This business of being a Christian is a serious business and needs all my powers at their best. I offer them to You. May others see You ruling and reigning in me. For Jesus' sake. Amen.

FURTHER STUDY

Rev. 19:1–10; Exod. 15:18; 2 Chron. 20:6; Ps. 24:10

1. What was the great multitude proclaiming?
2. What did it sound like?

SECTION THREE

We Give—He Gives

For reading & meditation—Ephesians 4:17–32

"... put on the new self, created to be like God ..." (v.24)

We have now examined phrase by phrase the matchless words of the Lord's Prayer. To be effective, prayer must flow out of a truly committed heart: it must be the definition of our spirit, our attitude to God.

An unknown author put it this way: "I cannot say 'our' if I live only for myself. I cannot say 'Father' if I do not try to act like His child. I cannot say 'who art in heaven' if I am laying up no treasure there. I cannot say 'hallowed be thy name' if I am not striving for holiness. I cannot say 'Thy kingdom come' if I am not doing all in my power to hasten that event. I cannot say 'give us this day our daily bread' if I am dishonest, or seeking something for nothing. I cannot say 'forgive us our trespasses' if I bear a grudge against another. I cannot say 'lead us not into temptation' if I deliberately place myself in its path. I cannot say 'deliver us from evil' if I do not put on the armor of God. I cannot say 'thine is the kingdom and the power and the glory' if I do not give the King the loyalty due to Him from a faithful subject. And I cannot say 'forever' if the horizon of my life is bounded completely by time." The whole thrust of the Lord's Prayer is that when we give God His rightful place, He gives us our rightful place. But not before.

FURTHER STUDY

Mark 6:45–56; 1:35;
Luke 11:1; 5:16;
6:12

1. What was the pattern of Christ's life?
2. What was the disciples' request? Make it yours today.

Father, thank you for sharing with me the insights of this prayer. May I bring my praying more in line with Your praying. For Jesus' sake. Amen!

SECTION FOUR

The Armor of God

The Armor of God

"Whether or not you believe in the devil, he most certainly believes in you."

Selwyn Hughes doesn't pull any punches when it comes to reminding us that we need to put on the whole armor of God. The reality of spiritual warfare demands that we make our hearts and minds into a fortress against evil. This section of *Treasure for the Heart* explores Paul's admonition to the church at Ephesus to prepare for the onslaught from enemies of God by protecting themselves with the spiritual weapons at their disposal.

The warlike imagery is none too strong. From the earliest chapters of the Bible, stories of battle fill the Scriptures. As early as the fourth chapter of Genesis, Adam and Eve's son Cain murders his brother Abel. Conflict — both physical and spiritual — is everywhere from then on. Even the helpless infant Jesus had to be hidden away to avoid being slaughtered by a powerful king. Early churches and missions were as much fortresses as they were places of worship, their high towers and thick walls protecting local residents from danger as they sheltered them during services.

Throughout history, the power of God has been challenged at every turn, and the forces of evil will continue to oppose His divine will physically and spiritually. If we stand there helpless, we can never hope to preserve and share the Word with a world that desperately needs it. In God's wisdom He has given us everything we need to repel attacks on our own spiritual fortress — truth, salvation, righteousness, and all the rest. Take them up, put them on, and be strong in the Lord!

The painting introducing this section is titled *Sharing the Faith*, and it has a special place in Larry Dyke's heart. Though the mission building is based on eighteenth-century Spanish colonial architecture, the face of the figure on the left is one many modern viewers will recognize: Pope John Paul II. It was Larry's privilege to present this painting to the Pope. It hangs today in the Vatican.

L.G.G.

A Call to Arms

For reading & meditation—Ephesians 6:10–13

"For our struggle is not against flesh and blood . . ." (v.12)

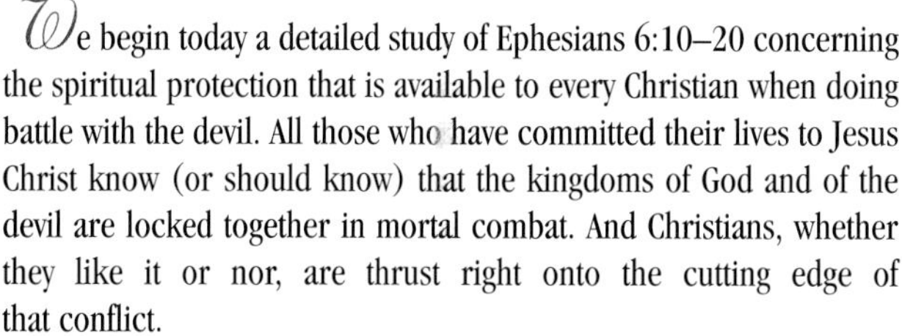

We begin today a detailed study of Ephesians 6:10–20 concerning the spiritual protection that is available to every Christian when doing battle with the devil. All those who have committed their lives to Jesus Christ know (or should know) that the kingdoms of God and of the devil are locked together in mortal combat. And Christians, whether they like it or nor, are thrust right onto the cutting edge of that conflict.

Many Christians are pacifists when it comes to the matter of earthly warfare, but no one can be a pacifist when it comes to the matter of spiritual warfare. Once we enlist in the army of God, we are then expected to train in the art of offensive and defensive spiritual warfare. At certain times and occasions in the Christian life, we find ourselves in a battle that demands fierce hand-to-hand combat with the forces of darkness, and unless we know how to handle these situations, we shall easily be overthrown.

The Bible shows us that the devil and his minions are bitter enemies of God, but because they are powerless against the Almighty, they turn their concentrated attention on those who are His followers—you and me. Did you notice how many times in the passage before us today the word *against* appears? It occurs six times in all, showing that when anyone comes over to the side of Jesus Christ, they are immediately identified as being for God and against the devil. There can be no compromise on this issue, no peaceful co-existence pact. To be for God is to be against the devil.

FURTHER STUDY

2 Cor. 10:1–5;
1 Tim. 1:18; 6:12

1. What does Paul say about our weapons of warfare?

2. What was Paul's charge to Timothy?

Prayer

Gracious and loving Father, help me get my perspectives clear. Train me in the art of spiritual warfare so that I will be able to resist every onslaught of the devil and come through every conflict victoriously. In Jesus' Name. Amen.

DAY 185

SECTION FOUR

Is There a Personal Devil?

For reading & meditation—John 8:36–44

"… He was a murderer from the beginning …" (v.44)

Surprising as it may sound, some Christians do not believe in a personal devil. A modern-day theologian writes: "Let us put to sleep this idea of a personal devil who walks about with a pitchfork seeking to tumble people into hell. Evil is not a personality but an influence—it is just the darkness where the light ought to be."

While I agree that the picture of a personal devil walking about with a pitchfork and with horns and a tail is not to be found anywhere in Scripture, the concept of a personal devil is found everywhere in Scripture. One evidence of this is the fact that many of the names given to him denote personality: Satan, deceiver, liar, murderer, accuser, tempter, prince of the power of the air, and so on. Listen to what someone has written on this subject:

Men don't believe in the devil now, as their fathers used to do,
They reject one creed because it's old, for another because it's new,
But who dogs the steps of the toiling saint, who spreads the net for his feet,
Who sows the tares in the world's broad fields where the Savior sows His wheat?
They may say the devil has never lived, they may say the devil has gone,
But simple people would like to know—who carries his business on?

Take it from me, whether or not you believe in the devil, he most certainly believes in you.

FURTHER STUDY

2 Cor. 11:1–14; 1 Thess. 3:5; 1 Pet. 5:8; Rev. 12:10

1. What are some of the guises in which Satan comes to us?
2. How does Peter describe him?

Prayer

Father, help me see that it is to Satan's advantage for me not to believe in him. Then he can do his evil work unresisted. Over these coming weeks, unfold to me the strategies I need to overcome him. In Christ's Name I ask it. Amen.

SECTION FOUR

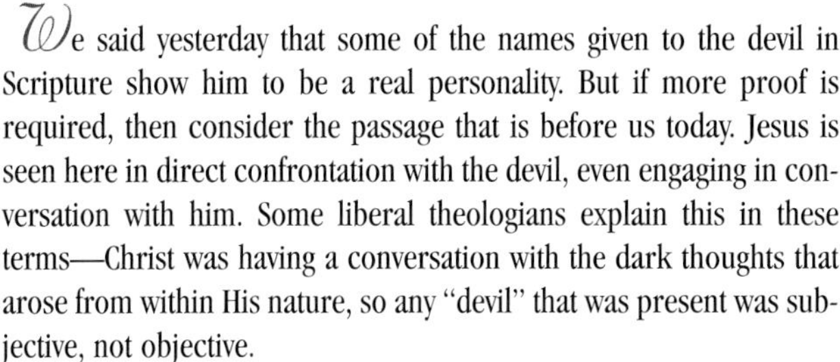

Satan—an Influence or an Intelligence?

For reading & meditation—Matthew 4:1–11

"Jesus said to him, 'Away from me, Satan! For it is written …'" (v.10)

We said yesterday that some of the names given to the devil in Scripture show him to be a real personality. But if more proof is required, then consider the passage that is before us today. Jesus is seen here in direct confrontation with the devil, even engaging in conversation with him. Some liberal theologians explain this in these terms—Christ was having a conversation with the dark thoughts that arose from within His nature, so any "devil" that was present was subjective, not objective.

If we allow that Christ had dark thoughts within His nature, then the whole scheme of redemption tumbles like a pack of cards, for a Savior who is not perfect could never fully atone for our sins. As Dr. Handley Moule puts it: "A Savior who is not perfect is like a bridge broken at one end and is not a reliable passage of access." Once we try to get around Scripture, we create endless difficulties for ourselves and finish up looking foolish. Far better to accept the Bible as it stands and believe its testimony on everything.

Actually it is to Satan's advantage to get us to believe that he is not a personal being, for if there is no personal devil, there can be no personal resistance. Don't allow yourself to be deceived into thinking that the term *devil* is a synonym for the evil influence that is in the world. The devil is more than an evil influence; he is an evil intelligence. Only when we recognize this fact will we be motivated to take effective steps to resist him.

FURTHER STUDY

1 John 3:1–8; Heb. 2:14; John 12:30–31

1. Why was Jesus made manifest?

2. What did He declare?

Prayer

Father, help me see that the first step in spiritual warfare is to "know the enemy." For until I know and understand my enemy, I will not be able to defeat him. Deepen my knowledge of these important truths, I pray. In Jesus' Name. Amen.

"Who Cleft the Devil's Foot?"

For reading & meditation—Isaiah 14:9–15 & Ezekiel 28:11–19

"You said in your heart ... 'I will make myself like the Most High.'" (Isa. 14:13–14)

New Christians often ask: just who is the devil, and where did he come from? The 17th-century poet John Donne wrote that there were two things he could not fathom: "Where all the past years are, and who cleft the devil's foot." The origin, existence, and activities of the devil have always been among man's most puzzling problems. The books of Isaiah and Ezekiel give us a very clear picture, however, of what someone has called "The Rise and Fall of the Satanic Empire."

Jesus said one day to His disciples: "I saw Satan falling from heaven as a flash of lightning" (Luke 10:18, TLB). Before he was known as the devil, Satan was called Lucifer and was created as a perfect angelic being. The passages before us today show him to have been a beautiful and morally perfect being. "You were the perfection of wisdom and beauty ... perfect in all you did from the day you were created" (Ezek. 28:12, 15, TLB).

Upright, beautiful, brilliant and with an enormous capacity for achievement, God entrusted Lucifer with the highest of all the offices in the interstellar universe: "You were anointed as a guardian cherub ... You were on the holy mount of God" (Ezek. 28:14). In his heart, however, arose a rebellious thought: "I will be like the Most High" (Isaiah 14:14 NKJV). Five times that phrase "I will" is used in this passage. Those two little words "I will," reveal what lies behind the awful blight of sin—a created will coming into conflict with the will of the Creator.

FURTHER STUDY

Prov. 16:1–18; 26:12; 3:7

1. What comes before a fall?

2. What attitude should we guard against?

Prayer

O Father, now that I see the real issue that lies behind sin—a created will colliding with the will of the Creator—help me constantly to align my will with Your will. In Jesus' Name I ask it. Amen.

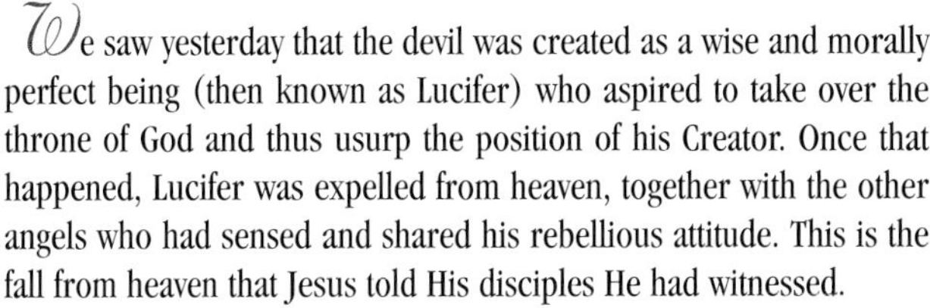

The Strength of Satanic Forces

For reading & meditation—Jude verses 1–13

"... angels who did not keep their positions of authority ... he has kept in darkness, bound with everlasting chains ..." (v.6)

We saw yesterday that the devil was created as a wise and morally perfect being (then known as Lucifer) who aspired to take over the throne of God and thus usurp the position of his Creator. Once that happened, Lucifer was expelled from heaven, together with the other angels who had sensed and shared his rebellious attitude. This is the fall from heaven that Jesus told His disciples He had witnessed.

Since his fall from heaven, Satan, apparently losing little of his administrative skill, has marshaled these fallen angels (now known as demons) into a hostile force to work against God and His creation. We do not know just how many angels fell with Satan, but doubtless it must have been a colossal number. Once when Jesus asked a demonic: "What is your name?" (Luke 8:30), the demons answered: "Legion." If they were telling the truth, the man was controlled by thousands of demons. A Roman legion contained 6,000 men!

It is little wonder, then, that the apostle Paul warned the Ephesians that they were involved in a tremendous spiritual conflict: "We are not fighting against people made of flesh and blood, but against persons without bodies—the evil rulers of the unseen world, those mighty satanic beings and great evil princes of darkness who rule this world" (Eph. 6:12, TLB). Is it any wonder our world is in the mess it is today? One of America's founding fathers said: "If men will not be governed by God, then they will be ruled by tyrants." How sad that people actually choose to be governed by Satan rather than by God.

FURTHER STUDY

Luke 10:1–19; Ps. 44:5; Rom. 8:31

1. What event did Jesus witness?

2. What power did He give to His disciples?

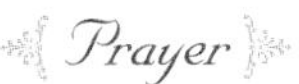

Prayer

O God my Father, I am so thankful that I have left the tyranny and rule of Satan to come under the sway of Your eternal and everlasting kingdom. May I come more and more under its sway hour by hour and day by day. In Jesus' Name I pray. Amen.

SECTION FOUR

"The Second Coming of Satan"

For reading & meditation—1 Timothy 4:1–16

"... in later times some will abandon the faith and follow deceiving spirits and things taught by demons." (v.1)

If we are to be effective in the art of spiritual warfare, then we must see that mankind's fiercest foe is not death or disease, but the diabolical deceiver we know as the devil. He is behind all our individual woes and international wars. He is the one who instigates all our crime and violence. He writes the script for human sorrow, sickness, and death. That is not to say that mankind does not bear some responsibility for the things I mention, but the motivation for these things springs directly from the devil. And there are signs that the devil's mission is heating up—just as our text for today predicted it would.

I think it is safe to say that in this generation, the devil is getting more exposure than ever before. Not so many years ago, *The Exorcist* broke all box office records, grossing over 150 million dollars. It was followed by a spate of films on the subject of the paranormal—*The Omen*, *The Antichrist* and many others—so much so that someone has described this age as the Second Coming of Satan.

In songs, in art, in the theatre, Satan is making his presence felt in a new and powerful way. The so-called science of parapsychology has given him admittance to the halls of academia. How sad that some universities offer courses on Satanism but bar any reference to the teachings of Jesus Christ. The devil is on the march. But don't let that thought trouble you too deeply, for the Scripture shows it to be a march to oblivion (Rev. 20:10).

FURTHER STUDY

Job 1, 2 & 42

1. Who was the source of Job's troubles?

2. What was the final outcome?

Prayer

O God, I am so grateful for the assurances of Scripture. They come to me at the moment I most need them and hold me fast when the strongest currents threaten to sweep me away from my spiritual moorings. Thank You, dear Father. Amen.

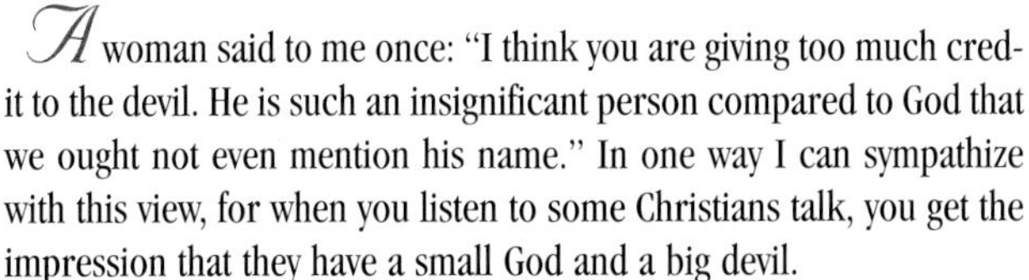

Danger—the Devil at Work

For reading & meditation—1 Peter 5:1–11

"... Your enemy the devil prowls around like a roaring lion ..." (v.8)

A woman said to me once: "I think you are giving too much credit to the devil. He is such an insignificant person compared to God that we ought not even mention his name." In one way I can sympathize with this view, for when you listen to some Christians talk, you get the impression that they have a small God and a big devil.

However, it would be unrealistic to think that we can go through life without coming into direct contact with Satan and his forces. And what is more unrealistic is to think that many (not all) of the problems which confront us day by day have no devilish strategy behind them. Satan is responsible for more of our troubles than we may believe. The late Dr. Martyn Lloyd-Jones said: "I am certain that one of the main causes of the ill state of the church today is the fact that the devil is being forgotten ... we have become so psychological in our attitude and thinking. We are ignorant of this great objective fact—the being, the existence of the devil, the adversary, the accuser and his fiery darts."

Does the thought of doing battle with the devil frighten you? Then heed the words of Corrie ten Boom who said: "The fear of the devil is most likely from the devil himself." God has given us all the protection we need to defend ourselves against the attacks of Satan, and when we know how to avail ourselves of this protection, we will no longer be afraid of the devil—rather, he will be afraid of us.

FURTHER STUDY

2 Cor. 2:1–11; 11:3; 2 Thess. 2:9

1. What did Paul say about his knowledge of the devil?

2. What was his reason?

Prayer

O God, as I go deeper into this subject, I am becoming increasingly aware of the intensity of the spiritual battle in which I am engaged. Dispel every fear that may arise in me and show me the way to power and victory. In Jesus' Name I pray. Amen.

SECTION FOUR

God's Armor—Our Only Protection

For reading & meditation—Ephesians 6:11–18

"Put on the whole armor of God, that you may be able to stand against the wiles of the devil." (v.11, NKJV)

The armor of God is our only protection against the wiles of Satan, but it will do us no good unless we avail ourselves of it in its entirety. Today we concentrate on the first of these two vital issues. We must constantly keep before us the fact that such is the might and power of Satan that nothing apart from the armor of God will protect us from his onslaughts. Mark that and mark it well, for there are many Christians who have tried to stand against Satan in their own strength and have found themselves not victors, but victims. One of the "wiles" of Satan is to get us to believe that we can resist him in our own strength, but when we think that—we are finished.

In my time I have seen many believers lulled by Satan into thinking that their long experience in the faith and their understanding of Christian doctrine were all they needed to protect them from satanic attack, but they found to their cost that this was inadequate and insufficient. We never live more dangerously than when we depend on our spiritual experience and understanding to protect us from the fiery darts of the enemy. One thing and one thing only can protect us from the attacks of Satan and that is the spiritual armor which God has provided. You see, in the devil we are dealing with a foe that is inferior in power only to the Almighty Himself. Therefore, nothing less than the protection that God provides is adequate for our need.

FURTHER STUDY

Rom. 13:1–12;
1 Thess. 5:8;
2 Tim. 2:4

1. What are we to put aside?
2. What are we to put on?

O Father, I need to get this matter straight, for I see that if my dependence is on anything other than You, then I am sunk. Drive this truth deep into my spirit this day. In Jesus' Name. Amen.

SECTION FOUR

How Not to Be a "Wobbly Christian"

For reading & meditation—Romans 13:8–14

"... So let us put aside the deeds of darkness and put on the armor of light." (v.12)

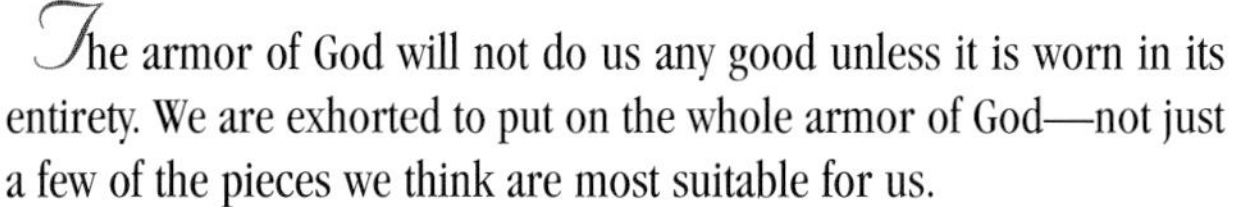

The armor of God will not do us any good unless it is worn in its entirety. We are exhorted to put on the whole armor of God—not just a few of the pieces we think are most suitable for us.

This again is something of crucial importance. If we are to be steadfast soldiers in the Lord's army, if we are to avoid becoming what John Stott calls "wobbly Christians who have no firm foothold in Christ," then we must put on the entire equipment which God provides for us. We cannot, we dare not select parts of the armor and say: "I don't really like the helmet of salvation, but I don't mind wearing the breastplate of righteousness." You can do that, of course, but if you do then you must know exactly what will happen to you—you will be overcome by Satan. The moment you say: "I need the breastplate, but I don't need the helmet"—you are defeated. You need it all—the whole armor of God.

You see, our understanding of what is involved in spiritual defense against Satan is extremely inadequate—we just don't have sufficient knowledge of what is involved. It is God alone who knows our enemy and it is God alone who knows exactly how to protect us so that we remain firm and steadfast when Satan and his forces hurl themselves against us. So learn this lesson now before going any farther—every single piece of God's armor is essential, and to select some and leave the others is to take the route to failure and defeat.

FURTHER STUDY

2 Cor. 6:1–10; Phil. 1:27; 1 Pet. 5:9

1. What did Paul include as a necessary requirement for his ministry?

2. What are we called to do?

Prayer

O God, deliver me from the attitude of pride that seeks to put my ideas ahead of Your ideas. You know more about what I need to protect me from the enemy than I do. Help me ever to trust Your judgment. In Jesus' Name I ask it. Amen.

SECTION FOUR

The Belt of Truth

For reading & meditation—Psalm 119:145–160

"Yet you are near, O LORD, and all your commands are true." (v.151)

Paul, in listing the six main pieces of a soldier's equipment, illustrates the six main ways by which we can defend ourselves against the power of Satan—truth, righteousness, steadfastness, faith, salvation, and the Word of God. Most commentators believe that the reason why Paul selected these six pieces of armor to illustrate the Christian's protective system against satanic attack was because he was chained to a soldier as he wrote the letter (Eph. 6:20). Although it is unlikely that the soldier would have worn the full armor of an infantryman on the battlefield, the sight of him would have kindled Paul's imagination.

The list begins with the belt of truth. Why, we ask ourselves, does the apostle start with such a seemingly insignificant item? Why did he not begin with one of the bigger and more important pieces of equipment, such as the breastplate, the shield or the sword of the Spirit? The order in which these pieces are given to us is an inspired order, and if we change the order we make our position extremely perilous. For example, the reason why many Christians fail to wield the sword of the Spirit effectively is because they have not first girded their waist with truth. If we reverse the order, we succeed only in weakening our spiritual defense.

It is very important that we grasp this. Girding our waist with truth is always the place to start whenever we are under satanic attack. If you don't start right, then you will not finish right. You cannot do battle with the devil until you first gird your waist with truth.

FURTHER STUDY

2 Pet. 1:1–12; Prov. 23:23; 3 John 1–4

1. In what are we to be established?

2. In what did John rejoice?

Prayer

Gracious and loving Father, help me to absorb this thought into my inner being this day so that it will stay with me for the rest of my life: I cannot do battle with the devil until I first gird my waist with truth. Amen.

SECTION FOUR

The Power and Importance of Truth

DAY 194

For reading & meditation—Psalm 51:1–17

"Surely you desire truth in the inner parts . . ." (v.6)

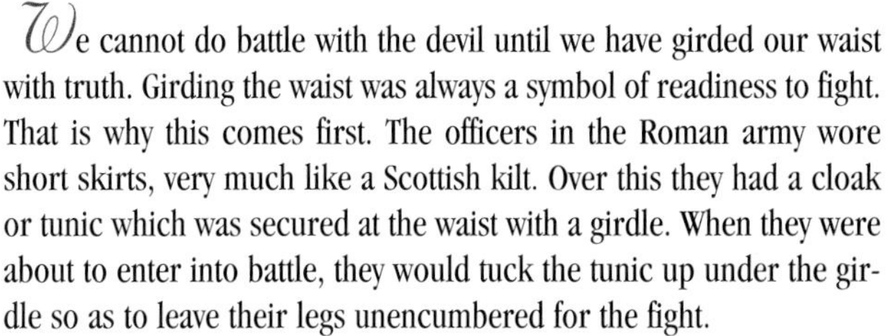

We cannot do battle with the devil until we have girded our waist with truth. Girding the waist was always a symbol of readiness to fight. That is why this comes first. The officers in the Roman army wore short skirts, very much like a Scottish kilt. Over this they had a cloak or tunic which was secured at the waist with a girdle. When they were about to enter into battle, they would tuck the tunic up under the girdle so as to leave their legs unencumbered for the fight.

What does Paul's phrase, "gird your waist with truth" really mean? What significance does it have for us today? The word *truth* can be looked at in two ways: one, objective truth, as it is to be found in Jesus Christ, and two, subjective truth as it is to be found in the qualities of honesty and sincerity. The Puritan, William Gurnall, points out that whether the word implies truth of doctrine or of heart, one will not do without the other.

I believe that in Ephesians 6, Paul is emphasizing subjective truth—truth in the inner being. When we are deceitful or hypocritical, or resort to intrigue and scheming, we are playing the devil's game. And you will never be able to beat the devil at his own game! What Satan despises is transparent truth—he flees from it as quickly as darkness runs from the dawn. Having our waist girded with truth, then, means being possessed with truth, guided by truth and controlled by truth. No truth—no power over Satan. It is as simple as that.

FURTHER STUDY

John 8:34–45; Col. 3:9; Prov. 12:22

1. What can protect us from the devil?

2. Where should we desire truth?

Prayer

O Father, I see that You have set standards by which I rise or fall. When I fulfil, them I rise, when I break them I fall. Give me the strength I need to fulfil, all Your laws, especially the law of truth. In Jesus' Name. Amen.

Under the Searchlight of Truth

For reading & meditation—Psalm 139:1–24

"Search me [thoroughly], O God, and know my heart! Try me, and know my thoughts!" (v.23, Amp. Bible)

We remind ourselves of what we said yesterday—that to have our "waist girded with truth" means to be possessed by truth. If we are to defend ourselves effectively against the attacks of Satan, then truth and honesty are vital necessities.

The mental health experts tell us that being willing to face the truth about ourselves is an important part of our growth toward maturity; the same is true in the realm of the spiritual. How easy it is to hide from the truth and imagine ourselves to be truthful when really we are not. Whatever his personal idiosyncrasies and his rebellious attitude toward Christianity, Sigmund Freud made an interesting contribution to our understanding of human personality when he documented with true genius the incredibly subtle ways in which we lie to ourselves. Psychologists call them "defense mechanisms," but a more biblical view of them would be "lying mechanisms."

We would all much prefer to be called defensive than dishonest. But whenever we allow ourselves to be self-deceived, we not only impede our spiritual growth—we also lower our defenses against Satan. He thrives on deception, and if he can push us toward self-deception, he maintains a definite advantage over us. Many of us might react with horror to the suggestion that we may be dishonest, for we would not dream of doing or saying anything that was not according to the truth. Yet it is possible to be open and honest on the outside and yet hide from truth on the inside. All of us, even mature and experienced Christians, are capable of hiding from truth.

FURTHER STUDY

2 Chron. 7:1–14;

Isa. 44:20;

James. 1:22

1. What are God's people to turn from?

2. What does James warn against?

Prayer

O Father, I see that if I am to overcome Satan, then I must know truth inwardly as well as outwardly. Search my heart today, dear Lord, and bring to the surface the things within me that are untrue. In Jesus' Name I ask it. Amen.

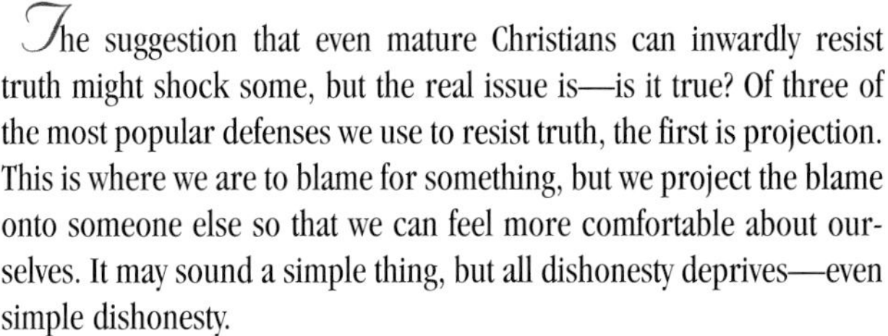

Three Forms of Dishonesty

For reading & meditation—1 John 1:1–10

"If we claim to be without sin, we deceive ourselves and the truth is not in us." (v.8)

The suggestion that even mature Christians can inwardly resist truth might shock some, but the real issue is—is it true? Of three of the most popular defenses we use to resist truth, the first is projection. This is where we are to blame for something, but we project the blame onto someone else so that we can feel more comfortable about ourselves. It may sound a simple thing, but all dishonesty deprives—even simple dishonesty.

Then take the defense of denial. How many times do we refuse to face the fact that we may be angry about something, and when someone says: "Why are you angry?" we reply with bristling hostility: "I'm not angry!" We fail to recognize what others can plainly see. And denial, no matter how one looks at it, is a form of inner deceit.

Another dishonest defense is rationalization. We do this whenever we persuade ourselves that something is what it is not. C. S. Lewis points out that when our neighbor does something wrong, it is obviously because he or she is "bad," while if we do something wrong it is only because we did not get enough sleep, or someone gave us a rough time, or our blood chemistry is at fault, and so on.

All defense mechanisms deprive us of inner honesty, and apart from hindering our spiritual growth (as we said) they lower our defenses against Satan. This is why over and over again in Scripture we are bidden to open up to honesty. The more honest we can be, the more spiritually powerful and effective we can be.

FURTHER STUDY

Rev. 3:14–22;
James. 1:26;
Gal. 6:3

1. How did the Laodiceans see themselves?

2. How did God see them?

Prayer

Lord Jesus, help me to open up to honesty. For I see that the more honest I am, the more authority I can wield over Satan. I want to be able to say, as You said: "The ruler of this world is coming, and he has nothing in me." For Your own dear Name's sake. Amen.

Without Truth—We Get Nowhere

For reading & meditation—Hosea 10:1–12

"… it is time to seek the LORD …" (v.12)

The phrase "gird your waist with truth" clearly suggests that this is something we must do and not expect God to do for us. Clinton McLemore says: "Whenever any one of us embodies and promotes personal honesty, we are knowingly or unknowingly doing God's work." So ask yourself: "Am I an honest person?" If there are areas of your life where you are not sure, then spend some time before God in prayer today asking Him to help you root out all dishonesty. For honesty is our first line of defense against Satan. If we are not willing to be honest, then the devil will soon disable us.

We live in an age which, generally speaking, evades the truth. We seem to take it for granted that advertisements distort, contracts contain fine print that no one draws our attention to, and professionals conceal one another's malpractice. There are few domains of life that are uncompromised, few social structures that are not tainted, few relationships that retain any semblance of wholesomeness.

The Christian Church is not without blame either. Consider the endless maneuverings of some church boards and committees. God put the Church in the world, but somehow the devil has put the world in the Church. Our text for today sums up the present Church situation: "It is time to seek the Lord." Am I speaking too strongly? I think not. If we don't get things straightened out at the start, then how can we hope to be victorious in the war against Satan? Always remember that sin, at its root, is a stubborn refusal to deal with truth.

FURTHER STUDY

1 Pet. 4:12–19;
Rom. 12:17;
Jer. 17:9

1. What is the natural condition of the heart?
2. Where must things be put right first?

Prayer

O God, forgive us that we, Your redeemed people, sometimes pursue our own interests and allow truth to be dragged in the gutter. Help us, dear Lord. For without truth we have no power. In Jesus' Name we ask it. Amen.

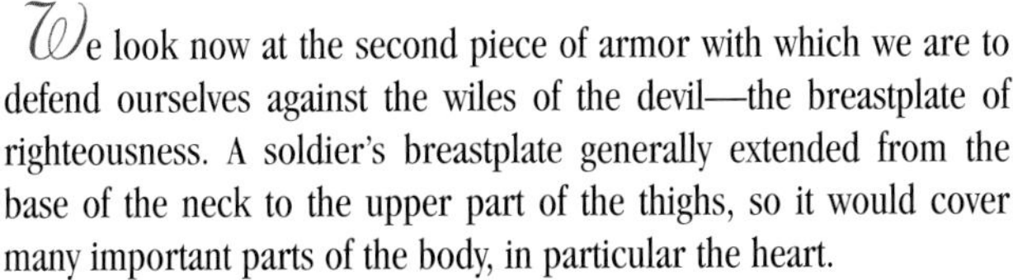

SECTION FOUR

The Breastplate of Righteousness

For reading & meditation—Psalm 132:1–18

"May your priests be clothed with righteousness; may your saints sing for joy." (v.9)

We look now at the second piece of armor with which we are to defend ourselves against the wiles of the devil—the breastplate of righteousness. A soldier's breastplate generally extended from the base of the neck to the upper part of the thighs, so it would cover many important parts of the body, in particular the heart.

Some commentators think that the word *breastplate* suggests that this piece of equipment covered only the front of the chest and thus gave no protection for the soldier's back. They deduce from this that a Christian should face the devil and never turn his back on him or else he will expose a part that is unguarded. It is an interesting idea but it must not be given too much credence, for the soldier's breastplate often covered his back as well as his front.

What spiritual lesson can we draw from the "breastplate of righteousness"? Most commentators believe that because a soldier's breastplate covered mainly his heart, the spiritual application of this is that in Christ we have all the protection we need against negative or desolating feelings—the heart being seen as the focal point of the emotions. What an exciting thought—by putting on the breastplate of righteousness, we have the resources to deal with all those debilitating feelings that tend to bring us down into despair—unworthiness, inadequacy, fear, and so on. When I mentioned this to a friend who asked me what I thought the breastplate of righteousness was for, he said: "It sounds too good to be true." I replied: "It's too good not to be true."

FURTHER STUDY

Matt. 15:10–20; Mark 7:21; Prov. 4:23; 28:9

1. What comes out of the heart?

2. How are we to guard our hearts?

Prayer

Gracious Lord and Master, how can I sufficiently thank You for providing a defense against this most difficult of problems—emotional distress. Show me how to apply Your truth to this part of my personality. In Jesus' Name. Amen.

SECTION FOUR

Nothing Wrong with Christ

For reading & meditation—Romans 8:31–39

"Who then will condemn us? Will Christ? No! For he is the one who died for us ..." (v.34, TLB)

Today we face the question: when Paul talks about the "breastplate of righteousness," is he talking about our righteousness or Christ's righteousness? I believe he is talking about Christ's righteousness. That is not to say, of course, that our own righteousness (or moral uprightness) is unimportant, for as Paul points out in 2 Corinthians 6:7, our personal righteousness can be a definite defense against Satan. In Ephesians 6, however, the emphasis is not on our righteousness in Christ, but Christ's righteousness in us.

So how does putting on the breastplate of righteousness act as a spiritual defense against the wiles of the devil? Take, for example, those people who have definitely surrendered their lives to Christ but whom Satan afflicts with a feeling that they are not good enough to be saved. Why do they have such feeling? The answer is simple—they have taken their eyes off Christ and His righteousness and have focused on themselves and their righteousness. And in doing that, they play right into the devil's hands.

You see, the devil can find all kinds of flaws and blemishes in your righteousness, but he can find nothing wrong with the righteousness of Christ. The way to withstand an attack like this is to put on the breastplate of righteousness. In other words, remind yourself and Satan that you stand not on your own merits but on Christ's. This may sound simple, even simplistic to some, but I have lived long enough to see people latch on to it and come from the depths of emotional distress to the heights of spiritual exaltation.

FURTHER STUDY

1 Cor. 1:19–31; Isa. 64:6; Phil. 3:9

1. What is our righteousness like?

2. What was Paul's declaration?

Prayer

Lord Jesus, help me to latch onto it. Make it crystal clear to my spirit that although the devil can find many flaws in my righteousness, he cannot find a single flaw in Yours. I rest my case—on You. Thank You, dear Lord. Amen.

SECTION FOUR

"The Tyranny of the Oughts"

For reading & meditation—Romans 5:1–11

"Therefore, since we have been justified by faith, we have peace with God through our Lord Jesus Christ." (v.1)

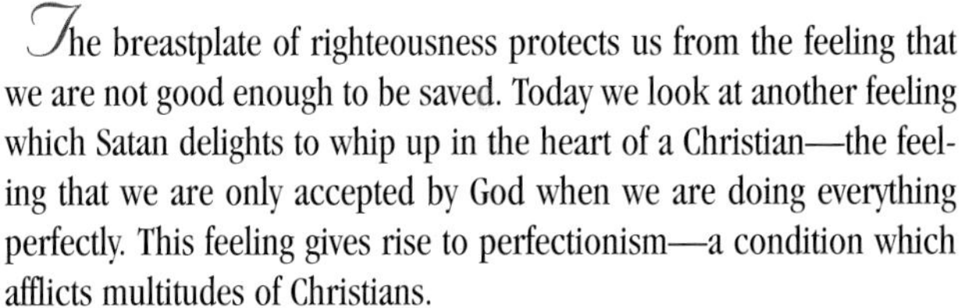

The breastplate of righteousness protects us from the feeling that we are not good enough to be saved. Today we look at another feeling which Satan delights to whip up in the heart of a Christian—the feeling that we are only accepted by God when we are doing everything perfectly. This feeling gives rise to perfectionism—a condition which afflicts multitudes of Christians.

The chief characteristic of perfectionism is a constant overall feeling of never doing enough to be thought well of by God. Karen Horney describes it as "the tyranny of the oughts." Here are some typical statements of those who are afflicted in this way: "I ought to do better," "I ought to have done better," "I ought to be able to do better." There is nothing wrong with wanting to do better, but in the twisted thinking of a perfectionist, he or she believes that because they could or ought to have done better, they will not be accepted or thought well of by God. They come to believe that their acceptance by God depends on their performance; they constantly try to develop a righteousness of their own rather than resting in the righteousness which Christ has provided for them.

If you suffer from this condition, then it's time to put on your spiritual breastplate. You need to remind yourself that the way you came into the Christian life is the way you go on in it—by depending on Christ and His righteousness, not on yourself and your righteousness. You are not working to be saved; you are working because you are saved.

FURTHER STUDY

Gal. 3; Gen. 15:6; Acts 13:39

1. What was the purpose of the law?

2. What does it mean to be "justified"?

Prayer

Lord Jesus, I see that when I stand in Your righteousness, I stand in God's smile. But when I stand in my own righteousness, I stand in God's frown. Help me move over from frown to smile. In Your dear Name. Amen.

Paul's Breastplate in Place

For reading & meditation—1 Corinthians 15:1–11

"But by the grace of God I am what I am …" (v.10)

Another feeling which Satan can arouse in a heart that is unprotected by a spiritual breastplate is that of a subtle form of discouragement in which he draws our attention to what other Christians may be saying or thinking about us.

The apostle Paul was a particular target of Satan in this respect, but see how he used the breastplate of righteousness as his spiritual defense. Paul's background was anti-Christian, and he could never get completely away from that. He had been the most hostile persecutor of the church, and he must therefore have constantly run across families whose loved ones he had put to death. Some might even have doubted his claim to be an apostle. Some commentators claim that in 1 Corinthians 15:9, he was replying to such an accusation.

How does Paul react to the criticism? Does he succumb to discouragement? Does he say: "What's the use of working my fingers to the bone for these unappreciative people? They don't do anything but hurl recriminations in my face!" This is what the devil would have liked him to do. But look at what he does. He says: "By the grace of God I am what I am." Can you see what he is doing? He is using the breastplate of righteousness. He is saying, in other words: "I don't need to do anything to protect myself; what I am is what Christ has made me. I am not standing in my own righteousness, I am standing in His." What a lesson in how to use the spiritual breastplate. You and I need to learn this lesson too.

FURTHER STUDY

Ps. 73:1–28; 2 Cor. 5:7–21

1. What brought discouragement to the psalmist?

2. How did Paul encourage the Corinthians?

Prayer

O God, day by day I am catching little glimpses of what You are trying to teach me—that the more I depend on Your righteousness and the less I depend on my own, the better off I will be. Help me to learn it—and learn it completely. Amen.

SECTION FOUR

How to Handle Confusion

For reading & meditation—Romans 8:29–39

"... nothing will ever be able to separate us from the love of God demonstrated by our Lord Jesus Christ ..." (v.39, TLB)

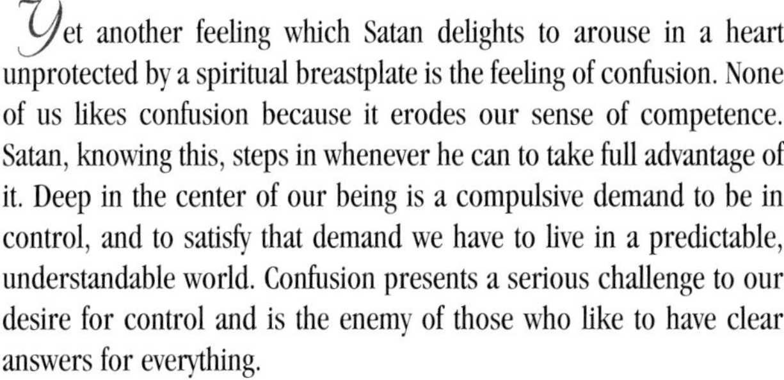

Yet another feeling which Satan delights to arouse in a heart unprotected by a spiritual breastplate is the feeling of confusion. None of us likes confusion because it erodes our sense of competence. Satan, knowing this, steps in whenever he can to take full advantage of it. Deep in the center of our being is a compulsive demand to be in control, and to satisfy that demand we have to live in a predictable, understandable world. Confusion presents a serious challenge to our desire for control and is the enemy of those who like to have clear answers for everything.

Whenever Satan sees that we are not wearing our spiritual breastplate, he comes to us and says something like this: "Look at the great problems that are all around you—earthquakes, famines, violence, cruelty to children ... how can you believe in a God of love when these things are going on in the world?" Sometimes he presses home these arguments with such power that you have no clear answers.

There is only one clear answer against such assaults; it is to put on the "breastplate of righteousness." You cannot understand particular happenings, you cannot give any explanation, but you do know that the God who clothed you with His righteousness and saved you from a lost eternity must have your highest interests and those of His universe at heart. When you hold on to that, your heart is protected from despair, even though your mind struggles to comprehend what is happening. You can live in peace even though you do not know all the answers.

FURTHER STUDY

2 Tim. 1:1–7; 1 Cor. 14:33; Isa. 26:3

1. Where does our peace stem from?

2. Where does confusion come from?

Prayer

Father God, I see that I can experience security in my heart even when my mind cannot understand Your ways. Hidden in Christ and His righteousness, I am safe. I am so thankful. Amen.

Satan as an Angel of Light

For reading & meditation—Philippians 1:1–11

"… he who began a good work in you will carry it on to completion …" (v.6)

Yet another feeling which the devil delights to arouse in an unguarded heart is the feeling that God does not love us. He times his attack to coincide with those moments when everything is going wrong and we are beset by all kinds of difficulties. Then he whispers in our ear: "Do you still believe that God is love?" When you respond by saying that you do, he transforms himself into an angel of light and tries another tactic. "Well," he says, "it is obvious that He does not love you, for if He did then He would not allow you to go through these difficult situations."

There is only one protection against such an assault; it is to put firmly in place the "breastplate of righteousness." Nothing else will avail at this point. You must point him to the truth of Romans 8:28—"We know that in all things God works for the good of those who love him." Paul does not say "we understand," but "we know."

This brings you directly to the theme of justification by faith, which is in fact the righteousness of Christ. You rest on that, and that is all you need. You must say to yourself: "He would never have clothed me with His righteousness if He had not set His love upon me and saved me. I will have courage. I do not know what is happening to me now. I cannot fathom it. But if He has begun His work in me, then I know He will go on to complete it."

FURTHER STUDY

Jer. 31:1–3; Eph. 2:1–7; 3:16–19; Rom. 5:8

1. How has God demonstrated His love?

2. What was Paul's desire for the Ephesians?

Prayer

O God, what wondrous power there is in Your Word. I can feel it doing me good even as I read and ponder it. Give me a greater knowledge of Your Word, for only through that can I maintain an advantage over the devil. In Jesus' Name. Amen.

SECTION FOUR

What Happens When We Sin?

For reading & meditation—1 John 1:5–10 & 2:1–2

"If we confess our sins, he … will forgive us our sins and purify us from all unrighteousness." (v.9)

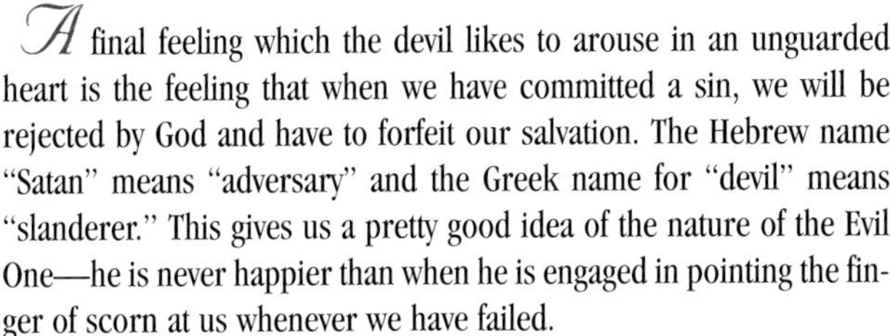

A final feeling which the devil likes to arouse in an unguarded heart is the feeling that when we have committed a sin, we will be rejected by God and have to forfeit our salvation. The Hebrew name "Satan" means "adversary" and the Greek name for "devil" means "slanderer." This gives us a pretty good idea of the nature of the Evil One—he is never happier than when he is engaged in pointing the finger of scorn at us whenever we have failed.

It is part of the doctrine of the Church that a Christian may sometimes fall into sin. We are saved, but we are still fallible. God forbid that we should fall into sin, but when we do, we must remember that we have "an advocate with the Father, Jesus Christ the righteous." You can be sure, however, that when you fall into sin, the devil will come to you and say: "You were forgiven when you became a Christian because you sinned in ignorance, but now that you are a Christian you have sinned against the light. There can be no forgiveness for you now. You are lost—forever."

The answer to this, as with all of Satan's accusations, is to put on the "breastplate of righteousness." You must remind him that God's righteousness not only covers us at our salvation but continues to cover us for time and eternity. Never allow the devil to use a particular sin to call into question your whole standing before God. That is something that has been settled in heaven, not in the debating chamber of the devil.

FURTHER STUDY

Isa. 55:1–7; 43:25; Eph. 1:7–8; Acts 13:38

1. What does God do when He blots out our sin?

2. How does the Lord respond when we return to Him?

My Father and my God, my heart overflows at the revelation of Your full and free forgiveness. Help me not to take it for granted but to take it with gratitude. In Jesus' Name I pray. Amen.

SECTION FOUR

The Shoes of Peace

For reading & meditation—Philippians 1:12–30

"... stand firm in one spirit, contending as one man for the faith of the gospel" (v.27)

We come now to the third piece of armor—having our feet shod "with the readiness that comes from the gospel of peace" (Eph. 6:15). Shoes are absolutely essential to a soldier. Imagine a barefoot soldier. The rough ground would tear his feet to pieces and would soon render him unfit for duty. But with a stout pair of shoes, he would be ready to face anything that came.

Markus Barth, a Bible commentator, says that a Roman soldier in Paul's day would have worn not so much a shoe as a sandal. They were known as *caligae* (half boots), which consisted of "heavy studded leather soles and were tied to the ankles or shins with more or less ornamental straps." These equipped the soldier for a solid stance and prevented his feet from slipping or sliding.

What is the spiritual application of all this? What did the apostle Paul have in mind when he penned the words: "Stand ... having ... shod your feet with the preparation of the gospel of peace" (NKJV). The New English Bible brings home the point of the passage in a most effective way: "Let the shoes on your feet be the gospel of peace, to give you firm footing." The shoes we are to put on are the gospel of peace—the tried and tested truths of the gospel—and their purpose is to prevent us from slipping and sliding when we do battle with our wily and nimble adversary, the devil. What are you like when under attack from Satan? Firm and resolute—or unsteady and unsure?

FURTHER STUDY

Ps. 40:1–5; 1 Sam. 2:9; Isa. 52:1–7

1. What was the psalmist's testimony?
2. Is that your testimony?

Prayer

O Father, I see that if I am to stand firm and resolute when under enemy attack, my feet must be securely shod. Show me what is expected of me, dear Lord—and help me apply it. In Jesus' Name I pray. Amen.

SECTION FOUR

Don't Miss the Point

For reading & meditation—2 Timothy 2:1–15

"Do your best to present yourself to God as one approved ... who correctly handles the word of truth." (v.15)

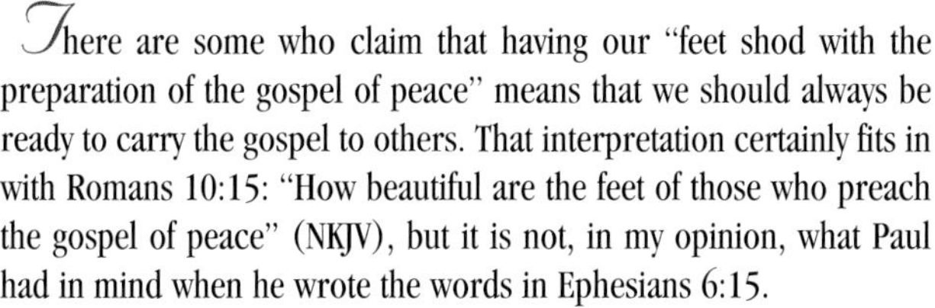

There are some who claim that having our "feet shod with the preparation of the gospel of peace" means that we should always be ready to carry the gospel to others. That interpretation certainly fits in with Romans 10:15: "How beautiful are the feet of those who preach the gospel of peace" (NKJV), but it is not, in my opinion, what Paul had in mind when he wrote the words in Ephesians 6:15.

In Ephesians 6 the apostle here is dealing with one thing only—the Christian's engagement with the devil. "We do not wrestle against flesh and blood, but against principalities, against powers ..." (v.12, NKJV). His purpose is to show us how to stand against the "wiles" of the devil. Although Paul was an evangelist with a strong evangelistic spirit, he was not thinking here of evangelizing, vital though that is. He was rather picturing a Christian who is under attack by Satan and warning us that unless our feet are firmly shod, we can easily be knocked down and disabled.

Those who claim that the phrase "the readiness of the gospel of peace" relates to evangelism miss the point of his exposition. No one would deny the importance of always being ready to share Christ with others, but the readiness Paul is referring to here is the readiness to stand firm on the truths of the gospel. In other words, he is saying: don't get into a fight with the devil in your bare feet. Make sure you are well shod, for if you are not, he will most certainly get the better of you.

FURTHER STUDY

Ps. 119:97–105; Isa. 40:8; 1 Pet. 1:23–25

1. How did the psalmist view God's Word?

2. Why is God's Word a sure foundation?

O Father, I am so grateful that You breathed into Your servant Paul to write these illuminating words. They are inspired, for they inspire me. Continue to teach me, dear Lord. I am hungry for more and more of Your truth. Amen.

SECTION FOUR

Nothing to Hold On To

For reading & meditation—1 Corinthians 16:1–18

"Be on your guard; stand firm in the faith; be men of courage; be strong." (v.13)

The point we made yesterday, that having our "feet shod with the preparation of the gospel of peace" means being ready to stand firm on the truths of the gospel, is brought out also in the text before us today.

One of the great tragedies today is that large numbers of Christians do not have their feet shod with the preparation of the gospel of peace. They are slipping and sliding in all directions because they do not know what to believe. I once met a few Christians from the area in South Wales where I was brought up, Christians who at one time were on fire for God and had a solid confidence in Scripture. As I talked with them, however, I saw that they no longer thought of the Bible in the way they once did, for their conversation about Christ and His Word was filled with doubts. How sad.

If my correspondence is anything to go by, as well as my conversations with Christians in all denominations, there are signs that large numbers of men and women are no longer standing for the truths of the gospel—they no longer know what to believe or what to hold on to. How the devil must rejoice as he sees Christians slipping and sliding in their faith. Here in Britain we see evidence of it, not just in ordinary believers but in some of our notable theologians and bishops. Do you know what you believe? Do you stand firm on the truths of the gospel? Remember, if you don't stand for something, then you will fall for anything.

FURTHER STUDY

Ps. 17:1–15 ; Phil. 4:1; 1 Thess. 3:8

1. What was the psalmist's prayer?

2. What was Paul's exhortation to the Philippians?

Prayer

Dear Father, help me to keep close to the words of Scripture, for they take me beyond the words to You, the Living Word. Strengthen me so that I might hold fast to the truths of the gospel, for without them I cannot help but stumble and fall. Amen.

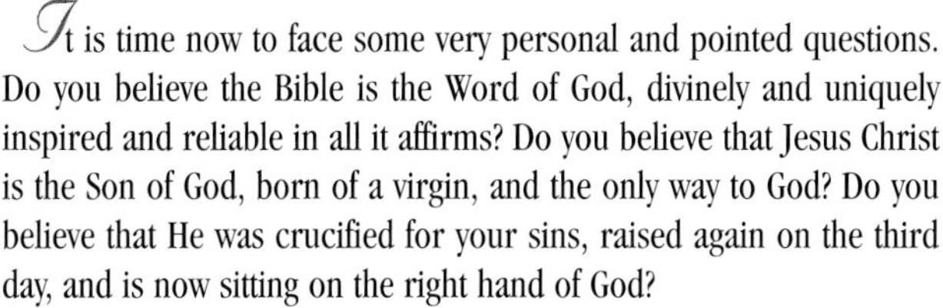

For reading & meditation—2 Corinthians 1:12–24

"For no matter how many promises God has made, they are 'Yes' in Christ...." (v.20)

It is time now to face some very personal and pointed questions. Do you believe the Bible is the Word of God, divinely and uniquely inspired and reliable in all it affirms? Do you believe that Jesus Christ is the Son of God, born of a virgin, and the only way to God? Do you believe that He was crucified for your sins, raised again on the third day, and is now sitting on the right hand of God?

I could go on raising more questions, but the ones I have mentioned are what I consider to be the irreducible minimum of Christianity. In other words, these are the basic truths of the gospel and if you don't take your stand on these truths, then you cannot call yourself a Christian. This is what is meant by having your feet shod with the preparation of the gospel of peace—you are ready to stand for the authority of Scripture, the deity of Christ, His substitutionary death, His resurrection from the dead, and His return to earth in power and glory.

Do you know where you stand on these matters? Are you sure of your spiritual position? How can you fight the enemy if you do not know what you believe? As I write, some of the daily newspapers here in Britain are calling on church leaders to give a spiritual lead. But many of our leaders do not have a high view of Scripture. How can they give a lead when they don't know where they are going? They don't know where they stand, and no one else knows either.

FURTHER STUDY

2 Pet. 1; Col. 2:7; 1 Cor. 3:11

1. Why are we given so many great and precious promises?

2. What should our foundation be?

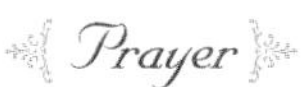

O Father, Your Word promises to be a lamp to our feet and a light for our path. Bring those whose feet are slipping and sliding in the faith back to an unshakeable confidence in the gospel. In Jesus' Name I ask it. Amen.

A Word to New Christians

For reading & meditation—2 Thessalonians 2:13–17

"... stand firm and hold to the teachings we passed on to you ..." (v.15)

Christians need to stand with their feet shod with the preparation of the gospel of peace. The moment we begin to compromise on the Word of God and the great truths of the gospel, we shall not only slide in the understanding of our faith but also in its practice.

Permit me to say a word to those who have been in the Christian life for just a short time. Now that you are a Christian, take your stand unflinchingly on the Lord's side. When you meet your old friends, those you used to hang around with in the days before you came to know the Lord, and they propose that you go on doing the things you used to do which you know are not in harmony with God's Word, then be resolute and refuse. Take a firm stand; and watch that you do not slip toward them. Have your feet shod with the preparation of the gospel of peace.

The first thing that strikes everyone who comes into the Christian life is that it is entirely different from one's former life. You must determine to take your stand with Jesus Christ and when others tempt you, say: "I cannot betray my Lord. I am bound to Him for all eternity. My feet are shod and I am not moving." You have to know what you believe and be resolute and determined to stand for it, come what may. If I had not done this in the days following my conversion, then I would have forfeited an adventure that has taken me deeper and deeper into God.

FURTHER STUDY

Gal. 5:1–13; Phil. 1:27; 1 Pet. 5:7–11

1. What did Paul say to the Galatians?

2. How should we conduct ourselves?

Prayer

O God, how can I have faith in You unless I have faith in the words You have spoken to me in the Bible? Help me stand firm in the faith—today and every day. In Jesus' Name. Amen.

SECTION FOUR

A Spiritual Adventure

For reading & meditation—Judges 7:1–22

"The Lord said to Gideon, 'With the three hundred men that lapped I will save you ...'" (v.7)

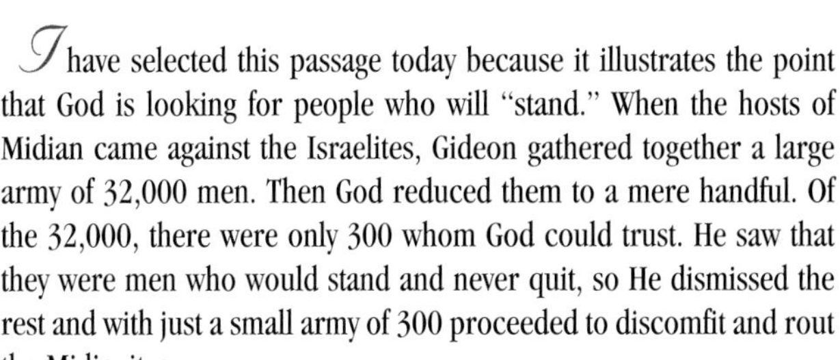

I have selected this passage today because it illustrates the point that God is looking for people who will "stand." When the hosts of Midian came against the Israelites, Gideon gathered together a large army of 32,000 men. Then God reduced them to a mere handful. Of the 32,000, there were only 300 whom God could trust. He saw that they were men who would stand and never quit, so He dismissed the rest and with just a small army of 300 proceeded to discomfit and rout the Midianites.

God has always done His greatest work in and through a comparatively small number of people. When it comes to spiritual victories, forget the idea of numbers—what God wants is men and women who are prepared to "stand," whose feet are "shod with the preparation of the gospel of peace." He will not entrust great responsibility to people whom He knows will not "stand," for that would be an exercise in fruitlessness.

Are you standing for God—in the environment in which God has put you? Or, are you ready to stand? You see, you cannot stand until you are prepared to stand. It begins with a firm attitude which then issues in resolute action. As in Gideon's day, the Lord is looking for people who will take their stand on His Word, come what may, and commit themselves to doing what He asks even though they may not feel like it or see the sense of it. Are you such a one? If you are, then I predict that ahead of you is an exciting spiritual adventure.

FURTHER STUDY

Gal. 6:1–9; 1 Cor. 15:58; Eph. 4:15

1. What is the result of remaining steadfast?

2. What can hinder our spiritual success?

Prayer

O God, help me not to miss the highest because of my spiritual unpreparedness. Help me to be ready for all that You have for me—even before I see it. In Jesus' Name I pray. Amen.

SECTION FOUR

Peace that Does Not Go to Pieces

For reading & meditation—Colossians 3:1–17

"... let the peace of God rule in your hearts ..." (v.15, NKJV)

Why the phrase "the gospel of peace?" Well, the Gospel is first and foremost a message about peace. First we experience peace with God, and then we experience the peace of God.

A soldier in battle has to be certain about a number of things or else he will be distracted and become an easy prey for the enemy. He needs to be certain that he is fighting in a just war, that his commander is a wise strategist and that he has the constant support of those under whose authority he fights. He needs to know also that his loved ones are being cared for and that they are being protected by a defense force. So too the Christian soldier has to be certain about his relationship with God, the truth and reliability of the Bible, the resources that are available to him, and so on. How can his heart be at peace if he is not assured of these things?

At this point that we Christians have an advantage over every other soldier, for not only are we led by the wisest military strategist in the universe, but we have inside information on how the battle against Satan will end—we win! We would never be able to stand against the "wiles" of the devil unless we enjoyed peace with God and the peace of God. Even in the midst of the hottest conflict, we know that although the devil may win some of the battles, he will most definitely lose the war. If you have peace about the outcome, then you have peace all the way—period.

FURTHER STUDY

Phil. 4:1–7; Ps. 29:11; John 16:33; Rom. 14:17

1. What keeps our hearts and minds?

2. How does this relate to battle?

O Father, I see so clearly that if I have doubts about You or about my salvation, then I will not be able to fight the enemy. I shall have to spend the whole time struggling with myself. But there are no doubts. I have peace with You and peace within. I am so thankful. Amen.

SECTION FOUR

The Shield of Faith

For reading & meditation—1 John 5:1–12

"... This is the victory that has overcome the world, even our faith." (v.4)

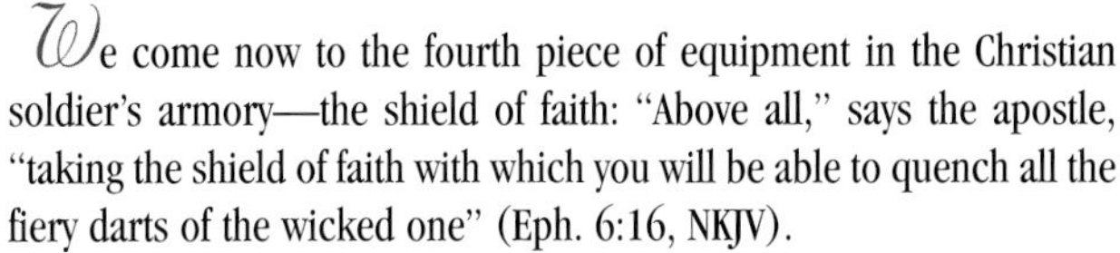

We come now to the fourth piece of equipment in the Christian soldier's armory—the shield of faith: "Above all," says the apostle, "taking the shield of faith with which you will be able to quench all the fiery darts of the wicked one" (Eph. 6:16, NKJV).

Some take Paul's use of the expression "above all" to mean, "above everything else in importance" and from this, they go on to argue that the last three pieces of armor are more important than the first three. But the phrase really means "in addition to all this" (NIV). It is a transition phrase designed to introduce us to a section of the armor which has a different purpose.

The six pieces of armor fall clearly into two main groups, the first consisting of the belt of truth, the breastplate of righteousness, and the shoes of the preparation of the gospel of peace. The second group comprises the shield of faith, the helmet of salvation, and the sword of the Spirit. The first three pieces of armor were fixed to the body by a special fastening, and hence, to a certain degree, were immovable. But the shield was not fixed to the body; it was something quite separate. The same applies to the helmet; that, too, was something that could be put on or taken off quite easily. And obviously the same was true of the sword of the Spirit. The lesson, quite clearly, is this—the first three pieces of equipment should be worn at all times, while the other three are to be taken up when and where necessary.

FURTHER STUDY

1 Tim. 1:12–20; 6:12; 1 Thess. 5:8

1. What had some rejected?

2. What was the result?

Prayer

Gracious and loving Heavenly Father, I am so thankful for the care and design that have gone into providing for me a sure defense against Satan. I have learned much, yet I see there is still much more to learn. Teach me, my Father. Amen.

SECTION FOUR

"Having" and "Taking"

For reading & meditation—Hebrews 11:1–16

"And without faith it is impossible to please God ..." (v.6)

We ended yesterday with the thought that the first three pieces of the Christian armor should be worn at all times, while the last three should be taken up and used when and where it is necessary. Evidence for this can be seen when we look at Paul's use of the words having and taking.

Listen again to the passage: "Stand therefore, having girded your waist with truth, having put on the breastplate of righteousness, and having shod your feet with the preparation of the gospel of peace" (NKJV). Then, in the second section, the word changes: "Above all, taking the shield of faith ... take the helmet of salvation, and the sword of the Spirit" (NKJV). The difference between the first and last three pieces of equipment is that "having" and "taking."

The "shield" referred to in Ephesians 6 was extremely large, about four feet long and about two and a half feet wide, designed to give as much protection as possible to the front of the body. More important, the front surface was covered with a sheet of fireproof metal so that the fiery darts of the enemy would have little or no effect.

Clearly Paul thought that, in addition to the first three items, a further defense was needed to protect us from the devil's preliminary attacks. When we consider the lengths to which God has gone in order to give us the protection we need against satanic attack, one wonders why we ever allow ourselves to be defeated by the devil.

FURTHER STUDY

Heb. 11:17–40; Rom. 10:17; Phil. 3:8–9

1. How does faith come?

2. List some of the things accomplished through faith.

O Father, once again I want to record my gratitude for the way in which You have provided for my defense against satanic attack. Help me to see, however, that it will do me no good just to appreciate it; I must use it. In Christ's Name I will use it. Amen.

"Fiery Darts"

For reading & meditation—2 Timothy 4:1–18

"... the Lord stood at my side and gave me strength ... And I was delivered from the lion's mouth." (v.17)

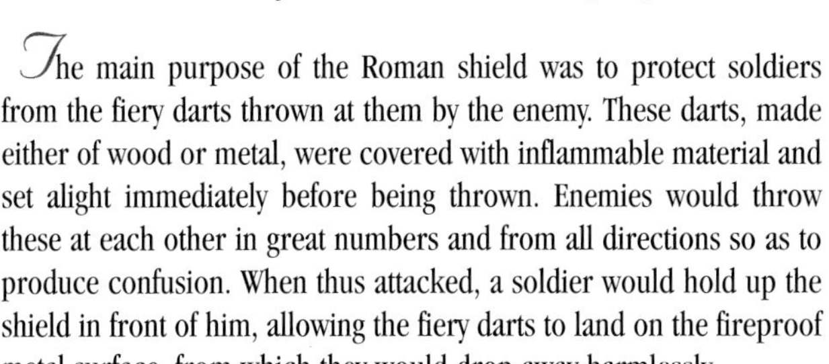

The main purpose of the Roman shield was to protect soldiers from the fiery darts thrown at them by the enemy. These darts, made either of wood or metal, were covered with inflammable material and set alight immediately before being thrown. Enemies would throw these at each other in great numbers and from all directions so as to produce confusion. When thus attacked, a soldier would hold up the shield in front of him, allowing the fiery darts to land on the fireproof metal surface, from which they would drop away harmlessly.

The apostle says that we Christians need a "shield of faith"—in order "to quench all the fiery darts of the wicked" (KJV). An understanding of what these "fiery darts" are is essential if we are to stand firm against the adversary. Have you ever gone to bed at night feeling perfectly happy, only to wake in a sad mood? If there was no obvious physical or psychological reason for that, the chances are that you have experienced one of Satan's "fiery darts."

Sometimes they come as evil thoughts which intrude suddenly into our thinking, often at the most incongruous times. We may be reading the Bible, we may be praying, when all of a sudden some filthy thought flashes into our mind. It is a "fiery dart" from the devil. They do not come from inside us but from outside us. They strike us. Some thoughts arise from within our carnal nature but these come from without—from Satan. And we are foolish if we do not recognize this and deal with them in this light.

Further Study

Jas. 1:1–22; 1 Cor. 10:13; 2 Cor. 11:3

1. What is the progression in temptation?

2. What was Paul's concern?

Prayer

O Father, help me to be alert and able to recognize the "fiery darts" of Satan when they are hurled at me. For I see that it is only when I recognize them that I can deal effectively with them. Give me insight and understanding. In Jesus' Name. Amen.

SECTION FOUR

The Satanic Strategy

For reading & meditation—John 13:1–11

"... the devil had already put it into the heart of Judas Iscariot ... to betray him." (v.2, RSV)

We are seeing that the "fiery darts" of the devil are quite different from the thoughts that are generated by our carnal nature. They come at us, rather than from within us. A satanic attack can usually be differentiated from something that arises from within by the force with which the thought hits us. Thoughts that arise out of the carnal nature are offensive, but the thoughts that come as "fiery darts" from the devil burn.

Many Christians have told me that they often experience these attacks when they go to read their Bibles or to pray. When they read a newspaper nothing seems to happen, but when they turn their attention to something spiritual, they find it almost impossible to concentrate by reason of the shameful thoughts that occupy their minds.

The other thing one notices about these attacks is that they seem to come in cycles. They are not there permanently, but they come at certain times and seasons. I once counseled a man for one hour a week over a period of a whole year and got him to write down in his diary the times and dates when he felt under satanic attack. When we looked through his diary together at the end of the year we discovered an amazing thing—every single attack took place immediately prior to him doing something special for the Lord, like leading a Bible study, conducting a service, visiting the sick, or giving a public testimony. I shall never forget the expression on his face as he looked at me and said: "Who says that Satan isn't a strategist?"

FURTHER STUDY

Gen. 3; Matt. 4:1–10

1. How did Satan seek to penetrate Eve's mind?

2. How does this correlate with the temptation of Christ?

Prayer

My Father and my God, I realize that even though Satan is a strategist, he is no match for You. You know how to out-maneuver his every move. Help me to stay close to You that I might experience Your strategy and not his. Amen.

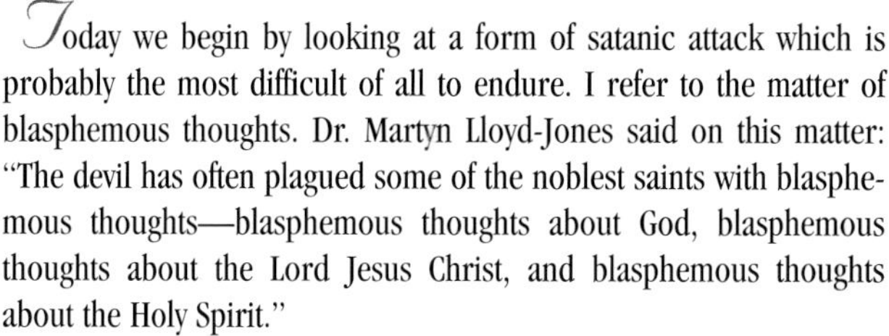

Blasphemous Thoughts

DAY 216

For reading & meditation—2 Corinthians 2:1–11

"… For we are not unaware of his schemes." (v.11)

Today we begin by looking at a form of satanic attack which is probably the most difficult of all to endure. I refer to the matter of blasphemous thoughts. Dr. Martyn Lloyd-Jones said on this matter: "The devil has often plagued some of the noblest saints with blasphemous thoughts—blasphemous thoughts about God, blasphemous thoughts about the Lord Jesus Christ, and blasphemous thoughts about the Holy Spirit."

How horrible and terrifying such thoughts can be. Sometimes the devil hurls the most awful words and phrases into the mind, but again, it is important to see that these do not arise from within the heart of the believer—they come from the devil, who is trying to confuse and demoralize you. How grateful we should be to the saints down the ages who have recorded these satanic attacks, for otherwise we would be tempted when experiencing them to believe that they have never happened to anyone else. Many masters of the spiritual life have described these satanic attacks in great detail—John Bunyan and Martin Luther being the two best examples.

But how do we deal with these "fiery darts" of Satan? What action must we take to repel these devilish attacks? There is only one answer—we must take and use the shield of faith. Faith alone enables you to meet and overcome this particular type of attack. What you must not do is expose your chest and expect the breastplate of righteousness to deal with this problem. Each piece of the equipment is designed to deal with a particular attack. And the answer here is—faith.

FURTHER STUDY

2 Cor. 10:1–5; Matt. 22:37–38; Eph. 1:22–23; James 4:7–8

1. In what ways does Satan attack the mind?

2. What is the scriptural antidote?

Prayer

Heavenly Father, I understand the problem—now show me how to apply the answer. The answer, I see, is faith. But how does it work? How can I apply it? Teach me more. In Jesus' Name. Amen.

SECTION FOUR

Prompt Action

For reading & meditation—Romans 10:1–18

"... faith comes by hearing, and hearing by the word of God."
(v.17, NKJV)

Prayerfully, we ask ourselves the question—how does faith act as a protective shield? First of all, we must understand what faith is and how the word is being used by Paul in Ephesians 6:16. A little boy, when asked to give a definition of faith, said: "Faith is believing something you know isn't true." Well, that is precisely what faith is not. Faith is believing what you know to be true. But it is even more than that—it is acting on what you know to be true. Some people see faith as something vague and mysterious, but faith is one of the most practical commodities in the Christian faith. Take this verse, for example: "Faith without deeds is dead" (James 2:26). There is always the element of activity in faith; it always prompts us to action. "Faith is the assurance of things hoped for, the conviction of things not seen" (Heb. 11:1, NASB).

Taking the shield of faith, then, is responding to the things the devil hurls at us by the quick application of what we believe about God and His Word, the Bible. When Satan sends his "fiery darts" in our direction, we can either stand and lament the fact that we are being attacked, or quickly raise the shield of faith and remind ourselves that the devil is a liar from the very beginning, and because we are redeemed by the blood of Christ, he has no legal or moral right to taunt us. But believing that is not enough; it must be acted on—and acted on quickly.

FURTHER STUDY

James 2:14–26;
Heb. 11:1;
1 John 5:4

1. How are we justified?

2. Write out your definition of faith.

Prayer

Father, I see that when Satan throws his "fiery darts" at me I must act, and act quickly. Help my faith to be so strong that it will not need a "jump start" to get it going. This I ask in Jesus' Name. Amen.

SECTION FOUR

"I Am Your Shield"

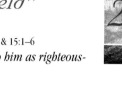

For reading & meditation—Genesis 14:18–24 & 15:1–6

"Abram believed the LORD, and he credited it to him as righteousness." (v.6)

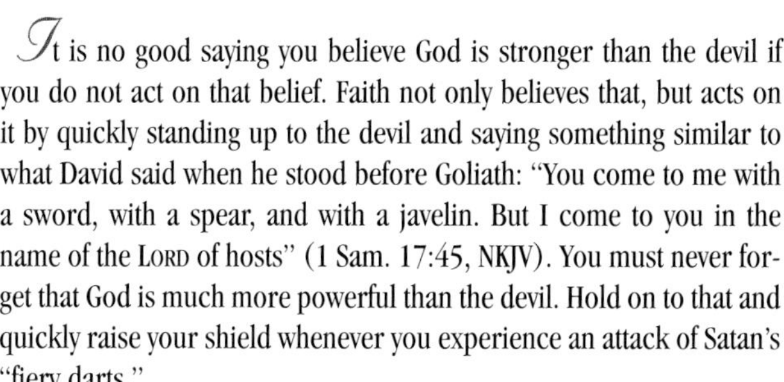

It is no good saying you believe God is stronger than the devil if you do not act on that belief. Faith not only believes that, but acts on it by quickly standing up to the devil and saying something similar to what David said when he stood before Goliath: "You come to me with a sword, with a spear, and with a javelin. But I come to you in the name of the LORD of hosts" (1 Sam. 17:45, NKJV). You must never forget that God is much more powerful than the devil. Hold on to that and quickly raise your shield whenever you experience an attack of Satan's "fiery darts."

Our passage today focuses on an incident in Abraham's life which took place when he was exhausted after making a great stand. Doubtless Satan would have attacked him with thoughts like: "What is the point of all this action of God on your behalf, and all these promises, when you do not have an heir to carry on your line? God doesn't seem to have as much power as it would appear."

Abraham was fearful at this point until the Lord came to him and gave him these glorious words: "Do not be afraid, Abram. I am your shield, your exceedingly great reward" (15:1, NKJV). "I am your shield." Hold on to that great truth, my friend, and when under attack, quickly lift it up and remind the devil that you belong to One whose power is endless and eternal. His promises are ever sure. That is what it means to hold up the shield of faith.

FURTHER STUDY

Prov. 30:1–5; Deut. 33:29; Pss. 33:20; 59:11; 84:9

1. Why was Israel blessed?

2. What was the psalmist's continual testimony?

Prayer

O God, how grateful I am for the sureness and certainty of Your Word. Once again I feel it entering into the core of my being. Help me to put these truths into practice the very moment I come under satanic attack. In Jesus' Name I pray. Amen.

SECTION FOUR

The Helmet of Salvation

For reading & meditation—2 Corinthians 11:1–15

"... I am afraid that just as Eve was deceived ... your minds may somehow be led astray ..." (v.3)

The second piece of armor which is not tied or fixed to the body but which a Christian soldier has to take up and put on is "the helmet of salvation" (Eph. 6:17). The helmet worn by a Roman soldier was usually made of bronze or iron with an inside lining of felt or sponge. In some cases, a hinged visor added frontal protection. When a Roman soldier saw an enemy coming, he would take hold of his shield, put on his helmet, take his sword in hand, and stand alert and ready to do battle.

The figure of a helmet immediately suggests to us that this is something designed to protect the mind, the intelligence, the ability to think and reason. Just as the breastplate of righteousness protects us from emotional distress, so the helmet of salvation protects us from mental distress. This helmet can help us keep our thinking straight and preserve us from mental confusion.

As you look out at the world, has there ever been a time when we needed something to keep our thinking straight more than we do now? Politicians vacillate and oscillate between despairing pessimism and unrealistic optimism. Just think of the staggering complexities of the issues we face in our generation—AIDS, violence, nuclear missiles, international tension, economic instability, inner-city slums, and so on. The intelligentsia of our day confess to being utterly baffled in dealing with the problems with which human society is confronted. Where can we turn to ease the pressure on our minds? The only answer is God—and in the helmet of salvation which He provides.

FURTHER STUDY

Eph. 4:1–17; Rom. 8:7; Col. 1:21

1. How were the Ephesians not to live?

2. How powerful is the influence of the mind?

O Father, I am so grateful that You have provided freedom from that most terrifying of human problems—mental distress. Teach me all I need to know in applying Your truth to the important area of my mind. In Jesus' Name. Amen.

SECTION FOUR

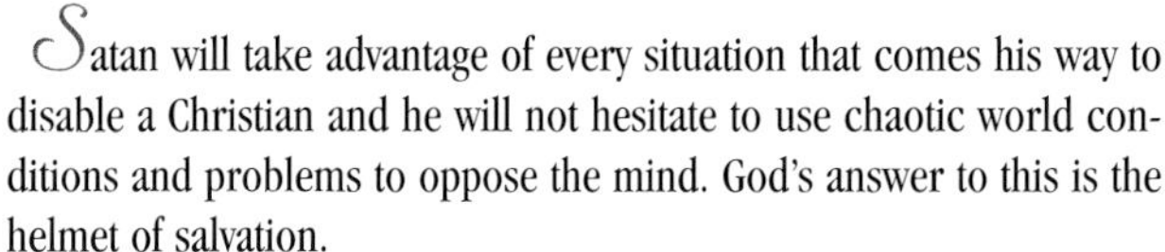

The Tenses of Salvation

DAY 220

For reading & meditation—1 Thessalonians 5:1–11

"… let us be self-controlled, putting on faith and love as a breastplate, and the hope of salvation as a helmet." (v.8)

Satan will take advantage of every situation that comes his way to disable a Christian and he will not hesitate to use chaotic world conditions and problems to oppose the mind. God's answer to this is the helmet of salvation.

Paul is not talking here about the salvation of the soul. He is not referring to salvation as regeneration or conversion. This is the mistake that many make when attempting to interpret this verse. They say: "Whenever the devil attacks your mind and seeks to oppress it, remind yourself that you have been saved." Well, there is nothing wrong with that, of course, and this explanation is mistaken, not because it is untrue, but because it does not go far enough.

The best way to interpret a verse of Scripture is with another verse of Scripture. Thus the text before us today throws a shaft of light on Paul's statement in Ephesians 6:17, for it shows salvation, not just as something in the past but something that is also future. He uses the word in the same way in Romans when he says: "Our salvation is nearer now than when we first believed" (Rom. 13:11).

In the Bible, the word *salvation* has three distinct tenses—past, present and future. At conversion, we are saved from the penalty of sin. Now, day by day, we are being saved from the power of sin. And one day in the future, we will be saved from the presence of sin. It is to the future Paul is looking when he invites us to put on the helmet of salvation.

FURTHER STUDY

Pss. 27:1–14; 37:39; Isa. 12:2; 25:9

1. What was the psalmist's conviction?

2. What is the prophet proclaiming?

Prayer

O Father, thank You for reminding me of the tenses of salvation. I see that in order to live effectively, I must view the present tense by the future tense. Help me lay hold on this. In Jesus' Name. Amen.

SECTION FOUR

"An Atheist Who Lost His Faith"

For reading & meditation—Romans 8:18–30

"For in this hope we were saved ..." (v.24)

What is Paul talking about in our passage today? He is talking about the time when Christ will return, when the kingdom of God will be established and when creation will be delivered from its bondage. The helmet of salvation, therefore, is the recognition that all human schemes, all human disorder, and all human chaos will one day be ended, and when that happens, the whole universe will see that God has been quietly working out His purposes in and through everything.

That truth, when understood and embraced, is the one thing above all others that will enable us to keep our thinking straight in a world that is full of confusion and darkness. Why is it that thoughtful minds like H.G. Wells, Bernard Shaw, and others were and are so bewildered by what they see in the world? It is because they pin their hopes on unreliable and unrealistic resources. As the Dean of Melbourne wrote about H.G. Wells: "He hailed science as a panacea for all ills and the goddess of knowledge and power."

But what were H.G. Wells's conclusions about the world before he died? He wrote this: "The science to which I pinned my faith is bankrupt. Its counsels, which should have established the millennium, led instead directly to the suicide of Europe. I believed them once. In their name I helped destroy the faith of millions of worshipers in the temples of a thousand creeds. And now they look at me and witness the great tragedy of an atheist who has lost his faith." There is no protection in the world for the mind.

FURTHER STUDY

Titus 2; Prov. 14:32; Acts 24:15; Col. 1:5

1. How should we live?

2. What are we to look for?

Prayer

Something, my Father, is being burned into my consciousness—there is just no hope outside of You. If I break with You, I break with sanity. Help me to walk closely with You so that Your mind becomes my mind. In Jesus' Name. Amen.

SECTION FOUR

Everything Is Under Control

For reading & meditation—Ephesians 1:3–14

"... according to His purpose who works all things after the counsel of His will." (v.11, NASB)

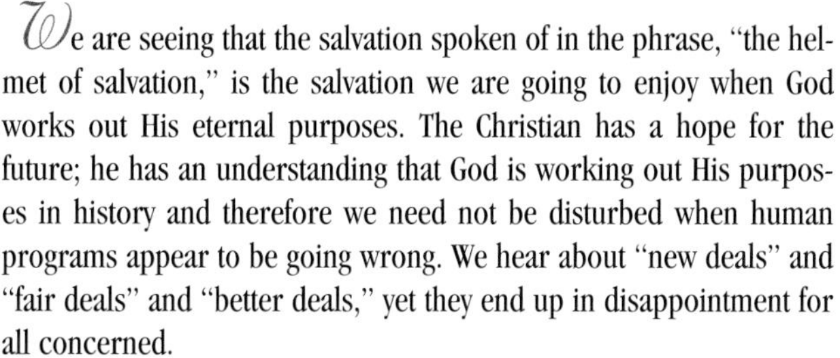

We are seeing that the salvation spoken of in the phrase, "the helmet of salvation," is the salvation we are going to enjoy when God works out His eternal purposes. The Christian has a hope for the future; he has an understanding that God is working out His purposes in history and therefore we need not be disturbed when human programs appear to be going wrong. We hear about "new deals" and "fair deals" and "better deals," yet they end up in disappointment for all concerned.

The Christian expects the world to get worse and worse, for that is what the Bible tells us will happen. He expects false teachings to abound. He expects the world's systems to fail, for anything that is not built on Christ has no guarantee of success. The Christian knows that wars and international tension are unavoidable, even though every effort is made to avoid them. The world is in such a state and such a condition that the more attention we give it, the more weary our minds become.

What is a Christian to do in such a world as ours? How are we to react when the devil takes advantage of our sensitivity to world conditions and focuses our thoughts upon them? Shall we give up? Shall we withdraw from life? No, we put on the helmet of salvation and remind ourselves that in the face of everything that appears contrary, God is working out His eternal plan and purpose. History is His-story. The Almighty God is at work in the very events that appear to be filled with darkness and confusion.

FURTHER STUDY

Heb. 6; 1 Pet. 1:3; 1 John 3:3

1. What does this hope provide for us?

2. How does Peter describe our hope?

O God, help me see that although You are apart from the events of history, You are also in the events of history. Ultimately all things are going to glorify You. Thank You, Father. Amen.

SECTION FOUR

"Not a Private Fight"

For reading & meditation—2 Chronicles 20:4–26

"... Do not be afraid or discouraged ... For the battle is not yours, but God's." (v.15)

As I have been saying, the spiritual application of the helmet of salvation is not so much the enjoyment of our present salvation (though it includes that) but the assurance that a sure salvation is coming and is even now at work.

This is what we need to know if we are to prevent the devil from bringing us into a state of mental distress—not merely that things will finally end right but that God's plan is being worked out now. "History," writes Ray Stedman, an American Bible teacher, "is not a meaningless jumble but a controlled pattern, and the Lord Jesus Christ is the one who is directing these events." The attack of Satan on the mind proceeds differently: "Just look around you at the state of the world. God seems powerless to put things right. He has given lots of promises that things will one day get better, but none has come to pass. Hadn't you better give up this foolish idea that it's all going to work out right?"

If you were to let your mind dwell on that kind of satanic argument, you would soon find yourself in distress. The answer is to put on the helmet, the hope of salvation. You must remind yourself that things are not as they appear. The battle is not ours, but the Lord's. We may be individual soldiers fighting in the army of God, but the ultimate cause is sure and the end is certain. We need not be unduly troubled by what is happening in the world—our commander is not just winning; He has already won.

FURTHER STUDY

Luke 21:10–28;
John 14:1–4; 16:33

1. How did Jesus describe the world?
2. What did He say to His disciples?

Prayer

Lord Jesus, I am grateful that the cross is the guarantee that neither sin nor Satan will ever defeat You. Your victory at Calvary has settled forever the question of who has the final word in the universe. I am so deeply, deeply thankful. Amen.

SECTION FOUR

We See Jesus

For reading & meditation—Hebrews 2:1–15

"… we do not see everything subject to him. But we see Jesus …" (vv.8–9)

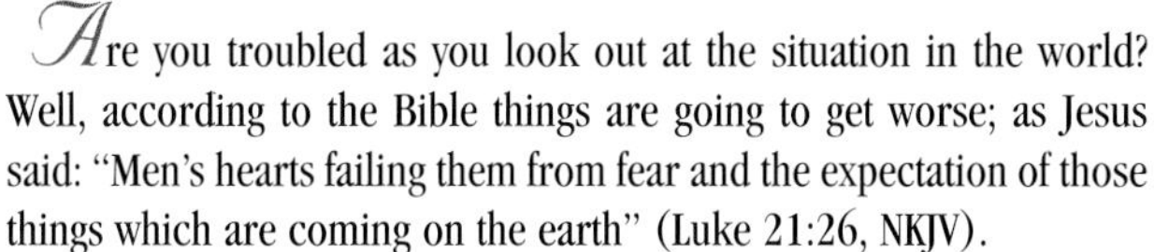

Are you troubled as you look out at the situation in the world? Well, according to the Bible things are going to get worse; as Jesus said: "Men's hearts failing them from fear and the expectation of those things which are coming on the earth" (Luke 21:26, NKJV).

How are Christians going to stand when the darkness deepens and things get very much worse? What will we do when international tension increases? Christians have a glorious hope—the hope of salvation. It is this, and this alone, which enables believers to live out their lives free from mental distress. I am sure you have already discovered that after reading the morning newspaper, you move into the day feeling somewhat depressed. Why is this? It is because almost daily, our newspapers are filled with murder, rape, violence, economic distress, and child abuse. And our conscience, which through conversion has been sensitized to the moral laws of God, begins to reverberate as it comes up against the reports of things we know are contrary to the divine principles.

Satan, seeing our concern, attempts to exploit it to his own ends. "Things are getting worse, aren't they?" he says. "Why don't you just admit that God has lost control of His world?" If we did not have the helmet of salvation to put on at such a moment, we would finish up with the same attitude as H.G. Wells, who, after the Second World War, wrote: "The spectacle of evil in the world has come near to breaking my spirit." Again I say, there is no protection in the world for the mind.

FURTHER STUDY

John 17; Rom. 8:35–37; 1 John 5:4

1. What did Jesus pray for His disciples?

2. What was Paul's conviction?

My Father and my God, where would I be if I could not cling to a text such as that in my reading for today? My spirit too would be near to breaking. I am so thankful that in You there is hope—hope with a capital H. Amen.

SECTION FOUR

The Way to an Undisturbed Mind

For reading & meditation—Colossians 1:9–28

"... Christ in you, the hope of glory." (v.27)

In the British Isles we are relatively free from much of what concerns and distresses others. We have much to be sad about, but we have much to be glad about also. We can still preach the gospel in our churches and can still enjoy freedom of speech. But I know that these pages will be read in areas of the world where this is not possible, where Satan is openly worshiped and where faith is not allowed to be expressed openly.

What do Christians living in these places do to prevent themselves from becoming wearied by their adverse circumstances? There is only one thing they can do—they must put on the helmet of the hope of salvation. This, more than anything, will help keep their thinking straight. But no matter where in the world we live, those of us who have enlisted in the army of God must do the same. We must not succumb to the popular delusion that the working out of all human problems lies just around the corner through the application of humanistic ideas.

Almost from the dawn of history, men and women have been grasping after the elusive hope that something can be worked out here. But God has never said that. Consistently throughout the Scriptures, He has said that fallen humanity is totally unable to work out its problems. We know, however, that He has reserved a day of salvation when all wrongs will be righted, and it is only in the strength of the hope of that day of salvation that our hearts and minds can be kept undisturbed.

FURTHER STUDY

Gal. 2; John 14:20; 1 John 3:24

1. How did Paul describe his Christian walk?

2. How would you describe your Christian walk?

Prayer

O Father, how can I ever be grateful enough that I am caught up in an eternal purpose. I live in the present, yet I draw also from the certainties of the future. Nourish this hope within me until it drives out every fear. In Jesus' Name. Amen.

SECTION FOUR

The Sword of the Spirit

For reading & meditation—James 4:1–10

"... stand firm against the devil; resist him and he will flee from you." (v.7, Amp. Bible)

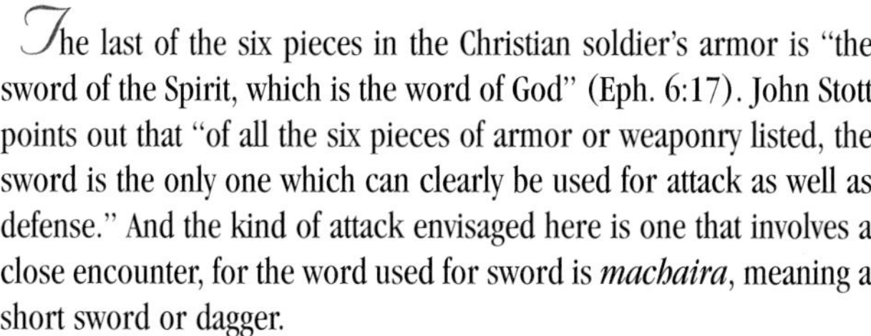

The last of the six pieces in the Christian soldier's armor is "the sword of the Spirit, which is the word of God" (Eph. 6:17). John Stott points out that "of all the six pieces of armor or weaponry listed, the sword is the only one which can clearly be used for attack as well as defense." And the kind of attack envisaged here is one that involves a close encounter, for the word used for sword is *machaira*, meaning a short sword or dagger.

There is much more to spiritual warfare than standing up to the devil—we have, according to our text today, the potential to make him "flee." The word *flee* is a very strong word in the original Greek. It means much more than a strategic withdrawal; it means beating a swift retreat. What an amazing truth! It is possible for a Christian so to resist the devil that he races away as fast as he can.

This truth must not be seen in any way as limiting the devil's power, for he is a strong and determined foe. It means rather that a Christian able to wield the sword of the Spirit can ensure that he is overpowered. We are right to develop a healthy respect for the devil's wiles, but we are wrong when we allow him to terrorize us. We must have the assurance, given everywhere in the New Testament, that to engage in conflict with the devil is not a hopeless task. We are not to indulge in over-confidence but, at the same time, we are not to be frightened by him.

FURTHER STUDY

Luke 10:1–20; Acts 3:6–8; 16:16–18; 1 Pet. 5:8–9

1. How much authority over Satan have we been given?

2. How did the early Church exercise this authority?

Prayer

O Father, the thought that I, a sinner saved by grace, am able to send Satan into retreat almost overwhelms me. Yet I must believe it, for Your Word tells me so. Help me understand even more clearly the authority I have in Christ. In His Name I ask it. Amen.

SECTION FOUR

The Power of Precise Scripture

For reading & meditation—Matthew 4:1–11

"... It is written ... It is also written ..." (vv.4 & 7)

We must now focus on what is meant by the phrase—"the sword of the Spirit, which is the word of God." The sword is the Word of God, the Bible, the inspired Scriptures.

In the passage before us today we see a perfect illustration of how Jesus used the sword of the Spirit when rebutting the temptations of the devil. Notice how, prior to the temptation, Jesus was anointed by the Holy Spirit (Matt. 3:13–17). Next we are informed that Jesus was "led by the Spirit into the desert to be tempted by the devil" (4:1). During the temptation our Lord, filled with the Spirit, resisted every one of the devil's statements by using the precise words of Scripture. Follow me closely, for this is extremely important: Christ did not merely utter a newly formed statement or something that came to Him on the spur of the moment, but quoted a text which had already been given by God and written down. The weapon used by our Lord was the Word of God, the Scriptures.

Can you see the point I am making? Satan is not rebuffed by clever phrases that are made up on the spur of the moment and may sound theologically sophisticated and refined; he is defeated only when we quote to him the precise words of Scripture. If this was the strategy Jesus had to use, then how much more you and I. Nothing defeats Satan more thoroughly and effectively than the sword of the Spirit, which is the Word of God.

FURTHER STUDY

1 Pet. 1:13–25; Ps. 119:89 & 103; Jer. 15:16

1. What did Jeremiah do with God's word?
2. How did the psalmist describe it?

Prayer

O God, open my eyes that I might see more clearly than ever the power and authority that lies in Your sacred Word, the Bible. Help me to know it better. For Your own dear Name's sake. Amen.

The Bible—An Inspired Book

For reading & meditation—John 16:1–15

"... when he, the Spirit of truth, comes, he will guide you into all truth ..." (v.13)

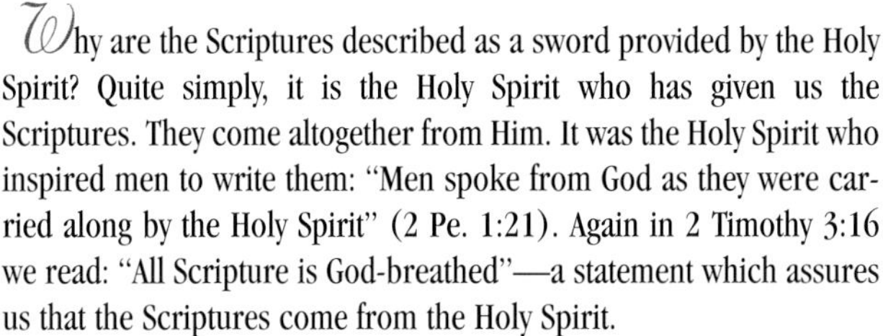

Why are the Scriptures described as a sword provided by the Holy Spirit? Quite simply, it is the Holy Spirit who has given us the Scriptures. They come altogether from Him. It was the Holy Spirit who inspired men to write them: "Men spoke from God as they were carried along by the Holy Spirit" (2 Pe. 1:21). Again in 2 Timothy 3:16 we read: "All Scripture is God-breathed"—a statement which assures us that the Scriptures come from the Holy Spirit.

The Bible is not a mere human document. The Holy Spirit breathed into men and inspired them to write the way they did. This does not mean that the people who wrote the Scriptures did so mechanically, in the way that someone would dictate into a dictating machine. The Holy Spirit used their natural way of expression but gave them an additional ability to write without error. It is vital, if you are to win the battle against Satan, that you not only see this but believe it. When you consider how powerful Satan is, then you need something that is even stronger. And the Bible, the inspired Word of God, is your strength.

One step further—only the Holy Spirit can enable us truly to understand God's Word: "We have not received the spirit of the world but the Spirit who is from God, that we may understand what God has freely given us" (1 Cor. 2:12). Without the Holy Spirit, we would be no more able to understand the Scriptures than a blind man could judge a beauty contest.

FURTHER STUDY

Col. 3:1–16; Deut. 6:6; 11:18; Heb. 10:15–16

1. What does the word "dwell" mean?

2. Where must God's word be written?

Prayer

Gracious Holy Spirit, just as You breathed into the Bible to give it its life and power, breathe also into my heart today so that I might know and understand its truth. I ask this in Jesus' Name. Amen.

SECTION FOUR

"Divide and Conquer"

For reading & meditation—1 Corinthians 2:1–16

"... the things that come from the Spirit of God ... are spiritually discerned." (v.14)

Only the Holy Spirit can help us can help us properly to interpret the Word of God. A person may have a fine mind, a good seminary training, even a theological degree, but that is not a sufficient foundation on which to attempt to interpret the Word of God. Truth, as our text for today tells us, is "spiritually discerned."

But there is one more thing we need to understand—only the Holy Spirit can show us how to use it aright. Doubtless this was the consideration in the mind of the apostle when he penned the statement we are considering: "the sword of the Spirit, which is the word of God." It is one thing to know the contents of Scripture; it is another thing to know how to use those contents in a way that defeats the devil. Only the Holy Spirit can enable us to do this.

The relationship between the Holy Spirit and the Word of God is an important one. Some tend to put the emphasis on one side or the other. But the moment we separate the Spirit and the Word, we are in trouble. The late Donald Gee once said: "All Spirit and no Word, you blow up. All Word and no Spirit, you dry up. Word and Spirit—you grow up." Without the Spirit, the Word is a dead letter; with the Spirit, it is a living and powerful force. The devil has a policy of "divide and conquer," and if he can get us to separate the Word from the Spirit, then he has us just where he wants us.

FURTHER STUDY

2 Cor. 3:1–6; John 6:63; 1 Pet. 3:18

1. What "gives life"?
2. What made Paul an able minister of truth?

Prayer

My Father, I see that when I separate the Spirit from the Word and the Word from the Spirit, I am in trouble. Help me to be as open to the Spirit as I am to the Bible, and as open to the Bible as I am to the Spirit. In Jesus' Name. Amen.

SECTION FOUR

The Divine Design

For reading & meditation—John 14:15–27

"... the Holy Spirit ... will teach you all things and will remind you of everything I have said to you." (v.26)

When we come to God's Word, laying aside all preconceived ideas and depending entirely on the Holy Spirit to reveal its truth to us, we put ourselves in a position where the Holy Spirit can impress the truth of the Scriptures into our innermost being. There it takes root within us, and whenever we stand in need of a word with which to rebut the devil, the Holy Spirit brings it to our remembrance.

And here's the most wonderful thing—the Word of God on our lips will have the same effect upon the devil as if he were hearing it from the lips of Jesus Himself! Every time we open the Bible, we must be careful to pray for the illumination of the Spirit so that we don't finish up making the Bible mean what we want it to mean. When we receive that help, we are following the divine design—letting the Spirit bring home to our hearts the truth and meaning of His own Word.

This attitude of humility and receptivity gives the Holy Spirit the opportunity He needs to build the truth of the Word of God into our spirits. Approaching the Bible in this way, said the late J. B. Phillips, "is like rewiring a house where the electricity has not been turned off." You touch something that lets you know there is a current of power flowing through its pages that was not put there by any man. The Holy Spirit has gone into it, so is it any wonder that the Holy Spirit comes out of it?

FURTHER STUDY

John 15:18–27;
Luke 12:11–12;
Rom. 8:14

1. What did Jesus declare about the Holy Spirit's ministry?

2. What promise did Jesus give to His disciples?

My Father and my God, I know the Spirit dwells in Your Word. I come now to ask that He might dwell also in me, to open up my whole being to the truth and power that lies in its inspired pages. In Jesus' Name I ask it. Amen.

SECTION FOUR

The Coal Miner and the Ph. D.

For reading & meditation—Hebrews 4:1–13

"For the word of God is living and active. Sharper than any double-edged sword ..." (v.12)

Some of you reading these lines today may not have had the benefits of a good or extensive education. You may be deficient in your knowledge of many things. But here is the encouraging thing—none of these issues are important when it comes to the matter of defeating Satan.

I remember being present some years ago in a church in South Wales when a debate was held between a university professor and an ordinary coal miner. The subject was: "Is the Bible true?" The university professor presented his arguments in a clear fashion, and I remember feeling quite sorry for the miner as I envisaged some of the difficulties he might have when making his reply. After the professor had finished, the miner stood to his feet and for over an hour I witnessed one of the most amazing demonstrations of the Holy Spirit at work that I have ever seen in my life.

The miner began by asking everyone to bow their heads as he prayed a prayer which went something like this: "Lord, I have not had much education, but You know that I love Your Word and have spent my life searching its pages. Help me now to say something that will convince my friends here that Your Word is true." He then proceeded to demolish the arguments of the professor simply by quoting appropriate Scriptures without making even a simple comment. When he finished, there was thunderous applause. The professor's highly intellectual arguments had been torn to pieces by the sharp edges of the sword of the Spirit—by that, and by that alone.

FURTHER STUDY

Jer. 5:1–14; 23:29;
Ps. 119:105 & 130

1. What was God's word in Jeremiah's mouth?

2. What was it to the psalmist?

Prayer

O Father, the more I hear, the more I want to hear. For I was created by Your Word, designed according to Your Word, and I can never remain content until I am indwelt with Your Word. Teach me even more. In Jesus' Name. Amen.

Go Still Deeper

For reading & meditation—John 17:1–19

"... your word is truth." (v.17)

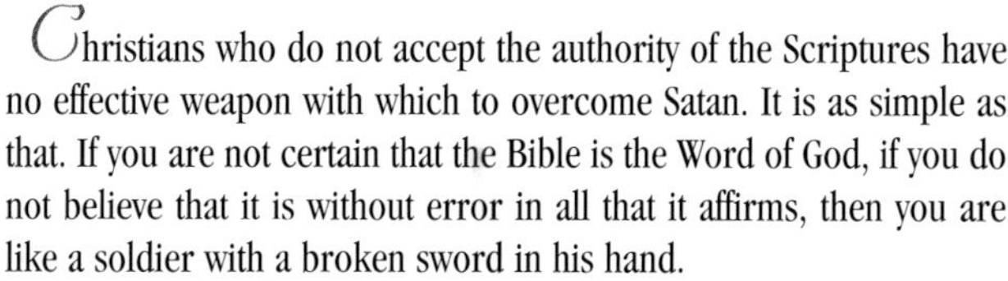

Christians who do not accept the authority of the Scriptures have no effective weapon with which to overcome Satan. It is as simple as that. If you are not certain that the Bible is the Word of God, if you do not believe that it is without error in all that it affirms, then you are like a soldier with a broken sword in his hand.

To use the sword of the Spirit effectively, we need to have as wide a knowledge of the Bible as possible. Let me take you back to Christ's encounter with Satan in the wilderness of temptation once again. When Satan advanced, Jesus took up the sword of the Spirit and knew exactly which particular Scriptures to use to rebut each of the three separate temptations of the devil.

If we are to conquer Satan in the same way that Jesus conquered him, then we must know the Bible in its entirety. It is no good saying to the devil: "The verse I want to use against you is somewhere in the Bible." You must quote it to him and quote it precisely. I hope you do not think that reading these pages will do this for you, because it won't. These daily readings will help you start the day, but you need a deeper and more intensive program of study if you are to become proficient in the use of the Scriptures against Satan. Decide right now to commit yourself to exploring the Bible more deeply and thoroughly than you have ever done before.

FURTHER STUDY

Ezek.37:1–10; Acts 17:11; Rom. 10:8

1. What was the result of the spoken word through Ezekiel?

2. What did Paul say of the Bereans?

Prayer

O Father, I see that the more I know of Your Word, the more effective I will be in resisting Satan. Show me how to go more deeply into the Scriptures than I have ever done before. In Jesus' Name I pray. Amen.

SECTION FOUR

A Final Exhortation

For reading & meditation—Luke 21:20–36

"Be always on the watch, and pray . . ." (v.36)

One might think that, having examined in detail the six pieces of the armor of God, this would be a natural place to end our discussion, but there is one more verse to consider: "Praying always with all prayer and supplication in the Spirit, being watchful to this end with all perseverance and supplication for all the saints" (Eph. 6:18, NKJV).

What is the meaning of this further and final exhortation? Well, it is not, as so many Christians believe, an additional but unnamed piece of armor. One commentator writes: "Paul is giving us in this verse the final piece of armor for the Christian who is in conflict with the devil: praying always with all prayer . . . ." This surely cannot be so, for Paul's reference to "praying always with all prayer," although closely related to the six pieces of armor, is quite different from them and does not fall within the bounds of the careful and close analogy that he has been making.

What then does he mean? He is saying (so I believe) that "praying in the Spirit" is something that ought to pervade all our spiritual warfare and is something we have to do and keep on doing if we are to win the battle against Satan and his forces. Paul is saying: "Put on the whole armor of God, every single piece, and in the proper order; but in addition to that, at all times and in all places, keep on praying." In other words, the armor which is provided for us by God cannot be used effectively unless it is worn by a praying Christian.

FURTHER STUDY

Luke 18:1–8; 1 Chron. 16:11; Col. 4:2; 1 Thess. 5:17

1. What was Jesus teaching in this parable?

2. How did Paul exhort the Colossians?

Prayer

O Father, thank You for inspiring Your servant Paul to give us this insight, for we see that without it we would be defeated by the devil. Help me become a watchful and praying Christian. In Jesus' Name. Amen.

SECTION FOUR

Not a Postscript

For reading & meditation—Colossians 1:1–12

"We always thank God, the Father of our Lord Jesus Christ, when we pray for you" (v.3)

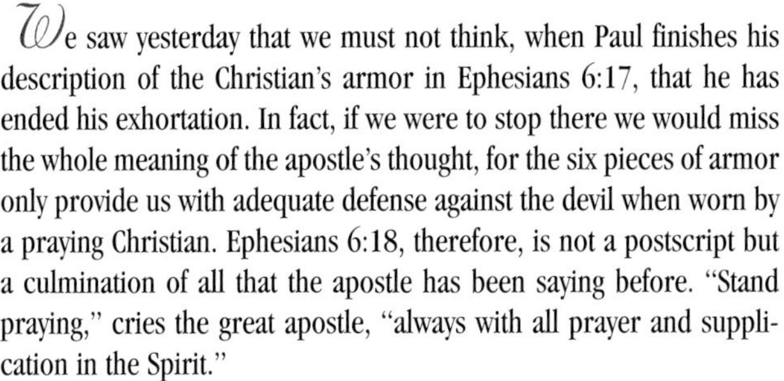

We saw yesterday that we must not think, when Paul finishes his description of the Christian's armor in Ephesians 6:17, that he has ended his exhortation. In fact, if we were to stop there we would miss the whole meaning of the apostle's thought, for the six pieces of armor only provide us with adequate defense against the devil when worn by a praying Christian. Ephesians 6:18, therefore, is not a postscript but a culmination of all that the apostle has been saying before. "Stand praying," cries the great apostle, "always with all prayer and supplication in the Spirit."

The danger facing us is that we can feel, once we have our spiritual armor on, that we are safe, we can relax, all is well, that the armor will protect us. But that is the height of folly and something Satan would love to get us to believe. And if we do believe it, then it means we are already defeated. The armor of God and its spiritual application must always be thought of in terms of our relationship with God. If there is no communion with Him, then the six pieces of armor will be ineffective. The armor of God is not something that is magical or mechanical; it functions as a spiritual defense only when worn with prayer. One of the great hymns of our faith expresses the thought most beautifully when it says:

To keep your armor bright
Attend with constant care
Still walking in our Captain's sight
And watching unto prayer.

FURTHER STUDY

John 15:1–7; Jer. 29:13; Matt. 26:41; Mark 11:24

1. Why can we pray with confidence?

2. What must accompany prayer?

Prayer

Father, I see that with all I have learned about defending myself against the devil, I must still go a step further. Help me to understand this step, for it is vital that I am not just protected against Satan, but fully protected. Amen.

And Yet . . .

For reading & meditation—1 Thessalonians 5:11–24

"Be unceasing in prayer—praying perseveringly" (v.17, Amp. Bible)

John Stott, in his commentary on Ephesians, says: "Equipping ourselves with God's armor is not a mechanical operation; it is in itself an expression of our dependence upon God."

Note the phrase, "is not a mechanical operation." Some Christians like to begin each day by going through the motions of dressing themselves in the armor of God. In their minds they put on the belt of truth, the breastplate of righteousness, the shoes of the preparation of the gospel of peace, and so on. I have no objection to this myself, but I do see a danger that it can become merely a mechanical operation in which they look just to the armor to protect them from the wiles of the devil, and think that nothing more needs to be done. Let me remind you again—every single piece of armor, excellent and valuable though it is in itself, will not work for us unless always, and at all times, we are in a close, prayerful relationship with God.

Cast your mind back once again over the six pieces of the Christian soldier's equipment: the belt of truth, the breastplate of righteousness, the shoes of peace, the shield of faith, the helmet of salvation, and the sword of the Spirit. What strong protection our Lord has provided for us in this conflict against Satan and his forces. And yet, having all this great and wonderful equipment available, we can still suffer defeat if we do not stand in the strength and power which God provides. And that power can flow only along the channel of fervent, believing prayer.

FURTHER STUDY

Col. 1:1–12; Phil. 4:13; Eph. 3:16; 1 Pet. 5:10

1. What was Paul's prayer for the Colossians?

2. Where does our strength come from?

Prayer

Father, day by day it is becoming increasingly clear that unless I am continually linked to Your resources through believing prayer, the armor You have provided for me gives me only a limited defense. Help me never to forget this. Amen.

SECTION FOUR

Standard Operating Procedure

For reading & meditation—1 Timothy 2:1–10

"I want men everywhere to lift up holy hands in prayer, without anger or disputing." (v.8)

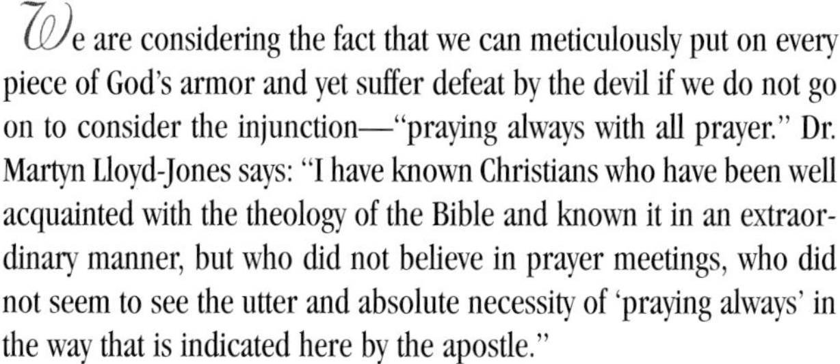

We are considering the fact that we can meticulously put on every piece of God's armor and yet suffer defeat by the devil if we do not go on to consider the injunction—"praying always with all prayer." Dr. Martyn Lloyd-Jones says: "I have known Christians who have been well acquainted with the theology of the Bible and known it in an extraordinary manner, but who did not believe in prayer meetings, who did not seem to see the utter and absolute necessity of 'praying always' in the way that is indicated here by the apostle."

It is possible to be orthodox in your doctrine and still, as far as spiritual warfare is concerned, be a defeated Christian. You cannot fight the devil, even with orthodoxy, if you know nothing of a vital, day-by-day relationship with God through prayer. Many people have a wonderful understanding of Scripture and are experts at pointing out the errors in other people's teaching, but because they do not have a close relationship with God in prayer, they fall easy prey to the devil.

A whole church or community of Christian people can experience the same problem; they can have a good, sound knowledge of the Bible, yet know nothing of a strong corporate ministry of prayer in their midst. Such a church can be easily paralyzed by the devil. It may seem that I am laboring the point, but it is absolutely imperative we understand that our effectiveness in spiritual warfare depends not on the armor alone, but on our ability to maintain a close and intimate relationship with God through prayer.

FURTHER STUDY

Luke 11:1–13; 6:12; Mark 1:35; 6:46–47

1. What was the disciples' request?

2. What was Jesus' pattern?

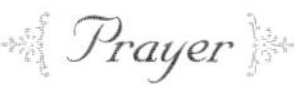

Prayer

Father, I think I have it now—no prayer, and everything else fails to work the way You designed it to. Drive this truth so deeply into my spirit that for the rest of my life, it will be standard operating procedure. Amen.

SECTION FOUR

The Four "Alls"

For reading & meditation—Matthew 14:22–33

"... he went up on a mountainside by himself to pray ..." (v.23)

If, as we have seen, the effectiveness of our spiritual warfare depends not just on wearing the six pieces of armor, but also on constant believing prayer, then we must ask ourselves: what can we do to make our prayer lives more contributive?

The place given to prayer in both the Old and New Testaments is remarkable. All the great saints of the Old Testament knew how to pray—Abraham, David, Daniel, Jeremiah, Isaiah, to mention just a few. The same prowess in prayer can be seen also in the New Testament saints. But of course the greatest prayer was none other than our Lord Jesus Christ. Although He possessed great knowledge and wisdom, He found it essential to turn aside time and time again to pray. On certain occasions He would spend whole nights in prayer or rise long before dawn in order to pray and maintain His communion with God. Is it surprising, therefore, that being so dependent on prayer, He should have told His disciples:

"Men ought always to pray, and not to faint" (Luke 18:1, KJV). Praying is the only alternative to fainting—we must pray or else we faint.

Paul's teaching with regard to prayer in Ephesians 6:18 revolves around four "alls." We are to pray at all times, with all prayer, with all perseverance, and for all the saints. Most Christians, however, pray at some times, with some prayer, and some degree of perseverance for some of God's saints. When we replace "some" by "all" in these expressions, we are on our way to effective praying.

FURTHER STUDY

1 Sam. 7:1–10;
1:27;
Exod. 15:24–25;
1 Kings 18:37–38

1. List some prayers God answered.
2. List some answers to prayer you have received.

My Father and my God, I see that through prayer, You offer me the most breathtaking power. Help me humbly to take it and use it wisely. In Jesus' Name I pray. Amen.

SECTION FOUR

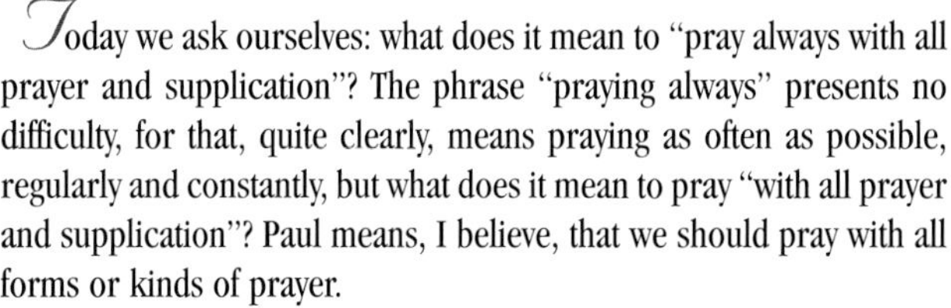

The Various Forms of Prayer

DAY 238

For reading & meditation—Colossians 4:1–12

"Devote yourselves to prayer, being watchful and thankful." (v.2)

Today we ask ourselves: what does it mean to "pray always with all prayer and supplication"? The phrase "praying always" presents no difficulty, for that, quite clearly, means praying as often as possible, regularly and constantly, but what does it mean to pray "with all prayer and supplication"? Paul means, I believe, that we should pray with all forms or kinds of prayer.

You see, there are many different forms of prayer that are available to us. First, there is verbal prayer when we present our prayer to God in carefully chosen words and phrases. Second, there is silent prayer, when no words cross our lips but prayer flows directly from our hearts. Third, there is ejaculatory prayer, when we express sounds rather than words, as when we sigh or groan in prayer. Then there is public prayer, common prayer, or "praying together"—or, as some prefer to call it, "praying in concert." So praying with all prayer means using every form of prayer available to us and praying in every way and manner that we can. We are to be at it always, and in endless ways.

But there is a certain form of prayer to which the apostle refers which deserves closer examination—the prayer of supplication, or "petition," when we pray with regard to special requests and needs. We must not overlook this, for it is so easy to be caught up in adoration and praise that we neglect to focus our prayers on the various needs that arise from time to time, not only in our own lives, but also in the lives of others.

FURTHER STUDY

Matt. 7:1–12; Acts 1:14; 4:24; 12:12; 21:5

1. What is evident about the early Church?

2. How does Jesus relate fatherhood to prayer?

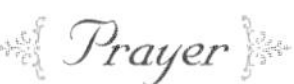

Prayer

Father, help me to see the senselessness of trying to muddle through life in my own strength when You have made Your power and resources available to me through prayer. Help me grow in prayer. In Jesus' Name. Amen.

SECTION FOUR

"Praying in the Spirit"

For reading & meditation—Romans 8:18–30

"... We do not know what we ought to pray for, but the Spirit himself intercedes for us ..." (v.26)

What does it mean to pray "in the Spirit"? Here again, there is a good deal of misunderstanding among Christians as to the true meaning of this phrase.

There are times when one feels deeply affected emotionally as one prays, but this is not the meaning of the phrase "praying in the Spirit." It has no relationship to the emotions that we feel in prayer. I am not saying that feelings are unimportant in prayer; I am simply saying that I do not believe this is what Paul had in mind when he used the phrase "praying in the Spirit." The "spirit" spoken of here is not the human spirit, but the Holy Spirit. Some believe that "praying in the Spirit" takes place when we pray in other tongues, and although it can include that, I believe it is much more than that.

Prayer that is "in the Spirit" is prayer that is prompted and guided by the Spirit. One commentator puts it this way: "It means that the Holy Spirit directs the prayer, creates the prayer within us, and empowers us to offer it and to pray it." Dr. Martyn Lloyd-Jones calls praying in the Spirit "the secret of true prayer" and goes on to say: "If we do not pray in the Spirit, we do not really pray." I would hesitate to make such a sweeping statement myself, but I would go so far as to say that if we do not know what it means to pray in the Spirit, our prayers will have little impact upon Satan and his forces.

FURTHER STUDY

Rom. 8:1–17; Luke 11:13; 24:49

1. To what does the Spirit bear witness?
2. What was Christ's promise to His disciples?

Prayer

Dear Father, I have so much to learn about prayer that unless You take my hand and guide me, I can soon lose my way. Teach me how to enter the deeper levels of prayer. In Jesus' Name. Amen.

SECTION FOUR

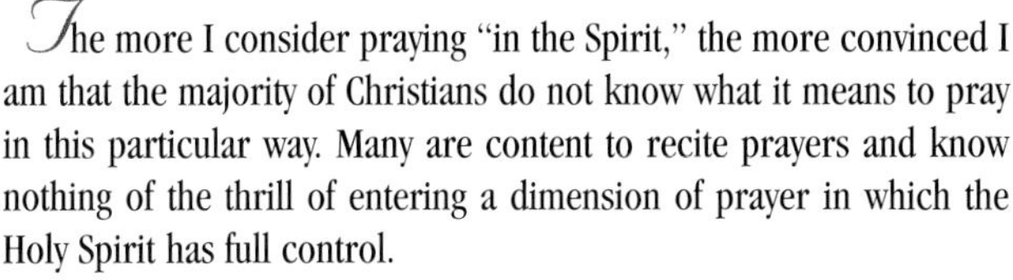

Spirit-Aided Praying

DAY 240

For reading & meditation—John 6:56–69

"The Spirit gives life . . ." (v.63)

The more I consider praying "in the Spirit," the more convinced I am that the majority of Christians do not know what it means to pray in this particular way. Many are content to recite prayers and know nothing of the thrill of entering a dimension of prayer in which the Holy Spirit has full control.

Not that there is anything wrong with liturgical or written prayers—they can be a wonderful primer for one's spiritual pump. Many people tell me that the prayers I frame at the bottom of each page of *Every Day with Jesus* have sometimes helped them more than the actual notes I have written. Using written prayers can be helpful, but we must heed the apostle's exhortation to move on into that dimension which he calls "praying in the Spirit." The best description of "praying in the Spirit" I have ever heard is that given by some of the old Welsh preachers, like Daniel Rowlands, Christmas Evans, and others. They describe it as "praying with unusual liberty and freedom."

There is hardly anything more wonderful in the Christian life than to experience liberty and freedom in prayer. I can remember the minister and elders of the church in which I was converted in South Wales saying after a prayer meeting in which there had been great liberty and power: "Tonight we have prayed in the Spirit." Have you not experienced moments when, after struggling and halting in prayer, you were suddenly taken out of yourself and words just poured out of you? At that moment, you were "praying in the Spirit."

FURTHER STUDY

2 Cor. 3:6–18; Matt. 6:7–8; 1 Cor. 14:15; Jude 20

1. What does the Spirit of the Lord bring?

2. What are we to avoid when we pray?

Prayer

O Father, forgive me that I try to do so much in my own strength instead of learning how to let You do it in me. Teach me how to let go and let You take over in everything—particularly my praying. In Jesus' Name. Amen.

First Principles

For reading & meditation—Luke 5:1–11

"… Put out into deep water …" (v.4)

I find myself compelled to spend another day discussing Paul's pregnant phrase "praying in the Spirit." There are times in my own life, as I am sure there are in yours, when I struggle in prayer and find it difficult to concentrate, only to discover that suddenly I am taken out of myself and given a freedom that transforms my prayer time from that point on. When that happens, I know I have been praying in the Spirit. This is the kind of thing about which the apostle Paul is exhorting us in Ephesians 6:18. Formal prayer is fine and has its place, but oh, how we need to experience more times of praying in the Spirit.

But how do we attain these times? Is it the Spirit's responsibility to bring us there or do we have some responsibility in the matter too? I believe we can learn to pray in the Spirit. Some first principles are these: (1) Come to God in an attitude of dependence. This means recognizing that your greatest need in prayer is not an ability to put words together or form fine phrases, but the Holy Spirit's empowerment. (2) Yield yourself totally to the Spirit for Him to guide and direct your praying. Be continually aware that He wants to have the bigger part in your prayer life. Start with these two principles, and learn to depend less and less on your own experience or ability, and more and more on the Spirit's enabling. Once you experience what it means to "pray in the Spirit," you will long to experience it more and more.

FURTHER STUDY

John 3:22–27;
2 Chron. 20:12;
2 Cor. 3:3–5

1. What was John's declaration?

2. How did Paul express his dependence on God?

Prayer

O Father, my appetite is being whetted. Help me "launch out into the deep" and give myself to You in the way that You are willing to give Yourself to me. In Christ's Name I ask it. Amen.

SECTION FOUR

Not Some . . . But All

For reading & meditation—Ephesians 4:17–32

". . . for we are all members of one body." (v.25)

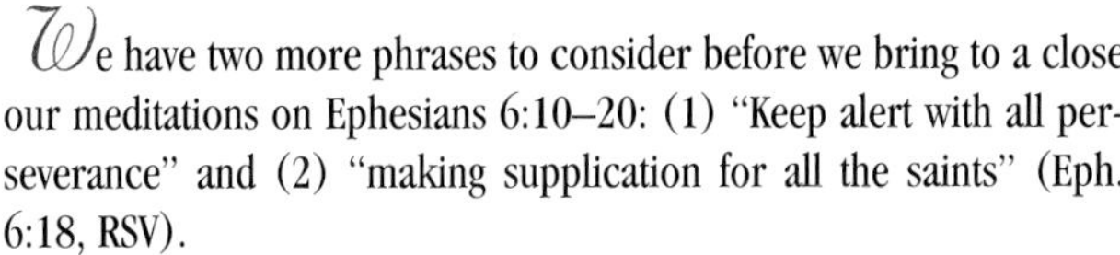

We have two more phrases to consider before we bring to a close our meditations on Ephesians 6:10–20: (1) "Keep alert with all perseverance" and (2) "making supplication for all the saints" (Eph. 6:18, RSV).

The first phrase draws our attention to the fact that we should never allow ourselves to become indolent and lethargic in relation to the matter of prayer, but always eager and ready to make our requests known to Him. But what is the purpose of this spiritual watchfulness? This question brings us to the second phrase: "making supplication for all the saints." Our watchfulness and concern must not be only on our own behalf, but on behalf of all other Christians also.

Why does Paul exhort us to pray for all rather than some Christians—those, for example, whom we know are enduring a particular attack of Satan? The answer is because all Christians need praying for. Every believer is under attack; no one is exempted. The Letter of Jude tells us that we are partakers of a "common salvation." But not only do we enjoy a common salvation: we are fighting a common enemy, and in this we experience common difficulties—hence the need to be intensely aware of each other's needs. We cannot, of course, take the armor of God and put it on another Christian, but we can pray for one another and thus call in spiritual reinforcements. We can pray that their eyes might be opened to the danger they are in and that they might be able to equip themselves to stand against Satan and his powerful forces.

FURTHER STUDY

Gen. 18:23–33;
Matt. 15:21–28;
Acts 12:5

1. How did Abraham intercede?

2. How did the Syrophoenician woman demonstrate persistence?

Prayer

O Father, forgive me, I pray, that sometimes I am so taken up with my own spiritual struggles that I forget my brothers and sisters face the same difficulties also. Save me from my self-centeredness, dear Lord. In Jesus' Name I pray. Amen.

SECTION FOUR

Satan's Pincer Movement

For reading & meditation—Luke 22:24–34

"... I have prayed for you, Simon, that your faith may not fail ..." (v.32)

Another reason why the apostle Paul bids us pray for one another is because the failure of any one of us is going to have some effect upon the spiritual campaign which, through the Church, God is waging against the devil. As we said on the first day of our meditations: all those who have committed themselves to Jesus Christ should know that the forces of the two kingdoms of God and the devil are locked together in mortal combat. And Christians, whether they like it or not, are thrust right onto the cutting edge of that conflict.

The battle line between the forces of God and the forces of Satan is the Church—and that means you and me. What is Satan's best tactic in attempting to bring about the Church's spiritual defeat? He probes at every point he can, looking for the weakest part. When he finds a weak Christian (or a group of weak Christians), he calls for reinforcements and in what military strategists call "a pincer movement," he attempts to break through at that point. And when one Christian fails, all of us to some extent are affected, for we are all part of the one line of defense.

How the devil rejoices when an individual Christian falls—especially a church leader. We are called to a ministry of prayer, not just for ourselves but for one another also, that we might stand perfect and complete in the will of God and that our faith will not fail when under attack by the devil.

FURTHER STUDY

Gal. 6:1–10; 1 Cor. 9:27; Phil. 3:12; James. 5:16

1. What are we to carry in prayer?

2. Of what was Paul conscious?

Prayer

Father, I am encouraged as I think that today, millions of Christians around the world will be praying for me. Help me never to fail in my responsibility to pray for them. In Christ's peerless and precious Name. Amen.

Pray for Me That . . .

For reading & meditation—Romans 12:1–13

"... be transformed by the renewing of your mind. Then you will be able to ... approve ... God's ... perfect will." (v.2)

The apostle ends his section on spiritual warfare (Eph. 6:10–20) on the following personal note: "Pray on my behalf, that utterance may be given to me in the opening of my mouth, to make known with boldness the mystery of the gospel ... that in proclaiming it I may speak boldly, as I ought to speak" (vv.19–20, NASB).

Paul was wise enough to know his own need of supernatural strength if he was to stand against the enemy, and was humble enough to ask his brothers and sisters to pray for him in this matter. Imagine this great apostle, probably the most powerful and effective disciple of Christ the world has ever seen, asking his friends to pray for him. And why not? The greater a Christian is, the more he realizes his dependence on the prayers of others. Paul knew full well the power that was against him, and he did not hesitate to ask for the prayers of the church in Ephesus.

Notice that his request for prayer is clear and specific. Whenever you ask someone to pray for you, be equally specific. Don't just say, "Pray for me," but "Pray for me that ..." Note, too, that Paul's request was not that he might be delivered from prison, but that through his testimony in prison the gospel of Christ might be advanced. He knew that the most important thing was not to triumph over prison but to triumph in it. He knew he was where God wanted him for that time, and he would allow no self-interest to interfere with the divine schedule.

FURTHER STUDY

2 Thess. 3; 1 Thess. 5:25; Heb. 13:18–19

1. What was Paul's request?

2. Whom are you praying for regularly?

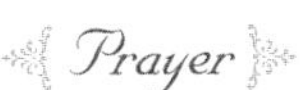

O Father, teach me, as You taught Your servant Paul, to know Your will and purpose so clearly that I might know just how and what to pray for. I ask this in and through the strong and mighty Name of Jesus. Amen.

SECTION FOUR

The Final Word

For reading & meditation—Ephesians 3:8–21

"... now, through the church, the manifold wisdom of God should be made known to the ... authorities in the heavenly realms" (v.10)

On the last day of this study of "The Armor of God," we gather up what we have been saying on this important theme. Once we become Christians, we are involved in a fight against Satan and his forces. God, however, has given us a defense against Satan and his wiles, which consists of six separate pieces of spiritual equipment.

First, He has given us the belt of truth—a willingness to let God's truth govern every part of our lives. Second, the breastplate of righteousness—seeing clearly that we are not saved by our own righteousness but Christ's. Third, we must have our feet shod with the preparation of the gospel of peace—our determination to stand firmly in the faith.

Fourth, we must raise the shield of faith—the quick action by which we act upon God's truth and refuse Satan's lies. Fifth, we must put on the helmet of salvation—the glorious hope that, one day, God will right all wrongs and establish His eternal kingdom. And sixth, we must take up the sword of the Spirit, the Word of God, and wield the written Scriptures in the same way that our Lord did in His wilderness temptations.

Yet we noted also that having done all this, it is still possible that we could be defeated by the devil unless we know how to pray in the power of the Spirit. And we must pray not only when things go wrong, but continuously, fervently, powerfully, and perseveringly. Our prayers must catch alight and burst into flame. Against such praying, the principalities and powers are helpless.

FURTHER STUDY

Pss. 18:1–50; 65:6;
Hab. 3:19;
Isa. 41:10

1. With what was David armed?
2. Have you put on your armor today?

Prayer

My Father, now that I have seen the resources that are available to me in Christ, I realize that my responsibility to avail myself of those resources is greater than ever. Help me to put everything I have learned into action. For Your own dear Name's sake. Amen.

SECTION FIVE

Hinds' Feet on High Places

Hinds' Feet on High Places

We all like to imagine ourselves being sure-footed in our faith, dutifully and responsibly following wherever God leads. But the reality, which Selwyn Hughes underscores here, is that following the Savior is a difficult and treacherous task requiring diligence, prayer, and God's boundless mercy.

The female deer, or hind, is one of the most sure-footed creatures on earth, nimbly climbing through rough mountainous terrain where the slightest slip can mean a quick and violent end. Her ease and confidence on a rocky slope are encouraging metaphors for the way we should approach our spiritual journey. If only it were that easy! We could simply hop from one rock to the next, steadily working our way up to the summit, where God rewards us for our diligence.

In real life, though, our spiritual path is filled with loose boulders and slippery gravel, unseen crevasses and disappointing dead ends that we're often ill-prepared to negotiate. Even the most beautiful mountain scenery can appear serene and inviting while concealing many hidden dangers. The only way to get through safely is to follow God's way precisely, like the hind, putting each foot in exactly the right place.

Of course, we can't actually do that. As fallible sinners, we're bound to make mistakes and find ourselves stuck clinging to the face of a sheer cliff, holding on for dear life. The great message of Psalm 18 is that God's way is perfect. He makes our feet like hinds' feet and sets us upon the high places. As we struggle in our sin to climb toward Him, He reaches down to pull us up.

Admitting we need God's help goes against our stubborn commitment to independence. It's human nature to want to do everything ourselves. But without God, we'll slip and fall. With Him, our spiritual sure-footedness is assured.

L.G.G.

SECTION FIVE

Spiritual Sure-Footedness

For reading & meditation—Psalm 18:16–33

"He makes my feet like hinds' feet, and sets me upon my high places." (v.33, NASB)

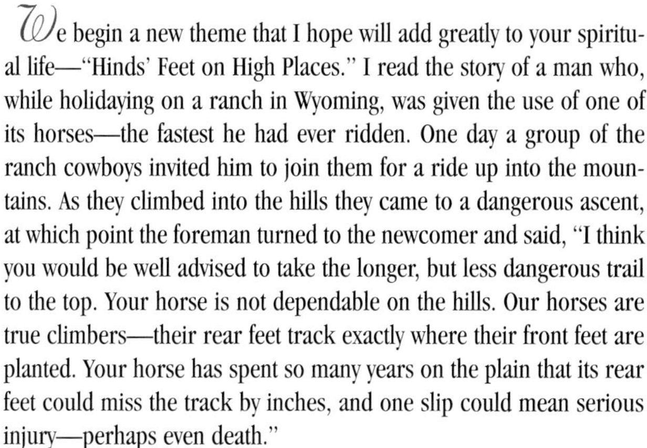

We begin a new theme that I hope will add greatly to your spiritual life—"Hinds' Feet on High Places." I read the story of a man who, while holidaying on a ranch in Wyoming, was given the use of one of its horses—the fastest he had ever ridden. One day a group of the ranch cowboys invited him to join them for a ride up into the mountains. As they climbed into the hills they came to a dangerous ascent, at which point the foreman turned to the newcomer and said, "I think you would be well advised to take the longer, but less dangerous trail to the top. Your horse is not dependable on the hills. Our horses are true climbers—their rear feet track exactly where their front feet are planted. Your horse has spent so many years on the plain that its rear feet could miss the track by inches, and one slip could mean serious injury—perhaps even death."

When I read those words, my thoughts turned immediately to the verse before us today, for no animal has such perfect correlation of its front and rear feet as the deer. When it leaps from rock to rock, its back feet land exactly where its front feet had been placed. If we are to climb higher with God than we have ever gone before, then more is needed than just speed—we must know spiritual sure-footedness also. Let's determine we will let nothing stand in the way of making our feet like hinds' feet and climbing with God to the "high places."

FURTHER STUDY

Phil. 3:1–14; Isa. 54:2; Eph. 3:17–19

1. What was the deep desire of Paul's heart?

2. What did he pray for the Ephesians?

Prayer

My Father and my God, hear my prayer as I begin perhaps a new chapter in my spiritual experience. Help me to climb higher with You than I have ever gone before, and do it not only with speed, but with sure-footedness also. In Jesus' Name. Amen.

SECTION FIVE

Climbing Higher with God

For reading & meditation—Habakkuk 3:12–19

"... He has made my feet like hinds' feet, and makes me walk on my high places." (v.19, NASB)

We continue learning how to become as sure-footed in the spiritual realm as a deer is in the natural realm. There are numerous references in Scripture where the pursuit of God is likened to a deer climbing steadily and sure-footedly toward the high mountain peaks—today's text being just one of them—and the more we consider the simile, the more rich and rewarding are the truths that flow out of it.

Why does God liken the pursuit of Himself to a deer making its way upward to the high places? And why does He focus so much attention upon the deer's feet? Well, as we said yesterday, the deer has an amazing ability, when climbing a steep mountain slope, of ensuring that its back feet alight on the exact spot where its front feet were positioned. This perfect correlation between its front and back feet enables the deer to avoid the dangers that would befall a less coordinated animal.

The Bible writers, in drawing attention to the sure-footedness of the deer, are attempting to show (so I believe) that what the deer experiences in the natural realm, we can experience in the spiritual realm. Do you really want to climb higher with God than you have ever gone before? Is there a deep longing in your heart to ascend, like the prophets and seers of old, into the mountain of the Lord? Then take heart—you can. This can be the greatest time of spiritual advance you have ever known. You supply the willingness, and I promise you—God will supply the power.

FURTHER STUDY

Isa. 55; Pss. 42:2; 63:1; 143:6

1. What did the psalmist express continually?

2. What does God promise?

Prayer

O Father, my prayer is—make this the greatest time of my life. I long more than anything to ascend into the mountain peaks with You. I am willing—now send the power. In Jesus' Name I ask it. Amen.

SECTION FIVE

DAY 248

God Has the Biggest Part

For reading & meditation—Psalm 40:1–17

"... he set my feet upon a rock and gave me a firm place to stand." (v.2)

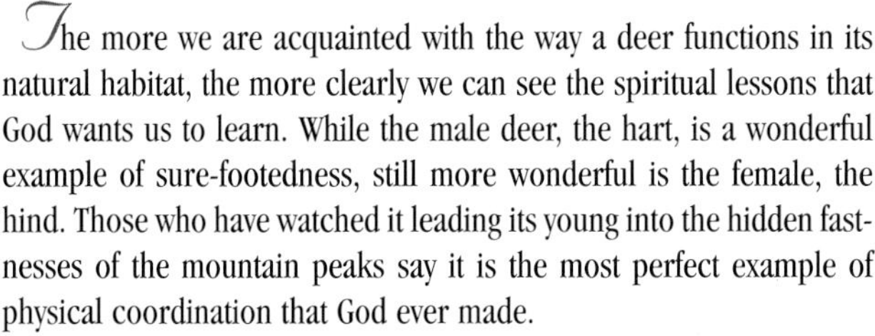

The more we are acquainted with the way a deer functions in its natural habitat, the more clearly we can see the spiritual lessons that God wants us to learn. While the male deer, the hart, is a wonderful example of sure-footedness, still more wonderful is the female, the hind. Those who have watched it leading its young into the hidden fastnesses of the mountain peaks say it is the most perfect example of physical coordination that God ever made.

Why is this physical coordination so important? When a deer moves upwards over a steep mountain slope, it proceeds by leaping from one spot to another, so it needs to be certain that its back feet will land on something solid. By positioning its front feet on something secure, it instinctively knows that if its rear feet land there also, it will proceed upwards in safety. If this were not so, and the deer's back feet were to land on a loose rock, then it would slip and meet with serious injury—perhaps even death.

This sense of perfect coordination is not something the deer learns; it is an instinctive ability given to it by its Creator. And what God has done for the deer in the natural realm, He is able to do for us in the spiritual realm. Listen again to the words of the psalmist: "He makes my feet like hinds' feet." Note the word *makes*. I find that deeply encouraging. It is not something I have to achieve on my own; He has a part in it too. And, may I add—the biggest part.

FURTHER STUDY

Isa. 26:1–4; Pss. 92:15, 61:2; Matt. 7:24–29

1. What did Isaiah declare?

2. What was Jesus teaching?

Prayer

O Father, help me understand that although You have the biggest part in making my feet like hinds' feet, it cannot be accomplished unless I, too, do my part. Thus I willingly surrender to Your divine purposes. In Jesus' Name I pray. Amen.

DAY 249

SECTION FIVE

Togetherness

For reading & meditation—Mark 11:12–26

"... whoever says to this mountain, 'Be removed ...,' and does not doubt ... but believes ... will have whatever he says." *(v.23; NKJV)*

What is the spiritual lesson we can draw from the deer's amazing ability to ensure that its back feet land on the exact spot where its front feet had been positioned? Just as the creature which has the most perfect correlation between its front and rear feet makes its way swiftly and safely to the mountaintop, so the Christian who has a perfect coordination between the head and heart will rise to new heights with God. For you see, unless the head and heart are properly coordinated and move purposefully together, it is possible to miss one's step on the steep slopes of Christian experience and become a spiritual casualty.

I have known many Christians in my time who, because they lack coordination between what they ask for with their lips and what they want deep down in their hearts, stay in the same place spiritually year after year. They are not bad people, they just lack spiritual coordination and thus never know what it is to ascend into the mountain peaks with God.

Perhaps nowhere in Scripture is this truth more clearly portrayed than in the verse before us today. We are told that things happen in the spiritual realm when there is a perfect coordination between what we ask for and what we believe. When our mind and our heart are in alignment, when they track together with the sure-footedness of a mountain deer, then nothing shall be impossible to us. How many of us, I wonder, miss our step on the slopes of the Christian life because our hearts and minds are not properly and perfectly coordinated?

FURTHER STUDY

Isa. 58:1–11;
Matt. 23

1. Why was the Lord displeased with Israel?
2. How did Jesus depict the Pharisees?

Prayer

Gracious and loving Heavenly Father, slowly I am beginning to see the truth that underlies Your promise to make my feet like hinds' feet. Show me how to be as coordinated in the spiritual realm as the deer is in the natural realm. In Jesus' Name. Amen.

SECTION FIVE

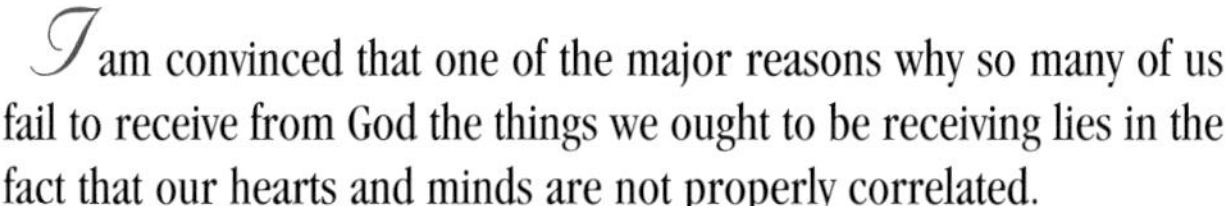

Not Just What You Say

For reading & meditation—Proverbs 4:10–27

"Keep your heart with all diligence, for out of it spring the issues of life." (v.23, NKJV)

I am convinced that one of the major reasons why so many of us fail to receive from God the things we ought to be receiving lies in the fact that our hearts and minds are not properly correlated.

Do you find yourself continually praying for things you never receive? I don't mean things about which there may be some doubt, but things you definitely know the Almighty longs to give you—love, joy, peace, wisdom, patience, the Holy Spirit, and so on. Maybe your mind is asking for one thing and your heart another. You see, it is possible to want something with the mind which is not supported by the heart. The mind is a much easier part of the personality to deal with than the heart, but, as our text for today states: "Keep your heart … for out of it spring the issues of life" (NKJV).

We can approach God with our minds and think that because we have a clear idea of what we want; God will give it to us, but the heart may contain hidden doubts which prevent us from being fully integrated people. We fail to receive because we are not asking out of a fully integrated personality. As someone has put it: "God does not just answer prayer—He answers you." Those who wish to receive from God the things He delights to give ought always to remember that who we are is just as important (if not more so) than what we ask. God is not just listening to your words; He is listening to you.

FURTHER STUDY

Matt. 15:1–20; Prov. 3:5; 23:7; Luke 8:45

1. What did Isaiah prophesy?

2. How did Jesus respond to Peter's request?

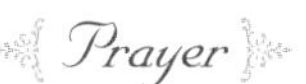

Prayer

O Father, the more I meditate on the need for heart and mind to be in perfect coordination, the more I am set on fire to become a fully integrated person. I know You are eagerly reaching down to me; help me to be as eager to reach up to You. In Jesus' Name. Amen.

SECTION FIVE

"The Seemingly Trivial Inches"

For reading & meditation—Jeremiah 29:1–14

"You will seek me and find me when you seek me with all your heart." (v.13)

We are looking at what I consider one of the greatest truths about receiving from God that we can discover: "God does not just answer prayer—He answers you."

The Almighty does not just listen to the words we weave into the air when we pray; He listens also to the attitude of our heart. If the two are not properly correlated, then we miss out on many of God's blessings. And this missing out is not because God is stingy about the way He dispenses His blessings, but because we short-circuit our own spiritual system and become imperfect receivers. To put it another way, our failure to receive isn't due to the fact that God is not good at giving, but because we are not good at receiving. The fault is always in us, never in Him.

We are far enough along in our meditations, I believe, for me to ask you: are you a fully integrated person? When you present your requests to God, are your heart and mind at one? Is what you ask with your lips fully supported by what you are saying in your heart? If not, then when you attempt to climb higher with God, you will not have the precise coordination you need to scale the precipitous heights. The awesome fact that has to be faced by all those who want to climb the mountains of God is this—it is possible to miss your step on those steep slopes, not by feet, but merely by inches. And it is in those seemingly trivial inches that our spiritual direction is often determined.

FURTHER STUDY

Joel 2:1–13; Deut. 6:5; Ps. 119:2

1. What was God's message through Joel?

2. When are we blessed?

Prayer

O Father, I am seeing more and more the perils that come from being inwardly at cross purposes. Help me, however, to see that although the challenge is great, the power behind me is greater than the challenge in front of me. In Jesus' Name. Amen.

SECTION FIVE

The Peril of a Missed Step

For reading & meditation—Psalm 18:32–50

"You enlarged my path under me; so that my feet did not slip" (v.36; NKJV)

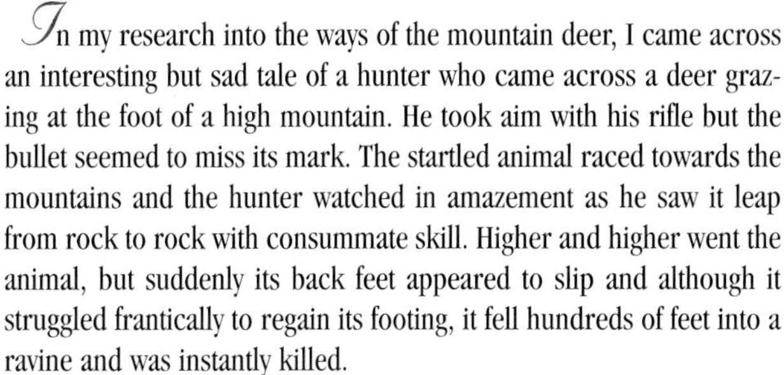

In my research into the ways of the mountain deer, I came across an interesting but sad tale of a hunter who came across a deer grazing at the foot of a high mountain. He took aim with his rifle but the bullet seemed to miss its mark. The startled animal raced towards the mountains and the hunter watched in amazement as he saw it leap from rock to rock with consummate skill. Higher and higher went the animal, but suddenly its back feet appeared to slip and although it struggled frantically to regain its footing, it fell hundreds of feet into a ravine and was instantly killed.

When the hunter arrived at the spot where the animal lay, he noticed a small burn on its flank caused by the bullet he had fired, which had simply grazed the animal without penetrating its flesh. The hunter says, "It was obvious what had happened. The graze had affected the deer's coordination and in a moment when it needed to move swiftly and safely to the mountain height, it did not proceed with its usual perfect correlation. Its back feet did not land on the precise spot where its front feet had been, and although it was only an inch off it was enough to bring about its fall."

This illustration must not be pushed too far and made to mean that a missed step on the mountain of God will bring about our spiritual death. A missed step, however, will undoubtedly hinder our spiritual progress and prevent us from climbing as swiftly as we ought into the heights of God.

FURTHER STUDY

Ps. 40:1–5; Isa. 52:7; Eph. 6:15

1. What was the psalmist's testimony?
2. What are we to have on our feet?

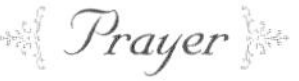

Prayer

O Father, make me the kind of person whose heart and mind move forward into Your purposes with perfect unity and coordination. Help me not to miss my step—not even by inches. In Jesus' Name I pray. Amen.

DAY 253

SECTION FIVE

Commitment Means Cohesion

For reading & meditation—Luke 11:14–28

"... a house divided against itself will fall." (v.17)

Today we look at a scriptural illustration of the need for a proper correlation between our heart and our mind based on the life of the Old Testament character, Amaziah. In 2 Chronicles 25:2 we read: "He did what was right in the eyes of the Lord, but not wholeheartedly." His mind gave itself to doing right in the sight of the Lord, but his heart did not support his actions.

This lack of coordination proved to be his undoing: "When Amaziah returned from slaughtering the Edomites, he brought back the gods of the people of Seir ... set them up as his own gods, bowed down to them and burned sacrifices to them" (25:14). Now look at how the life of Amaziah ends: "From the time that Amaziah turned away from following the Lord, they conspired against him ... and ... sent men after him to Lachish and killed him there" (25:27).

Notice the steps: (1) outwardly correct but inwardly uncoordinated; (2) the inner disunity shows itself in outer disloyalty; (3) failure and death. At the beginning, Amaziah does not appear to be a particularly bad individual—he just failed to be wholehearted in his commitment. He did all the right things outwardly, but his heart was not in them—hence spiritual ruin. We could say he missed his step by inches, but his fall was one of the worst ever recorded. If we are not held together by a single-minded devotion, our spiritual life can quickly go to pieces. Commitment to God demands cohesion—the cohesion of heart and mind.

FURTHER STUDY

James. 1:1–8, 4:8; Heb. 13:9

1. What makes us unstable?

2. What was the word of the Lord to the Hebrews?

Prayer

O God my Father, help me to live a life of single purpose, with heart and mind moving together as one. Let me will the highest with all my being. In Jesus' Name I ask it. Amen.

SECTION FIVE

Spoiled by Ulterior Motives

For reading & meditation—James 4:1–12

"When you ask, you do not receive, because you ask with wrong motives ..." (v.3)

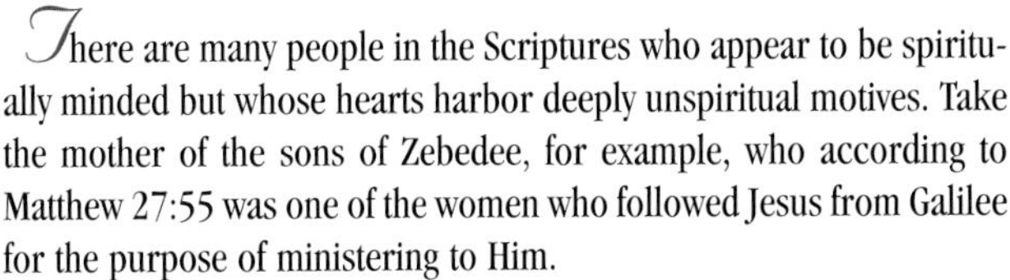

There are many people in the Scriptures who appear to be spiritually minded but whose hearts harbor deeply unspiritual motives. Take the mother of the sons of Zebedee, for example, who according to Matthew 27:55 was one of the women who followed Jesus from Galilee for the purpose of ministering to Him.

Most commentators believe this small band of women were devotees of Christ and assisted Him and the disciples by the preparation of meals, washing and repairing of clothes, and so on. Those looking on would have classified them as deeply spiritual women, willing to give up their time to minister to Jesus—and of course, in the main, they were. However, in one place the Scripture draws aside the veil over the heart of one of them, the mother of James and John, and shows her approaching Jesus with the request: "Grant that one of these two sons of mine may sit at your right and the other at your left in your kingdom." "You don't know what you are asking," Jesus said (Matt. 20:21–22).

She served Jesus, of that there can be no doubt, but she had a secret and selfish motive in her heart—a privileged position for her sons. It is easy to excuse her action, as many have done, on the grounds that she was doing only what any other concerned mother would have done—attempting to get the best for her children. But Jesus saw right into her heart and said: "You don't know what you are asking." How sad that her beautiful ministry to Jesus was spoiled by ulterior motives.

FURTHER STUDY

James 2; Eph. 2:3; 1 John 2:15–16

1. What motive was James exposing?

2. What did he say about the law?

Prayer

My Father, help me to see that I cannot be a fully integrated person when I harbor within me two mutually exclusive loves. I cannot love You fully when I love my own interests fully. Set me free, dear Lord, to live only for You. Amen.

SECTION FIVE

The Heart of the Matter

For reading & meditation—Proverbs 3:1–18

"Trust in the Lord with all your heart and lean not on your own understanding." (v.5)

What is the essential difference between the heart and the mind? Many believe there is no difference and that they are really the same thing. I see a clear difference between the heart and the mind: the mind is the part of us that thinks and reasons; the heart is the part of us that contains our deep longings and desires. Although the mind is important, the heart is even more important because that is the engine room of our personality—the part from which comes our drive and motivation. That is why our Lord says, "Out of the overflow of the heart, the mouth speaks" (Matthew 12:34).

Christ said that the words He spoke were the words given to Him by His Father (John 14:24). Does that mean the Father wrote out the words which He wanted Christ to say and got Him to learn them by heart? No—the motivating center of the heart of Jesus Christ was the very heart of God the Father; consequently the words Christ spoke were the exact expression of God's thought. In our Lord, the tongue was always in its right place. He spoke not just from His head, but from His heart; His heart and mind were one.

Oswald Chambers put it like this: "The heart is the central altar and the mind the outer court. What we offer on the central altar will show itself in due course through the outer extremities of the personality." In the search for unity of purpose and integration, there is no doubt that the heart of the matter is the matter of the heart.

FURTHER STUDY

Mark 7:14–23; Prov. 4:23; Rom. 10:10

1. What comes from the heart?

2. What was Jesus teaching?

O God, help me to be like Jesus and to pass on to others, not just the things that come into my head but the things that flow out of my heart. Bring my heart in closer contact with Your heart, dear Father. In Jesus' Name I pray. Amen.

SECTION FIVE

An Honest Look

DAY 256

For reading & meditation—Luke 8:1–15

"... those with a noble and good heart, who hear the word, retain it, and by persevering produce a crop." (v.15)

We turn now to consider some of the steps we must take in order to bring about a more perfect coordination between heart and mind. The first step is this—prepare to take an honest, straightforward look at what is going on beneath the surface of your life.

Over the years in which I have been writing *Every Day with Jesus*, I have from time to time invited my readers to spend a few days taking an honest look at themselves. The reactions I have got to this suggestion have been quite interesting. Some Christians hear in my words a call to self-preoccupation and become concerned that I am pushing people toward becoming engrossed with their aches and pains. One of my readers put it like this: "What people need is to forget about themselves and concentrate on reaching out to others, then their personal problems will quickly be forgotten." Others have taken an opposite position and said, "We need more of this, for our hearts are so self-deceived that unless we are constantly challenged in this way, we will never get through to a close relationship with God."

I am unhappy about both those reactions, for both are unbalanced positions. The first one fears that taking a look beneath the surface of our lives leads to unhealthy self-preoccupation, and the second assumes that constant self-examination is the only way forward. An occasional honest and straightforward look at what is going on beneath the surface of our lives contributes greatly to our spiritual progress, providing it is done in a proper and balanced way.

FURTHER STUDY

Pss. 51:1–6; 15:1–2; Rom 8:27

1. Where does God require truth?

2. What must we allow God to do?

O God, help me to see that in inviting me to examine myself, You are not seeking to demean me, but to develop me; not to take away from my spiritual stature, but add to it. Make me an honest person—honest with You, honest with myself, and honest with others. Amen.

Going Below the Waterline

For reading & meditation—Psalm 51:1–17

"... you desire truth in the inner parts ..." (v.6)

We are considering the proposition that a balanced, honest look at what is going on beneath the surface of our lives is something that contributes greatly to our spiritual health. Think of your life as an iceberg. We are told that the visible part of an iceberg, that is, the part we see above the water line, is about one-tenth of its total size. Its bulk lies hidden beneath the surface and is revealed only to those who are equipped to go down below the waterline. Our lives are like that; there is much more to them than we see on the surface. Think of the visible part above the waterline as representing the things you do, the thoughts you consciously think, and the feelings you sense going on within you. Let the mass below the waterline represent the things that go on inside you that cannot be clearly seen or understood, such as motives, attitudes, impulses, and so on.

Facing what goes on above the waterline, our visible behaviors and actions, is a whole lot easier than delving below the surface, and this is why many Christians (not all) concern themselves with only what they can see, know, and understand. These people can be described as "surface copers," who cope with life by dealing with whatever they can see and ignoring all the rest. If, however, we are to enjoy a deeper relationship with God, then we will do so only as we come to grips with the tough issues that lie beneath the surface of our lives.

FURTHER STUDY

Isa. 11; 1 Kings 3:1–10; John 5:30

1. How does Jesus judge and reprove?

2. What did Solomon ask for?

Prayer

God, help me this day to stand before You in complete and utter honesty. Save me from becoming a "surface coper" and give me the grace I need to face the things that normally I would avoid. In Jesus' Name I pray. Amen.

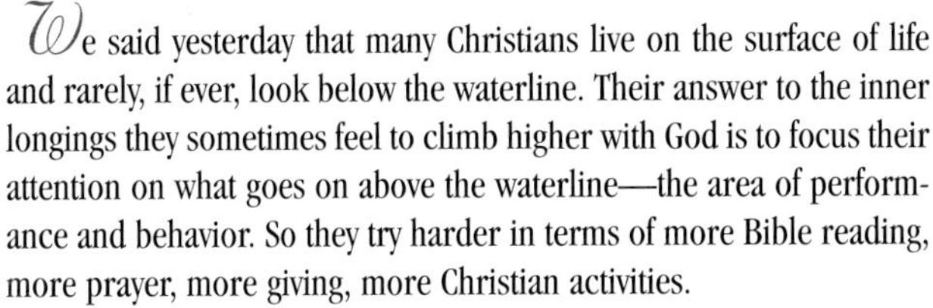

More Needed Than Performance

DAY 258

For reading & meditation—Proverbs 23:12–28

"My son, give me your heart, and let your eyes keep to my ways" (v.26)

We said yesterday that many Christians live on the surface of life and rarely, if ever, look below the waterline. Their answer to the inner longings they sometimes feel to climb higher with God is to focus their attention on what goes on above the waterline—the area of performance and behavior. So they try harder in terms of more Bible reading, more prayer, more giving, more Christian activities.

I would be the last person to view greater obedience as unimportant, but it is not the only, or indeed the final answer. A great mistake made by many Christians who recognize they are not receiving from God the things they ought to be receiving is to think that the solution lies solely in more spiritual effort, the assumption being that as we do more above the waterline, the problems that lie below the waterline will all come right.

Now sometimes greater obedience and more responsible effort do have this result. I have often found, for example, that when a man who falls out of love with his wife chooses a change in behavior and deliberately sets out to do loving things for her, the loving behavior can trigger loving feelings. However, there is more to spiritual change than a change on the surface. It can begin there, but it is not complete until the focus moves from the surface down into the depths. Those who remain above the waterline in their Christian living and resist the invitation to look beneath the surface soon become legalists—good at performing but bad at being.

FURTHER STUDY

2 Tim. 3:1–5; Isa. 29:1–13

1. What did Paul say would be a characteristic of the last days?

2. What was the Lord's complaint against the children of Israel?

Prayer

My Father and my God, I see that if change is to take place in me, then it must take place in all of me. Help me to see even more clearly that while what I do is important, what I am in the depth of my being is even more important. In Jesus' Name. Amen.

SECTION FIVE

"There Must Be No Pretense"

For reading & meditation—Matthew 23:13–28

"... You are like whitewashed tombs ... beautiful on the outside but on the inside are full of dead men's bones ..." (v.27)

We ended yesterday with the thought that Christians who live on the surface and refuse to take a look below the waterline soon become legalists—more concerned about doing good than being good.

The Pharisees of Jesus' day were like that. They specialized in looking good. Sin was defined by them in terms of visible transgressions, and as long as they did nothing to violate the standards which they so carefully defined, they regarded themselves as being free from sin. And there can be little doubt about it—they were good performers. Their level of disciplined conformity to external expectations was very high. They impressed many by their performance, but there was someone they failed to impress—Jesus. He told them that they were nothing more than whitewashed tombs and called them "blind leaders of the blind" (Matt. 15:14, NKJV).

In His rebuke to the Pharisees, our Lord established a principle that must guide us in our effort to become the people He wants us to be, and that principle is this—there must be no pretense. Christ's teaching seems to be that we can't make it as His followers unless we are willing to take an honest and straightforward look at what is going on beneath the surface of our lives. To look honestly at those parts of our being which we would rather not know about is not, as some would have it, a sign of morbid introspection but a sign of healthy spirituality. Always remember, our Lord reserved His harshest criticism for those who, like the Pharisees, made pretense and denial into a trademark.

FURTHER STUDY

Col. 2:1–20;
Isa.1:11–17;
Gal.4:10

1. What did Paul bring to the Colossians' attention?
2. How similar was it to Isaiah's word centuries before?

Prayer

O Father, You are boring deep—help me not to wriggle and squirm. Love me enough to overcome all my resistances, all my antipathies and all my fears. For I don't just want to be a better person; I want to be a whole person. In Jesus' Name. Amen.

The Awful Consequences of Pretense

For reading & meditation—Acts 5:1–11

"When Ananias heard this, he fell down and died. And great fear seized all who heard what had happened." (v.5)

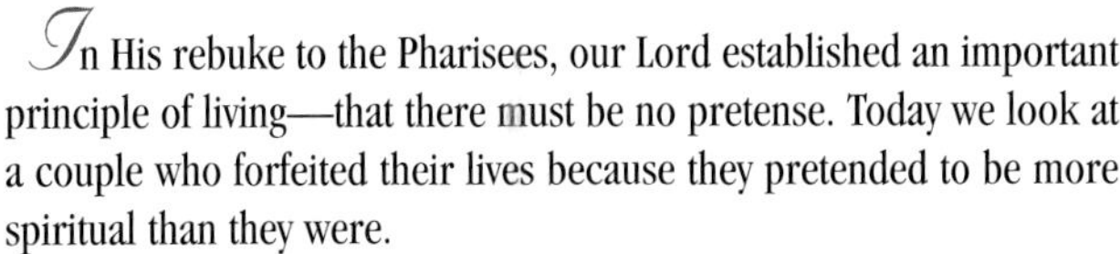

In His rebuke to the Pharisees, our Lord established an important principle of living—that there must be no pretense. Today we look at a couple who forfeited their lives because they pretended to be more spiritual than they were.

Ananias and Sapphira were highly respected members of the early Church and appeared on the surface to be deeply committed disciples of the Lord Jesus Christ. Doubtless they had a fairly high degree of dedication, and easily went along with the idea of selling their possessions and putting the proceeds into the treasury of the early Church. Their mistake, of course, was to pretend they had given their all when they hadn't, and the consequences of this pretense were swift and dramatic.

God deals harshly with dishonesty, but He is most compassionate to those who see themselves as they really are, confess that to Him, and request His help in becoming the person they know He wants them to be. I have known people who have stood up in front of a Christian audience and talked about how wonderful it is to live a victorious Christian life when in reality they were inwardly messed up. And I have known others get up before their brothers and sisters, confessing that though they love the Lord, they are experiencing great struggles and difficulties in seeking to live for Him. Who do you think is the closer to God? I will tell you—it is the one who is honest and open. Pretense repels God—openness and honesty draw Him quickly to our side.

FURTHER STUDY

Acts 19; Eph. 1; Rev. 2:1–5

1. Why did the word of the Lord spread rapidly in Ephesus?

2. What words did Christ bring to them some years later?

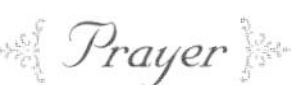

Father, help me to be a sincere and transparent person. Save me, I pray, from adopting an air of pretense and masquerading as someone I am not. You delight in openness and honesty—help me to delight in them too. Amen.

SECTION FIVE

"Ostrich Christians"

For reading & meditation—Proverbs 20:15–30

"The spirit of a man is the lamp of the LORD, searching all the inner depths of his heart." (v.27, NKJV)

Most of us (myself included) are not good at observing ourselves and reflecting honestly on what goes on beneath the surface of our lives. Why is this so? I think one of the reasons is fear—fear of the unknown, fear of losing control, fear of spoiling a comfortable existence or fear of having to face some unpleasant discoveries about ourselves. I have met many Christians in my time who adopt the attitude: however things are, good or bad, they could be worse, so it is better to leave well enough alone.

When we read the Bible, however, what do we find? We discover texts like the one before us today, that show us God has designed us with the ability to explore our deepest parts. Also we hear men like the psalmist crying out to God: "Search me [thoroughly], O God, and know my heart! Try me, and know my thoughts! And see if there is any wicked or hurtful way in me, and lead me in the way everlasting" (Ps.139:23–24, Amp. Bible).

I want to stress once again that too much introspection is unhealthy, but occasionally and in proper doses, it is "good medicine." Those who resist this and pretend everything is well when it isn't are what a friend of mine calls "ostrich Christians." They have peace, but it is a peace built on unreality. When they lift their heads out of the sand, the peace they possess somehow falls to pieces. God's peace can keep our hearts and minds intact while we face whatever is true—outside and inside.

FURTHER STUDY

Mark 2:1–8; Matt. 12:25; Luke 6:8; John 2:25

1. How deeply did Jesus see into people's lives?

2. How deeply do you let Him penetrate into your life?

Prayer

Father, save me from becoming an "ostrich Christian"—someone who pretends everything is well when it isn't. Nothing, dear Lord, must be allowed to hinder the work that You want to do in my heart. Corner my soul and make me what You want me to be. Amen.

SECTION FIVE

Why Take an Inside Look?

For reading & meditation—Isaiah 33:10–24

"This is the man who will dwell on the heights, whose refuge will be the mountain fortress ..." (v.16)

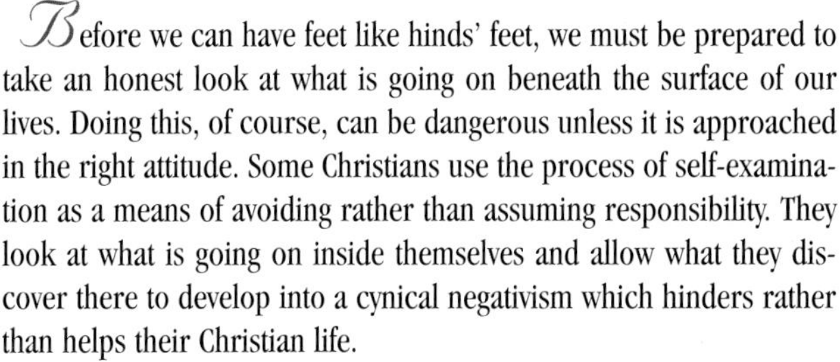

Before we can have feet like hinds' feet, we must be prepared to take an honest look at what is going on beneath the surface of our lives. Doing this, of course, can be dangerous unless it is approached in the right attitude. Some Christians use the process of self-examination as a means of avoiding rather than assuming responsibility. They look at what is going on inside themselves and allow what they discover there to develop into a cynical negativism which hinders rather than helps their Christian life.

Those who do this fail to understand the purpose of godly self-examination, which is to bring what is discovered to the Lord so that He can deal with it. Many commentators have pointed out, in the incident when the Israelites in the wilderness were bitten by the snakes, that when they looked at themselves and recognized their condition, they were then highly motivated to look to the brass serpent for help (see Num. 21:4–9).

The purpose of taking an honest look at what is going on beneath the surface of our lives is to promote a deeper dependence on the Lord and thus contribute to our spiritual effectiveness. Recognition of our true condition provides a strong motivation to look away from ourselves and turn in simple faith to the Lord Jesus Christ. As we take this journey into the core of our being, let me encourage you to be willing to face yourself in a way that you have never done before. I cannot promise you it will be painless, but I can promise you it will be profitable.

FURTHER STUDY

1 Cor. 11:23–33; Lam. 3:40; Gal. 6:4

1. How does Paul admonish us?

2. How does the writer of Lamentations put it?

Prayer

Father, give me the courage to overcome all those fears that would rise within me saying: "I am not sure that I can face it." Deepen the conviction within me that with You, I can face anything. In Jesus' Name. Amen.

SECTION FIVE

Honesty Put to the Test

For reading & meditation—Psalm 15:1–5

"He whose walk is blameless and who does what is righteous, who speaks the truth from his heart" (v.2)

Today we move to the second step toward producing a perfect coordination between our head and our heart by facing the question: when I pray or seek the Lord, is my heart fully and enthusiastically behind what I am asking for with my lips? If not, we will fail to surmount the heights of God "with all four feet."

One of the things that used to puzzle me greatly in the early days of my pastoral ministry was to sit down with people who were not getting what they longed for spiritually and, after hours of counseling, sometimes to discover that although they were asking God for something with their lips, they were not really desiring it deep down in their hearts. I am thinking as I write of a woman I knew who prayed earnestly (and loudly) in church for the conversion of her non-Christian husband.

One day, however, in a moment of great openness and honesty (such as often occurs in counseling) she admitted that deep down in her heart, she didn't really want her husband to be converted because she was afraid that if he was, the attention and sympathy she was getting from her brothers and sisters in the church would no longer be there. Once she realized what was going on inside her, she was able to deal with it and became one of the most spiritually released women I have ever known. Her whole life (not just her prayer life) became one of deep, quiet conviction and eventually, many years later, she had the joy of seeing her husband surrender to Christ.

FURTHER STUDY

Jer. 17:1–10; 23:24; 1 Cor. 3:20

1. How does Jeremiah describe the heart?

2. How does the Lord view the thoughts of the worldly wise?

Prayer

My Father, one thing is clear—such are the subterfuges of the human heart that without Your light and guidance, I can be self-deceived. Help me to apply the test of honesty and openness to my own spiritual life. In Jesus' Name. Amen.

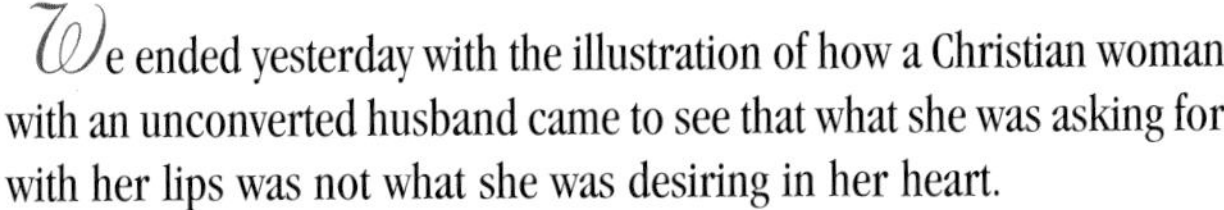

For reading & meditation—Matthew 7:1–14

"Ask and it will be given to you; seek and you will find; knock and the door will be opened ..." (v.7)

We ended yesterday with the illustration of how a Christian woman with an unconverted husband came to see that what she was asking for with her lips was not what she was desiring in her heart.

Although, in her case, she had the joy of seeing her husband become a Christian, this must not be taken to mean that we have here a guaranteed formula for bringing a non-Christian spouse to the Lord. It is right to pray with passion for those in our families who are not converted, but we must remember that each man and woman must personally surrender their wills to Christ if they are to be converted. People are admitted into the family of God only as they give up their commitment to independence and say, in effect: "Heavenly Father, I can do nothing to save myself; save me, in Jesus' Name."

A man came to me complaining that he was not getting what he wanted spiritually. He told me that he had a deep sense of unworthiness and although he prayed desperately for God to take it away, it stayed with him. After many hours of talking, praying, and heart-searching, he came to see that although in his head he was asking for God to take it away, deep down in his heart he was not desiring it. He had lived with it for so long that he was afraid of the new positive feelings he would have to face if the negative feelings were not there. He preferred the safety of the old to the adventure of the new.

FURTHER STUDY

Luke 18:1–8; Deut. 4:29; Prov. 8:17

1. What characteristic did the woman display?

2. How can we be sure of finding God?

Father, day by day I am seeing more clearly than ever the subtle devices of the human heart. Give me the insight I need to probe my own heart and track down those things that may be preventing me from climbing into the heights with You. In Jesus' Name I pray. Amen.

SECTION FIVE

Why We Cling to Unforgiveness

For reading & meditation—Psalm 86:1–17

". . . give me an undivided heart, that I may fear your name." (v.11)

A friend of mine who is a minister and Christian counselor shared with me about a woman who told him that she spent thirty to forty-five minutes every day asking God to take away from her an unforgiving spirit. She told Him that what she wanted more than anything in the world was the ability to forgive those in her family who had brought her hurt.

The minister joined her in prayer, but the Holy Spirit spoke to his heart and showed him that deep down, the woman did not want a forgiving spirit. The minister waited for the Spirit to show more, but nothing came. Realizing that he had enough information to pursue the matter, the minister invited the woman to explore the possibility that what she was asking for with her lips was not what she was asking for in her heart.

At first, the woman seemed annoyed and upset by the suggestion that deep down she might not want what she was asking for, but gradually she agreed to take an inside look. In the hour or two that followed, this came out—despite her claim that she wanted to forgive, deep down in her heart she clung to an unforgiving spirit as it gave her the justification she felt she needed when she was the cause of hurt to someone else. In other words, she was saying to herself: "Other people have hurt me, so it won't matter so much when I hurt them." When she saw what she was doing, she immediately surrendered it to God and found inner release and freedom.

FURTHER STUDY

Luke 17:1–5; Mark 11:25; Eph. 4:32

1. How did the apostles respond to Christ's challenge?

2. How did Paul admonish the Ephesians?

Prayer

God, I am deeply challenged by this, yet deeply relieved to know that whatever might elude me can never elude You. I open up my heart right now for inspection and examination. Search me and make me whole. In Jesus' Name. Amen.

SECTION FIVE

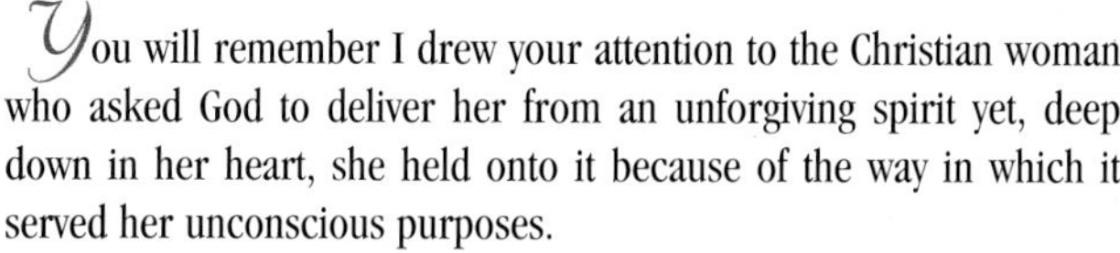

For reading & meditation—Luke 11:1–11

"Forgive us our sins, for we also forgive everyone who sins against us ..." (v.4)

You will remember I drew your attention to the Christian woman who asked God to deliver her from an unforgiving spirit yet, deep down in her heart, she held onto it because of the way in which it served her unconscious purposes.

I want to suggest that you read the next sentence carefully, for in it lies the secret of the failure of many Christians to walk with "hinds' feet" to the high places which God has prepared for them. If you harbor resentment or hatred toward just one individual in the world, by that much you are separated from God Himself. By just that much do your rear feet fail to track with your front feet and, in the pursuit of God, you are in danger of slipping over the edge to spiritual failure. Let me put it even more clearly—if anyone has sinned against you and you have not forgiven them from the depths of your heart, then the attitude of unwillingness is a sin against God.

Listen to what the apostle John says about this: "If anyone says, 'I love God,' yet hates his brother, he is a liar. For anyone who does not love his brother, whom he has seen, cannot love God, whom he has not seen" (1 John 4:20). The very first thing we must do if we are to climb higher with God is make sure there is no bitterness or resentment lingering in our hearts. If you have not done so before, turn now in thought to all those who have trespassed against you and forgive them—fully and completely.

FURTHER STUDY

1 John 4; 3:14–24; John 15:12

1. What was Christ's commandment?

2. Why not memorize 1 John 3:16?

God, once again I plead for the insight and courage to see myself truly, for I may be cloaking my resentments with garments of piety. I would harbor no dangerous Trojan horses within me. Help me to be free of all resentment. In Jesus' Name. Amen.

SECTION FIVE

"The Familiar Feelings of Failure"

For reading & meditation—Psalm 145:1–21

"The Lord is near to all who call on Him, to all who call on Him in truth." (v.18)

Many years ago, a young man came to see me and said: "I am not making a success of my life spiritually. I want with all my heart to become a successful Christian, but I seem to be failing in everything I do." At that time I was not as aware of the subtleties of the human heart as I am today, and I encouraged him to keep trying. I said,"Responsible effort and dogged obedience will bring you what you need; keep going no matter what." The advice I gave him was good, but it was not complete.

About a year later, after God had allowed me to see the subtleties and deceptions of my own heart, and after putting some personal things right before Him, I sat down once again with the young man and asked him how things were going. "A little better," he said, "but even though I keep asking God to help me become a successful Christian, I am still failing."

I took a deep breath and tentatively suggested that perhaps, deep down in his heart, he preferred failure to success. He looked at me in amazement and after a few seconds said, "Say some more about that. I feel you are touching something very vulnerable inside me." We talked for hours, and he told me how all his life he had lived with failure, and it soon became obvious that he preferred the familiar feelings of failure to the unfamiliar feelings of success—even spiritual success. That one insight was all he needed to open up the whole of his being to God.

FURTHER STUDY

Exod. 16:1–3; Num. 11:1–6; 13:17–33

1. What was the problem of the children of Israel?

2. Why were they not prepared to move forward?

Prayer

O Father, if I, too, need something to trigger off a deeper openness and self-awareness in my heart, then give it to me today. I want nothing more than to be an honest person—honest, not only on the surface but also at the depths. Help me—in Jesus' Name. Amen.

SECTION FIVE

The Danger of Denial

For reading & meditation—John 8:21–36

"Then you will know the truth, and the truth will set you free." (v.32)

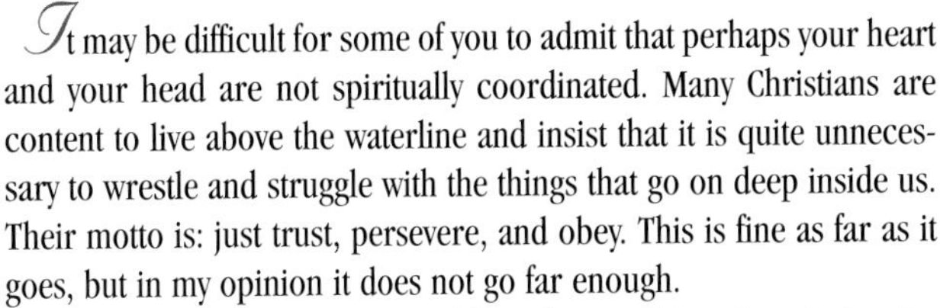

It may be difficult for some of you to admit that perhaps your heart and your head are not spiritually coordinated. Many Christians are content to live above the waterline and insist that it is quite unnecessary to wrestle and struggle with the things that go on deep inside us. Their motto is: just trust, persevere, and obey. This is fine as far as it goes, but in my opinion it does not go far enough.

The effect of this teaching is to blunt the painful reality of what the Bible says about the condition of the human heart: "The heart is deceitful above all things, and desperately wicked; who can know it? I, the LORD, search the heart" (Jer. 17:9–10, NKJV). It is possible for even mature Christians to be self-deceived, and this is why we must live in constant dependence on God and invite Him from time to time, as did the psalmist, to "search me and know my heart" (Ps. 139:23).

There is a word to describe the attitude of those who ignore what may be going on deep inside them and concentrate only on what they can see above the water line, and that word is—*denial*. In many Christian circles, maintaining a comfortable distance from what may be going on deep down inside is strongly encouraged. But nothing can be gained from denial. In fact, I would say it is one of the major reasons why our feet are not like "hinds' feet" and why we slip and slide on the slopes that lead upward to a deeper understanding and knowledge of God.

FURTHER STUDY

Gal. 6;
Rom. 6:16–23

1. What was Paul's word to the Galatians?

2. How are we to walk?

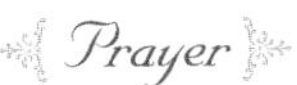

Prayer

God, I realize I am dealing with something too devastating to pass over quickly or lightly. Help me to be aware of the tendency that is in me to deny that I deny. Stay close to me at this moment, dear Father, for without You I can do nothing. Amen.

DAY 269

SECTION FIVE

The Stark Choice Facing Us

For reading & meditation—Luke 16:1–13

"... unless you are honest in small matters, you won't be in large ones. ..." (v.10, TLB)

What is denial? It is the attitude that avoids looking realistically at issues and pretends that things are not the way they are.

Most Christians, myself included, are, to varying degrees, held together by denial. Deep down we sense that if we were to face the realities of life openly and honestly, we might not be able to cope, and so we pretend things are not what they are. I know Christians who pretend that what they have satisfies more than it does, or pretend they haven't been hurt as badly as they have. They refuse to face and feel what is going on inside them, due to the strange belief that it is lack of faith on their part to admit to anything that is negative.

The teaching that we ought to ignore what is going on inside us instead of facing it and dealing with it is responsible for more casualties in the Christian life than anything I know. A Christian psychologist says: "I am convinced that much of what we admire as spiritual maturity is a fragile adjustment to life based on the foundation of denial." My own observation would lead me to say that I have found some non-Christians to be more open and honest in facing what is going on inside them than some Christians. Is denial a wise plan for life? Absolutely not. The choice, then, is stark: either to deny and live comfortably, or face every issue painfully—and go on to climb the heights with God.

FURTHER STUDY

Eccl. 5:1–7; Isa. 29:13; Matt. 15:1–9

1. What do fools do?

2. What prophecy was fulfilled by the Pharisees?

Prayer

Father, help me to see that I need never be afraid to face anything, for in You I have the resources to resolve all problems, not just skirt them. Show me how to blast denial right out of my life—once and for all. In Jesus' Name. Amen.

DAY 270

A Heart That Pants for God

For reading & meditation—Psalm 42:1–11

"As the deer pants for streams of water, so my soul pants for you, O God." (v.1)

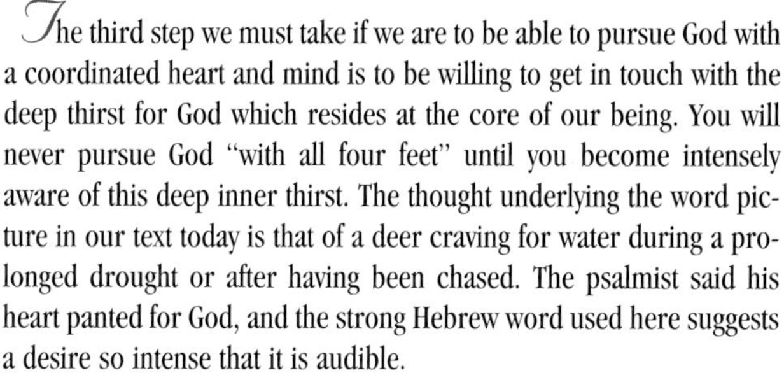

The third step we must take if we are to be able to pursue God with a coordinated heart and mind is to be willing to get in touch with the deep thirst for God which resides at the core of our being. You will never pursue God "with all four feet" until you become intensely aware of this deep inner thirst. The thought underlying the word picture in our text today is that of a deer craving for water during a prolonged drought or after having been chased. The psalmist said his heart panted for God, and the strong Hebrew word used here suggests a desire so intense that it is audible.

Do you pant after God in the way the psalmist described? Do you pursue Him in such a way that everything else in your life takes second place? I have to confess that I don't. Oh yes, I long after God. But I know I don't pant after Him in the way the psalmist described. And neither, I am convinced, do most other Christians.

Now don't react defensively and say: "Whatever does he mean? My heart pants after God, and I will not let anyone try to tell me differently." Let me ask you to reserve any judgment you have on the statement I have just made, and I think I will be able to show you that although you have a deep desire to know God, you still might not have got to the place where your heart pants after Him in the way the psalmist described. But take heart—you can.

FURTHER STUDY

Pss. 73:15–28; 27:4;
2 Chron. 15:15

1. What was the psalmist's confession?

2. What happened when Israel sought the Lord wholeheartedly?

Prayer

God my Father, I would be rid of all that hinders my pursuit of You. Help me to see clearly into my heart, for I am so prone to defend myself. If there is something here that I need to know, then help me to look at it—openly and honestly. In Jesus' Name. Amen.

SECTION FIVE

The DIY Syndrome

For reading & meditation—Daniel 5:13–28

"... you did not honor the God who holds in his hand your life and all your ways." (v.23)

Yesterday I said that most Christians do not pant after God in the way the psalmist described in Psalm 42:1. Now I must attempt to make clear what I mean.

First, let me pull into focus the major problem with which we all struggle as soon as we are born. When God created us in the beginning, He designed us to have a relationship with Himself. This means that deep within our being is a thirst for God which will not go away. It can be ignored, disguised, misunderstood, wrongly labeled, or submerged under a welter of activity, but it will not disappear. And for good reason. We were designed to enjoy something better than this world can give us, particularly in the sphere of relationships. No human relationship can satisfy in the way that a relationship with God satisfies.

This deep thirst for God that resides within us makes us dependent on God for satisfaction, and that is something our sinful human nature deeply resents. You see, due to Adam and Eve's sin in the Garden of Eden, we have all been left a legacy called, "Do It Yourself." There is something within every single one of us that wants to take charge and have a hand in bringing about our own salvation. So here is the problem: to face the fact realistically that we inwardly thirst after God puts us in touch with a level of helplessness from which our sinful human nature shrinks. It reinforces the conviction that we are dependent on someone outside of ourselves for satisfaction. And that is something we don't care to acknowledge.

FURTHER STUDY

Pss. 143:1–6; 42:2; 63:1

1. What did the psalmist recognize?

2. What does it mean to "thirst"?

Prayer

O my Father, I recognize this elemental drive in my nature which causes me to resist standing in utter helplessness before You. But I sense that there can be no breakthrough in my life until I face this issue and deal with it. Help me, Father. In Jesus' Name. Amen.

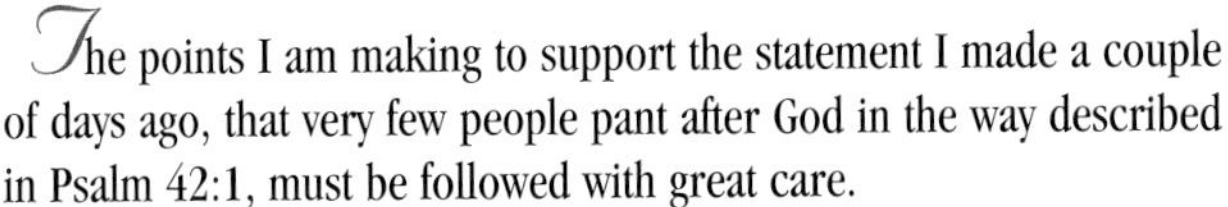

Looking in the Wrong Places

For reading & meditation—Jeremiah 2:1–13

"My people have committed two sins: they have forsaken me, the spring of living water, and have dug ... broken cisterns ..." (v.13)

The points I am making to support the statement I made a couple of days ago, that very few people pant after God in the way described in Psalm 42:1, must be followed with great care.

I said yesterday that the major problem with which we are all confronted when we come into this world is that we have at the core of our being a deep thirst for God which makes us entirely dependent on God for satisfaction. Our sinful human nature resents this because it dislikes the feeling of helplessness that such dependence brings, and prefers to have a hand in bringing about its own satisfaction. This terrible tendency of the human heart to try to satisfy its own thirst independently of God is brought out most clearly in the passage before us today. The prophet Jeremiah indicts the people of God for depending on broken cisterns in their efforts to quench their spiritual thirst, cisterns which they themselves made but which can hold no water.

Note carefully the two observations our text for today suggests: first, the people were thirsty, and second, they moved in the wrong direction to satisfy their thirst. God said it was as if they walked right past the clear waters He provided and chose instead to dig their own well. They wanted to run their own lives and refused to come to God and allow Him to quench their deep thirst. This stubborn commitment to independence is responsible more than anything else for preventing us having feet like "hinds' feet."

FURTHER STUDY

Judg. 17:1–6; 21:25; Prov. 28:26; 1 Cor. 10:12

1. How does the Book of Judges sum up the human heart?

2. What was Paul's admonition to the Corinthians?

Prayer

Gracious Father, I see that the problem You had with the nation of Israel is my problem too. For far too often I try to dig my own well. You are searching deeply into my life. Help me not to evade or avoid any issue. In Jesus' Name. Amen.

SECTION FIVE

How Problems Occur

For reading & meditation—John 7:32–44

"... If anyone is thirsty, let him come to me and drink." (v.37)

Yesterday we put our finger on what, in my opinion, is the biggest single preventative to us having feet like "hinds' feet"—a stubborn commitment to independence. This reflects itself in every one of our lives—even those who have been on the Way for several decades. In the Garden of Eden, Adam and Eve, who were designed to experience fulfillment by being dependent on God, decided to act independently of Him. Sin can be summed up as: "A Declaration of Independence"—an attempt to do for ourselves what only God can do for us.

What happened in the Garden of Eden is duplicated millions of times daily, not only in the lives of unbelievers, but in the lives of Christians also—Christians who use self-centered strategies to satisfy the deep thirst that is in their heart for God. Almost every spiritual or psychological problem has at its roots this condition—the person is failing in some way to let God satisfy their deep inner thirst.

This might sound like a simplistic explanation to some, but after many years of experience working in the field of counseling, I am convinced that it is this which underlies such conditions as anorexia, sexual perversions, worry, hostility, depression, homosexuality, and so on. You see, if we are not conscious that God is meeting the deep thirst that we have for Him on the inside of our being, then the inner emptiness will move us in one of two directions—to work to fill the emptiness in any way we can, or to withdraw and protect ourselves from the possibility of any further pain.

FURTHER STUDY

Matt. 5:1–6; John 4:1–42

1. What was the message of Jesus to the woman?

2. How was this reinforced through the teaching of the Sermon on the Mount?

Father, I see yet again that until and unless my deep thirst for You is being quenched, I am in deep trouble and vulnerable to all kinds of problems. I simply must get this issue straightened out. Help me, dear Father. In Jesus' Name. Amen.

SECTION FIVE

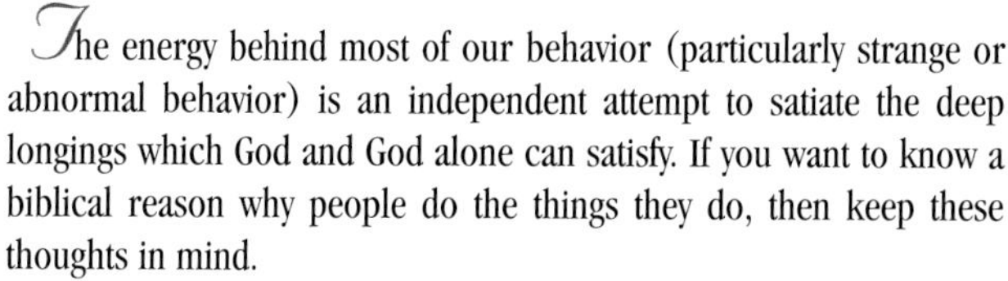

The Purpose of Living

For reading & meditation—Luke 10:25–37

"... 'Love the Lord your God ...' and, 'Love your neighbour as yourself.'" (v.27)

The energy behind most of our behavior (particularly strange or abnormal behavior) is an independent attempt to satiate the deep longings which God and God alone can satisfy. If you want to know a biblical reason why people do the things they do, then keep these thoughts in mind.

A man said to me some time ago: "Why do I browbeat my wife and make demands on her which I know are not loving? And why, despite my best efforts to change, do I fall back into my usual patterns?" I told him: "Your legitimate longings for impact and respect are not being met by God, and as you can't function very well when these longings go unmet, you set about trying to get your wife to meet them." He saw the point, asked God to forgive him for drinking at the wrong well, and turned in a fresh way to Christ for life and power and reality.

But what about the person who goes in the other direction and withdraws from others, manifesting such symptoms as extreme shyness and some forms of depression? This person is someone who has little awareness of their thirst being quenched by God—hence a degree of inner emptiness—and is motivated to avoid moving toward loving involvement with others for fear he or she might be rejected. Self-enhancement (a selfish attempt to quench our own thirst) or self-rejection—these are the two styles of relationship which characterize many Christians' lives. And both are a violation of the law of love.

FURTHER STUDY

John 13:1–35; 15:12; Matt. 22:39; 1 Thess. 3:12

1. How do we show that we belong to Jesus?

2. What was Paul's desire for the Thessalonians?

Prayer

Loving Lord, Your Word is crystal clear—the purpose of living is simply to love as I am loved. If I am not loving others, then quite simply, I am not allowing You to love me. I am sinning in both directions. Help me, my Savior. Amen.

SECTION FIVE

"Much Easier to Pretend . . ."

For reading & meditation—John 5:24–40

". . . you refuse to come to me to have life." (v.40)

Why do most Christians not pant after God in the way described by the psalmist? Because to pant after God means we have to get in touch with the deep thirst which is at the center of our being, and acknowledge our basic helplessness—a feeling which our fallen human nature deeply dislikes.

Most of us instinctively draw back from dealing with this stubborn commitment to independence, and pretend we are all right as we are. It is much easier to pretend we are thirsting after God than it is to face the challenge of giving up our commitment to independence. I am conscious that the challenge I am putting before you is one I want to deny in my own life. There is something in me that would like to think—and would like you to think—that I have a heart that pants after God. But I know that if I stop short of identifying my independent strategies for finding life on my own and giving them up, I will never get in touch with the deep thirst for God that exists at the core of my being.

What is the answer? I must ask God to search my heart, expose my self-centered motivations, and help me see just where it is that I stop short of panting after Him. You see, the more deeply we sense our thirst, the more passionately we will pursue water—but we will never sense that thirst until we are willing to face the fact that we may be drinking more from our own self-constructed wells than from the wells of God.

FURTHER STUDY

Exod. 32:1–9;
Isa. 28:12; 30:15;
2 Chron. 24:19

1. How did God describe the children of Israel?
2. What is said of them time and time again?

Prayer

Father, I tremble as I recognize this terrible tendency within me to walk right past the fountain of living water and drink from a well of my own making. But help me to recognize it for what it really is—not just a terrible tendency, but a terrible sin. In Jesus' Name I pray. Amen.

SECTION FIVE

The Word That Irritates

For reading & meditation—2 Chronicles 7:11–22

"If my people ... will humble themselves and ... turn from their wicked ways, then I will ... forgive their sin ..." (v.14)

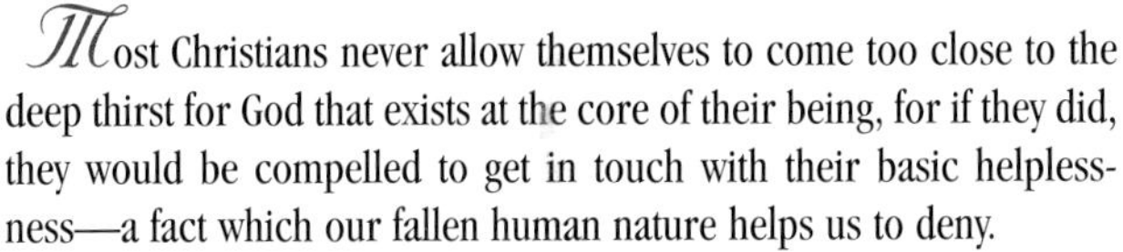

Most Christians never allow themselves to come too close to the deep thirst for God that exists at the core of their being, for if they did, they would be compelled to get in touch with their basic helplessness—a fact which our fallen human nature helps us to deny.

Why would we want to deny our basic helplessness? Because to recognize it puts us in a position where we have to repent of it—and that is something our fallen human nature pulls back from doing. Believe me, the one word which grates and irritates our carnal nature is the word *repent*. It is much easier to be given advice like: "Read more of the Bible every day," "Add extra minutes to your prayer time," or "Seize more opportunities to share your faith," than to be told to repent. All these things I have just mentioned may be excellent in themselves, but more is required if we are to get in touch with the deep thirst for God which exists at the core of our being—we must repent.

But repent of what? Our stubborn commitment to independence; the awful desire and practice of choosing to dig our own wells. A passionate pursuit of God demands this. Believe me, no matter what we say with our lips, we will never begin to pant after God until we are prepared to repent of the self-sufficiency that has made its home deep within our hearts. This, in my opinion, is the biggest single step we can take in our pursuit of God and the experience of having feet like "hinds' feet."

FURTHER STUDY

Ps. 34:1–18; Joel 2:12; Luke 13:1–3

1. What was the central message of Jesus?

2. How does the psalmist express it?

Prayer

Gracious and loving heavenly Father, help me to repent deeply. May I know at this moment a turning from self-dependence to God-dependence. I give You my willingness—now give me Your power. In Jesus' Name I ask it. Amen.

SECTION FIVE

"Faith in Two Minds"

For reading & meditation—Matthew 21:18–27

"... if you have faith ... you can say to this mountain, 'Go, throw yourself into the sea,' and it will ..." (v.21)

The fourth step we must take if we are to have feet like "hinds' feet" is to learn how to face and handle any doubts that may arise in our heart. Most of us have to face the problem of doubt at some time or another, and unless we have a clear understanding of what is involved when we doubt and how to deal with it, our pursuit of God can be greatly hindered.

The English word *doubt* comes from the Latin *dubitare*, which is rooted in an Aryan word meaning "two." To doubt means to take two positions on something or to have a divided heart. A major misconception concerning doubt—and one that has brought great anxiety to many a Christian's heart—is to view doubt as the opposite of faith, which clearly it is not. Unbelief is the opposite of faith. Os Guinness puts it like this: "To believe is to be 'in one mind' about accepting something as true; to disbelieve is to be 'in one mind' about rejecting it. To doubt is to waver between the two, to believe and disbelieve at once, and so to be 'in two minds.'"

Donald Bridge, in his book *When Christians Doubt*, refers to doubt as "faith asking questions." Some might think this definition elevates doubt to a position it does not deserve and masks its true nature—but not so. It is only when we understand what doubt really is that we can deal with it in the way we should.

Doubt is, as Os Guinness puts it, "faith in two minds."

FURTHER STUDY

Matt. 14:22–33;
Luke 24:13–35

1. How does Peter illustrate the principle of being in two minds?

2. What did Jesus mean by "slow of heart?"

Prayer

My God and Father, I would be at my best—at Your best. But Your best cannot get across to me if doubt remains in my heart. Show me the steps I must take to overcome doubt. In Jesus' Name I pray. Amen.

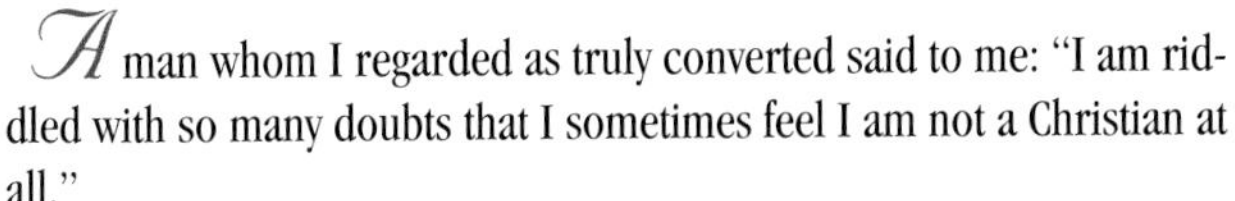

The True Nature of Doubt

DAY 278

For reading & meditation—Matthew 28:1–20

"When they saw him, they worshiped him; but some doubted." (v.17)

A man whom I regarded as truly converted said to me: "I am riddled with so many doubts that I sometimes feel I am not a Christian at all."

When I pointed out to him the nature of doubt—that it is not the same as unbelief—I saw a new expression appear on his face. He grasped me by the hands and said: "How can I ever sufficiently thank you? You have released a pressure that has been building up inside me for years." I met him years later, and he told me that the simple insight I had given him concerning the nature of doubt was all he needed to face his doubts and deal with them in a spiritual way. I say again, no misunderstanding causes more anxiety to the heart of a Christian than that which concerns the nature of doubt.

Let's put unbelief under the microscope for a moment, for by doing so we will see the nature of doubt still more clearly. "Unbelief is a willful refusal to believe, resulting in a deliberate decision to disobey. It is a state of mind which is closed against God, an attitude of heart which disobeys God as much as it disbelieves the truth. It is the consequence of a settled choice." Doubt is not a willful decision to disbelieve, but a suspension between faith and unbelief. To believe is to be in one mind, to disbelieve is also to be in one mind, but to doubt is to be caught in the halfway stage between the two—suspended between the desire to affirm and the desire to negate.

FURTHER STUDY

John 20:24–29;
11:16; 14:5; 21:2;
Matt. 10:3

1. How did Thomas display his total commitment?

2. Why then did he doubt?

Prayer

Father, while I am relieved to discover that doubt is not the same as unbelief, I nevertheless long to live a doubt-free existence. Break down any barriers within me that would hinder the flow of faith. In Christ's Name I ask it. Amen.

SECTION FIVE

Doubt Must Be Corrected

For reading & meditation—Matthew 14:22–36

"... Jesus reached out his hand and caught him. 'You of little faith,' he said, 'why did you doubt?'" (v.31)

While it is possible for us to distinguish between doubt and unbelief in theory, it is not so easy in practice. Doubt can eventually move in the direction of unbelief and cross the borderline, but when it does it ceases to be doubt. The idea of "total" or "complete" doubt is a contradiction in terms, for doubt that is total can no longer be classified as doubt; it is unbelief.

Os Guinness points out that when we attempt to undertake a biblical analysis of doubt, we can come out with either a "hard" or "soft" view of the subject. Those who take a "soft" view of doubt point to how vastly different doubt is from unbelief, and those who take a "hard" view of doubt point out its similarities. Both views can be drawn out of the Scriptures. Error is usually truth out of balance, and it is important, therefore, that we get a balanced view of what the Bible has to say about doubt. In my view it can be summarized like this—doubt is not the same as unbelief, but unless corrected, can lead naturally to it.

This view has helped me avoid what I consider to be the extremes of being too hard or too soft on doubt. It is a condition which must be regarded as serious but it need not be fatal. Don't allow your doubts to bring you into condemnation, for when faced and brought into clear perspective, they can be the catalyst to a deeper pursuit of God.

FURTHER STUDY

Matt. 8:1–26; 6:30; 16:8

1. What phrase did Jesus often use?
2. What did He say of the centurion?

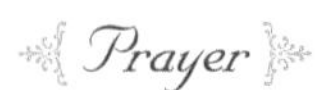

Father, when will I learn that in You all things serve—even doubt? Show me how to make my doubts into stepping stones and use them to come into an even closer relationship with You. Amen.

Doubt Keeps Faith in Trim

For reading & meditation—John 8:34–47

"... he is a liar and the father of lies." (v.44)

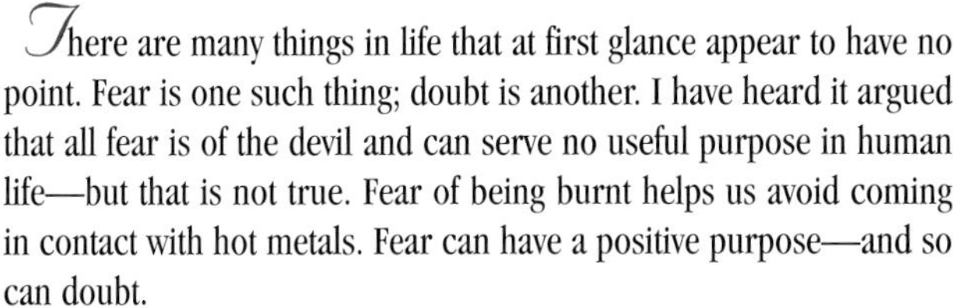

There are many things in life that at first glance appear to have no point. Fear is one such thing; doubt is another. I have heard it argued that all fear is of the devil and can serve no useful purpose in human life—but that is not true. Fear of being burnt helps us avoid coming in contact with hot metals. Fear can have a positive purpose—and so can doubt.

Doubt can be used to help us detect error. We live in a world of which at the moment Satan is "prince," and he tries his utmost to get us to believe his lies. Jesus was not being poetic when He described Satan as the "father of lies." The devil's stock-in-trade is half-truths and half-lies that masquerade as the whole truth. So because all things are not true, not everything should be believed. Some things ought to be doubted. One writer says: "The inescapable presence of doubt is a constant reminder of our responsibility to truth in a twilight world of truth and half-truth." It acts like a spur to challenge us to find out the truth about a situation.

It is precisely because all is not certain that we have to make certain. Francis Bacon put it like this: "If a man will begin with certainties, he shall end in doubts; but if he will be content to begin with doubts, he shall end in certainties." Doubt can act as a sparring partner both to truth and error; it keeps faith trim and assists us in shedding the paunchiness of false ideas.

FURTHER STUDY

2 Pet. 2:1–10; Titus 1:9–11; 2 Tim. 4:1–5

1. What will come in the last days?

2. How did Paul exhort Timothy?

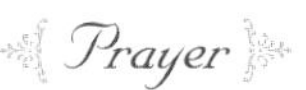

Prayer

Gracious and loving Father, thank You for reminding me yet again that I can take anything that comes and use it to positive ends—even doubt. Help me to use my doubts as a sparring partner to keep my faith trim. In Jesus' Name I pray. Amen.

SECTION FIVE

The First Thing to Do

For reading & meditation—1 Timothy 2:1–15

"I want men everywhere to lift up holy hands in prayer, without anger or disputing." (v.8)

Although doubt can be turned destructively against error, it is also possible for it to be turned destructively against truth. How do we deal with the darker side of doubt? The first thing we must do is to bring every doubt into the open and examine it.

Most Christians fail to do this; they do nothing with their doubts and just hope that they will go away. The way people react to their doubts is an excellent indication of their attitude to doubt itself. Many feel ashamed when they experience doubt and thus push the doubts below the surface of their minds and refuse to recognize them. Some even regard doubt as the unpardonable sin. Others treat it as an unmentionable subject and never refer to any doubts they have for fear they are letting the side down. I myself sometimes struggle with doubt—even after over fifty years in the Christian life.

In the months following my conversion, I had doubts about the inspiration and inerrancy of the Bible until I decided to accept it by faith. When I did, all my doubts concerning it were immediately dissolved, and from that day to this I have never had one doubt about the reliability of Scripture. But I have doubted other things—particularly in the area of personal guidance. I have learned, however, not to let doubts threaten or intimidate me, and when they come I simply look them in the face and say: "I am going to put you in harness and make you work to bring me closer to God." Now my doubts get fewer and fewer.

FURTHER STUDY

1 John 2:1–20; 3:24; 1 Cor. 13:12

1. What did Paul admit to?

2. What did John affirm?

Father, how can I sufficiently thank You for showing me how to take the negative things of life and turn them into positives? Nothing need work against me when I have You within. I am so thankful. Amen.

SECTION FIVE

Talk to Yourself

For reading & meditation—Hebrews 4:1–13

"For the word of God is living and powerful … and is a discerner of the … intents of the heart." (v.12, NKJV)

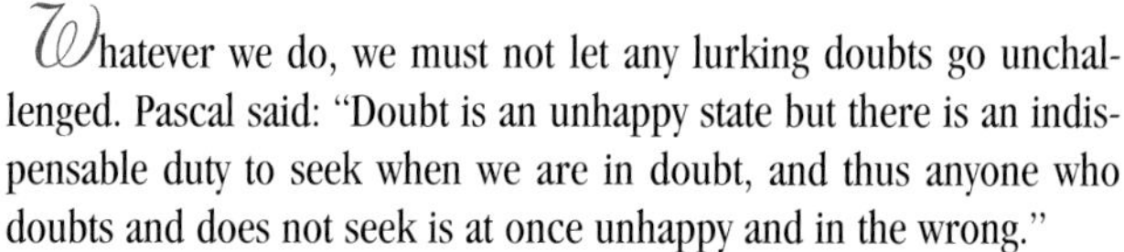

Whatever we do, we must not let any lurking doubts go unchallenged. Pascal said: "Doubt is an unhappy state but there is an indispensable duty to seek when we are in doubt, and thus anyone who doubts and does not seek is at once unhappy and in the wrong."

How do we go about resolving doubts? One way is to bring them to the Lord in prayer and ask Him to help you overcome them. If prayer does not dissolve them, apply the tactic which Nehemiah adopted: "But we prayed to our God and posted a guard" (Neh. 4:9). Take a verse of Scripture that is the opposite of your doubt and hold it in the center of your mind, repeating it to yourself many times throughout the day. Dr. Martin Lloyd-Jones once said: "Have you realized that most of your unhappiness in life is due to the fact that you are listening to yourself instead of talking to yourself? We must talk to ourselves instead of allowing 'ourselves' to talk to us!"

In listening to our doubts instead of talking to them, we fall prey to the same temptation which caught Adam and Eve off guard in the Garden of Eden. The order of creation was stood on its head when the first human pair allowed themselves to be dictated to by the animal world (in the form of the serpent) when, in fact, they had been put in a position to dictate to it. Don't let your doubts dictate to you. Turn the tables and dictate to them. Talk to them with words from the Word of God.

FURTHER STUDY

Gen. 3; Ps. 53:5; James. 1:6

1. What was Satan's strategy?

2. What did Adam confess?

Prayer

Father, help me never to be nonplussed, for in You there are ways to overcome every problem. Drive the truth I have learned today deeply into my spirit so that I may apply it whenever I am faced with doubt. In Jesus' Name. Amen.

SECTION FIVE

"The Doubter's Prayer"

For reading & meditation—John 20:19–29

"... Stop doubting and believe." (v.27)

If, after facing your doubts, praying about them and developing the habit of talking to yourself with a Scripture passage that refutes them, they still persist, then seek the help of a minister or a Christian counselor. God has given us three resources to help us whenever we get into spiritual difficulties: the Word of God, the Spirit of God, and the people of God. The final answer to doubt may come as you share with an experienced Christian the things that are going on in your heart.

If you are not able to get the kind of help I am suggesting, then get in touch with your nearest Christian bookshop and ask them to recommend some helpful reading on the subject. Whatever you do, don't allow yourself to settle down into a complacent attitude about your doubts. Adopt a positive approach and determine to do something about resolving them. This will ensure that even though your doubts may take some time to get resolved, they will not degenerate into unbelief. Let me remind you of "The Doubter's Prayer" compiled by Martin Luther:

Dear Lord, although I am sure of my position,
I am unable to sustain it without Thee.
Help me or I am lost.

Remember this—if the only thing you are able to do is pray, then that by itself will prevent doubt from becoming unbelief. If you go further, however, and adopt the principle of "talking to yourself" from the Word of God, then you have in your hands the strategy for overcoming every single doubt.

FURTHER STUDY

Mark 9:14–29; Matt. 9:29–30; 21:21

1. What was the father's request?

2. Do you need to pray that prayer today?

Prayer

Father, help me, whenever I don't know what to do, to turn naturally to prayer. Then no moment will be empty or fruitless. But help me also to utilize the power of Your Word, the Bible. Let these two things become my central strategy. Amen.

SECTION FIVE

Another Dip into the Depths

For reading & meditation—Psalm 24:1–10

"Who may ascend the hill of the Lord? ... He who has clean hands and a pure heart ..." (v.3–4)

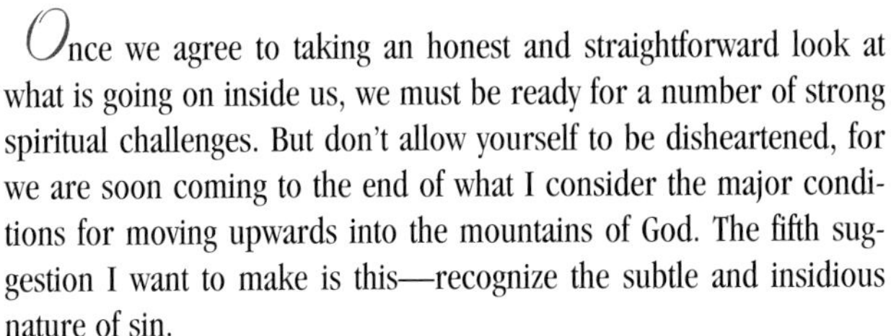

Once we agree to taking an honest and straightforward look at what is going on inside us, we must be ready for a number of strong spiritual challenges. But don't allow yourself to be disheartened, for we are soon coming to the end of what I consider the major conditions for moving upwards into the mountains of God. The fifth suggestion I want to make is this—recognize the subtle and insidious nature of sin.

There is a view in the Christian church that as long as we focus on the sins that are obvious (i.e., sins of behavior), then we can forget any hidden sins that may be in the heart and trust God to deal with them in His own way. Dealing with obvious sin is extremely important—don't hear me minimizing this fact. Moral discipline is part of the Christian commitment. We are expected to resist the temptations that come our way and correct any spiritual violations that may occur, but to concern ourselves only with obvious sin and avoid facing the sins of the heart will cause us to miss our footing on the slopes of God.

Someone has put it like this: "The grime has been so embedded in the carpet that a simple vacuuming will not do the job. We need a scrubbing brush and a strong detergent." Diligence in putting right the things that are obviously wrong is good, but without a clear understanding of how sin has penetrated our heart, we will be nothing more than surface-copers.

FURTHER STUDY

Jer. 17:1–11; Gen. 3:8; Prov. 28:13

1. What is the tendency of the human heart?

2. What is one condition for us to prosper spiritually?

Prayer

Father, forgive me that I have been so content to live on the surface of life. Help me see that in turning my gaze at what is going on inside me, You are not seeking to demean me but to develop me. Give me grace not to shrink from the task. Amen.

DAY 285

SECTION FIVE

A Little-Known Sin

For reading & meditation—Psalm 7:1–17

"... For the righteous God tests the hearts and minds."
(v.9, NKJV)

Focusing only on correcting obvious sin (i.e., sins of behavior) without understanding what it means to deal with the issues of the heart will bring about a condition akin to that of the Pharisees—more smug than spiritual.

One of the things I have noticed about myself is that whenever I feel I am not pursuing God in the way I should, I tend to focus on the surface issues of my life, above-the-water-line problems, and work at them all I can. But sin involves far more than what goes on above the surface; there is also something going on in the deep recesses of my heart.

As there is little need for me to discuss the sins that are obvious, I want to focus now on those that are not. I imagine that those of you who have been Christians for some time will expect me at this stage to identify the hidden sins of the heart under such categories as resentment, lukewarmness, impatience, jealousy, and so on. My concern, however, is with a category of sin that is not easily recognized and not very well known. This sin is probably more deeply buried in our hearts than any other and acts, in my opinion, as a trigger to them. The sin I refer to is—demandingness. You won't find the word in the Bible, but you will certainly see it illustrated there. Demandingness is insisting that our interests be served irrespective of others. Clearly, if Christ is to live in us, then this has to die in us.

FURTHER STUDY

Gal. 2:15–21; Isa. 29:15; 30:1–2; 1 Cor. 10:24

1. How did Paul describe demandingness?
2. What were the children of Israel doing?

Prayer

Father, I see that again You are about to face me with a strong and serious challenge. Forgive me if I draw back when Your lance plunges deep. I have lived with demandingness for so long that I might not even be able to recognize it. Help me. In Jesus' Name. Amen.

SECTION FIVE

The Example of Jacob

For reading & meditation—Genesis 27:30–38 & 28:10–22

"... If God will ... watch over me ... so that I return safely ... then the Lord will be my God ..." (vv.20–21)

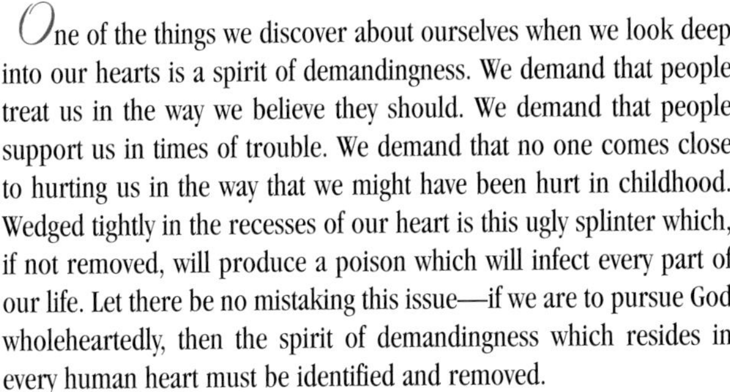

One of the things we discover about ourselves when we look deep into our hearts is a spirit of demandingness. We demand that people treat us in the way we believe they should. We demand that people support us in times of trouble. We demand that no one comes close to hurting us in the way that we might have been hurt in childhood. Wedged tightly in the recesses of our heart is this ugly splinter which, if not removed, will produce a poison which will infect every part of our life. Let there be no mistaking this issue—if we are to pursue God wholeheartedly, then the spirit of demandingness which resides in every human heart must be identified and removed.

Jacob is probably one of the clearest biblical illustrations of a demanding spirit. He insisted on having his father's blessing for himself and took advantage of his brother's hunger, buying his birthright for a plate of stew. Later, Jacob went through a kind of half conversion, making God his God and giving Him a tenth and so on, but deep in his heart there was still the spirit of demandingness.

It shows itself again at Paddan Aram where, after marrying Rachel, Laban's daughter, he worked out a scheme to make himself rich at his father-in-law's expense (Gen. 30:41–43). He was still Jacob—the man who demanded to have his own way. He had talked about himself in terms of honesty: "my honesty will testify for me in the future" (Gen. 30:33), but it was nothing more than above-the-water-line honesty. His mind was changed, but not his heart.

FURTHER STUDY

Luke 15:11–32;
Matt. 20:1–16

1. How did the prodigal's brother display demandingness?

2. How did Jesus illustrate it?

Prayer

O Father, I am so grateful that You have recorded in Scripture so many illustrations of the truths You want me to know. I see so much of myself in Jacob. Help me from this day forward to be less and less like him. In Jesus' Name I pray. Amen.

SECTION FIVE

"What Is Your Name?"

For reading & meditation—Genesis 32:22–32

"So Jacob was left alone, and a man wrestled with him till daybreak." (v.24)

The way in which God helped Jacob to be rid of his spirit of demandingness is revealing—"a man wrestled with him till daybreak." Like the Hound of Heaven, the love of God pursued him down the years, awaiting the hour when he would be ready to admit that he was beaten.

The man (probably an angelic representative) wrestled with him until Jacob's strength was diminished, at which point he asked him: "What is your name?" To us it seems a simple question, but in those days one's name was the expression of one's character; if the character changed, the name was changed. So Jacob, after a tremendous struggle, made the crucial confession: "My name is Jacob—the supplanter," he sobbed. The depths were uncovered. Jacob's heart was naked before God. The real problem was identified.

If you have not reached this place in your spiritual experience, then I suggest you stop everything and tell God your name. You might have to confess: "My name is Demandingness; I insist on having my own way in everything." For some of you it will be hard to get that name out. But get it out, no matter what the cost, for there will be no new name until you say the old name. The saying of the old name is a confession, a catharsis. When Jacob said his name, the angel said: "Your name will no longer be Jacob, but Israel" (v.28)—a striver with God. It was after Israel, the crooked man made straight, that the new nation of Israel was named. Jacob was buried and Israel was alive forevermore.

FURTHER STUDY

1 John 1:1–9; Ezra 10:11; 2 Sam. 12:13

1. What are we to do with our sin?

2. How did Nathan respond to David?

Prayer

God, help me to tell You my name—my real name. Help me to dodge no longer: the game is up. Take out of me the spirit of demandingness. Change my name and change my character. Save me from myself. In Jesus' Name I pray. Amen.

SECTION FIVE

How Demandingness Flourishes

For reading & meditation—Daniel 3:8–30

"... we want you to know, O king, that we will not serve your gods or worship the image of gold ..." (v.18)

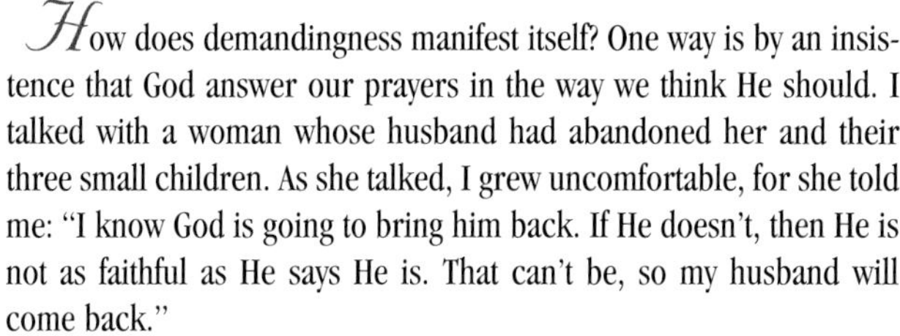

How does demandingness manifest itself? One way is by an insistence that God answer our prayers in the way we think He should. I talked with a woman whose husband had abandoned her and their three small children. As she talked, I grew uncomfortable, for she told me: "I know God is going to bring him back. If He doesn't, then He is not as faithful as He says He is. That can't be, so my husband will come back."

Can you hear the spirit of demandingness in these words? I sympathized with her hurt to such a degree that it was painful for me to have to explain that faith is one thing, but demandingness is another. Her "faith" in God was based, not on unconditional confidence in His character and sovereign purposes, but rather in the hope that He would relieve her suffering in the way she thought best.

Deep hurt is a most suitable environment in which to nourish a demanding spirit. Nothing convinces us more that God must answer our prayers in the way we think He should than when we are experiencing continued heartache. And the line between legitimate desiring and illegitimate demanding is a thin one which is easily crossed. How can we be sure our desiring does not turn to demanding? When we are willing to say: "If God does not grant what I desire, then I can still go on because I know that He will never abandon me, and in His love I have all the strength I need to handle whatever comes."

FURTHER STUDY

Matt. 26:36–46; Ps. 40:8; Eph. 6:6; Phil. 1:1

1. How did Jesus express desire without demandingness?

2. How did Paul express it?

Prayer

O God, save me from an insistent and demanding spirit. You who are always reaching out to me in love and awakening me, help me to recognize the difference between a desire and a demand. In Jesus' Name. Amen.

SECTION FIVE

Faith Is Not Demandingness

For reading & meditation—Hebrews 11:1–16

"Now faith is the substance of things hoped for, the evidence of things not seen." (v.1, NKJV)

About demandingness, I am frequently asked: "Doesn't what you say destroy the faith and confidence we ought to have when we approach God in prayer? Isn't powerful praying the ability to insist on God giving us the things we know we ought to be receiving?"

There is a world of difference between "praying in faith" and demandingness. When we "pray in faith," we have the assurance in our hearts that God wants to bring about a certain purpose for His own glory, whereupon faith reaches into heaven and pulls down the answer through fervent, believing prayer. Demandingness is another thing entirely—it insists on getting the answers that are in accord with its own desires rather than God's purposes. It is an attempt to bring God in line with our will rather than bringing our wills in line with His will.

Dr. Francis Schaeffer, when advised that he was suffering from a terminal illness, became assured that his work on earth was finished and that soon he would leave this world and go to his heavenly home. Thousands of people prayed for his healing and when he himself was asked why he did not claim the Bible's promises concerning health and wholeness, he replied: "When I am in the presence of God, it seems uniquely unbecoming to demand anything." Some have interpreted these words as a lack of faith but I think I understand what the great man meant. It is one thing to plead and pray with passion for something very personal; it is another thing to demand that the will of the Almighty be one with our own.

FURTHER STUDY

Ps. 143:1–10;
Matt. 12:50;
James. 4:1–15

1. What was the desire of the psalmist?
2. How does James put it?

Prayer

Father, I see the line between demandingness and faith is so fine that I can easily cross from one to the other without knowing it. Tune my spirit so that I will always be able to discern the difference between these two things. In Jesus' Name. Amen.

SECTION FIVE

The Cure for Demandingness

For reading & meditation—Hosea 14:1–9

"Take words with you and return to the Lord ..." (v.2)

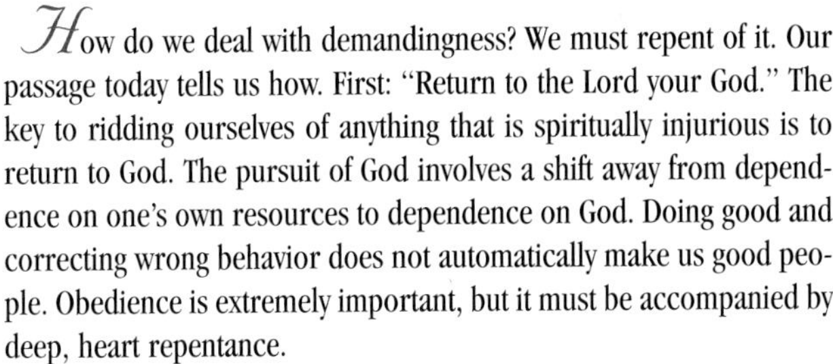

How do we deal with demandingness? We must repent of it. Our passage today tells us how. First: "Return to the Lord your God." The key to ridding ourselves of anything that is spiritually injurious is to return to God. The pursuit of God involves a shift away from dependence on one's own resources to dependence on God. Doing good and correcting wrong behavior does not automatically make us good people. Obedience is extremely important, but it must be accompanied by deep, heart repentance.

Second, the passage says: "Take words with you." This phrase means that we must put into words a clear description of what we are repenting of. If we are not clear about what is going on inside us, how can we repent of it? Next: "Forgive all our sins." Repentance puts us in touch with God's forgiveness. We can work to bring about change also, but the greatest catalyst for change is humbly positioning ourselves before God and asking for His forgiveness.

Then: "Receive us graciously, that we may offer the fruit of our lips." The thought here is: "Receive us that we may worship You more effectively." The purpose of all restoration is to worship God. We will be drawn into true worship when we give up insisting on our own way and learn to trust God for our happiness. When repentance moves us from a spirit of demandingness to absolute trust in God, then we are where God is able to make our feet like "hinds' feet" and equip us with the ability to ascend into the heights with Him.

FURTHER STUDY

Joel 2:12–18; Isa. 55:7; Pss. 34:18; 51:17

1. What does God not despise?

2. What does it mean to "rend your heart"?

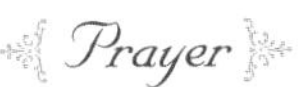

Tender and skillful Invader of my heart, I yield my stricken being to You for healing. "Be of sin the double cure": Drain every drop of demandingness from my being. For I want not only to be better, but whole. In Jesus' Name. Amen.

SECTION FIVE

"Too Good to Be True"

For reading & meditation—Luke 24:36–53

"... while they still did not believe it because of joy ... he asked them, 'Do you have anything here to eat?'" (v.41)

If we are to let nothing stand between us and the making of our feet into "hinds' feet," then we must understand the nature of disappointment and how it works to hinder our pursuit of God. All of us have been disappointed. Living in a fallen world means we have been subjected to experiences where we have been let down by others, even our loved ones at times. But this is not the problem—the problem occurs when we allow the hurts of the past to prevent us from reaching out to God and to others in an attitude of love.

A dramatic illustration of this is found in the passage before us today. It is the evening of the day of the resurrection and, without warning, Jesus suddenly enters the room where His disciples are assembled and makes Himself known to them. How did they respond? "They were still unconvinced, still wondering, for it seemed too good to be true" (v.41, NEB). It was obvious that the disappointment of Christ's crucifixion and death still reverberated within them, and now, faced with the reality of the resurrection, they did not want to believe it in case it was not true—and they would be disappointed again.

They wanted to believe, but they had difficulty in doing so because they knew that they could not cope with what would happen in their hearts if it turned out that what they were seeing was not true. Rather than take the risk of faith they preferred, for a little while at least, to withdraw into the safety of disappointment.

FURTHER STUDY

Luke 24:13–35;
Job 30:26

1. How did the disciples express their disappointment?

2. How did Jesus deal with them?

Prayer

God, forgive me that so often I allow the disappointments of life to deter me from moving toward You, in case something might happen that will disappoint me again. Help me to put everything I am and have in Your hands—with nothing held back. In Jesus' Name. Amen.

SECTION FIVE

"Surprised by Joy"

For reading & meditation—Psalm 30:1–12

"... weeping may remain for a night, but rejoicing comes in the morning." (v.5)

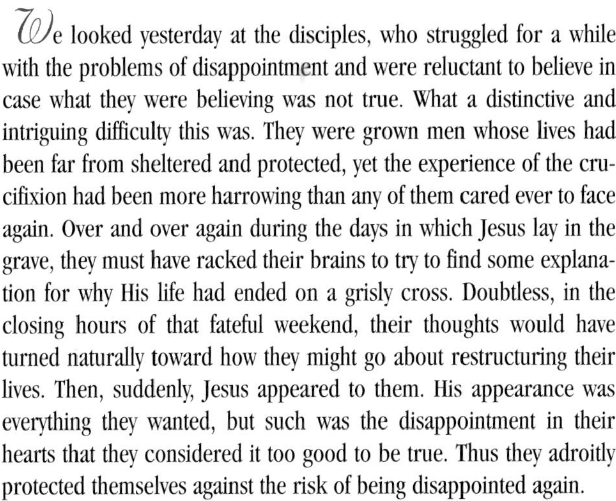

We looked yesterday at the disciples, who struggled for a while with the problems of disappointment and were reluctant to believe in case what they were believing was not true. What a distinctive and intriguing difficulty this was. They were grown men whose lives had been far from sheltered and protected, yet the experience of the crucifixion had been more harrowing than any of them cared ever to face again. Over and over again during the days in which Jesus lay in the grave, they must have racked their brains to try to find some explanation for why His life had ended on a grisly cross. Doubtless, in the closing hours of that fateful weekend, their thoughts would have turned naturally toward how they might go about restructuring their lives. Then, suddenly, Jesus appeared to them. His appearance was everything they wanted, but such was the disappointment in their hearts that they considered it too good to be true. Thus they adroitly protected themselves against the risk of being disappointed again.

This is the tragedy of disappointment—it can, unless looked at and dealt with, reverberate inside us and hinder us in our pursuit of God. When disappointment is put into its proper perspective and faith comes into its own, far from being too good to be true, one discovers that there is nothing else so good and nothing else so true. God proves Himself to be not just better than our worst fears, but better than our greatest dreams. Disbelieving for joy is quickly followed by being surprised by joy.

FURTHER STUDY

John 21:1–22; Ps. 126:5; Isa. 35:10

1. How did Peter respond to his disappointment?

2. What were Jesus' words to him?

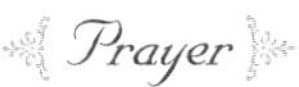

Prayer

Gracious and loving heavenly Father, give me insight into what I have been looking at today and show me how to press through all disappointments in the knowledge that beyond the hurts, I shall be "surprised by joy." Amen.

DAY 293

SECTION FIVE

"It's OK to Feel It"

For reading & meditation—Nehemiah 1:1–11

"When I heard these things, I sat down and wept ..." (v.4)

Why is it necessary to know to cope with disappointment? Because if it is allowed to reverberate in our hearts, however much we pretend with our minds that we do not care, our true feelings will prevent us from moving upward toward the peaks of God "with all four feet." Our back feet will not track where our front feet have been positioned, and thus we will miss our step on the steep slopes that lead upward to closer fellowship with God.

The first thing we should learn about disappointment is this—it's OK to feel it. The worst possible thing we can do with any problem that arises in our lives is to refuse to face it and feel it. Yet this is a typical response made by many Christians to life's problems.

I once counselled a young, unmarried woman who had gone through some bitter disappointments both in her childhood and in her adolescent years. Such was the pain these disappointments brought that the only way she could cope with them was to turn her mind to something else. She toyed with the idea of drink, sensual pleasures and several other things, but because she had a deep commitment to Christ, she decided to enroll in a Bible correspondence course. As we talked, it became clear to me that in doing this, her primary goal was not to learn more about Scripture but to relieve the pain of disappointment that was reverberating in her heart. Bible study became a way to escape from her problems rather than what it should have been—a way to confront them.

FURTHER STUDY

Jonah 1–4; Prov. 16:32; Eccl. 7:9

1. Why was Jonah disappointed?

2. How did demandingness come into it?

Prayer

Father, help me to see that You have made me in such a way that I function best when I go through problems rather than around them. Show me that maturity is me being in charge of my feelings, not my feelings being in charge of me. In Jesus' Name. Amen.

"Let's Not Stay Here Too Long"

For reading & meditation—Matthew 26:36–46

"... he said to them, 'My soul is overwhelmed with sorrow to the point of death. Stay ... keep watch with me.'" (v.38)

We said yesterday: "It's OK to feel disappointed." It is better to face disappointment and feel it than pretend it is not there. And when I say "feel it"—I mean exactly that. Most people, I find, just walk around the edges of their disappointment, in the way they would walk cautiously around the rim of a volcano, admitting they have been disappointed but working hard (often unconsciously) to blunt the feelings of disappointment with a "let's not stay here too long" attitude.

The usual response to what I am now saying is: "Surely there is no point in being willing to enter into all the pain of our disappointments? What is past is past; isn't it better to forget the hurts and disappointments of the past and get on with life?" Sounds rational and sensible, doesn't it? However, it is not the best way to deal with life. The more deeply we are willing to face our disappointments, the readier we will be to turn to Christ and draw from Him the strength we need to cope with them.

The danger we face when we are unwilling to feel as openly as possible the disappointments that come our way is that we will come to depend on our own strategies to cope with them, and turn only partially to Christ for succor and strength. Facing and feeling disappointment is a sure way of coming to recognize that God, and God alone, is the only one who can help us cope. When we face and feel our disappointments, we will cling more closely to Christ.

FURTHER STUDY

1 Kings 19; Heb. 4:15

1. What was Elijah's disappointment?
2. How did he respond to it?

Gracious and loving heavenly Father, I want to live fully and frankly. Help me to face whatever goes on inside me with complete honesty. Save me from all self-deception and subterfuges, for I would be a fit instrument for You. In Jesus' Name. Amen.

SECTION FIVE

The Sin of Self-Protection

For reading & meditation—1 John 3:11–24

"And this is his command: to believe in the name of his Son, Jesus Christ, and to love one another ..." (v.23)

Another advantage of being willing to feel disappointment is that it enables us to come in touch with another hidden sin of the heart—self-protection. Whenever we are disappointed, we naturally feel hurt and experience inner pain. Some people are so affected by disappointment that a pool of pain builds up inside them, and they say to themselves something like this: "People hurt: stay away from them and don't get too closely involved." These people see noninvolvement as the way to avoiding the pain of possible disappointment.

But this attitude is a violation of the law of love. Lawrence Crabb, a Christian psychologist, says: "Deficient love is always central to our problems." What does he mean? He means that behind most of our problems is a failure to love others as we love ourselves. If we refuse to move towards someone in the spirit of love because of the fact that they may disappoint us, then we are more interested in protecting ourselves from pain than we are in loving—and that is sin.

Did you ever think of self-protection as a sin? Well, it is, and in my estimation it is one of the most subtle of all. Many of our relationships are ruined by this—particularly marriage relationships. A man who shouts angrily at his wife early in his marriage is setting up a self-protective system that says: "Disappoint me and you will have to suffer the consequences." What is he doing? He is protecting himself more than loving his wife. And that, no matter how one might attempt to rationalize it—is sin.

FURTHER STUDY

Luke 10:25–37;
Rom. 13:10;
James. 1:27

1. What did the priest and Levite display?
2. What did the Samaritan display?

Prayer

Father, Your challenges are sometimes more than I can bear, yet I see the sense and wisdom that lies behind them. Reveal to me my own self-protective devices and help me to give them up in favor of loving as I have been loved. Amen.

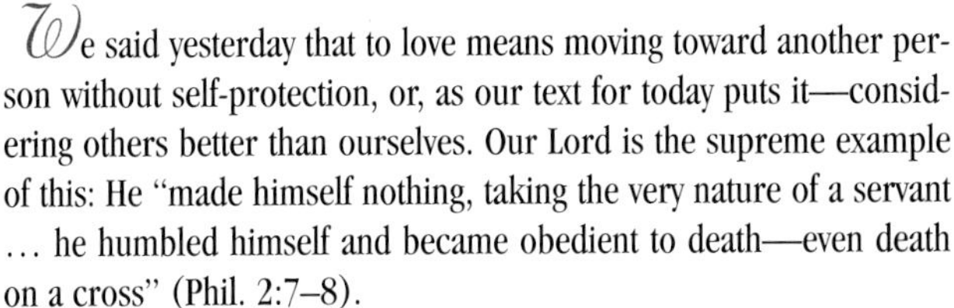

For reading & meditation—Philippians 2:1–13

"Do nothing out of selfish ambition or vain conceit, but in humility consider others better than yourselves." (v.3)

We said yesterday that to love means moving toward another person without self-protection, or, as our text for today puts it—considering others better than ourselves. Our Lord is the supreme example of this: He "made himself nothing, taking the very nature of a servant ... he humbled himself and became obedient to death—even death on a cross" (Phil. 2:7–8).

Disappointed people sometimes find it difficult to move out toward others. After all, people—even Christian people—can be rude, uncouth, obnoxious and sometimes downright disgusting. I sometimes think it might be helpful if we put a sign outside some churches saying: "Enter here at your own risk." Forgive my cynicism, but I have lived long enough to know that Christians can hurt! What are we supposed to do when we know that to move toward another person in love exposes us to the risk of being disappointed? We move forward in love: easy to say but more difficult to do. Making ourselves vulnerable to disappointment is frightening, but this has to happen if we are to love as we are loved.

Mature Christians are those who are willing to look fully into the face of disappointment and feel it, knowing that because they do, they will come to a deeper awareness that no one can comfort the heart like Jesus Christ. In the presence of such pain, one sees the uselessness of every attempt to find solace in one's own independent strategies. Facing and feeling the pain of disappointment underlies more than anything else the gripping truth that only in God can we trust.

Father, at times Your purposes seem to run diametrically opposite to my interests, but the more I ponder them, the more I see that You always have my highest interests at heart. Help me to trust You more—and myself less. In Jesus' Name. Amen.

FURTHER STUDY

Matt. 26; 2 Tim. 2:13

1. What disappointments must Jesus have felt?

2. How often do you disappoint Him?

SECTION FIVE

"Love Is Not Blind"

For reading & meditation—1 Corinthians 13:1–13

"Love never fails . . ." (v.8)

If we draw back from being willing to face and feel our disappointments, then a part of us will experience spiritual deprivation. The more deeply we enter into our disappointment, the more thoroughly we will be able to see how committed we are to self-protection and turn from that in repentance to a more complete dependence on our Lord Jesus Christ.

Where have you been disappointed the most, I wonder? Most people to whom I address that question tell me: "My parents." It's surprising, though, how so many will not admit to being hurt or disappointed by their parents, for fear they are failing to honor them or are being disloyal. Listen to what one writer has to say about this: "When someone appreciates his parents only because he overlooks the pain they caused him, his appreciation is not only superficial, it is self-protective. Love is never blind to others' faults. It sees them clearly and is not threatened. It admits disappointment, but forgives and continues to be warmly involved."

Sadly, for most of us love is not the bottom line—self-protection is. When we can look into the face of every disappointment and be willing to feel the pain it brings, there is no more powerful way of motivating our heart to turn in full dependence toward the Lord. If we are unwilling to do this, then (as we saw) we might cling more to our own ways of handling disappointments than His. And if we do, then in no way can we climb to higher and more distant spiritual peaks "with all four feet."

FURTHER STUDY

2 Cor. 12:6–10; Phil. 4:11; Eph. 3:16

1. What could have been a great disappointment to Paul?

2. What attitude did he take instead?

Father, the more I become aware of what is involved in climbing higher with You, the easier it is to become discouraged. I am a dull, blundering disciple. Help me, dear Lord. Your grace works miracles. Work one in me today. In Jesus' Name. Amen.

SECTION FIVE

Deliverance from Fear

For reading & meditation—1 Chronicles 28:9–21

"... Be strong and courageous ... Do not be afraid or discouraged, for the Lord God, my God, is with you ..." (v.20)

The seventh and last step we must take if we are to have feet like "hinds' feet" is toask God to rid your heart of all and every fear. I am convinced perhaps millions of Christians are held back from pursuing God by fear.

We saw earlier that not all fears are harmful. When fear is spelled with a small "f," it can have useful biological ends. Fear makes the frightened deer alert and fleet of foot; it makes the surgeon skillful, for he sees the dangers that beset him if he does the wrong thing. Fear harnessed to constructive ends may be constructive. When we use fear and control it, then it is good; when fear uses and controls us, it is bad. When fear becomes Fear, then it becomes fearsome. I am sure that you have known times, as I have, when God beckons to you, as He did with John in the Revelation, to "come up here" (Rev. 4:1), only to find that as your mind got ready to begin the journey, your heart suddenly became gripped with fear. You wanted to move upward, but your progress was halted because you could not mount "with all four feet."

Overcoming fear ought to be one of our greatest objectives. The first word of the Gospel was the voice of the angel: "Do not be afraid" (Luke 1:30). The first word of Jesus after His resurrection was: "Do not be afraid" (Matt. 28:10). Between that first word and the last word, the constant endeavor of Jesus was to help us get rid of fear. We must learn His secret.

FURTHER STUDY

Matt. 14:22–33; 17:1–8

1. What caused Peter to sink?

2. What did Jesus say to the disciples on the mountain?

O God, give me deliverance from every harmful and unproductive fear. I know this is a prayer that You delight to answer, for You have fashioned me for faith, not for fear. Help me, then, to surrender to what I am made for. In Jesus' Name I pray. Amen.

SECTION FIVE

Fear and Cold Feet!

For reading & meditation—2 Timothy 1:1–12

"For God has not given us a spirit of fear, but of power and of love and of a sound mind." (v.7, NKJV)

If we are to be free of unproductive fear, then we must examine its negative and pervasive influence. When Simon Peter stepped out of the boat and attempted to walk on the water to Jesus: "He was frightened, and ... began to sink" (Matt. 14:30, Amp. Bible). Fear makes you sink. When Jesus healed the paralytic, His first word was: "Take heart, son," and His second: "Your sins are forgiven" (Matt. 9:2). When Jesus lifted the guilt, that lifted the fear which, in turn, lifted the paralysis.

When the disciples fell on their faces at the top of the Mount of Transfiguration, terrified because they had heard the voice of God, Jesus said: "Rise, and have no fear" (Matt. 17:7, RSV). Fear puts you down; faith lifts you up. The man who brought back the unused talent said: "I was afraid and went out and hid your talent" (Matt. 25:25). His life investment was in a hole in the ground! Fear did it. Again, it was said of the disciples that they were gathered "with the doors locked for fear of the Jews" (John 20:19). Fear always puts you behind closed doors; it makes you an ingrown person. Joseph of Arimathea was "a disciple of Jesus, but secretly because he feared the Jews" (John 19:38). Fear always drives you underground.

One man I know says that fear gave him cold feet. Prior to the Lord delivering him from fear, his circulation was so bad that he always had to wear socks in bed. "Now," he says, "my circulation is normal. God took away my fear and gave me warm feet."

FURTHER STUDY

Mark 4:35–41; 5:25–34

1. What had Jesus said to His disciples?

2. What had this caused Him to do?

Prayer

God, I see that fear is indeed costly. It is so costly that I dare not keep it. But I cannot easily get rid of it, for it has put its roots deep within me. Help me tear it up, root and branch. In Jesus' Name I pray. Amen.

SECTION FIVE

Home-Grown Fears

For reading & meditation—Mark 4:35–41

"He said to his disciples, 'Why are you so afraid? Do you still have no faith?'" (v.40)

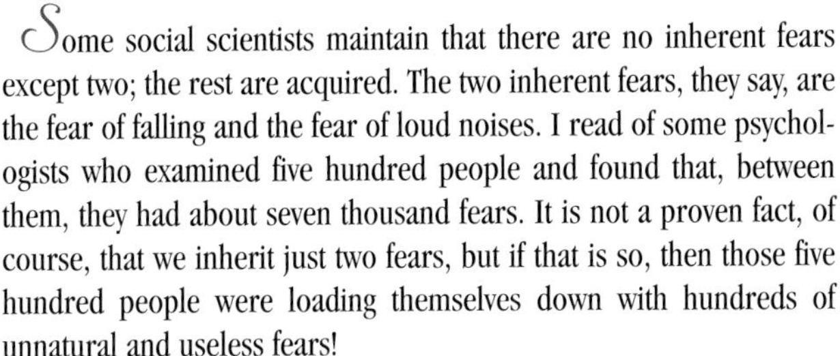

Some social scientists maintain that there are no inherent fears except two; the rest are acquired. The two inherent fears, they say, are the fear of falling and the fear of loud noises. I read of some psychologists who examined five hundred people and found that, between them, they had about seven thousand fears. It is not a proven fact, of course, that we inherit just two fears, but if that is so, then those five hundred people were loading themselves down with hundreds of unnatural and useless fears!

Once when I was in India, I was told of a caste where the women, on their birthdays, add four rings of heavy brass, one on each ankle and one on each arm. By the time they are in middle age, they walk with great difficulty under this senseless burden. But this is no more senseless than weighting oneself down with useless fears; fear of failure, fear of rejection, fear of the future, fear of growing old, fear of what other people might think, and so on. Most of our fears are home-grown—they come out of wrong home teaching and example. Parents who try to control their children by fear often succeed too well—their children grow up and are controlled by the fears themselves.

A woman wrote to me and said: "All my life I have been a victim of fear. My nightly prayer was: 'Lord, thank You for not letting anything too bad happen to me today.' You said if I turned to Christ, I could be rid of all fear. Well, I have—and He did."

FURTHER STUDY

Pss. 34:1–22; 23:4; Prov. 9:10; 19:23

1. What was David's testimony?

2. How can we find freedom from our fears?

Prayer

Father, we have filled Your world and our hearts with fear—needless, devastating fears. Help us, we pray, to find release from these fears, for they are not our real selves—they are an importation. In Jesus' Name. Amen.

SECTION FIVE

Two Basic Fears

For reading & meditation—Hebrews 2:5–18

"And free those who all their lives were held in slavery by their fear of death." (v.15)

Psychologists are at pains to point out that fear is different from anxiety. Fear has a specific object, whereas anxiety is a vague and unspecified apprehension. What, I wonder, is your biggest fear? Benjamin Rank, a social scientist, says that there are basically two forms of fear, the fear of life and the fear of death. The fear of life is the fear of having to live as an isolated individual. The fear of death is the fear of losing individuality. He says: "Between these two fear possibilities, these poles of fear, the individual is thrown back and forth all his life."

The first fear, the fear of life, is vividly illustrated by a small boy's comment: "I suppose the reason for twins is because little children don't like to come into the world alone." The fear of life makes many retreat into illness. It is a refuge out of responsibility. Freud found the cause of neurosis in the past—in childhood; Jung, a disciple of Freud, found it in the present. He said: "I ask, what is the necessary task which the patient will not accomplish?" Backing out of life's responsibilities through fear of life is a major cause of problems.

But with many, it is the fear of death that paralyzes them. Our verse today reads: "And might liberate those who, through fear of death, had all their lifetime been in servitude" (Heb. 2:15, NEB). Is it necessary to live under such servitude? Of course not. When Christ has all of you, then fear can have no part of you. It is as simple as that!

FURTHER STUDY

1 Cor. 15; 2 Cor. 5:1; John 11:25–26

1. What is the hope of every believer?

2. Is this your hope?

Prayer

Father, I am so thankful that You have made it possible for me not to be enslaved by fear. I can be free, gloriously free—and free now. Touch me in the deepest parts of my being this day and set me free from all and every fear. In Jesus' Name. Amen.

SECTION FIVE

Steps Out of Fear

For reading & meditation—Romans 8:1–17

"... you did not receive a spirit that makes you a slave ... to fear, but you received the Spirit of sonship ..." (v.15)

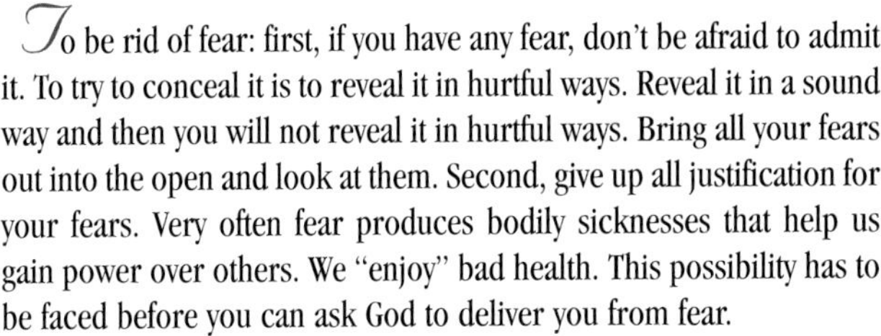

To be rid of fear: first, if you have any fear, don't be afraid to admit it. To try to conceal it is to reveal it in hurtful ways. Reveal it in a sound way and then you will not reveal it in hurtful ways. Bring all your fears out into the open and look at them. Second, give up all justification for your fears. Very often fear produces bodily sicknesses that help us gain power over others. We "enjoy" bad health. This possibility has to be faced before you can ask God to deliver you from fear.

Third, to be controlled by fear is a fool's business, so stop being a fool. One schoolteacher said: "I have been a teacher for thirty years, but I always have nervous indigestion a week before school begins." He was afraid of the children and probably the children were afraid of him. And neither had anything to fear except fear. Am I being too hard in urging you not to be a fool? No, I'm only echoing my Master, who said: "O foolish ones, and slow of heart to believe" (Luke 24:25, NKJV).

Fourth, remember every fear you face has been defeated by Jesus Christ. When any fear rises up within you, just calmly look it in the eye and say: "I am not afraid of you. You have been decisively beaten by my Lord. Bend your neck! There, I knew it. There is the footprint of the Son of God upon your neck." This confidence is your starting point. Nothing can touch you that hasn't touched Him and been defeated.

FURTHER STUDY

Luke 4:1–19; Isa. 61:1; John 8:31–32; Rom. 8:2

1. What was Christ's mission?

2. Will you let Him minister to you in this way today?

Prayer

Father, help me never to justify any unproductive fear, for when I do I cut myself off from Your redemption. I can live without all fear when I live with You. Set me free—gloriously free. In Jesus' Name I pray. Amen.

Love—Stronger Than Fear

For reading & meditation—1 John 4:7–19

"There is no fear in love. But perfect love drives out fear ..." (v.18)

Fifth, surrender all your fears into God's hands. This isn't as easy as it sounds, for it probably means the giving up of a whole life strategy. You may have been using your fears as a crutch—now I am asking you to renounce them.

Can you do that? You can if you are willing to depend on Christ for your life rather than depending on your own strategies. This means a life reversal. You will be tempted to compromise—half give them up and half keep them in your hands. This halfwayness will mean a whole failure. If you surrender your fears into God's hands, this means He has them, not you. This shifts the basis—you are not struggling to overcome them; you and God are working it out together. To look at God creates faith; to look at yourself creates more fear—fear of fear.

Sixth, keep repeating to yourself the verse at the top of this page: "Perfect love drives out fear." If there is no fear in love, then the obvious thing to do is to love. Fear can only come where love is not. Where love is, fear is not. How do you love? Well, don't try to work it up. Just open your heart to the love that is in God's heart. Remember His Word that says: "We love because he first loved us" (v.19). You will discover that as His love comes in, so fear will move out. Then, free of fear, your heart and mind will move, in a coordinated fashion, fleet-footed up into the hills of God.

FURTHER STUDY

Pss. 118:1–6; 3:6; 27:3; Isa. 12:2

1. What did the psalmist declare?

2. Why was Isaiah not afraid?

Prayer

Father, now all my fears are turned over to You, help me to open my heart to the great Niagara of Your love. Pour Your love into every corner of my heart until every one of my fears has been drowned. In Jesus' Name. Amen.

SECTION FIVE

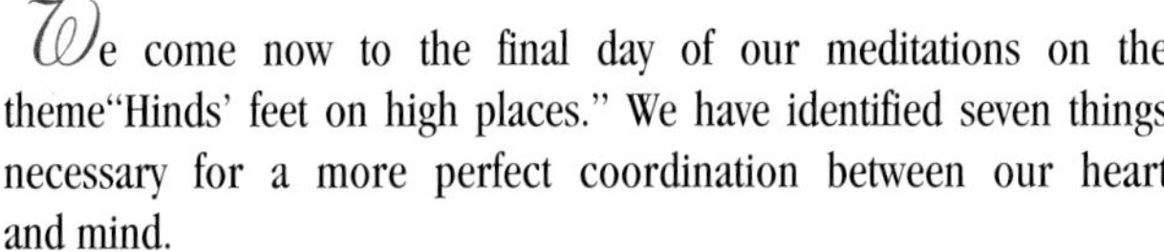

A Final Summary

DAY 304

For reading & meditation—Isaiah 35:1–10

"Then will the lame leap like a deer . . ." (v.6)

We come now to the final day of our meditations on the theme"Hinds' feet on high places." We have identified seven things necessary for a more perfect coordination between our heart and mind.

(1) Prepare to take an honest look at what is going on beneath the surface of your life. (2) Face the question: When I pray, is my heart enthusiastically behind what I ask? (3) Be willing to get in touch with the deep thirst for God which resides at the core of your being. (4) Learn how to face and handle any doubts that may arise in your heart. (5) Recognize the subtle nature of sin. (6) Understand the nature of disappointment and how it hinders your pursuit of God. (7) Ask God to rid your heart of all fear. Attend to any of these suggestions and your spiritual life will move into a new dimension. Attend to all of them and you are destined for the heights.

One word of caution, however—don't try to do too much all at once. Work on one suggestion at a time. Remember, growth in Christ is not arriving but moving upward in a godly direction. In these closing moments, catch again the dominant thought that has been presented in this theme: "Out of the heart spring the issues of life." And when the lips and the heart are in alignment, when they track together with the absolute certainty that the rear feet of the deer track with the front feet, then nothing is impossible, whether it be the climbing of mountains or the casting of mountains into the sea.

FURTHER STUDY

1 Cor. 2; Rom. 8:6; Phil. 2:5; Eph. 4:23

1. What does the Spirit reveal to us?

2. What has the Spirit revealed to you?

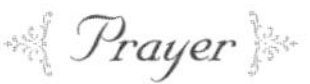

Prayer

Father, what can I say? I have heard Your call and I can never be the same again. I ask once more—make this year a time of rich and joyous discovery. Help me climb higher than I have ever gone before. In Jesus' Name. Amen.

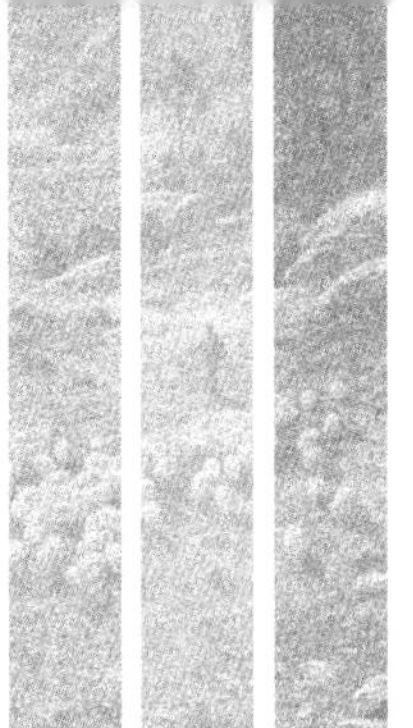

SECTION SIX

Your Father and My Father

Your Father and My Father

The Bible describes the Lord on one hand as the great, all-powerful creator to be respected and feared. On the other hand, the Lord is also our shepherd, our protector, and our Father in heaven. In this final section of *Treasure for the Heart*, Selwyn Hughes notes that the word "father" brings a variety of images to mind. A wide range of experience with our own earthly fathers gives us a world of different preconceptions about our heavenly one.

That may account in part for the fact that the Father portion of the Trinity has fallen out of favor in recent years. Unfortunately, some of us carry around negative images of fathers: demanding, overbearing, emotionally cold and unresponsive. Yet, as Hughes so convincingly tells us, unless we understand God as our Father, none of the other components of Christianity will have their proper place or meaning. Having a bad experience with our own earthly father might require us to step out in faith to establish a new and better relationship with our divine one. Knowing God the Father is essential to knowing how the Christian faith works, and what the relationship between God and humankind should be. Stifling the relationship stifles the ability to forge a spiritual connection between us and our Creator.

There's also the contemporary issue that a masculine God is out of sync with today's gender sensitivity. Hughes counters with the observation that God can be nurturing and tender without losing any of his "fatherliness." Furthermore, he says, God is masculine but not specifically male. Through Hughes' meticulous teaching and analysis, trendy sociological assumptions crumble in the presence of the true Gospel.

We are God's only by the gift of His grace. He is our good shepherd, our defender, our Father in heaven, because of His sacrificial love for us — sending His own perfect Son to die in order that we might all be His children.

L.G.G.

SECTION SIX

The Forgotten Father

For reading & meditation—John 20:10–18

"I am returning to my Father and your Father, to my God and your God." (v.17)

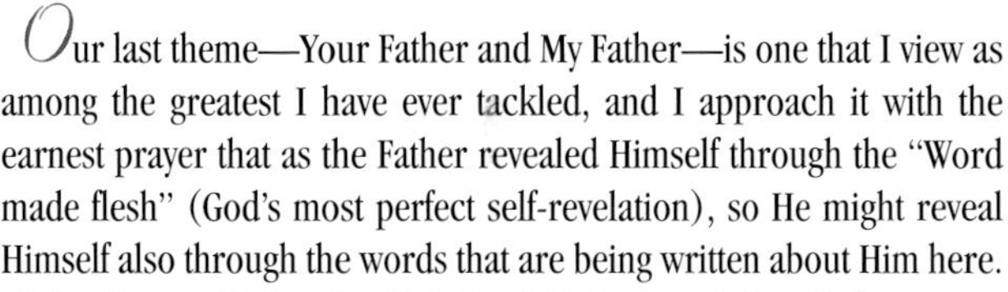

Our last theme—Your Father and My Father—is one that I view as among the greatest I have ever tackled, and I approach it with the earnest prayer that as the Father revealed Himself through the "Word made flesh" (God's most perfect self-revelation), so He might reveal Himself also through the words that are being written about Him here.

It has been said that the Christian faith is essentially a Father movement. Yet theologian Tom Smail suggested that in today's Church the Father is forgotten in precisely the same way that the Spirit was forgotten before the growth of the Pentecostal and charismatic movements. Can this be true? Are we in danger of focusing so much on the work of the Holy Spirit that we forget the Father? I think that in some sections of the Church there are evidences that this is the case. We hear much about the Son and much about the Spirit, but how much do we hear about the Father? When our Lord Jesus Christ lived on this earth He fulfilled many roles—Savior, Shepherd, Deliverer, Healer, Prophet, Life-giver—but the overall purpose of His being here was to restore us to relationship with the Father. Some of the greatest words He ever uttered are the words that form our text for today: "I am returning to my Father and your Father." Your Father.

Let those words sing their way into your consciousness. Through our Lord's redemptive work on the Cross God is not just the Father of Jesus. He is our Father too.

FURTHER STUDY

Acts 17:22–30; Deut. 32:18; Ps. 44:20–21; Isa. 17:10–11

1. In what way is God unknown today?

2. What are our modern-day idol substitutes?

O God my Father, over these coming weeks give me a new understanding of what it means to have You as my Father. I am standing on the shore of a great and wondrous truth. Help me launch out into the deep. In Jesus' Name. Amen.

SECTION SIX

"I Get By With That"

For reading & meditation—John 10:22–42

"My Father ... is greater than all; no one can snatch them out of my Father's hand." (v.29)

Can it really be true that our heavenly Father, though not denied, is largely forgotten in the contemporary Christian Church? Surely not. Millions of Christians all over the world recite the Lord's Prayer, which begins, as you know, with the words "Our Father." It is one thing, however, to recite the words; it is another to have a rich understanding of what divine Fatherhood really means.

Jim Packer, in his book *Knowing God*, says that knowledge of God as Father is at the heart of the Christian message. And by knowledge of God he doesn't mean merely intellectual knowledge, but an experiential knowledge—a deep awareness of what it means to have the God of the universe as our Father. "If you want to know how well a person understands Christianity," he says, "find out how much he makes of the thought of being God's child, and having God as his Father."

How real to you is your heavenly Father? Is the Fatherhood of God just an intellectual idea or is it a truth which warms your heart and fires your imagination? Once, during a counseling session, I asked a woman: "What does the idea of having God as your Father do for you?" She thought for a moment and said: "Not much I'm afraid. My earthly father tyrannized me, humiliated me, and abused me. One father is enough for me. I don't want another one." Then she added: "I just relate to Jesus. I get by with that." She may have been able to get by with that, but she certainly couldn't grow with it.

FURTHER STUDY

Matt. 6:1–3; Num. 12:8; Job 42:5; 1 John 1:1–3

1. How did the hypocrites and pagans know God?

2. How are we to know God?

Prayer

O God, I see that my spiritual growth can be stunted if I have no deep experiential knowledge of You as Father. Help me to enter into all that is involved in being Your child, and having the eternal God as my Father. In Christ's Name. Amen.

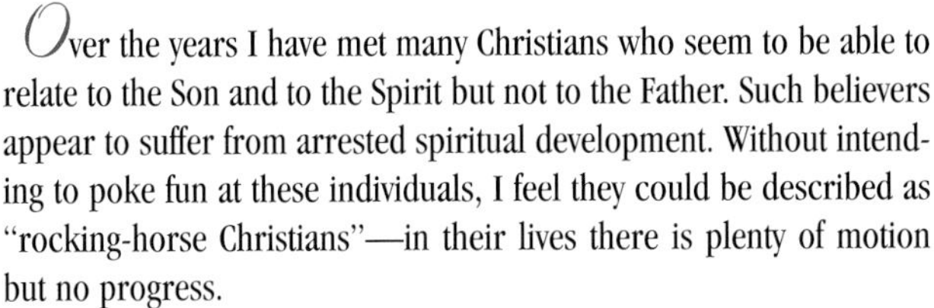

"Rocking-Horse Christians"

For reading & meditation—John 17:1–26

"Now this is eternal life: that they may know you, the only true God ..." (v.3)

Over the years I have met many Christians who seem to be able to relate to the Son and to the Spirit but not to the Father. Such believers appear to suffer from arrested spiritual development. Without intending to poke fun at these individuals, I feel they could be described as "rocking-horse Christians"—in their lives there is plenty of motion but no progress.

When I first noticed the link between a lack of spiritual growth and an inability to relate to God as Father, I thought it was just coincidence, but the more I researched the matter, the more evident it became that there was some kind of correlation. It is important to make the point that this is not the only reason for arrested spiritual development, but it is a major one.

There are a number of reasons why Christians do not find it easy to relate to God as Father (and we shall look at some of these later), but the point I want to make today is this: we live deprived lives spiritually if we do not have a rich and warm relationship with the Father. After all, as theologians point out, there is an established order in the Trinity. The Father is first, the Son second, and the Holy Spirit third. The delight of the Son and the Spirit is to initiate us into a relationship with the Father and to see us develop in that relationship. Christ and the Holy Spirit do not become envious or jealous when we make much of the Father. Our delight in Him is their delight.

FURTHER STUDY

Eph. 4:11–16; 1 Cor. 3:1–7; 13:11; 1 Pet. 2:2

1. Why do some Christians never grow up?

2. What helps us grow?

O Father, help me examine my life today to see if I enjoy a better relationship with Your Son and Your Spirit than I do with You. If this is so then clear the way for me to know You better. In Jesus' Name I pray. Amen.

DAY

308

SECTION SIX

"No One Ever Grows Up"

For reading & meditation—Matthew 6:1–15

"... your Father, who sees what is done in secret, will reward you." (v.4)

One of the failures of the evangelical Church, generally speaking, is that people who have been brought into a relationship with Christ are not taught how to go beyond Him and build a relationship with the Father. I have said many times before that we evangelicals are good obstetricians but bad pediatricians. We are good at bringing people into the Christian faith but we are not good at nurturing them. Unlike the first Christians, we do not devote ourselves to teaching (see Acts 2:42). There are, of course, some exceptions, and if you are in a church where training is given, then good. Far too many evangelical churches, however—even ones which are flourishing numerically—resemble the nurseries which the Argentinian pastor, Juan Carlos Ortiz, talks about: "places where the number of infants increase but no one ever grows up."

If you want to get an idea of how the reality of knowing God as Father affects our Christian growth then read through the whole of Matthew chapter 6, taking note of the verses I have drawn your attention to below. Knowing the Father affects the practice of our faith (v.1), our relationships (vv.14–15), our attitude towards money and possessions (vv.19–24), and gives deliverance from fear and anxiety (vv.25–34). As one theologian has put it: "Everything comes to the light so completely in relationship to Him [the Father] that His glory has to become the great goal of our conduct." The better we relate to God the Father the better we relate to all of life. The Bible makes this abundantly clear.

FURTHER STUDY

1 John 1:3; Jer. 31:33–34; Heb. 5:11–6:3; Gal. 4:19

1. What was the purpose of John's letter?

2. What is your spiritual age?

Prayer

My Father and my God, how I long to know You better. Whatever my knowledge of You and however rich my relationship with You, may they become richer and deeper day by day. In Jesus' Name. Amen.

SECTION SIX

Duty or Delight?

For reading & meditation—Psalm 43:1–5

"Then will I go to the altar of God, to God, my joy and my delight ..." (v.4)

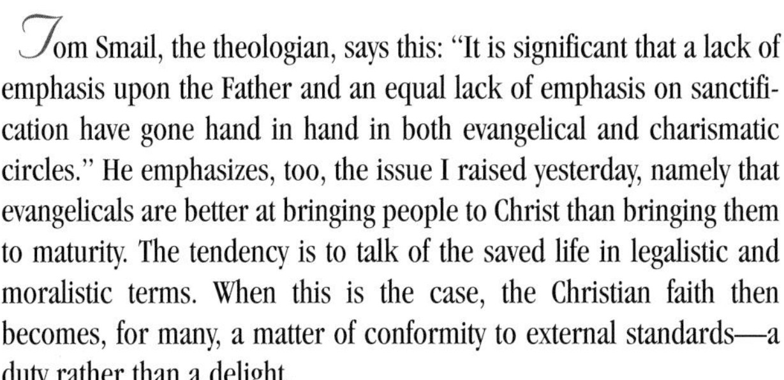

Tom Smail, the theologian, says this: "It is significant that a lack of emphasis upon the Father and an equal lack of emphasis on sanctification have gone hand in hand in both evangelical and charismatic circles." He emphasizes, too, the issue I raised yesterday, namely that evangelicals are better at bringing people to Christ than bringing them to maturity. The tendency is to talk of the saved life in legalistic and moralistic terms. When this is the case, the Christian faith then becomes, for many, a matter of conformity to external standards—a duty rather than a delight.

The charismatics, on the other hand, are inclined to encourage people to expect instant answers for everything, the resolution of all problems, and put an undue emphasis on power to the exclusion of purity. It should not escape our attention that the church which was perhaps the strongest in charismatic expression in the New Testament was also the weakest in holiness (see 1 Corinthians 3:1–3). There is nothing wrong with the manifestation of charismatic gifts, but unless there is an equal emphasis on holiness the gifts can be just spiritual playthings. "Christian maturity and holiness," says Smail, "are not to be found in a narrow pursuit of charismatic experiences and manifestations in and for themselves but in the existential rediscovery of Abba Father." Strong words you may think, but certainly worth pondering.

G. Kittel, a German theologian, puts it just as forcibly when he says: "Faith in the Father is an incentive to the sanctification of life." It is the incentive that every Christian needs if we are to grow.

Prayer

O Father, to be in a living relationship with You is to be trained and disciplined for perfection. You long for me to be perfect as You are perfect. That is my longing also. Help me, dear Father. In Jesus' Name. Amen.

FURTHER STUDY

Matt. 5:33–48;
2 Cor. 7:1; Ps. 40:8;
1 John 3:1–3

1. What is our incentive to be holy?

2. When can delight become duty?

SECTION SIX

The Divine Vinedresser

For reading & meditation—John 15:1–17

"I am the true vine, and my Father is the gardener." (v.1)

The more we know the Father the more we will yield to the sanctifying process that is an essential part of every Christian's life. The passage we have read tells us that the Father is the Gardener, or, as some translations have it, the Vinedresser: He is constantly at work cutting down the prolific growth of the branches so that they might yield more fruit. It is fruit the Divine Vinedresser is after, not more foliage.

This same Father, according to the writer to the Hebrews, disciplines those of us who are His true sons, not just for our own good, but that "we may share in his holiness" (Heb. 12:10). Many Christians struggle with their heavenly Father's disciplines because they do not see them as coming from His hand. My earthly father was a strong disciplinarian, but when he disciplined me I was left in no doubt it was for my benefit. I didn't like the discipline but I had sufficient faith in my father to know that he would not take a disciplinarian approach unless it was necessary. And the discipline gave me a view of life that went something like this: when I do wrong my father loves me enough not to let me get away with it.

When I became a Christian I found that my heavenly Father too loved me enough not to let me evade correction. I cannot say that I regarded His disciplines as my delight, but they certainly did me good. Anything that comes from God's hands has got to be good even though we may not think so at the time.

FURTHER STUDY

2 Kings 4:39–40; Matt. 21:18–19; Col. 1:10–12; Gal. 5:13–23

1. What is Christian foliage?
2. What is Christian fruit?

Father, I am so grateful that You love me enough to discipline me. Prune me that I may be more fruitful, and help me see that as I relate to You, so I live and grow. In Jesus' Name I pray. Amen.

SECTION SIX

"All in All"

For reading & meditation—1 Corinthians 15:12–28

"Then the end will come, when he hands over the kingdom to God the Father ..." (v.24)

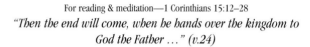

Are the theologians right when they say that the Christian faith is basically "a Father movement"? I am convinced that they are. One writer has expressed it like this: "The Gospel we preach is not first a Jesusology, or a Spiritology, but a Fatherology—a doctrine about God the Father." It starts not with Jesus coming to earth, or with the outpouring of the Spirit, but with the Father loving us so much that He was moved to send His one and only Son (John 3:16). And God's great purpose will be achieved not when the Church is wedded to Christ in eternity, not when sin is finally overcome, not even when Christ has subdued all His enemies and every knee has bowed at His Name. It will be achieved, as our text for today tells us, when Christ hands over the kingdom to God the Father. When this is done then the Son Himself will be made subject to the Father, "so that God may be all in all" (v.28).

This statement is one of the most powerful in the whole of the New Testament yet one which is rarely expounded. Just as the Father is the source of everything, so He is the goal of everything. Everything starts with Him, and everything finishes with Him. The mission of the Son and the Spirit is to advance the Father's glory so that He might be all in all. I think the theologians who say our faith is basically "a Father movement" sum up the matter well. This truth lies at the very heart of the Christian message.

FURTHER STUDY

John 3:13–21; 3:33–36; 2 Cor. 5:19; Eph. 3:1–15

1. Why is the Father both source and goal?

2. What is "the family in heaven and earth"?

Prayer

My Father and my God, help me see that by putting You first I am doing what Your Son and Your Spirit delight in doing. May I put the emphasis where Your Son and Spirit put it—on You. In Jesus' Name. Amen.

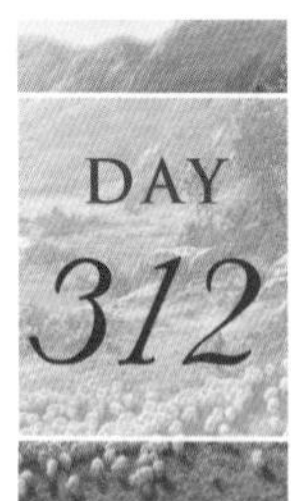

SECTION SIX

Wanted—A New Movement

For reading & meditation—John 14:1–14

"And I will do whatever you ask in my name, so that the Son may bring glory to the Father." (v.13)

The second half of the 20th century saw the rise of two great movements—the Jesus movement, and the charismatic movement which continue to this day. Perhaps now we are ready for a Father movement emphasizing more strongly the fact that the Godhead consists not only of the Son and the Spirit but, first and foremost, of the Father.

Some may have difficulty with this, knowing that the three Persons of the Trinity are equal. Why should there be an order of precedence? Well, though they are equal in power and love, there is a subordination in relation. D. Broughton Knox explains it in this way: "There is an order in the Trinity. This order does not imply inferiority but is an order among equals, yet it is not reversible, for irreversibility is of the essence of order."

In the New Testament we meet the same God three times. First, as the Father to whom Jesus prayed. Second, as the Son who showed us what God is like in a human form. Third, as the Holy Spirit whose main function is to relate us to Christ and the Father—and to each other. These are not three Gods side by side, but three revelations of the one God.

The truth of the "Trinity" should not be rejected because it is difficult to understand. Although the word Trinity is not found in the Bible, the doctrine of the Trinity is authentic Biblical revelation. There can be no Father without the Son, and no Son without the Father. And neither could have been revealed unless the Holy Spirit revealed Him.

FURTHER STUDY

Matt. 28:19; Isa. 48:16; John 16:12–15; Rev. 22:1

1. How do the Father, Son and Spirit relate to each other?

2. How do they relate to us?

Prayer

My Father, help me hold on to the fact that though the doctrine of the Trinity is a mystery, it is a clear Biblical truth nevertheless. May I always stand on Your Word even when I cannot understand. In Jesus' Name. Amen.

SECTION SIX

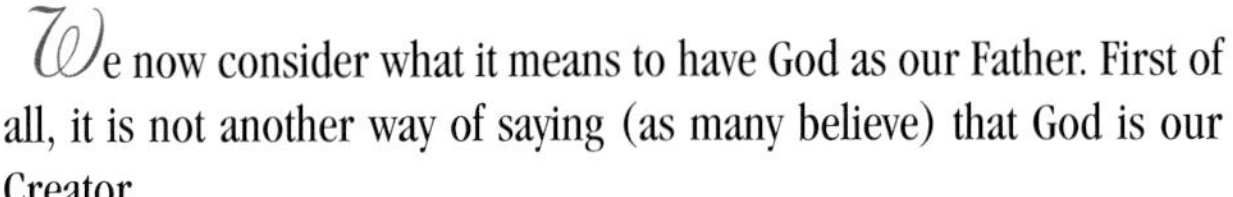

What Is a Christian?

DAY 313

For reading & meditation—John 1:1–18

"Yet to all who received him … who believed in his name, he gave the right to become children of God …" (v.12)

We now consider what it means to have God as our Father. First of all, it is not another way of saying (as many believe) that God is our Creator.

Once, after I had spoken at a church, several people came up to me and remarked that although they were not committed Christians they had appreciated what I had said. Later, a liberally minded bishop who was present told me that in his view everyone in the congregation was a child of God. When I pointed out that some who had approached me were clearly not Christians he replied: "I didn't say they were all Christians. I said they were all children of God." The bishop did what many seem to be doing these days—confusing God's role as Father with that of Creator. God is the Creator of all men and women, and in that sense they are His offspring, but when the Bible speaks of God's Fatherhood it reserves the term for those who are in a personal relationship with Him.

Jim Packer says that he defines a Christian as: "one who has God as Father." To be a child of God in the New Testament sense signifies much more than that we have been created as a human being; it means being related to Him through His Son Jesus Christ and experiencing an ongoing relationship of trust, obedience and love. The gift of sonship is ours not by natural birth but by supernatural birth. Only to those who receive His Son—and only to those—does He give the right to become children of God.

FURTHER STUDY

John 8:33–47; Matt. 13:38; Eph. 2:2–3 (NKJV)

1. Who is our "father" by natural birth?

2. What are the consequences?

Prayer

O God, how thrilling to know that my relationship with You is more than that of a creature to its Creator. I am Your child and You are my Father. Nothing in heaven or earth could be more wonderful. Thank You. Amen.

Now I Call Him "Father"

For reading & meditation—Galatians 3:15–29

"You are all sons of God through faith in Christ Jesus . . ." (v.26)

The idea of God being a universal Father is not Biblical. Neither Christ nor His apostles taught this. It is appropriate to speak of God as a universal Creator, for He brought all things into existence. It is right also to speak of Him as a universal King, for He not only made the world but He sustains it, orders it, and rules over it. But He is the Father only of our Lord Jesus Christ and of those whom He takes into His family when they receive His Son into their lives. As our text tells us, we are the children of God only when we are in Christ Jesus. So let us dispense with the idea of the universal Fatherhood of God. It has lulled many a person into a false sense of complacency.

Why would we need to come to Christ if we were already God's children by our natural birth? We are subjects of God by virtue of our natural birth but we are children of God by virtue of the new birth. I am a subject of the Queen of England, but I am not a member of her family. However, should she decide to adopt me into her family then my position would be entirely different. There was a time when I was a subject of the King of kings (and in a sense I still am), but now I am more—I am through faith in Christ a member of His family. His child. Once I could only refer to God as Creator or King. Now I can call Him "Father."

FURTHER STUDY

John 1:12–13; 3:1–8; James 1:17–18; 1 Pet. 1:23

1. Why do we need to be born again?

2. Praise God for the new birth.

Prayer

Father, I am so grateful for the words of the Bible that make my position clear. Once I was just one of Your subjects but now, through faith in Jesus, I am one of Your family. All glory be to Your precious Name. Amen.

God is Not Father of All

For reading & meditation—Hosea 1:1–11

"… where it was said to them, 'You are not my people,' they will be called 'sons of the living God.'" (v.10)

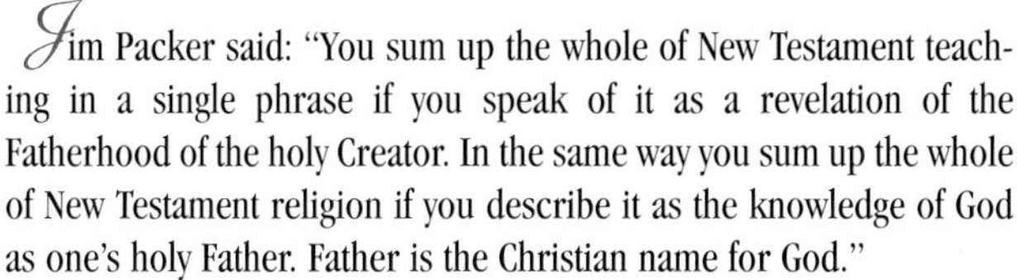

Jim Packer said: "You sum up the whole of New Testament teaching in a single phrase if you speak of it as a revelation of the Fatherhood of the holy Creator. In the same way you sum up the whole of New Testament religion if you describe it as the knowledge of God as one's holy Father. Father is the Christian name for God."

There are those who claim that the teaching given in the Old Testament is quite different. There, they say, God is viewed as being the Father of all. But is He? Consider this: "Israel is my firstborn son … 'Let my son go …'" (Ex. 4:22–23). There are many such passages. The Old Testament as well as the New shows God as the Father, not of all men and women, but of His own people, Abraham's descendants. The verse we looked at yesterday (Gal. 3:26) told us that God is not the Father of all, but only of those who know themselves to be sinners and have accepted His Son into their hearts. When we have done this, Paul says, we belong to Christ and are ourselves Abraham's offspring.

Divine sonship is not ours because we have been born into this world; it is ours because we have been born again into another realm—the kingdom of God. Sonship is a gift, a gift of grace. It is not a natural sonship but an adoptive sonship. God takes those who receive His Son and makes them His adopted children, to see and share His glory into which His one and only Son has already come.

FURTHER STUDY

Rom. 9:4–12; Jer. 31:9; Hosea 11:1; 2 Cor. 6:18

1. What makes people children of God?

2. What does "Abraham's children" mean?

Prayer

O Father, once again I want to record my deepest thanks that because of Your Son I am an heir of God and a joint heir with Christ. How wonderful. How truly wonderful. All honor and glory be to Your precious Name. Amen.

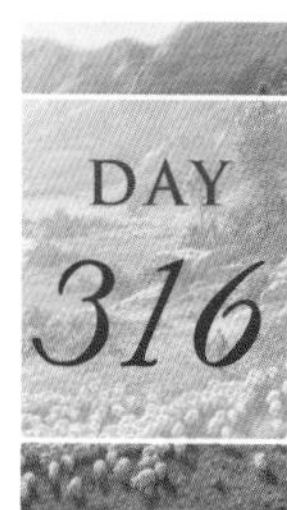

SECTION SIX

I'm Adopted!

For reading & meditation—Ephesians 1:1–14

"... he predestined us to be adopted as his sons through Jesus Christ ..." (v.5)

Once a believer has received the revelation that God is his or her Father, then, in a sense, the purpose of the Scriptures has been fulfilled. The new status of the believer is given in our text for today: "adopted." No one can really understand the wonder of what it means to be a child of the Father without understanding the meaning of adoption. So reflect with me for a few days on what it means to be an adopted child of God.

Before looking at some of the New Testament texts that talk about adoption, here is a formal definition of adoption from the Westminster Confession (chapter XII): "All those who are justified, God makes partakers of the grace of adoption by which they are taken into the number and enjoy the liberalities and privileges of the children of God, have His name put upon them, receive the spirit of adoption, have access to the throne of grace with boldness, are enabled to cry Abba Father, are protected, provided for and chastened by Him, as by a Father, yet never cast off, but sealed to the day of redemption and inherit the promises as heirs of everlasting salvation."

Whenever my thoughts turn to the theme of adoption I think of the little girl in the school playground who, taunted by her playmates that she was an adopted child, replied: "Your parents didn't choose you ... they had to take whatever came. My parents chose me out of everybody else." There you have it—Christians are chosen people, chosen to be adopted. How wonderful!

FURTHER STUDY

Deut. 10:15; 1 Cor. 1:27–28; 2 Thess. 2:13; 1 Pet. 2:9–10

1. Look up "choose" in a dictionary.

2. What does it mean and imply?

Prayer

O Father, how can I ever sufficiently thank You that I have been adopted into the family of God? Burn the wonder of this fact deeper and deeper into my soul. In Jesus' Name I pray. Amen.

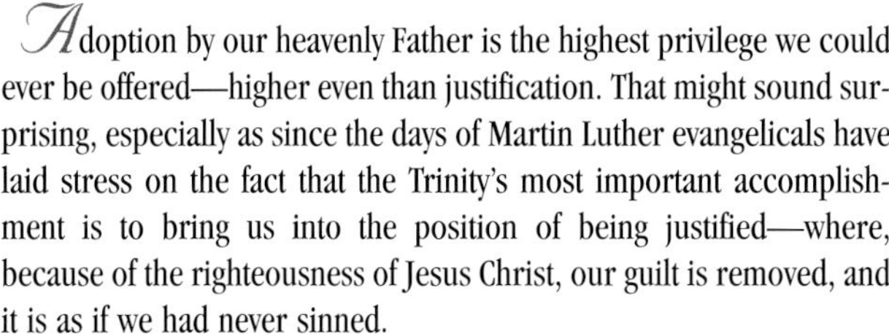

The Greatest Thing of All

For reading & meditation—Galatians 4:1–18

"So you are no longer a slave, but a son; … an heir." (v.7)

Adoption by our heavenly Father is the highest privilege we could ever be offered—higher even than justification. That might sound surprising, especially as since the days of Martin Luther evangelicals have laid stress on the fact that the Trinity's most important accomplishment is to bring us into the position of being justified—where, because of the righteousness of Jesus Christ, our guilt is removed, and it is as if we had never sinned.

Justification is a tremendous blessing, but adoption is a greater blessing because of the richer relationship with God involved. Justification is a forensic term, a legal word. Adoption is a family idea which views God not so much as a Judge but as a Father. In adoption God takes us into His family, elevates us to the same level as His Son, so that we become joint heirs with Christ. Closeness, warmth, generosity are all words associated with adoption. To be right with God is wonderful, but to be in a close relationship with God is even more wonderful.

No Christian can fully enter into the thrill of salvation until he or she understands that we have been transported not simply from condemnation to acceptance, but from destitution to, as one theologian describes it: "the safety, certainty and enjoyment of the family of God." In the chapter before us today, Paul contrasts the previous life of the Galatian converts, characterized by slavish legalism, with their present knowledge of the Creator as their Father. God has adopted us into His family and has made us joint heirs with Christ. Nothing could be more wonderful than that. Nothing.

FURTHER STUDY

John 15:15; Acts 26:15–18; Rom. 8:15–18; Col. 1:12–14

1. What is the essence of justification?

2. What is the essence of adoption?

Prayer

O Father, to be justified and seen by You as if I had never sinned is awesome. But to be adopted and made a partaker of the inheritance belonging to Your Son is mind-blowing. Help me take it all in I pray. In Jesus' Name. Amen.

SECTION SIX

A Foretaste of Heaven

For reading & meditation—Romans 9:1–15

"… Theirs is the adoption as sons; theirs the divine glory …" (v.4)

Yesterday we discussed the fact that adoption is the highest privilege the believer can enjoy. We saw how Paul, when writing to the Galatians, contrasted their previous life of slavish legalism with their present knowledge of their Creator as Father. "You are no longer slaves," he tells them, "instead you have received the adoption of sons."

When the great hymnwriter Charles Wesley found Christ, his experience of conversion was expressed in what is now called "The Wesleys' Conversion Hymn," in which the transition from slavery to sonship is the dominant theme. I have thrilled many times to these glowing words. Listen to them once again:

O how shall I the goodness tell,
Father, which Thou to me hast showed?
That I, a child of wrath and hell,
I should be called a child of God,
Should know, should feel my sins forgiven,
Blest with the antepast of heaven!

FURTHER STUDY

Rom. 7:14–8:2; Eph. 2:1–10; Titus 3:3–7

1. What are the characteristics of a slave?
2. What are the characteristics of a free person?

Shortly after Charles wrote this hymn, his brother John was converted. When John told him this wonderful news, Charles records in his diary: "We sang 'O how shall I the goodness tell?' with great joy."

Can you make Wesley's words your own? Can you too sing them with joy? If you are not sure you are God's then pray this prayer with me now:

Prayer

Father, as I open my heart to You at this moment, forgive my every sin, cleanse me, and make me a whole person. I receive Your Son as my Savior and Lord. Accept me and adopt me now into Your family. Thank You for hearing my prayer. In Jesus' Name. Amen.

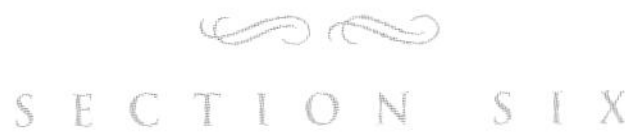

SECTION SIX

What Else Matters?

For reading & meditation—Mark 3:20–35

"Whoever does God's will is my brother and sister and mother." (v.35)

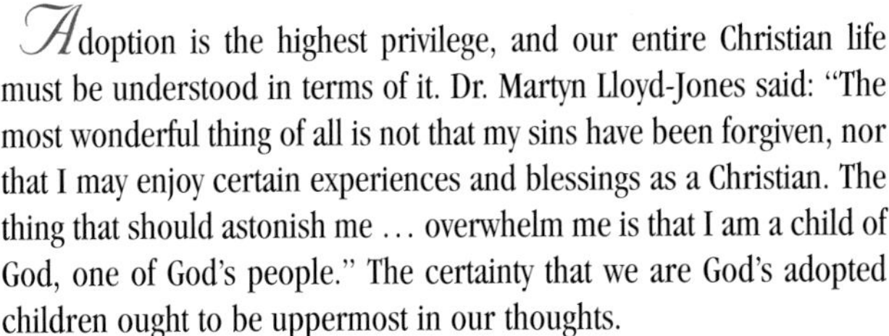

Adoption is the highest privilege, and our entire Christian life must be understood in terms of it. Dr. Martyn Lloyd-Jones said: "The most wonderful thing of all is not that my sins have been forgiven, nor that I may enjoy certain experiences and blessings as a Christian. The thing that should astonish me … overwhelm me is that I am a child of God, one of God's people." The certainty that we are God's adopted children ought to be uppermost in our thoughts.

Almost every day since I became a Christian, I have reminded myself that I have been adopted into the family of God. It has become the dominant thought of my life. Some time ago, when I mentioned this fact to a fellow Christian, he looked at me blankly and said: "So what?" So what? So not only is Jesus my Savior, He is my Brother also. Following His resurrection our Lord said: "Go … to my brothers and tell them, 'I am returning to my Father and your Father, to my God and your God'" (John 20:17). Then again, the writer to the Hebrews tells us that Jesus is not ashamed to call us brothers (Heb. 2:12).

When I was young I always wanted a brother. A sister came along twelve years after I was born but I never had a brother. Not until I became a Christian, that is. Then, by virtue of the fact that I was adopted into the royal family of heaven, I found a Brother. And what a Brother! God is my Father, Jesus is my Brother … what else matters?

FURTHER STUDY

Rom. 8:29; Eph. 3:14–15; 1 Tim. 5:1–2; 1 John 3:16–18

1. What are the privileges of being in the family of God?

2. What are the responsibilities?

Father God, forgive me that with such an inheritance as this I get taken up with trifling things. Help me make this the controlling thought of my life: I am a child of God. Nothing else matters. Amen.

DAY 320

SECTION SIX

One Dominant Thought

For reading & meditation—1 John 1:1–10

"...And our fellowship is with the Father and with his Son, Jesus Christ." (v.3)

Over and over again in His teaching our Lord makes clear that the knowledge of being one of God's children should control the way we live. "Love your enemies ..." He says, "that you may be sons of your Father in heaven." "Be perfect, therefore, as your heavenly Father is perfect" (Matt. 5:44–45, 48). "Let your light shine before men, that they may see your good deeds and praise your Father in heaven" (Matt. 5:16). What additional point is our Lord making in these verses? Isn't it that if we live out our lives in the consciousness that we are the children of a loving heavenly Father, then others, seeing our conduct, will realize that fact too?

Another point worth focusing on (though not directly related) is this: our knowledge that we are God's adopted children should govern not only our conduct, but (as we have seen) our approach to prayer also: "This, then, is how you should pray: 'Our Father ...'" (Matt. 6:9). The Father's constant accessibility to His children is the foundation on which we build our prayer lives.

There are many more texts I could list, but let me mention just one more: "Do not worry ... what you will eat or drink; or about your body, what you will wear ... Look at the birds of the air ... your heavenly Father feeds them..." (Matt. 6:25–26). Do you get the point? If God cares for the birds whose Father He is not, is it not plain that He will care for you, whose Father He is?

FURTHER STUDY

Ps. 73:1–28; 2 Cor. 6:18–7:1; Eph. 2:11–22; Phil. 4:8

1. How do thoughts of God change us?
2. Think now of your position as God's child.

Prayer

O God, help me, I pray, to let this thought dominate all my days—that I am the child of my heavenly Father. May it be my first thought when I awake and the last thought before I go to sleep. In Jesus' Name I ask it. Amen.

SECTION SIX

The Spirit's Voice

For reading & meditation—Romans 8:1–17

"… you received the Spirit of sonship. And by him we cry, 'Abba, Father.'" (v.15)

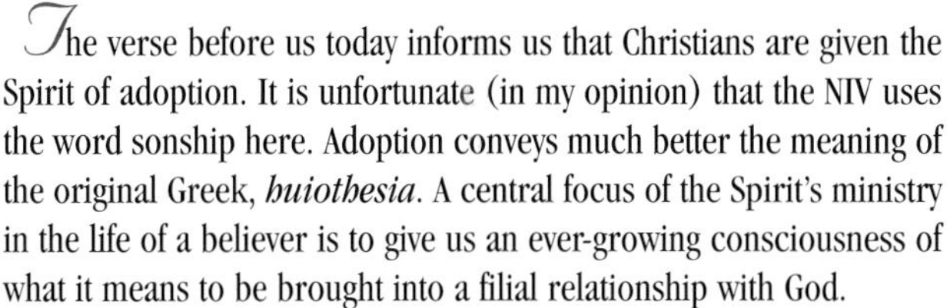

The verse before us today informs us that Christians are given the Spirit of adoption. It is unfortunate (in my opinion) that the NIV uses the word sonship here. Adoption conveys much better the meaning of the original Greek, ***huiothesia***. A central focus of the Spirit's ministry in the life of a believer is to give us an ever-growing consciousness of what it means to be brought into a filial relationship with God.

Just as our adoption as God's children is at the heart of the New Testament's message, so the truth that the Holy Spirit enters into us as the Spirit of adoption is central to the New Testament's teaching concerning the Spirit's work in the life of the believer. A major ministry of the Holy Spirit is to make us constantly aware that we are God's children. The Holy Spirit is at work in us to accomplish this task. Whatever other aspects of the Spirit's ministry are available to us—empowerment, sanctification, enlightenment—this is one of His most important ministries. He deepens our consciousness of our relationship to the Father even when the perverse and mulish parts of our nature rise up to counter the idea.

In these days when so much emphasis is being laid on the Spirit's power, how I wish that we would put an equal emphasis on the ministry He has to make us ever aware of the fact that we are God's children. Whatever else the Holy Spirit does, He can do nothing greater than bringing us into a relationship with the Father and assuring us that we are really His.

FURTHER STUDY

1 Cor. 2:9–14; Gal. 4:4–6; Eph. 2:18

1. How does the Holy Spirit reveal the Father?

2. Invite the Holy Spirit to reveal the Father to you now.

Prayer

O Father, how loving and considerate it is of You to keep me ever alert to the fact that I am Your child. Help me see that a primary work of Your Spirit is to remind me of this. May His voice sound out clearly in my soul. Amen.

SECTION SIX

The Abba Cry

For reading & meditation—Galatians 4:1–7

"... God sent the Spirit of his Son into our hearts, the Spirit who calls out, 'Abba, Father.'" (v.6)

The Holy Spirit prompts us to cry: "Abba, Father." What is the purpose behind this? The term *Abba* (an Aramaic word) is found three times in Scripture: here; by Jesus in His prayer in the Garden of Gethsemane (Mark 14:35–36); and by Paul in Romans 8:14–15. Some Bible teachers claim that what the Spirit does is to bring us into such a close relationship with the Father that we no longer need to use the formal designation "Father," but can use the more informal word, "Daddy." The explanation sounds very appealing, but is not in line with what Scripture is saying. Professor C.F.D. Moule (and many other scholarly Bible expositors) claim that the best translation of the word Abba is not "Daddy" but "Dear." The phrase is thus best translated "Dear Father."

Is this a distinction without a difference, as some claim? The Abba cry on the lips of Jesus in the Garden of Gethsemane as He waited for His betrayer was not so much a cry of closeness and familiarity (though that, of course, was there), but more the cry of obedience and utter trust. When the Spirit prompts us to cry out "Abba, Father," His real aim is to prompt us to reach the same level of commitment and surrender to the will of God that Jesus demonstrated in Gethsemane. The Abba cry is the cry of obedience. It says: "Dear Father, I don't understand all that You are doing, but because I am secure in Your love I offer You my deepest adoration, my fullest loyalty and my dependent trust."

FURTHER STUDY

Gen. 22:1–18; Heb. 11:17–19; Rom. 16:26

1. Describe how Abraham related to Abba Father.

2. What is the obedience of faith?

Prayer

O God, just as Your Spirit rose up in Jesus enabling Him to cry out "Dear Father, I delight to do Your will," so grant that the same cry shall be heard also in my soul. In Jesus' Name I ask it. Amen.

SECTION SIX

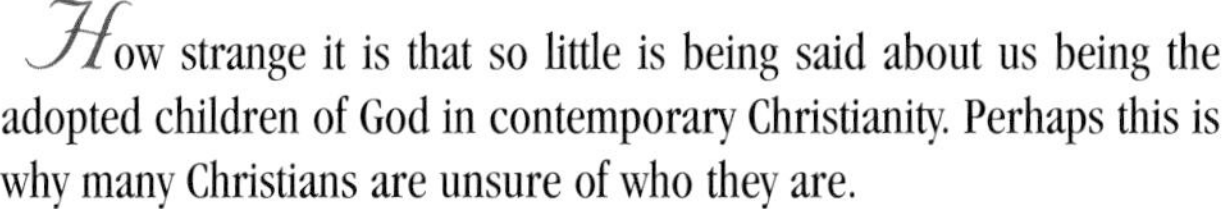

Who Am I?

DAY 323

For reading & meditation—1 John 3:1–10

"How great is the love the Father has lavished on us, that we should be called children of God! …" (v.1)

How strange it is that so little is being said about us being the adopted children of God in contemporary Christianity. Perhaps this is why many Christians are unsure of who they are.

A man once wrote to me: "I don't know who I am. Can you help me?" In my reply I said: "You won't know who you are until you know whose you are … and if you have received Jesus into your heart you are a child of God." I suggested he should reflect on the fact that he belonged to the family of God, and that he should say this to himself every day: "I am God's child. God is my Father, Jesus is my Savior, the Holy Spirit is my comforter, heaven is my home, the Bible is my guide, and the angels are my companions." Later I met that person. He told me that he had repeated the words to himself every morning and evening for a whole month, and they had served to bring him into a deep realization of who he was in Christ.

How thrilled are you at the fact you have been adopted into the royal family of heaven? Do you daily remind yourself of the great privilege that is yours of actually being drawn into a close relationship with your heavenly Father? Are you aware of the Spirit's cry in your heart prompting you to look up into the Father's face and say: "Your will is my will!" If, though you are a Christian, my words mean little to you, pray this prayer with me now:

FURTHER STUDY

Jer. 30:18–22; Heb. 4:14–16; 7:19; 10:16–22

1. How do we draw close to God?

2. Just do it!

Prayer

My Father and my God, set my heart on fire with a new understanding and awareness of what it means to belong to You. Draw me closer to You, Father, closer than I have ever been before. In Jesus' Name. Amen.

SECTION SIX

A Watershed Issue

For reading & meditation—Romans 15:1–13

"… so that with one heart and mouth you may glorify the God and Father of our Lord Jesus Christ." (v.6)

There is nothing even remotely sexist about the truth that God is our Father. This was never an issue in past centuries but now, with the rise of feminism and the trend towards inclusive language, the point has to be addressed.

Our text reminds us that God is the Father of our Lord Jesus Christ, and these words make it clear that the relationship between God and Christ is not that of Mother and Son, but Father and Son. When Anne Hepburn, president of the Women's Guild of the Church of Scotland, used the expression "Dear Mother God" in her prayer at the Annual Meeting of the Guild in April 1982, so intense was the reaction, both negative and positive, that a special committee was set up to examine the implications of what she had said. They concluded that though we should keep to the Scriptural term "Father" when addressing God, we should think of Him in terms of a Motherly Father. There are, they said (and with this no one can disagree), motherly qualities in God. But this does not give us the license to say He is Mother.

The matter of whether we call God "Mother" or "Father/Mother" is becoming a watershed issue in the contemporary Christian Church. Addressing God as "Mother" instead of "Father" is not what Jesus did when He prayed, and it is not the way He taught us to pray. "When you pray," He said to His disciples, say: "Father …" (Luke 11:2). We must be careful that we do not change what the Bible does say into what we think it should say.

FURTHER STUDY

2 Cor. 1:2–3; 11:31; Eph. 1:2–3; Col. 1:2–3

1. In what way is God the Father of our Lord Jesus Christ?

2. In what way is He our Father?

Prayer

O Father, save us at this critical hour from attempting to fit the Scriptures into our present-day culture. Help us see that culture changes but that You and Your Word never change. In Christ's Name. Amen.

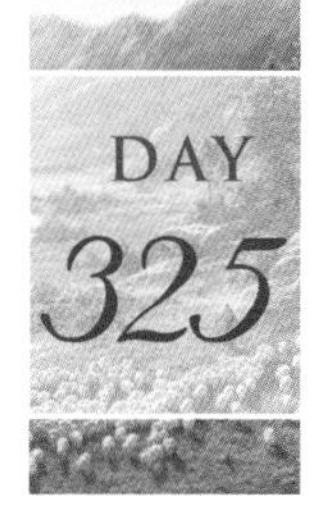

Are We Going Too Far?

For reading & meditation—2 Corinthians 1:1–11

"Praise be to the God and Father of our Lord Jesus Christ ..." (v.3)

We continue reflecting on what we are describing as a watershed issue in today's Church: The attempt by a growing number of Christian women (and men) to understand and speak of God in ways that reflect more fully the female experience. As we pointed out yesterday, the idea of addressing God as "Mother" has not been an issue in the Church until recent times, but with the rise of feminism and political correctness the matter is being raised in almost every section of the Church—the evangelical wing included.

I came across a new hymn which is being sung in a few liberal churches in the United States. This is how it is worded:

Who is she, neither male nor female, Maker of all things,
Only glimpsed or hinted, source of life and gender?
She is God, mother, sister, lover.
In her love we wake, move and grow,
Are daunted, triumph and surrender.

Is this going too far? Personally I believe it is. Unless we are careful, we will turn the God and Father of our Lord Jesus Christ into a goddess or female deity.

Those who are committed to a view of Biblical authority (as I am) will take the position that our Lord's use of the word *Father* when addressing God leaves no room for flexibility or discussion on how we ourselves may address the Almighty. When Christ told His disciples to address God as "Father" it was not a suggestion that He gave them but a command.

FURTHER STUDY

2 Tim. 3:15–4:4; 1 Tim. 1:3–11; Rom. 1:21–25

1. What does "Biblical authority" mean?

2. Is it important?

My Father and my God, help me put what Christ says before what my culture says. Keep me true to Your Word no matter what the consequences. In Christ's peerless and precious Name I pray. Amen.

DAY

326

SECTION SIX

God—Mother or Father?

For reading & meditation—Isaiah 66:7–16

"As a mother comforts her child, so will I comfort you ..." (v.13)

Many think that the reason why we use the term "Father" when addressing God, instead of "Mother" or "Father/Mother" is because from the dawn of time He has been defined in the context of a patriarchal society. Women have been considered as second-class citizens throughout most of history, and now that the situation is changing, God needs to be redefined in terms of feminine as well as masculine characteristics. That is how the argument goes.

No one can deny that throughout time women, generally speaking, have had a bad deal—suffering restrictive employment, commercial exploitation, abuse, repression, and so on. I am glad that there is a movement towards recognizing the importance of women in society and in the Church. But according to Scripture, when it comes to addressing God, the image we are to use and the term of address we are to employ is that of "Father."

It is true that several times in Scripture God is likened to a mother—the text before us today being one among many. And it must be admitted, also, that over the centuries most Bible teachers have been somewhat sexist in the way they have avoided any reference to the fact that the Almighty demonstrates motherly characteristics. When the love of God is denied its motherly quality and is portrayed in a masculine, authoritarian and sexist manner, we end up with a distorted picture both of the Deity and of humanity. But having said that, it does not follow that since God has motherly qualities, He should be addressed as "Mother." He has motherly qualities but He is Father.

FURTHER STUDY

Matt. 6:1–18; Num. 11:12; 1 Thess. 2:7

1. How many times does "Father" appear in Matthew 6?

2. What motherly qualities does the Father possess?

O Father, help me get this matter right, for I hear so many different opinions. Fix it clearly in my mind that though there are maternal qualities in You, it is not as "Mother" You have chosen to be called, but "Father." In Jesus' Name. Amen.

Compensating Images

For reading & meditation—Isaiah 49:8–15

"Can a mother forget the baby at her breast and have no compassion on the child she has borne?" (v.15)

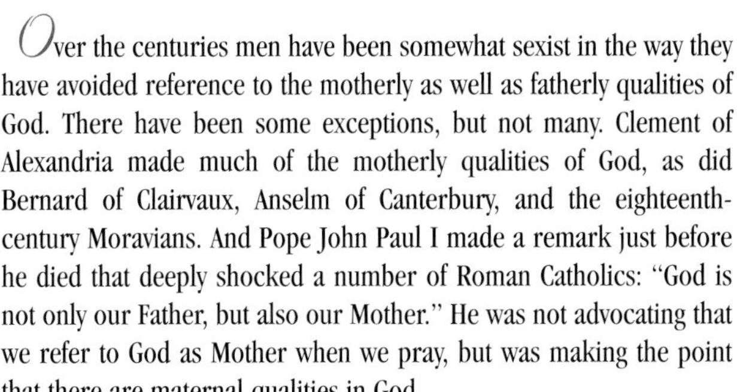

Over the centuries men have been somewhat sexist in the way they have avoided reference to the motherly as well as fatherly qualities of God. There have been some exceptions, but not many. Clement of Alexandria made much of the motherly qualities of God, as did Bernard of Clairvaux, Anselm of Canterbury, and the eighteenth-century Moravians. And Pope John Paul I made a remark just before he died that deeply shocked a number of Roman Catholics: "God is not only our Father, but also our Mother." He was not advocating that we refer to God as Mother when we pray, but was making the point that there are maternal qualities in God.

Many theologians believe that because preachers have been hesitant to focus on the maternal aspects of God's nature, compensating images such as that of the tender, gentle Jesus or the Virgin Mother have evolved. People run to such figures in order to get away from the harsh demands of the Father. "I like Jesus," said a young convert, "but I am afraid of God. He is too stern for me. I much prefer to talk to Jesus than to His Father."

It is not right to use Jesus or Mary, His mother, to compensate for what we perceive as missing in the heart of the Father. To quote Tom Smail again: "The love of God the Father revealed in Jesus is the original although not the projection of all our human loves … [it] fulfils and holds them all together … not only with the authority of the Father, but also with the tender care of a mother."

FURTHER STUDY

Ps. 105:23–45; Isa. 40:10–11; Rom. 11:22; 2 Pet. 3:9–10

1. How do you see the authority of God?

2. How do you see the care of God?

Prayer

Father, help me to see You not through sexist eyes but through spiritual eyes—eyes that have been opened to view You as You are, not as I think You should be. In Jesus' Name. Amen.

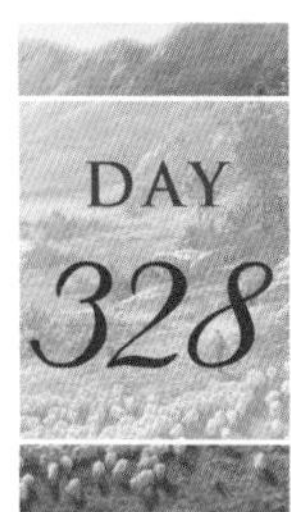

SECTION SIX

Not Just a Simile

For reading & meditation—Isaiah 40:18–31

"'To whom will you compare me? Or who is my equal?' says the Holy One." (v.25)

Many Christians actually believe that God is male. This led a famous feminist, Mary Daly, to say: "Since God is male, the male is God." No, the God of the Bible has no sexuality. God is completely "Other" than His creation. That is what is meant by His holiness. He is set apart. In the passage before us today God says to the prophet Isaiah: "To whom will you compare me?" The question expects the answer: "God can't be compared to anyone. He is 'Other.'" The reason God is spoken of in masculine terms is not to emphasize His sexuality but to maintain the distinction between Himself and His creation. He wants us to worship Him, not the things He has created.

The Almighty may be compared to a mother but that does not mean He is a mother. Nowhere in Scripture is the term "Mother" used of God. Again, God is said in the Old Testament to cry out like a woman (see, for instance, Isaiah 42:14), but that does not mean He is a woman.

As you will know, when one thing is likened to another the reference is called a simile. Sometimes a simile is used when describing the Fatherhood of God. One example is: "As a father has compassion on his children, so the Lord has compassion on those who fear him" (Ps. 103:13). But the idea of God's Fatherhood is not limited to similes. Over and over again (as in 1 John 1:3) the truth is stated categorically: "And our fellowship is with the Father …" Father!

FURTHER STUDY

Matt. 3:16; 23:37;
Rev. 1:13–16

1. Can you find the similes in these verses?

2. What truths are expressed?

Prayer

My Father and my God, I need divine insight if I am to form conclusions that are according to Your Word. Guide me in my thinking so that I emerge not with mere opinions but with divine convictions. In Christ's Name I pray. Amen.

SECTION SIX

Suspect Doxology

For reading & meditation—Genesis 1:1–13

"In the beginning God created the heavens and the earth." (v.1)

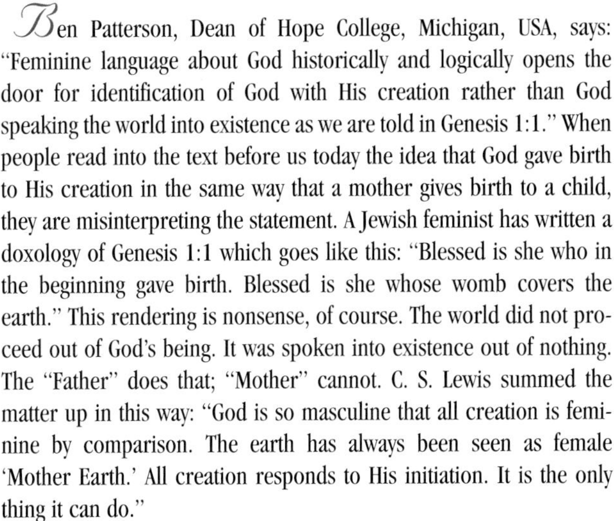

Ben Patterson, Dean of Hope College, Michigan, USA, says: "Feminine language about God historically and logically opens the door for identification of God with His creation rather than God speaking the world into existence as we are told in Genesis 1:1." When people read into the text before us today the idea that God gave birth to His creation in the same way that a mother gives birth to a child, they are misinterpreting the statement. A Jewish feminist has written a doxology of Genesis 1:1 which goes like this: "Blessed is she who in the beginning gave birth. Blessed is she whose womb covers the earth." This rendering is nonsense, of course. The world did not proceed out of God's being. It was spoken into existence out of nothing. The "Father" does that; "Mother" cannot. C. S. Lewis summed the matter up in this way: "God is so masculine that all creation is feminine by comparison. The earth has always been seen as female 'Mother Earth.' All creation responds to His initiation. It is the only thing it can do."

The main reason, then, why God is called Father and not Mother is not that we might think He is male but because His initiating qualities can best be described in terms of masculinity. The most appropriate way to define masculinity, said C. S. Lewis, is by the word *movement*. God is the great initiator, the great mover, who relates to the world He has made, orders it, and sustains it through His Word and by His Spirit. That's the impact made by the imagery of Father, as opposed to Mother.

FURTHER STUDY

Heb. 11:3; Rev. 4:11; Neh. 9:6; Ps. 102:25; Gen. 1:29

1. What is the difference between creation and reproduction?

2. What do they each produce?

Father, I am beginning to understand that if I see You as Mother rather than as like a Mother I border on regarding creation as coming out of You rather than being separate from You. Make things clearer to me. Amen.

SECTION SIX

"Sewage Treatment"

For reading & meditation—2 Timothy 1:1–14

"Guard the good deposit that was entrusted to you …" (v.14)

Paul urges Timothy to guard the good deposit that had been entrusted to him. In Paul's mind what had been delivered to the Christian community needed to be protected. And one matter, I suggest, that needs to be protected in our day is the doctrine we are discussing—the Fatherhood of God.

Jim Packer refers to a dimension of a theologian's work which he calls "sewage treatment"—the need to ensure that the spiritual water we drink is free from pollutants. As I am sure you are aware, the Word of God is being tampered with nowadays and the pure waters of Scripture are in danger of being contaminated. I invite you, therefore, to reaffirm with me now the basics of our faith.

Jesus is the Word of God incarnate. He is God in human form, revealed to us in space and time. Because He is who He said He is—the eternal Son of God—then what He says about His Father must be accepted as the first and last word on the Godhead. Jesus put it this way in John 13:20: "I tell you the truth … whoever accepts me accepts the one who sent me." Jesus said: God is Father. If nothing else was said on the subject that ought to be enough. Our Lord's words are not something to argue about; they are something we must submit to. When we seek to revise them we are no better than the false prophets of Jeremiah's day of whom God said: "[they] steal from one another words supposedly from me" (Jer. 23:30).

FURTHER STUDY

Ezek. 34:17–19; John 7:37; 15:3; Eph. 5:25–27; Heb. 10:22

1. How are we cleansed by the Word?
2. List some current pollutants.

Prayer

O God, give me grace to submit to Your Word and not seek to revise it. I have confessed You as Lord of my life, now I confess You as Lord of my language. It is to the Father I will pray, just as Your Son taught me. Amen.

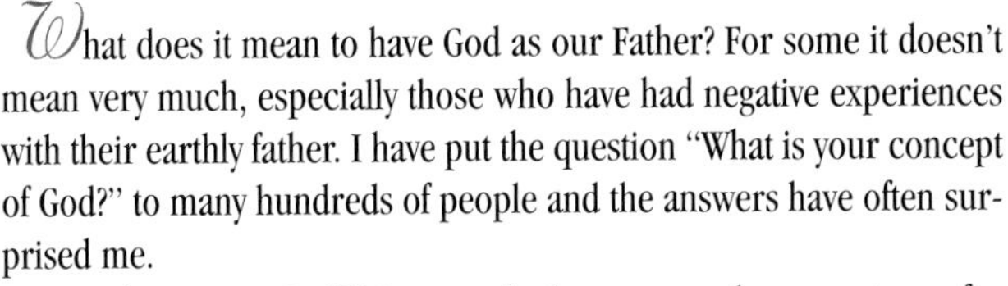

SECTION SIX

"How Much More!"

DAY 331

For reading & meditation—Luke 11:1–13

"... how much more will your Father in heaven give the Holy Spirit to those who ask him!" (v.13)

What does it mean to have God as our Father? For some it doesn't mean very much, especially those who have had negative experiences with their earthly father. I have put the question "What is your concept of God?" to many hundreds of people and the answers have often surprised me.

"How do you see God?" I once asked a woman who came to me for counseling. She replied: "I see God sitting behind a newspaper." Do you need three guesses to know where her father spent most of his time? To be fair, the father in this case may well not have spent all his time behind a newspaper, but that was how she perceived him. And that perception was projected on to God whenever she started to pray. "When I close my eyes in prayer to ask God for something," she said, "I am never sure that I have His attention. I always see Him as occupied with His own interests." There is, I have found, a close psychological connection between our experiences of human fatherhood and our approach to God's Fatherhood. And it is much more influential than many people think.

God's Fatherhood must not be defined by our understanding of human fatherhood. There are some similarities, of course, but we go astray if we think that divine Fatherhood is simply human fatherhood projected on to the screen of heaven and given infinite enlargement. Take the best in human fatherhood, multiply it a billion times, and you do not even come close to the passion, the love and concern which our heavenly Father has for His children.

FURTHER STUDY

Isa. 65:24; Dan. 9:20–23; Luke 12:22–30; Phil. 4:19

1. When does God know our needs?

2. When does He respond?

Prayer

My Father, help me see that the very best father-child relationship gives but a poor and faint picture of the care and interest You have for Your children. Your Fatherhood is perfect. I am so grateful. Amen.

A Highly Emotive Issue

For reading & meditation—Ephesians 6:1–9

"Fathers, do not exasperate your children; instead bring them up in the training and instruction of the Lord." (v.4)

One of the things that has astonished me as a Christian pastor and counselor is the way in which people react when the psychological connection between the experience of human fatherhood and our approach to our heavenly Father is raised. The question I mentioned yesterday—What is your concept of God?—has proved to be highly emotive.

"I see God as cold, distant, and punitive," said one man to me when I put that question to him. An hour later, when I asked him how he saw his father, he replied: "Cold, distant, and punitive." I am convinced that there are literally thousands of Christians who find it difficult to relate to God as their heavenly Father because of negative experiences they had with their earthly father. They are robbed of a rich relationship with Him because their thinking is influenced by a father-child relationship that was characterized by lack of love, disinterest, abuse. If the father was often absent there may have been no relationship at all.

Another thing that has intrigued me is to hear the adult child of an abusive father say: "I wish my father had been an absent father. That would have been easier to cope with." Then to hear the adult child of an absent father say the opposite: "I think I would have preferred to have had an abusive father than an absent father." For years I have puzzled over these opposing viewpoints and I think the answer is this: such is the human hunger for attention that in some cases (not all) abusive attention is better than no attention.

FURTHER STUDY

Deut. 12:29–32;
2 Kings 3:26–27;
Mark 10:13–16;
Rev. 21:3–4

1. What was your experience of your earthly father?
2. How has this influenced your view of your heavenly Father?

Prayer

O God, help me gain a picture of You that is unpolluted by my earthly relationships. The best of fathers is but a faint shadow of You. You are the perfect Father. For that I shall be eternally grateful. Amen.

SECTION SIX

"Too Busy for Me"

For reading & meditation—Psalm 103:1–22

"As a father has compassion on his children, so the Lord has compassion on those who fear him ..." (v.13)

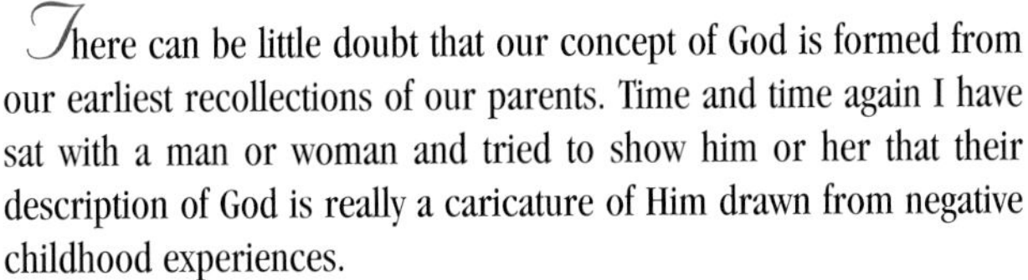

There can be little doubt that our concept of God is formed from our earliest recollections of our parents. Time and time again I have sat with a man or woman and tried to show him or her that their description of God is really a caricature of Him drawn from negative childhood experiences.

One day when I was a pastor I visited a lady in a Yorkshire village who was well into her eighties. During the course of the conversation she told me that she was having difficulties in a certain area of her life. I suggested that we pray together about it and invite the Lord to use His power on her behalf. "Oh, no," she retorted, "I don't want to worry God about such a relatively small problem. He is too busy for little old me." For a few moments I sat quietly, then I asked: "Am I right in thinking that your parents never had much time for you and never gave you the feeling that they were interested in the little details of your life?" The question appeared to leave her nonplussed and she said: "How did you know that?" "It's simple," I told her. "As you look at God you are thinking of your parents. God is never too busy for you. His love for you extends to the tiniest detail of your life." At this she burst into tears. After regaining her composure she remarked: "Think of it—almost all my life I have reckoned that God was too busy to make time for me. What a fool I have been." Indeed.

FURTHER STUDY

Ps. 34:15; 91:1–4;
Matt. 6:25–32;
10:29–31

1. Describe God's attitude to you.

2. Describe your attitude to God.

Prayer

O Father, can it be that my concept of You is a caricature and not one drawn from Your true nature? Set me free if I am worshiping a false image of You. In Jesus' Name. Amen.

DAY

334

SECTION SIX

"Honest to God"

For reading & meditation—Psalm 89:1–18

"O Lord God Almighty, who is like you?" (v.8)

Many hold the view that the concept of divine Fatherhood can mean little to those who had an abusive or absent father, or one who developed no emotional relationship with his child. There are exceptions, but I have generally found it a reliable rule. However, we must be careful not to use this as an excuse for not entering into the joys of a relationship with God as Father.

In 1963 a British bishop, John Robinson, wrote the controversial book *Honest to God*. In it, he omitted to mention the fact that God is our Father. An evangelical reviewer referred to this. In reply, a defendant of Bishop Robinson argued that as family life had largely broken down, it was a brilliant move to leave out any reference to God as Father. "It would be difficult for many in contemporary society to relate to God as Father," he said, "so why use an image that creates more difficulties than it solves?"

This is a nonsensical argument, as it simply is not true to suggest that someone brought up in a family where the father was not a positive figure cannot form a concept of God as a loving Father. If it cannot be done by comparison then it can be done by contrast. Many couples go into marriage resolved not to make the mess their parents made of it. The negative experiences they underwent do not stop them from developing a positive ideal. The same can happen in relation to negative experiences with an earthly father. Where we can't compare our earthly relationships with the divine, we can contrast them.

FURTHER STUDY

2 Chron. 28:22–29:11; Jer. 31:29

1. How does Hezekiah contrast to his father Ahaz?

2. Why was he so different?

Prayer

Father, I see that even if I carry a negative concept of You in my heart drawn from unhappy early relationships, I have no excuse for maintaining it. Where I can't compare I can contrast. Help me do this I pray. In Jesus' Name. Amen.

SECTION SIX

Tell Yourself This . . .

For reading & meditation—2 Corinthians 1:12–24

"For no matter how many promises God has made, they are 'Yes' in Christ." (v.20)

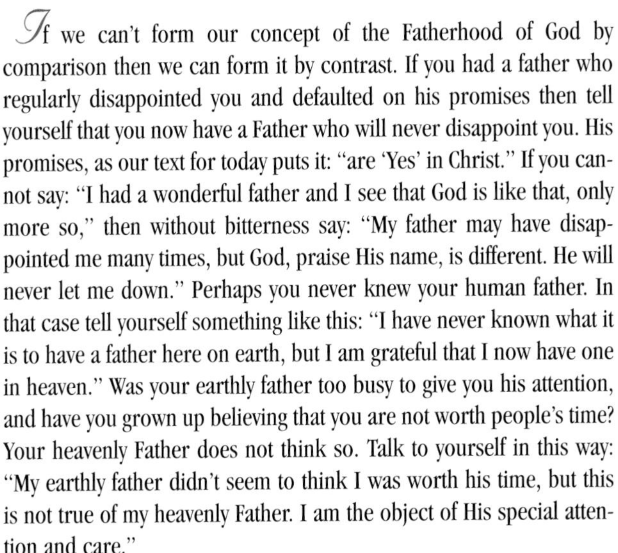

If we can't form our concept of the Fatherhood of God by comparison then we can form it by contrast. If you had a father who regularly disappointed you and defaulted on his promises then tell yourself that you now have a Father who will never disappoint you. His promises, as our text for today puts it: "are 'Yes' in Christ." If you cannot say: "I had a wonderful father and I see that God is like that, only more so," then without bitterness say: "My father may have disappointed me many times, but God, praise His name, is different. He will never let me down." Perhaps you never knew your human father. In that case tell yourself something like this: "I have never known what it is to have a father here on earth, but I am grateful that I now have one in heaven." Was your earthly father too busy to give you his attention, and have you grown up believing that you are not worth people's time? Your heavenly Father does not think so. Talk to yourself in this way: "My earthly father didn't seem to think I was worth his time, but this is not true of my heavenly Father. I am the object of His special attention and care."

And remember this also: God has not left us to guess what His Fatherhood is like by drawing analogies or contrasts from human fatherhood. He has revealed the full meaning of this relationship through Jesus. The better we know Him the better we shall know the Father.

FURTHER STUDY

John 14:6–14; Mark 1:40–41; 6:34–42; Luke 7:11–15

1. How does Jesus show us the Father?

2. What is the Father like?

Prayer

O Father, I see that no matter what my early relationships were like, good or bad, there is a way to make my relationship with You full of richness and meaning. Help me take it. In Jesus' Name. Amen.

DAY
336

SECTION SIX

Two Opposite Pairs

For reading & meditation—Proverbs 14:1–12

"There is a way that seems right to a man, but in the end it leads to death." (v.12)

I have met many people who have experienced such deep hurt in their early relationships that they cannot rid themselves of negative ideas about having God as their Father, and by God's grace have been able to help some of them. But the route to healing is not an easy one, and involves walking a path that is quite different from the one a secular counselor might suggest.

The route which the world usually advises victims of parental abuse to take consists of three steps: self-discovery, self-expression, and self-protection. Self-discovery is where the victim is encouraged to get in touch with his or her repressed emotions. Self-expression is the release and expression of those emotions. Self-protection is the establishment of boundaries around one's life so that one will never have to endure or experience serious hurt again.

The Biblical route to healing, while recognizing some truth in these ideas, starts from a different base and leads to a different goal. It begins with the question: Do I believe that a God who allowed me to be as deeply hurt as I was is good? And it ends with the question: Am I willing to give myself to those I am called to love, and to be more interested in loving well than in protecting myself against hurt?

Which sounds the easier path of these two? Undoubtedly, the way of the world. The way of Christ may seem as if it is the route to death, but really it is the route to life. To live we must be willing to die; to find we must be willing to lose.

FURTHER STUDY

Matt. 5:43–48; 7:13–14; 16:24–25; John 12:24–25

1. What is the Biblical way to life?
2. What makes the narrow way narrow?

Prayer

Father, help me take Your way in everything I pray. I don't want symptom relief, I want a complete cure. And if I don't need help on this particular issue, help me learn how to be of help to others. Amen.

SECTION SIX

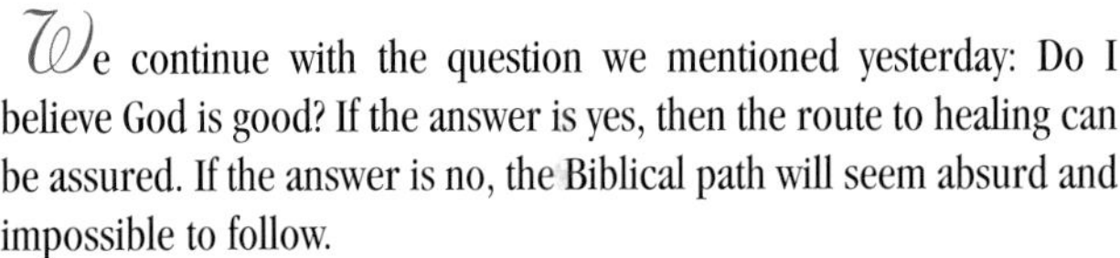

For reading & meditation—Psalm 100:1–5

"For the Lord is good and his love endures forever …" (v.5)

We continue with the question we mentioned yesterday: Do I believe God is good? If the answer is yes, then the route to healing can be assured. If the answer is no, the Biblical path will seem absurd and impossible to follow.

I once put this question to a woman who had been sexually abused by her father. Her reply was this: "No, I do not believe God is good. If He is good then He would have rescued me from my father's abuse and not stood by and let it happen." I had great sympathy for that woman for it is not easy coming to terms with the fact that God is good when one has suffered abuse at the hands of a brutal father. Yet it is an issue that has to be resolved, for one cannot get very far in the Christian life carrying the suspicion that God is not good. If we cannot trust God because of the past, how will we ever be able to trust Him for the future? Almost all of us have had experiences which have caused a question such as this to form in our minds: If God loves me, why did He let that happen to me? Unless we know how to deal with this issue we can become shipwrecked spiritually.

Let me tell you how I deal with doubts concerning the fact of God's goodness. I go to the Cross and remind myself that a God who gave His Son to die for me has got to be good, no matter how persuasive the evidence to the contrary.

FURTHER STUDY

2 Cor. 1:3–11; 4:7–11; Rom. 5:8; 8:28–32

1. Why does God allow us to feel pain?

2. How do we know God is good?

O Father, when doubts and circumstances combine to argue against the fact of Your goodness, help me to make my way to the Cross and light my torch there so that I can walk confidently into the dark. In Jesus' Name. Amen.

SECTION SIX

A Divine Wrestling Match

For reading & meditation—Genesis 32:22–32

"... you have struggled with God and with men and have overcome." (v.28)

Many Christians who have memories of deep trauma caused by unloving parents prefer to take the route the world suggests for healing: self-discovery, self-expression, and self-protection. I offer no criticism of those who choose this path, for to broken people, the world's route offers great appeal.

Some have told me that the prospect of taking the spiritual route to the healing of life's hurts can be frightening. One such person went as far as to say this: "The cure seems at first worse than the disease." This is why many Christian counseling approaches to the problem of past trauma dilute the Biblical process to make it more palatable. Symptoms are relieved, but the real problems of the soul continue and are expressed in other ways.

Trusting ourselves to a God whom we consider could have prevented, and indeed, should have prevented some hurtful experience we went through in the past is not easy, but it is not impossible. If we are open to considering the fact that God's intentions are always good, and that He allowed a painful experience because of some good purpose known only to Him, then we are at the point of spiritual breakthrough. Some energetic wrestling is required before we come through to trustful confidence in God, but the commitment to wrestle will be honored by God in the same way that Jacob's wrestling was honored. It is true that his wrestling resulted in a wounded hip. He never again walked without a limp. But he found that the freedom in his heart was well worth the cost of a displaced limb.

FURTHER STUDY

Gen. 37:23–28; 50:15–21; Isa. 1:18; Col. 4:12

1. Rewrite Genesis 50:20 in your own words.
2. What issue would you like to wrestle over with God?

Prayer

My Father and my God, help me wrestle with issues and not to take the easy way. Make it even more clear to me that You not only break, but bless. I draw near to You. Draw near to me. In Jesus' Name. Amen.

No Place For a Christian

For reading & meditation—Psalm 51:1–19

"Surely you desire truth in the inner parts; you teach me wisdom in the inmost place." (v.6)

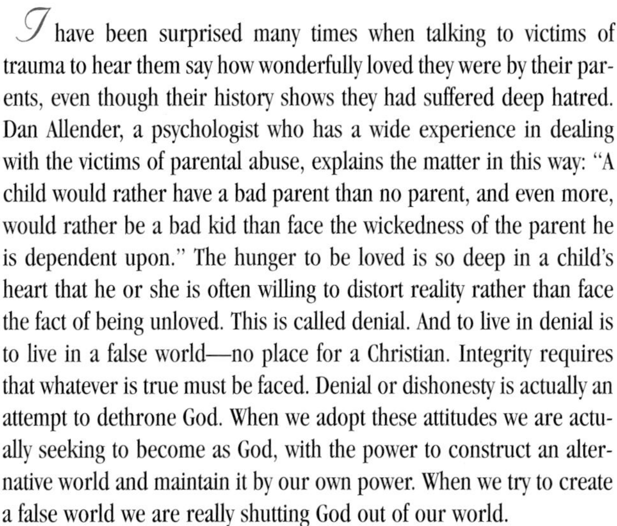

I have been surprised many times when talking to victims of trauma to hear them say how wonderfully loved they were by their parents, even though their history shows they had suffered deep hatred. Dan Allender, a psychologist who has a wide experience in dealing with the victims of parental abuse, explains the matter in this way: "A child would rather have a bad parent than no parent, and even more, would rather be a bad kid than face the wickedness of the parent he is dependent upon." The hunger to be loved is so deep in a child's heart that he or she is often willing to distort reality rather than face the fact of being unloved. This is called denial. And to live in denial is to live in a false world—no place for a Christian. Integrity requires that whatever is true must be faced. Denial or dishonesty is actually an attempt to dethrone God. When we adopt these attitudes we are actually seeking to become as God, with the power to construct an alternative world and maintain it by our own power. When we try to create a false world we are really shutting God out of our world.

There is no need to look back and distort reality, or reconstruct life's circumstances or situations in order to survive. God is well able to hold us and give us the security we need to face the reality of what has happened—no matter how traumatic it was. Truth at first may be hated, but only the truth can set us free.

FURTHER STUDY

John 3:19–21; 8:31–32; 15:22; 1 John 1:8–10

1. Why is denial and dishonesty dangerous?

2. Why is truth dangerous?

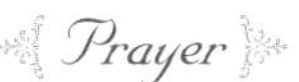

Prayer

Father, I see that the unreal world is no place for a Christian. Forgive me if I have tried to construct an alternative world and attempted to keep it spinning by my own power. Amen.

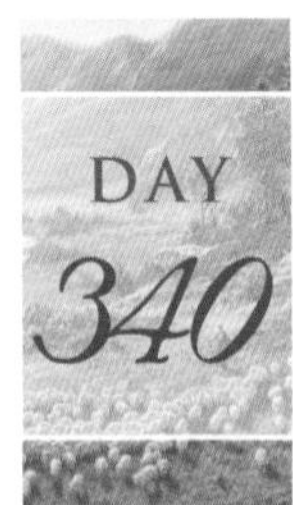

DAY 340

SECTION SIX

"Gnawing Dogs of Truth"

For reading & meditation—Psalm 86:1–17

"Teach me your way, O Lord, and I will walk in your truth ..." (v.11)

Facing the hurts of the past can, for some, be quite terrifying. It is much easier to say: "My parents loved me" than: "I was the object of their hatred and never really knew love." T.S. Eliot wrote: "Human kind cannot bear very much reality" and one can see why. Some have endured such physical and emotional torment in the world of reality that a world of unreality is much more palatable.

The soul, however, is never set free by dishonesty, and dishonesty is what denial is. Only truth can free the soul by removing the burden created by falsehood. I like what one psychologist says about the matter: "The work of keeping the gnawing dogs of truth at bay actually takes far more energy than admitting the awful reality." At first the wounded soul hates the taste of truth, but soon the taste becomes pleasant because it is accompanied by relief as the soul is set free and rejoices in knowing that in the presence of a loving God (forgive the change of metaphor) there is no need to hide.

When we are committed to honesty—to seeing the past as it is, without denial or distortion—we have only to knock on the door of truth to find that it opens and the Bread of Life is deposited in our hands. Recognizing the damage done to us is a necessary step if we are to pursue the Biblical route to healing. And if the road is too hard to travel alone then do it with the aid of a godly counselor.

FURTHER STUDY

Ps. 32:3–5; 41:4–13; Prov. 28:13; Gen. 3:8–13

1. Why is truth so painful?

2. Why is truth so necessary?

Prayer

O Father, I wonder how much denial there is in my life. All denial affronts You because it assumes that false reality is better than truth. I don't want to live a lie; I want to live according to truth. Help me my Father. In Jesus' Name. Amen.

SECTION SIX

The Greatest Commandments

For reading & meditation—Mark 12:28–34

"Love the Lord your God … Love your neighbor as yourself." (vv.30–31)

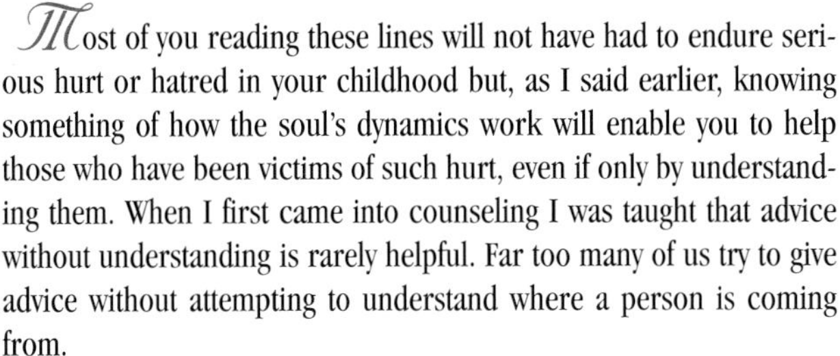

Most of you reading these lines will not have had to endure serious hurt or hatred in your childhood but, as I said earlier, knowing something of how the soul's dynamics work will enable you to help those who have been victims of such hurt, even if only by understanding them. When I first came into counseling I was taught that advice without understanding is rarely helpful. Far too many of us try to give advice without attempting to understand where a person is coming from.

Today I feel I must pause and ask those of you whose childhood was happy, and who have no faulty constructs of God in your heart: How aware are you of the fact that even the minor hurts and disappointments of life can drive you towards self-protection? My own childhood was very happy. There were some disappointments, some troubles, some forms of deprivation, but none that can be described as traumatic. I am aware, however, that those minor disappointments and troubles (very small compared to those experienced by individuals who have suffered physical and mental abuse) have produced a drive within me that says: "People hurt. Don't get too close to them." The result is that I tend to get close enough to be affirmed by people but not close enough to be hurt by them.

That is my problem. I wonder, is it yours too? I suspect you know what I am talking about. "Love," says Dr. Larry Crabb, "is moving toward others without self-protection." And all of us, not just the victims of trauma, are prone to do that.

FURTHER STUDY

John 13:34–35; 15:12–13; Acts 5:1–2; Gal. 2:11–14

1. How do we see self-protective love in Acts and Galatians?

2. Are you guilty of self-protective love?

Father, You have me cornered. Thank You for reminding me of my tendency to think more of myself than I do of others. Forgive me and help me so that I be of service to those with whom I have to do. Amen.

DAY 342

SECTION SIX

The Catalyst

For reading & meditation—Romans 2:1–16

"... God's kindness leads you towards repentance." (v.4)

The first step, if we are to replace a seriously faulty concept of God with a Biblical one, is to face the crucial question of whether or not we accept that God is good. Once we are assured of that, the next step, we agreed, is to confront the reality of the past. What next? The third step is to invite God to bring about change.

The catalyst is always repentance. The word *repent*, as you probably know, comes from the Greek word *metanoia* which means a change of mind. In a sense, as soon as someone begins to face the past realistically, the act of repentance has begun. One writer has defined repentance like this: "Repentance is an about-face movement from denial and rebellion to truth and surrender—from death to life." Honestly facing the distortions the mind makes in order to live comfortably with the past is a positive step—a repentant step. Please note that.

Now before talking further about repentance let me make clear that someone who has been the victim of hurt is never called by God to repent of the abuse that was inflicted on him or her. I have met some who, having suffered at the hands of abusive parents, believe it their responsibility to repent before God of not being sufficiently attractive or appealing for their parents to love them. Let me repeat: a person who has been the subject of cruelty and abuse in their childhood years is never called by God to repent of that. It is the perpetrators who should repent, not the victim.

FURTHER STUDY

2 Sam. 11:26–12:13; Luke 19:1–9

1. How did David move from denial to repentance?

2. How did Zacchaeus show repentance?

Prayer

Father, as the text for today says, it is Your kindness that leads us to repentance. You are a kind God. Help me to focus on Your kindness, and allow it to lead me to repentance. In Jesus' Name. Amen.

"I Want to Be Captain"

For reading & meditation—John 13:18–38

"... As I have loved you, so you must love one another." (v.34)

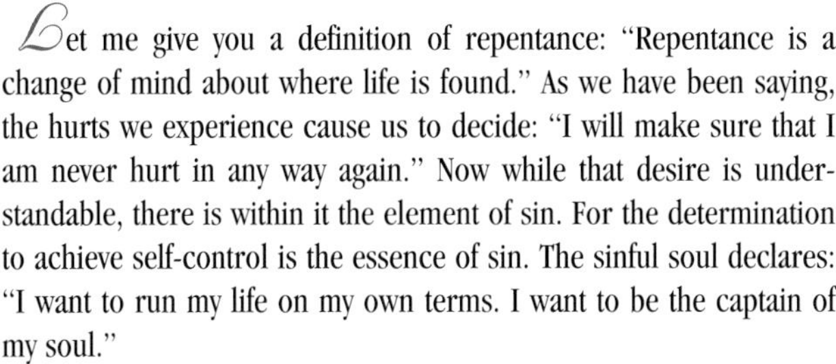

Let me give you a definition of repentance: "Repentance is a change of mind about where life is found." As we have been saying, the hurts we experience cause us to decide: "I will make sure that I am never hurt in any way again." Now while that desire is understandable, there is within it the element of sin. For the determination to achieve self-control is the essence of sin. The sinful soul declares: "I want to run my life on my own terms. I want to be the captain of my soul."

Our text for today, "As I have loved you, so you must love one another," unfolds for every one of us the real purpose of living, which can be described like this: we are to love as we are loved. How do we violate this law of love? We violate it when we move away from those we are called to love rather than moving towards them. But shouldn't those who have been seriously hurt be wary of people whom they think might harm them? Of course. God does not expect us to put ourselves in a position where we may experience violence or abuse. But He does expect us to move towards people to love them, care for them, and express to them the same love that He expresses to us. We must forfeit our self-protective, God-dishonoring ways of relating to others in order to fulfill the purpose of living—loving involvement with God and loving involvement with others. That is what has to be repented of.

FURTHER STUDY

Eph. 5:1–2; Acts 9:10–18; 9:26–28

1. How did Ananias and Barnabas love without self-protection?

2. Do you need to repent of self-protection?

Prayer

Father, again I must look into my heart to see how well constructed are the defenses of self-protection. Help me, for I cannot see myself clearly except in Your light. This I ask in Jesus' Name. Amen.

SECTION SIX

Sin in Its True Colors

For reading & meditation—Psalm 20:1–9

"Some trust in chariots and some in horses, but we trust in the name of the Lord our God." (v.7)

The Christian Church suffers from too superficial a view of sin and of repentance. Sin is often talked about in the Church in terms of wrong behavior. But we will never see sin in its true colors until we see it as a violation of the law of love.

When we adopt the attitude that because God didn't deflect a hurtful experience in the past and save us from it, He can't blame us too much when we don't trust Him to hold us in the area of relationships (an area in which we are almost guaranteed to get hurt), then we are guilty of self-protection. A man once said to me: "You talk and write a lot about self-protection. Where do you find that word in the Bible?" I replied (somewhat facetiously I am sorry to say): "In the same chapter as the term 'Trinity.'" You won't find the word self-protection in the Bible, but can you think of a better term to describe the dynamic that takes place when we fail to love as we are loved? There are those who think that an accumulation of hurts justifies a lack of trust. But when you look carefully into the wounded soul (or, for that matter, any human soul) you find something other than lack of trust. You find a determination not to trust.

How do you think God feels about our refusal to trust Him? I think He is grieved by it. I make the point again: it is that which has to be repented of. Not the hurts caused by others, but the determination not to trust.

FURTHER STUDY

James 2:10; 4:17;
1 John 4:7–21

1. Why is not loving sinful?
2. Compare your view of sin with the Bible's view.

Prayer

Father, forgive me that I am more preoccupied with the hurts that others have inflicted on me than the hurt I inflict upon You by my failure to trust. Forgive me and restore me to confident trust. In Jesus' Name. Amen.

Let's Be Close, But . . .

For reading & meditation—Isaiah 66:1–6

". . . This is the one I esteem: he who is humble and contrite in spirit, and trembles at my word." (v.2)

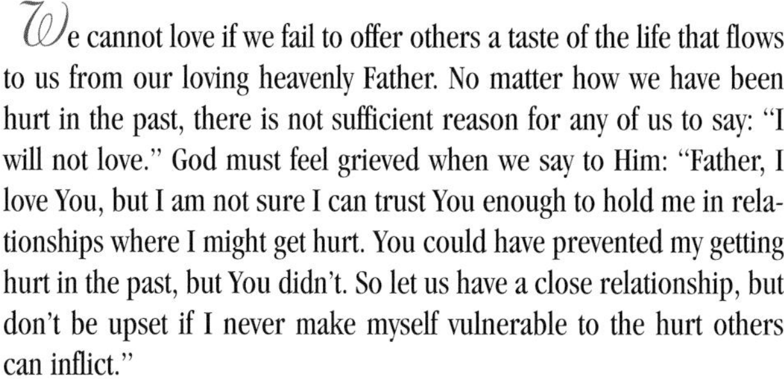

We cannot love if we fail to offer others a taste of the life that flows to us from our loving heavenly Father. No matter how we have been hurt in the past, there is not sufficient reason for any of us to say: "I will not love." God must feel grieved when we say to Him: "Father, I love You, but I am not sure I can trust You enough to hold me in relationships where I might get hurt. You could have prevented my getting hurt in the past, but You didn't. So let us have a close relationship, but don't be upset if I never make myself vulnerable to the hurt others can inflict."

That attitude is the sin of not trusting God and, if taken to its logical conclusion, is tantamount to making oneself God. God does not require anyone to repent of the wrong that was done to them, but He does require us to repent of our stubborn commitment to independence, our defensive strategies and refusal to trust. To repent is to experience a shift in our perceived source of life. We recognize that the law of love removes all excuses, and that the pain of the past is no reason for maintaining a position of unloving self-protection in the present.

The weight of this requirement may be heavy, but it is designed to humble us and bring us in brokenness before God. Ultimately repentance involves perceiving that there are no excuses for maintaining an attitude of distrust towards God and moving towards Him humbly with prayer and a broken spirit.

FURTHER STUDY

2 Kings 18:1–16;
Jer. 2:13; 17:13;
John 7:37–39

1. Why did Hezekiah move from trust to a self-protective strategy?

2. Where do people find their source of life?

Prayer

O Father, how ugly my self-protective strategies must appear to You. And how hurt You must be by my stubborn refusal to trust. Yet You do not reject me. Help me throw myself upon You in trust. In Jesus' Name. Amen.

DAY

346

SECTION SIX

Hate—A Virulent Germ

For reading & meditation—Colossians 3:1–17

"... Forgive as the Lord forgave you." (v.13)

The next step that has to be taken on the road to overcoming a negative concept of God is the step of forgiveness. This is the point where we struggle the most. The greater the damage, the more difficult it is for people to forgive. Is God being harsh and lacking in sensitivity when He commands us in our text for today to forgive? Many have told me that when wrestling with memories of hurt and abuse, God's demand that they should forgive is infuriating.

There are many reasons, of course, why God insists on us forgiving, and over the years I have approached this subject from different viewpoints. Permit me now to come at it from this angle: the damage we do to ourselves by harboring unforgiveness is greater than any damage that may have been done to us. One of the most virulent germs which can enter the human soul is resentment, and it is all the more dangerous because it often does its deadly work without being identified. When allowed to remain, it breeds bitterness, depression and disease. It causes nervous breakdowns and mental unbalance. It demolishes joy and develops self-pity.

A woman I knew had been deeply hurt by cruel and violent parents, and her heart burned with concentrated hate towards them. I told her that there was a cure for her condition but she refused it, and I watched her maintain her hate until eventually it killed her. She cultivated the germ of resentment in her heart, and in the end it caused her more harm than the hurts she had received over the years.

FURTHER STUDY

Heb. 12:15; Matt. 18:21–22; Luke 15:25–30; Eph. 4:31–32

1. Try to read Hebrews 12:15 in as many versions as you can.

2. How does resentment damage us?

Prayer

Father, I see that I cannot hate another without wronging myself. I know the fire of hate consumes; it consumes everything—myself included. Quench it within me. Let no smouldering embers remain. In Jesus' Name. Amen.

If Only . . .

For reading & meditation—Luke 23:26–43

"Jesus said, 'Father, forgive them, for they do not know what they are doing.'" (v.34)

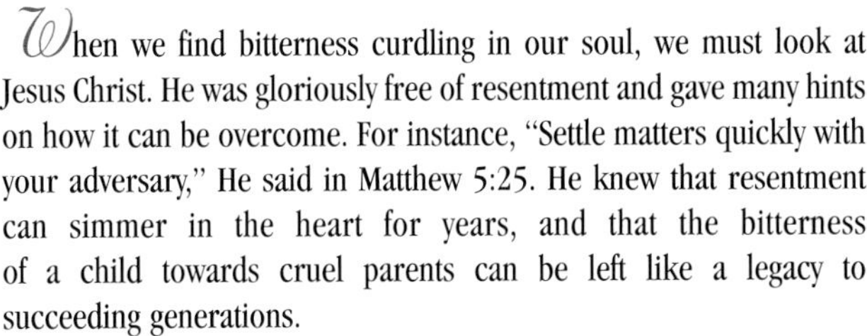

When we find bitterness curdling in our soul, we must look at Jesus Christ. He was gloriously free of resentment and gave many hints on how it can be overcome. For instance, "Settle matters quickly with your adversary," He said in Matthew 5:25. He knew that resentment can simmer in the heart for years, and that the bitterness of a child towards cruel parents can be left like a legacy to succeeding generations.

But His teaching and example were most powerful at the time of His death. The "first word" spoken from the Cross is among the most sublime Jesus ever uttered. Studying this will teach us more about how to deal with resentment than reading many volumes. Notice first that He forgave His foes and prayed as the blood spurted from His wounds: "Father, forgive them . . ." There is nothing like honest prayer to scour hate out of the heart. Second, He made allowances for them: "They do not know what they are doing." Who was He thinking of? Pilate? The people? The priests? The Pharisees? The soldiers? Who can tell? Forgiveness does not deny the evil that has been done, but spreads over foul deeds the kindly judgment that if those who caused the harm had known what they were really doing, they would not have done it. Third, He kept on loving. Their wickedness could not defeat His love. He could have come down from the Cross if He wanted, but having made love the principle of His life He went on loving to the end. If only at our lesser Calvaries we could rise to this!

FURTHER STUDY

Matt. 5:38–45; Luke 9:51–56; 1 Pet. 2:19–24

1. How did Jesus teach forgiveness?

2. How did Jesus model forgiveness?

Prayer

O Father, Your Son has revealed love as the secret. We have lost that secret, hence we spend our days griping and groping. Help us to see Your way, then we will find ours. In Jesus' Name. Amen.

The First Christian Martyr

For reading & meditation—Acts 7:54–60

"Lord, do not hold this sin against them." (v.60)

If Christ lives in you then He can love in you. You too can forgive injuries, pray for your enemies, and make every allowance for their wickedness.

The first man ever to die for Christ was Stephen. Our reading makes it clear that he was unjustly murdered. But Christ lived in Him. His last words were a magnificent echo of Calvary: "Lord, do not hold this sin against them." Remember Stephen was stoned to death. Imagine how painful that must have been. It was almost as cruel as crucifixion. One by one the stones pounded the life from his body, but though they battered the life out of him they could not batter the love out of him. Like his Lord he kept on loving to the end. Christ was in his mind up until his last moments. "Lord," he said, "Lord, do not hold this sin against them."

The chapter ends with a lovely sentence: "When he had said this, he fell asleep." But don't let these words lead you to think there was no hurt, no pain, no physical agony. He would have felt it all; you can be certain of that. But the love of Christ poured into him and through him and, taken up with Him in his heart and mind, his soul was taken up to be with Him. Some words ring in my mind as I write—words spoken by one who stood holding the coats of those who threw the stones: "Let this mind be in you, which was also in Christ Jesus …" (Phil. 2:5, KJV).

FURTHER STUDY

1 Sam. 24:1–25;
Acts 22:19–21;
Rom. 12:14–21

1. How did David have the mind of Christ?
2. How are we to treat those who treat us badly?

Prayer

Heavenly Father, I must not perpetuate the treatment people give to me. I must echo Your words and treat people as You do. But I can't do this except by Your grace. May Your love melt all my resentments and heal all my hurts. Amen.

SECTION SIX

Slow Growth—Good Growth

For reading & meditation—2 Peter 3:8–18

"But grow in the grace and knowledge of our Lord and Savior Jesus Christ." (v.18)

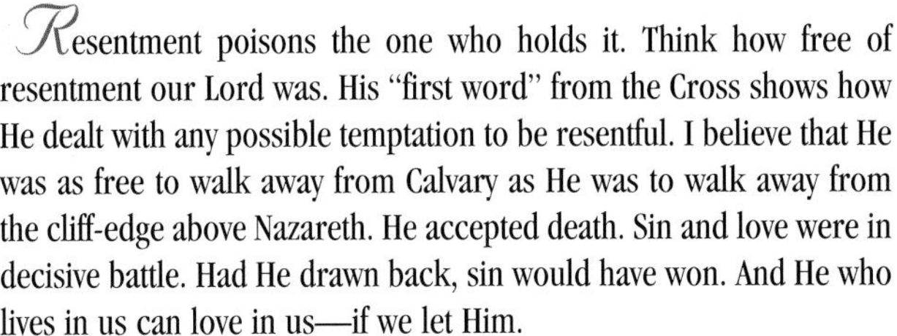

Resentment poisons the one who holds it. Think how free of resentment our Lord was. His "first word" from the Cross shows how He dealt with any possible temptation to be resentful. I believe that He was as free to walk away from Calvary as He was to walk away from the cliff-edge above Nazareth. He accepted death. Sin and love were in decisive battle. Had He drawn back, sin would have won. And He who lives in us can love in us—if we let Him.

What is the next step we must take? We must allow time for change. Change is more often than not a process. I want to emphasize this because many, when once they see the way out of their dilemma, want change to take place too quickly. Some changes in our lives take place quickly. The night I surrendered my life to Jesus Christ a lot of my sinful habits left me. But some didn't, and the process of change was long and tedious. Deep healing and supernatural change can take place in a moment, but often it takes months of struggle, trial and error, learning and unlearning.

All of us have different timetables when it comes to growing, and no one should judge another's timetable. There is an assumption that when God is involved then all change will be instantaneous. It can happen that way, but be prepared also for it to take place over a period of time. A gardener friend of mine says: "Slow growth is good growth." It is the same in the garden of the soul.

FURTHER STUDY

2 Pet. 1:2–8; Ps. 1:1–3; Jer. 17:7–8; Ezek. 31:3–9

1. What do we grow in?

2. Compare spiritual growth to a tree growing.

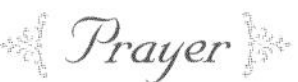

Father, help me to be content with Your timetable for my spiritual growth. Sometimes I want to grow more quickly than is good for me. Help me be patient with Your patience. In Jesus' Name. Amen.

SECTION SIX

Is All Suffering Good?

For reading & meditation—Hebrews 2:1–13

"In bringing many ... to glory, it was fitting that God ... should make the author of their salvation perfect through suffering." (v.10)

The Biblical route to change requires a degree of suffering, pain, even death—a prospect that the carnal nature abhors. As our text for today tells us, even Jesus was required to suffer in order to fulfil His mission. Why is suffering so necessary for growth? I like the way Dan Allender puts it: "Suffering ... is necessary for us because it strips away the pretence that life is reasonable and good, a pretense that keeps us looking in all the wrong places for the satisfaction of our souls."

Let me make it clear that I do not think all suffering is profitable. Many people suffer as a result of their own foolishness. I knew a man who complained that he was being persecuted by his neighbors. When I looked into the situation with him I found that all his neighbors did was simply to avoid him. Why? Every time he met them he told them they were going to hell. With a little more tact his suffering could have been avoided. He said he was suffering for the cause of Christ, but the truth was he was suffering as a result of his own foolishness.

There are others, too, who suffer under the weight of their sinful self-contempt. I call it sinful because self-contempt is a human effort to deal with the pain that is going on in our personality when we should be bringing it to God and letting Him deal with it. Once again it is a case of the self trying to be in control. Some may call such suffering good. Personally, I would not.

FURTHER STUDY

Rom. 5:3–5; 1 Pet. 3:14–18; 4:12–19; Heb. 12:11

1. Why can suffering be good for us?
2. Why can people suffer because of their own foolishness?

Prayer

Father, I acknowledge the reality that so often I have to be drawn to You on the raft of suffering. Help me face the fact that it is through pain that my soul matures. I would not ask You to save me from it, but to be with me in it. Amen.

SECTION SIX

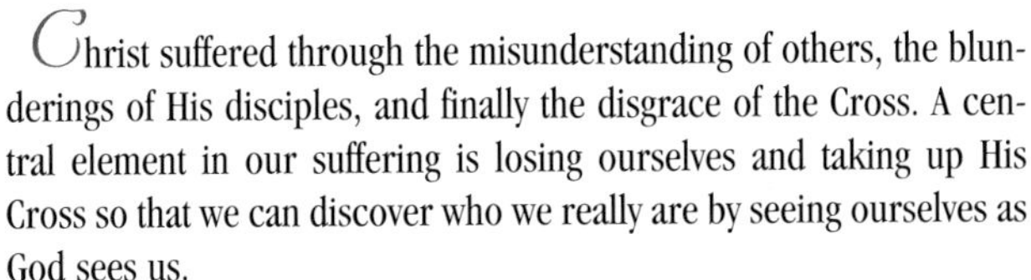

Three Great Purposes

For reading & meditation—Matthew 16:21–28

"For whoever wants to save his life will lose it, but whoever loses his life for me will find it." (v.25)

Christ suffered through the misunderstanding of others, the blunderings of His disciples, and finally the disgrace of the Cross. A central element in our suffering is losing ourselves and taking up His Cross so that we can discover who we really are by seeing ourselves as God sees us.

One writer said: "The purposes of God for us are threefold: to enjoy the thrill of being sensitive to the needs of others, a deepened capacity to relate to others from the depth of our souls, and the ability to make the right choices even though those choices may cause us to be unpopular." He encouraged his readers to ask themselves: How sensitive am I to the needs of others? How deeply do I give myself to people? How free am I to make decisions that may cause me to be unpopular?

There is a great enjoyment in being sensitive to the needs of others. One person described it: "I feel like a lovely tree that invites creatures to come and nest, whose leafy arms hold out the promise of comfort and rest." There is great satisfaction, too, in offering one's self to another. Not just in doing good, but in giving of one's self to others for their supreme good. And there is also great joy in not being driven by people's expectations. The capacity to act on conviction, no matter how unpopular the decision may be, enlivens the soul. Would you like to become such a person? The condition is simple but painful. It involves losing yourself in order to find yourself, dying in order to live.

FURTHER STUDY

2 Cor. 1:3–7; 2 Tim. 1:15–18; 1 Pet. 4:1–4

1. How do these passages bring out the three great purposes?

2. How does your life demonstrate them?

Prayer

O Father, I see You intend me to be such a person—sensitive, giving, and with fearless convictions. You have put this potential within me. Now do whatever is necessary to draw it out. In Jesus' Name. Amen.

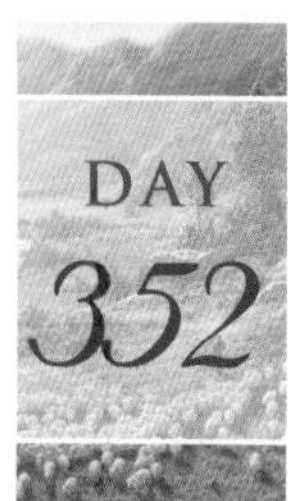

The Only Way

For reading & meditation—1 Peter 2:13–25

"He himself bore our sins … so that we might die to sins and live for righteousness …" (v.24)

The joy of being the person God designed you to be is beyond words. The ability to give sensitively to another from your heart brings deep bliss. And the freedom to act on conviction instead of being bound by fear gives pleasure that has to be experienced to be believed.

Life has damaged us so much that few of us function like this. All of us have numbed our souls in order to cope with the pain of not being loved in the way we cry out for. Our souls will come alive not by self-effort but by self-renunciation. A radical commitment to seeing our whole existence in terms of furthering God's purpose in other people's lives involves dying to self-interest and coming alive to God's interests. Self-interest is seeing our existence in terms of what we can get from people. God's interests for our lives are completely the opposite. Instead we ask: What can I give to people? The only way to change from pursuing self-centered interests to other-centered interests is to die. We lose our lives in the cause of others and then we find them. We die to self-interest and our souls come alive for the explicit purpose of having more to give to others for their well-being and God's glory.

Going against our carnal nature involves us in a good deal of suffering. Nobody would say it is easy. But when we decide to die to ourselves, no matter how much our fallen human nature cries to be relieved, we will come alive and enter into the nature of ultimate reality—other-centered relating.

FURTHER STUDY

1 Cor. 10:23–24; 10:33; 2 Cor. 5:13–21; Phil. 2:1–8

1. Define self-interest.

2. How do we move to other-centered relating?

Prayer

Father, I have come a long way with You over these past days. Don't let me balk now. Help me see that Your intention is that I should give, not get. Today I want to die to all self-interest and come alive to Your interests. In Jesus' Name. Amen.

SECTION SIX

Divine Re-parenting

For reading & meditation—1 John 5:1–15

"... the confidence we have in approaching God: that if we ask anything according to his will, he hears us." (v.14)

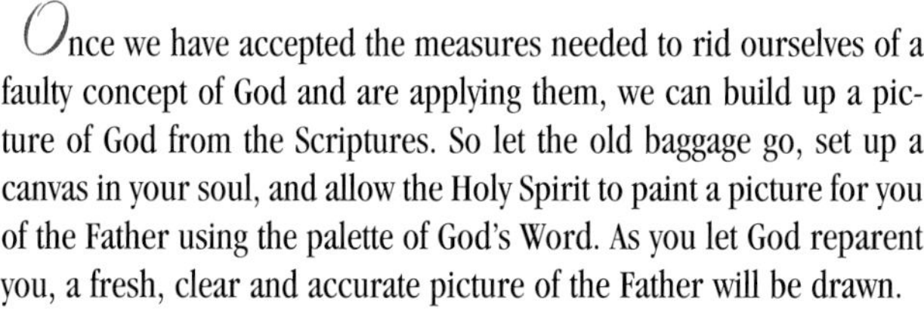

Once we have accepted the measures needed to rid ourselves of a faulty concept of God and are applying them, we can build up a picture of God from the Scriptures. So let the old baggage go, set up a canvas in your soul, and allow the Holy Spirit to paint a picture for you of the Father using the palette of God's Word. As you let God reparent you, a fresh, clear and accurate picture of the Father will be drawn.

The first thing you need to know about your heavenly Father is: He is never too busy for you. Were your parents ever too busy for you? Were there occasions when you cried out for them and they were not there? Well, be assured that your heavenly Father is not like that. Even though He has a million and one things calling for His attention, and a gigantic universe to run, He pays as much attention to you as if you were the only person on the face of the earth. Such is His relationship with you that it is as if there were not another soul in the universe. You don't have to share His attention with anyone—except, of course, when you are in prayer or fellowship with others. And even then He relates to you as if You were the only being in existence.

You may be too busy for your heavenly Father but, take it from me, your heavenly Father is never too busy for you. Look once again at the text at the top of this page. It is written specially for you.

FURTHER STUDY

2 Sam. 22:7; Ps. 139:11–18; Matt. 6:6–8; 1 John 3:21–22

1. Why can we pray with confidence?

2. Now pray confidently!

Prayer

O Father, burn this thought deep into my soul—I am Your special child. You relate to me as if I was the only one on the face of the earth. How wonderful. How truly wonderful. Thank You, Father. Amen.

SECTION SIX

"Tear Bottles"

For reading & meditation—Psalm 56:1–13

"Record my lament; list my tears on your scroll—are they not in your record?" (v.8)

Your heavenly Father feels for you in your deepest sorrows. Did you ever cry yourself to sleep as a child, believing that your parents were insensitive to your hurts? That could never be said of your heavenly Father. He collects all our tears in His bottle. Though the NIV doesn't use that expression in our text for today, many other translations do. The wording in the New King James Version is: "You … put my tears into Your bottle; Are they not in Your book?" Incredible, isn't it? Your heavenly Father collects your tears, and records every one of them. He doesn't stay emotionally uninvolved with His children. He shares our sorrows.

Somewhere I read that in Bible times there were bottles known as "tear bottles." It is believed that loved ones and mourners collected their tears in these bottles and buried them with the person who had died. They did this so that everyone would know how much the deceased person was loved.

Have you shed any tears recently? Did you wonder if anyone cared? Well, God cares. He is concerned about your every worry, your every concern, and when you cry He collects your tears and puts them in His bottle. The psalmist is speaking metaphorically, of course, but what a beautiful word-picture he uses to convey the fact that God does not consider it beneath His dignity to become emotionally involved with every one of His children. Whoever else may withdraw from you in your relationships, when you become tearful you can be sure of this: it will not be your heavenly Father.

FURTHER STUDY

Gen. 21:9–20; Isa. 25:8; 1 Pet. 5:7; Rev. 7:17

1. How does God respond to our tears?
2. Why?

Father, how comforting it is to know that though my emotions may cause others to withdraw or misunderstand me, You never do that. And You not only observe me, You feel for me. How wonderful. Thank You, dear Father. Amen.

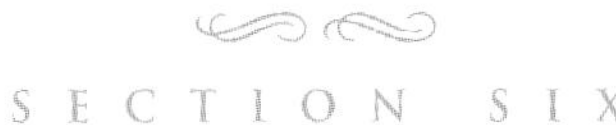

SECTION SIX

Never Abandoned

For reading & meditation—Psalm 27:1–14

"Though my father and mother forsake me, the Lord will receive me." (v.10)

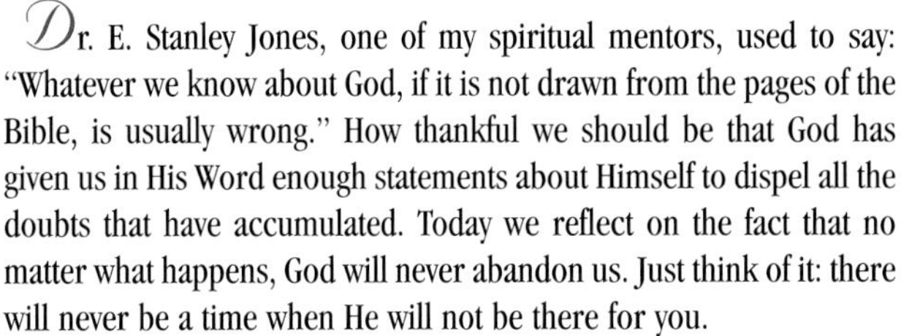

Dr. E. Stanley Jones, one of my spiritual mentors, used to say: "Whatever we know about God, if it is not drawn from the pages of the Bible, is usually wrong." How thankful we should be that God has given us in His Word enough statements about Himself to dispel all the doubts that have accumulated. Today we reflect on the fact that no matter what happens, God will never abandon us. Just think of it: there will never be a time when He will not be there for you.

Some of you know what it is like to be brought up without having your father around. A father may be absent for one of many different reasons: the need to work away from home, divorce, illness, or even death. With your heavenly Father, however, there is nothing that can cause Him to be absent. As well as taking note of the text at the top of this page, think about this one: "For the Lord will not reject His people; he will never forsake his inheritance" (Ps. 94:14). Over the years I have talked to many people who were abandoned by a parent. I have a picture in my mind as I write of a young girl who, having been abandoned by her father, sobbed and sobbed as she told her story: "He promised he would never leave me," she cried, "but he did."

Think back to our very first parents—Adam and Eve. It was not God who left them; it was they who left God. You may leave Him but He will never leave you.

FURTHER STUDY

Ps. 139:1–12; Isa. 41:8–18; Heb. 13:5–6; John 14:16–22

1. Why will God never abandon us?

2. How is He always with us?

Prayer

Gracious and loving heavenly Father, how wonderful it is to know that You are not a God who pulls out of relationships when the going gets tough. I am so grateful that I will never be abandoned by You. Amen.

DAY 356

SECTION SIX

"Solid as a Rock"

For reading & meditation—James 1:1–18

"... coming down from the Father of the heavenly lights, who does not change like shifting shadows." (v.17)

Our heavenly Father never changes. Human beings struggle to be consistent. It has been said that the only consistent quality in the human heart is inconsistency. God is not like that; He is like His Son: "the same yesterday and today and forever" (Heb. 13:8).

Did one of your parents have mood swings? One adult child of inconsistent parents told me in a counseling session: "I had to wait for my father to be in a good mood before I dared ask him if I could go fishing. Sometimes I had to wait for weeks." Well, God never has mood swings, never brings home a bad attitude from work, and never takes His frustrations out on anyone. He just doesn't act like that, for He is God. A phrase that still echoes in my mind is one my former pastor used when referring to the unchanging character of God: "He is as solid as a rock." He is.

Admittedly at times we may think we perceive inconsistency in our heavenly Father. Perhaps He responds to a prayer of ours one day and then, when we pray the same prayer again, no answer seems to come. But be assured of this: it is only a perceived inconsistency. It does not mean He is inconsistent; it simply means we can't see His consistency. I am convinced that when we get to heaven and see our lives in retrospect, we will have no reason to believe that God has been inconsistent. For, as one theologian has said: "Consistency is the way God is." Always. You can count on it.

FURTHER STUDY

Ps. 18:2; 18:31; 18:46; 102:25–27; Mal. 3:6; Heb. 1:12

1. List aspects of God's unchanging character.
2. When can God appear inconsistent?

Prayer

O Father, how can I sufficiently thank You for reminding me that You are a model of consistency? Forgive me if there have been times when I thought You were inconsistent. The fault was in me, not in You. I am sorry. Amen.

Tough Love

For reading & meditation—Hebrews 12:1–11

"... the Lord disciplines those he loves, and he punishes everyone he accepts as a son." (v.6)

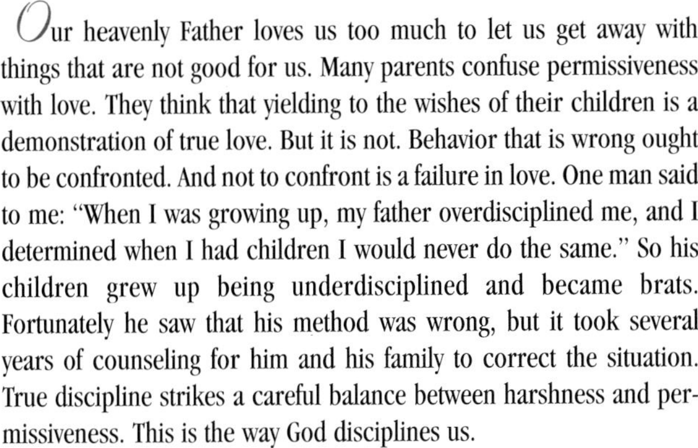

Our heavenly Father loves us too much to let us get away with things that are not good for us. Many parents confuse permissiveness with love. They think that yielding to the wishes of their children is a demonstration of true love. But it is not. Behavior that is wrong ought to be confronted. And not to confront is a failure in love. One man said to me: "When I was growing up, my father overdisciplined me, and I determined when I had children I would never do the same." So his children grew up being underdisciplined and became brats. Fortunately he saw that his method was wrong, but it took several years of counseling for him and his family to correct the situation. True discipline strikes a careful balance between harshness and permissiveness. This is the way God disciplines us.

But just how does God go about the task of disciplining us? His main method is through the Bible (see 1 Timothy 3:16). That is why it is important to spend time regularly studying His Word. If we neglect to read the Word, or fail to heed His Word, then He arranges circumstances that will get our attention. Sometimes He puts us in a spiritual wilderness and, as He did with the children of Israel, He lets us go around and around until we have got the point. Then at other times He blocks a promotion, makes our money run out, or delays a healing. Good parents understand that proper discipline is necessary for the development of their children. Could we expect less of our heavenly Father?

FURTHER STUDY

1 Sam. 2:12–17; 2:22–25; 3:11–18

1. How was Eli a bad father?

2. How is God a good Father?

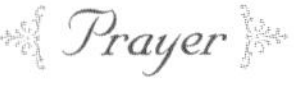

Father, I am so grateful that You care enough to discipline me, cherish me enough to point out where I am going wrong, and love me enough to confront me. And You do all this not for Your good but for mine. Amen.

DAY 358

SECTION SIX

The Face of the Father

For reading & meditation—Hebrews 1:1–14

"The Son is the radiance of God's glory and the exact representation of his being ..." (v.3)

One of our Lord's missions on this earth was to provide us with a perfect view of the Father. "The Son," our text tells us, "is the radiance of God's glory and the exact representation of his being ..." Eugene Peterson in *The Message* paraphrases this: "The Son perfectly mirrors God and is stamped with divine nature." A theologian writes: "We would not know God was a Father if the Son had not revealed Him. God without a Son would be the remote God of the philosophers, the anonymous and abstract ground of being who is everything in general and nothing in particular, the First Cause, a Force, a concept, a presence ... someone who would belong more to the debating society than the Church."

When I was young I heard a preacher say: "If God isn't like Jesus then I am not interested in Him." The statement took my breath away. His text was: "Anyone who has seen me has seen the Father" (John 14:9). Amazing words. The moment when Jesus declared that was one of the greatest in history.

In the former Belgian Congo (now the Democratic Republic of Congo) as some local people were about to pull an idol from an idol pit, those nearby hid their faces saying: "If we look on the face of our father we will die." But as we look on the face of our Father in Jesus, we do not die, we live. And how. We see that God is not terrible but tender, not forbidding but forgiving. We see God in Jesus as He is—really is.

FURTHER STUDY

John 8:18–19; 8:23–30; 10:30–38; 14:9

1. How does the Son mirror the Father?

2. What does Jesus show us about the Father?

O God, I realize I would never have known You were a Father had You not sent us Your Son. Seeing You in Your Son's face has not only satisfied me but stirred me—stirred me to be more like Him. Amen.

"Oh How I Wish . . ."

For reading & meditation—John 14:1–14

"Philip said, 'Lord, show us the Father and that will be enough for us.'" (v.8)

The Father has come to us in the Person of His Son to make us His children. Dr. E. Stanley Jones used to tell the story, which I have often repeated, of a little boy who stood before a picture of his absent father and then turned to his mother and said wistfully: "Oh, how I wish father would step out of the picture." That little boy expressed in his own way the deepest longing of all those who lived before Christ. The psalmist declared: "As a father has compassion on his children, so the Lord has compassion on those who fear him …" (Ps. 103:13). The Old Testament saints must have thought many times as they looked up to the heavens through the lattice of the law and creation: "How I wish the Father would step out of the picture." Well, He has stepped out of the picture. He stepped out at Bethlehem. The Word became flesh and dwelt among us.

Christianity is not a religion of influences or values or principles. It is much more. It is a religion of events. God came at a certain hour in history and to a certain place on earth, a town called Bethlehem, and revealed Himself to us. The Father has stepped out of the picture.

Yea, Lord, we greet Thee, born this happy morning;
Jesus, to Thee be glory given,
Word of the Father, now in flesh appearing:
O come, let us adore Him, Christ the Lord.

FURTHER STUDY

John 1:1–14; Matt. 1:23; 1 Tim. 3:16; 1 John 1:1–2

1. Why did God become flesh?

2. Take time to praise Father, Son and Holy Spirit.

Prayer

O Father, we see You faintly through nature but we see You clearly through the Person of Your Son. I am thankful that You were born in Bethlehem, but even more thankful that through You I have been born again. Amen.

SECTION SIX

He Never Stops Loving

For reading & meditation—Isaiah 43:1–13

"Fear not, for I have redeemed you; I have summoned you by name; you are mine." (v.1)

Consider this: the Father is not against you for your sin, but for you against your sin. Many people are afraid of God. I don't mean in the sense of reverencing Him or respecting Him, but being full of raw, naked fear. They view Him as harsh, judgmental, and angry, always trying to find some fault with them in an effort to keep them out of heaven. That's the kind of picture the devil wants us to have of God. Some Christians give the devil a lot of help. And so, also, do some parents. This is not to say, of course, that God does not get angry, but we must distinguish between His righteous anger and the kind of rage we often see people getting into. One difference between human beings and God is this: when God gets angry He doesn't stop loving. He hates the sin that we engage in but He loves us. It was said of Jesus when He was here on earth that He was a friend of sinners (see Matthew 11:19). Does that mean He condoned sin? The people of His day knew that though He denounced their sin He wanted to help them.

What a difference it makes to our daily living when we know that God is not like some parents who are harsh or vindictive with their children when they do wrong. He is kind, compassionate and full of grace. "Let us then approach the throne of grace with confidence, so that we may receive mercy and find grace to help us in our time of need" (Hebrews 4:16).

FURTHER STUDY

Ps. 86:5–15; John 3:16–17; 8:1–11; 2 Cor. 5:18–19

1. How does God view sin?

2. How does God view sinners?

Prayer

O God, what a relief it is to know that though You are against my sin You are for me. You are on my side. Some may see You as merciless and vindictive, but I see You as merciful and gracious. Thank You dear Father. Amen.

SECTION SIX

Perfect but Not Perfectionist

For reading & meditation—Romans 8:28–39

"Who will bring any charge against those whom God has chosen? It is God who justifies." (v.33)

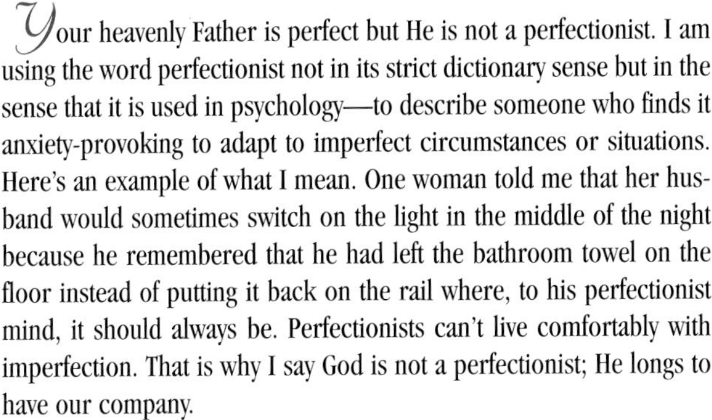

Your heavenly Father is perfect but He is not a perfectionist. I am using the word perfectionist not in its strict dictionary sense but in the sense that it is used in psychology—to describe someone who finds it anxiety-provoking to adapt to imperfect circumstances or situations. Here's an example of what I mean. One woman told me that her husband would sometimes switch on the light in the middle of the night because he remembered that he had left the bathroom towel on the floor instead of putting it back on the rail where, to his perfectionist mind, it should always be. Perfectionists can't live comfortably with imperfection. That is why I say God is not a perfectionist; He longs to have our company.

God, of course, desires perfection, and wants us to be perfect. In Matthew 5:48 He tells us: "Be perfect, therefore, as your heavenly Father is perfect." However, the lack of perfection in us does not cause Him to become so disturbed that He withdraws. Those raised by perfectionist parents, who grew up feeling that though they did everything possible to please them, but never came up to their expectations, need to understand that their heavenly Father is not like that.

A missionary I know experienced a mental and emotional breakdown due to having internalized his parents' impossible-to-please attitude and projected it on God. He thought he had to work himself to death in order to find God's approval, and became what is called "a missionary casualty." You don't need to strive to earn God's love. You already have it.

FURTHER STUDY

Gen. 12:10–20; 20:1–11; Gal. 3:6–29; Heb. 11:6–10; James 2:23

1. Was Abraham perfect?

2. Was God pleased with him?

Prayer

Heavenly Father, how thankful I am that You are not an impossible-to-please Parent—demanding, critical and condemning. You desire perfection, but You are patient with me even when I am far from perfect. Amen.

SECTION SIX

Suspect Theology

For reading & meditation—1 Peter 4:12–19

"Dear friends, do not be surprised at the painful trial you are suffering, as though something strange were happening ..." (v.12)

Our heavenly Father will not keep us from trouble but He will keep us in it. Some suffer from misperceptions of their heavenly Father, drawn not so much from a dysfunctional family but from a dysfunctional local church.

One man told me while I was in the Far East that he had been brought up in a church where the evangelistic thrust was based on this theme: become a Christian and you will never have any troubles again. He became a Christian on that basis and found that whatever troubles he had before were as nothing compared to those he experienced following his conversion. He lost his job, his family turned their backs on him, and his girlfriend jilted him at the altar—all because he would not renounce his belief in Christ. When Christian leaders hold out the hope that becoming a Christian means freedom from trouble, they push converts towards disillusionment. The theology appears attractive and may help draw people towards Christianity—but it is not true. As our text for today shows, our Lord made it clear that we should expect trouble in this world.

Followers of Christ suffer as much as others, sometimes moreso. Those who believe that being a Christian will insulate them from adversity may well find their faith collapsing when they are under stress. What Scripture teaches is this: God will not save us from hardship, but He will save us in it. Whatever heartache you experience, He will be there to hold you fast, and will not allow into your life any more trouble than you can bear.

FURTHER STUDY

Luke 21:12–19; John 16:33; 1 Cor. 10:13; 2 Cor. 12:8–9

1. Are difficulties normal or unusual for a Christian?

2. What does God promise in trouble?

Prayer

Father, more and more I see how important it is that I have a clear profile of You. Help me understand that the world is a battleground, not a playground. You are with me whatever the pain or heartache. I am so grateful. Amen.

SECTION SIX

A Father Who Hugs

For reading & meditation—Luke 15:11–31

"... he ran to his son, threw his arms around him and kissed him." (v.20)

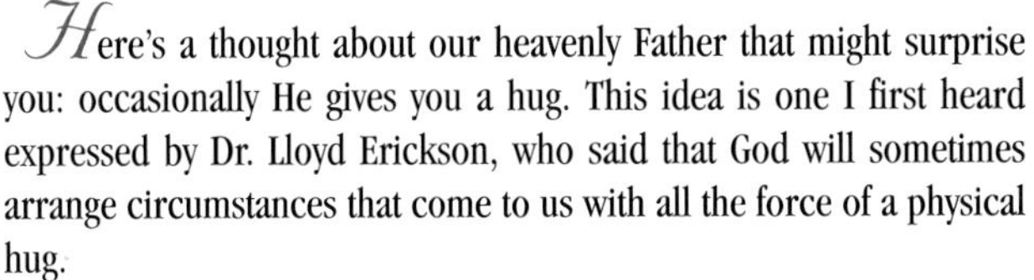

Here's a thought about our heavenly Father that might surprise you: occasionally He gives you a hug. This idea is one I first heard expressed by Dr. Lloyd Erickson, who said that God will sometimes arrange circumstances that come to us with all the force of a physical hug.

I found that thought quite intriguing, especially as my father never once hugged me. I remember looking down into my father's grave as we laid him to rest, and saying to myself: "You will never be able to hug me now." That's why, I suppose, the story of the Prodigal Son is one of my favorites. It tells of a father who ran to meet his erring son, threw his arms around him, and hugged him.

How does God hug us? When He surprises us by sending something delightful to let us know that He is thinking about us. It could be a friend calling unexpectedly, a child saying, "I love you," a stranger stopping to help you when your car has broken down. Late at night and on a lonely road in the United States, my car broke down miles from anywhere. I panicked as I thought of all the things that might happen. Within ten minutes or so a car driven by a woman drew to a halt and she asked: "Do you need any help?" I said: "Isn't it risky to stop like this to check on someone? What made you do it?" She answered: "I wouldn't normally, but I'm a Christian and the Lord told me to help you." It was one of my heavenly Father's hugs.

FURTHER STUDY

Acts 20:37; 28:14–15; 2 Cor. 8:1–5; 2 Tim. 1:16–18

1. How did Paul experience God's hugs?

2. Who can you hug this week?

Prayer

Father, I know You long to hold me in Your arms and give me a special hug. Help me see that this is what You are doing when you use others to bless me and encourage me. Give me a hug today, Lord. In Jesus' Name. Amen.

Known by Name

For reading & meditation—John 10:1–21

"He calls his own sheep by name and leads them out." (v.3)

One more thing about your heavenly Father: He knows you by name. A shepherd in Bible times knew every sheep by name. Max Lucado, in an imaginative encounter with a shepherd, pictures him describing his sheep in this way: "The one with the sad eyes, that's Droopy. And the fellow with the one ear up and the other down, I call him Oscar." When we see a crowd we just see a mass of people. But God sees us as individuals and knows every one of us by name.

A wonderful verse in Isaiah reads: "See, I have engraved you on the palms of my hands" (Isa. 49:16). The figure of speech is of more than ordinary interest. It suggests the permanence of a mark made by tattooing. The palm of the hand has passed into our language as a symbol of familiarity. We often hear people say if we doubt their familiarity with a place: "I know it like the palm of my hand." And that is where God carries the reminder of His people's needs—where it cannot be overlooked. Quite a thought, isn't it? Your name is on God's hands.

Perhaps you have seen your name in a special place, such as on a trophy or a roll of honor. Feels good, doesn't it? Or perhaps you have heard your name mentioned by someone famous. That too feels good. But listen. The most important person in the universe—your heavenly Father—knows your name too. It is written on His hands, whispered by His lips. Ask Him to reassure you today that He knows you by name.

FURTHER STUDY

Luke 10:20; Heb. 12:22–24; Rev. 20:12; 21:27

1. What is the book of life?

2. Is your name there?

Prayer

O Father, I often need reminding about people's names, but what a joy to know that You never need a reminder of my name. It is constantly before You—graven on Your hands. Reassure me today that You know my name. Amen.

Face to Face

For reading & meditation—1 Corinthians 13:1–13

"Now we see but a poor reflection as in a mirror; then we shall see face to face." (v.12)

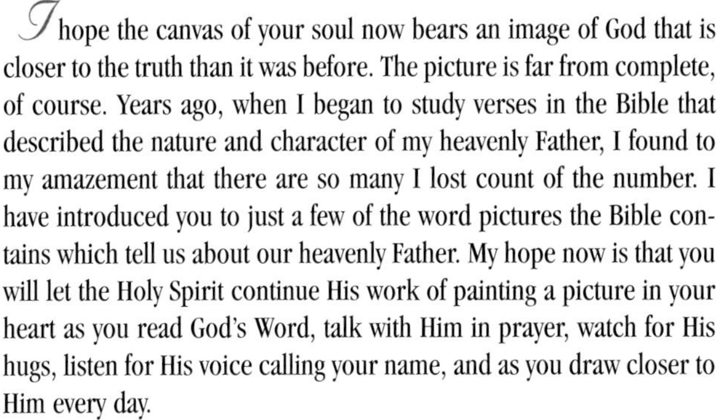

I hope the canvas of your soul now bears an image of God that is closer to the truth than it was before. The picture is far from complete, of course. Years ago, when I began to study verses in the Bible that described the nature and character of my heavenly Father, I found to my amazement that there are so many I lost count of the number. I have introduced you to just a few of the word pictures the Bible contains which tell us about our heavenly Father. My hope now is that you will let the Holy Spirit continue His work of painting a picture in your heart as you read God's Word, talk with Him in prayer, watch for His hugs, listen for His voice calling your name, and as you draw closer to Him every day.

But here's the best news of all. One day you are going to meet your heavenly Father—the Parent who loved you and drew you to Himself, taught you, encouraged you, sympathized with you, and went through tough times with you. Make time to read the Bible, for this is His love letter to you. Focus on those passages that tell you about your heavenly Father's characteristics. If you can't compare Him to anyone you know, then contrast Him. However good your earthly parents were, He is better. If your parents were cruel and vindictive then remind yourself that He is not. In your heavenly Father you have the One for whom your heart has always ached. And He stands ready to re-parent you.

FURTHER STUDY

John 20:17; 14:1–4;
Rev. 21:1–7; 22:1–6

1. What are you looking forward to in heaven?

2. Express your appreciation to your heavenly Father.

Prayer

Heavenly Father, I appreciate You, Heavenly Father, I appreciate You, I love You, adore You, I bow down before You, Heavenly Father, I appreciate You.

HOW TO USE THE BIBLE

A question I am often asked especially by young Christians is this: Why do I need to read the Bible?

We need to read the Bible in order to know not only God's mind for the future but how to develop a daily walk with Him. God uses His Word to change people's lives and bring those lives into a deeper relationship with Himself and a greater conformity to His will. For over four decades now I have spent hours every week reading and studying the Scriptures. God has used this book to transform my life and to give me a sense of security in a shifting and insecure world.

How do we read the Bible? Do we just start at Genesis and make our way through to the Book of Revelation? There are many ways to go about reading the Scriptures; let me mention the three most popular approaches.

One is to follow a reading plan such as is included in the *Every Day with Jesus Devotional Bible* or *Through the Bible in One Year.* The great advantage of following a reading plan is that your reading is arranged for you; in a sense you are being supervised. You are not left to uncertainty: what shall I read today, where shall I begin, at what point shall I end?

A second approach is to thread your way through the Scriptures by following a specific theme. It is quite staggering how many themes can be found in Scripture and what great spiritual rewards can be had by acquainting yourself with them. When I started writing *Every Day with Jesus* in 1965, I decided to follow the thematic approach and I wondered how long I would be able to keep it up. Now, over thirty years later, I am still writing and expounding on different themes of the Bible, and the truth is that I have more biblical themes and subjects than it is possible to deal with in one lifetime!

A third approach is by reading through a book of the Bible. This enables you to get into the mind of the writer and understand his message. Every book of the Bible has something unique and special to convey and, as with any book, this can only be understood when you read it from start to finish.

It is important to remember that all reading of the Bible ought to be preceded by prayer. This puts you in a spiritually receptive frame of mind to receive what God has to say to you through His Word. The Bible can be read by anyone, but it can only be understood by those whose hearts are in tune with God—those who have come into a personal relationship with Him and who maintain that relationship through daily or regular prayer. This is how the Bible puts it: "The man without the Spirit does not accept the things that come from the Spirit of God, for they are foolishness to him, and he cannot understand them, because they are spiritually discerned" (1 Cor. 2:14).

Praying before you open your Bible should not be a mere formality. It is not the act that will make the Bible come alive but the *attitude.* Prayer enables us to approach the Scriptures with a humble mind. The scientist who does not sit down before the facts of the universe with an open mind. He must first be prepared to give up every preconceived idea and be willing to follow wherever nature will lead him. It is the same with the reading of the Scriptures; we must come to it with a humble and receptive mind or we too will get nowhere. Prayer enables us to have the attitude that says, "Speak, for your servant is listening" (1 Sam. 3:10).

If we are to grow in the Christian life, we must do more than just *read* the Bible—we must *study* it. This means that we must give time to poring over it, considering it, thinking about what it is saying to us, and assimilating into our hearts and minds its doctrines and its ideas.

I have already pointed out that one of the ways of reading the Bible is by taking a theme and tracing it through the various books of the Bible. The pleasure this brings can be greatly enhanced by using this as a regular means of Bible study. When we study the Bible with the aid of concordances, lexicons and so on, we feed our minds. But when we study the Bible devotionally, we apply the Word of God to our hearts. Both exercises are necessary if we are to be well-rounded people, but we must see that it is at the place of the devotional that we open up our hearts and expose ourselves to God's resources.

Let me encourage you also to take advantage of a reading plan as a further basis of study. Following this will enable you to cover the whole Bible in a set period. Those who have used this method tell of the most amazing spiritual benefits. One person who had read through the whole Bible in a year said to me, "It demanded more discipline than I thought I was capable of, but the rewards have been enormous." When I asked her what these rewards were, she said, "I used to have a partial view of God's purposes because I dipped into my Bible just here and there as it suited me. Now, however, I feel as if I have been looking over God's shoulder as He laid out the universe, and I feel so secure in the knowledge that He found a place for me in that marvelous plan." There can be no doubt that reading through the entire Bible in a set period enables one to gain a perspective that has tremendously positive spiritual consequences.

The third form of study—reading through a book of the Bible at a time—has the advantage of helping you understand the unity and diversity of the Bible. It is quite incredible how so many writers sharing their thoughts at different times of history combine to say similar things and give a consistent emphasis. Reading and pondering on this gives you such an appreciation of the wisdom of God in putting together this marvelous volume that it fires your soul and quickly brings praise and adoration to your lips.

I have found the best way to study a book of the Bible is to read it through once for a sense of the whole, and then to read it again, making a note of anything that strikes me such as a principle to be applied, an insight to be stored away in my heart, or a thought to be shared with someone who is struggling.

One thing is sure, time spent with the Bible is not wasted. The more one loves God the more one will love the Bible. And the more one loves the Bible the more one will love God. Always remember this unique volume—God's one and only published work—yields its treasures only to those who read it, study it, and obey it.

Selwyn Hughes

Selwyn Hughes—A Brief Biography

Born in Wales to Christian parents who were significantly impacted by the Welsh revivals, Selwyn Hughes trained in theology and counseling in both the UK and USA. During his 18 years pastoring churches around the UK he was asked by a few of his congregation to share his method of daily Bible study. From this inconspicuous start grew *Every Day with Jesus* and for 30 years Selwyn has authored these daily Bible notes which are read by some 500,000 people around the world. In addition to writing, Selwyn travels extensively in many countries presenting a wide range of seminars on different aspects of the Christian life including counseling, marriage, relationships, and personal development.

Larry Dyke

Larry Dyke is a native Texan who has traveled, often with his wife and daughter, to some of the world's most beautiful places, underlying his painting is his deep Christian faith. "When I became a full-time artist, I was impressed to put a scriptural notation on each of my paintings," Dyke states. "It's an expression of what I think the true answer to life is." Dyke's paintings hang in the White House, the Vatican, and the homes of distinguished personalities including Billy and Ruth Graham.

Crusade for World Revival—A Brief History

Founded by Selwyn Hughes in 1965 as a charity, the commission statement of CWR states the purpose of the organization as "Applying God's Word to everyday life and relationships." Today CWR employs 45 people and from its base in the beautiful setting of Waverley Abbey House at Farnham in the south of England provides inspiration, training, and support to many Christians throughout the world through an extensive international publishing and training ministry.

For more information about CWR and the training and publishing products available, please apply to your nearest distributor listed elsewhere in this publication or to:

CWR, Waverley Abbey House, Waverley Lane, Farnham, Surrey,
England GU9 8EP
Tel: 44 1252 784700
E mail: CWRMarketing@compuserve.com
Or visit our Web Site at: www.cwr.org.uk